D1707014

MARKETING MODERNITY

Marketing Modernity is a cultural history of the early British film industry. It explains the social and institutional continuities that underpinned the market for popular entertainments in the late nineteenth and early twentieth centuries.

In this innovative study of early film exhibition, **Joe Kember** reveals a rich landscape of performance and business practices taking place in venues ranging from the magic lantern lecture to the fairground and variety theatre. Uncovering new sources, including previously neglected films, industrial documentation, memoirs, trade and popular periodicals, the book charts the development of film institutions in relation to this complex social and commercial context.

Joe Kember is Senior Lecturer in Film at the University of Exeter.

Exeter Studies in Film History

Published by University of Exeter Press in association with the Bill Douglas Centre for the History of Cinema and Popular Culture

Series Editors: **Richard Maltby,** Professor of Screen Studies, Flinders University, South Australia and **Steve Neale,** Professor of Film Studies and Academic Director of the Bill Douglas Centre, University of Exeter

UEP also publishes the celebrated five-volume series looking at the early years of English cinema, *The Beginnings of the Cinema in England*, by John Barnes.

Marketing Modernity
Victorian Popular Shows and Early Cinema

Joe Kember

UNIVERSITY
of
EXETER
PRESS

First published in 2009 by
University of Exeter Press
Reed Hall, Streatham Drive
Exeter EX4 4QR
UK
www.exeterpress.co.uk

British Library Cataloguing in Publication Data
A catalogue record for this book is available
from the British Library.

ISBN 978 0 85989 801 0

Mixed Sources
Product group from well-managed
forests and other controlled sources
www.fsc.org Cert no. SA-COC-002112
© 1996 Forest Stewardship Council

Typeset in Caslon
by XL Publishing Services, Tiverton
Printed in Great Britain by SRP Ltd, Exeter

Contents

List of Illustrations

Acknowledgements

This book has been several books. At various stages it has been a history of early British film narrative, of Victorian performance practices and mediation, and an analysis of the development of early film institutions; its final shape I owe to the encouragement and scrutiny of numerous colleagues. Erica Sheen's guidance when this project began as a thesis at the University of Sheffield has stuck with me, and continues to inform my thinking. The structure and scope of the book are the consequence of a great many conversations with friends and colleagues. I thank them all: Vanessa Toulmin, for telling me about the many greatest shows on earth, for directing me to so much fascinating and wonderful material, and for her helpful reading of extracts of the final draft of the manuscript; Steve Neale, for convincing me, twice in writing and numerous times in between, that it was all worth saying; Simon Popple, for encouraging me to speak about so many bits of it to so many excellent people; John Plunkett, for understanding the manuscript, and for information on the doorknob at the Egyptian Hall; Patricia Zakreski, for steering me through the wilds of Victorian popular culture and for constructive ridicule of my longest sentences. Among the many helpful contributions I have received at conferences and seminars, I would particularly like to mention the generosity of film historians Richard Brown and Tony Fletcher. Many thanks go to all of my colleagues at the Universities of Exeter and Teesside. The Film Studies team and the Centre for Victorian Studies at Exeter have provided a diverse and stimulating research environment in which to think, and write, and learn.

But I could not have completed this book without the help of numerous other individuals and institutions. My series editor, Richard Maltby, has been generous and insightful and provided me with as eloquent an evaluation of my analysis as you could possibly hope for. Simon Baker and Helen Gannon at the University of Exeter Press have been rigorous, attentive, and helpful throughout. Thanks go to the AHRC, British Academy, and the Universities of Sheffield and Teesside, all of which have funded my research for this book at various times. I also owe a great many thanks to the imagination and flair of librarians and curators at the Bill Douglas Centre and Special Collections at the University of Exeter, the National Fairground Archive at Sheffield, the National Film and Television Archive in London, the National Media Museum at Bradford, the John Johnson collection at the Bodleian Library, the Guildhall Library, Templeman Library Special Collections at the University of Kent, the Tampa Library at the University of South Florida, and The British Library. Special thanks go to Peter Jewell, who more than once has pointed me to gems in the Bill Douglas Centre, and to Noel Chanan, who has generously granted me access to his extensive collection of books and ephemera.

Earlier versions of extracts from Chapters 3, 4, and 5 have appeared in the journals, *Living Pictures, Early Popular Visual Culture, The Velvet Light Trap,* and in the book *The Showman, the Spectacle, and the Two-Minute Silence: Performing British Cinema Before 1930,* eds Alan Burton and Larraine Porter (Trowbridge: Flicks Books, 2001).

To my Mum, Dad, and brother, thank you. And Tricia, again: you know by now that I could not have finished this book so often without you!

This book is dedicated to Will and Merry who seem to know everything already.

Exeter, August 2009

Introduction

> There is not, there never was, an inventor of the Living Picture. Say that
> it grew from an infinitely small germ, as unlike its present form as the
> butterfly is unlike the egg from which it evolves; say that many minds
> have each contributed, and still are contributing their mite towards the
> realisation of that perfection yet to be attained; say that the Living
> Picture is the work of nineteenth-century civilised man—and the state-
> ment will be as true as any generalisation can be. [1]

The living picture, as Hopwood incisively remarked, already had a long and
complex history by the end of the nineteenth century. Its origins were nebu-
lous and difficult to define, and its 'perfection' had been and would remain
a cherished ambition. Cutting through the competing claims for pioneership that by 1899 were already being made by a number of inventors and
entrepreneurs, Hopwood sketches a much grander evolutionary schema, in
which the moving pictures appear as the logical outcome, even the epitome
of nineteenth-century ingenuity, enthusiasm and labour.

The question of origins has remained controversial within studies of early
film ever since. Occasionally, early squabbles concerning invention and
pioneership persist within scholarly work on what are now more often called
only tentatively and conditionally, the 'pre-' and 'early' cinemas. However,
in the past twenty-five years, new debates concerning the accretion of technologies and visual conventions governing the production of moving images
and of associated conventions for viewing such images have come to dominate research. In place of a developmental teleology, which inevitably
privileges the formation of what selected kinds of cinema would become,
work concerning cinema's antecedents has increasingly been seen as a contribution to an 'archaeology of cinema', uncovering multiple lines of influence
and seeking to demonstrate that cinema was not a privileged form, but developed amongst a heterogeneous collection of other media practices.[2]
Similarly, early film historians, publishing on an increasingly broad range of
topics from the 1980s, have justifiably opposed the commonly held idea that

1

early cinema was merely a primitive precursor of the advanced classical aesthetics of later cinema. Instead, early film texts and associated models of spectatorship have been celebrated for their complexity and diversity, their variation not only from place to place, but also from week to week and screening to screening.

Cumulatively, the many micro-historical projects that have been generated by such approaches have tended to resituate discourses of primitivity and invention onto earlier media or, like Hopwood, have celebrated early film as the epitome of representational media under conditions of modernity at the *fin de siècle*.[3] In doing so, however, they have often tended to emphasise the differences between early and classical cinemas, as if the early cinema 'belonged' more naturally to nineteenth- rather than twentieth-century media cultures. In this sense, though such studies have done much to establish the sophistication of early film practices, they have done little to challenge the dichotomous relationship that was proposed by earlier generations of film historians between early and classical cinemas. Much work, mostly conducted in the context of early US filmmaking, has therefore emphasised the differences to be found between the majority of mainstream film texts either side of (approximately) 1908, but has paid less attention to similarities between the institutional and social practices of the industry across the same period.[4] For the same reason, the continuities which can be traced from nineteenth-century entertainment industries through early cinema and into later cinema have also been underestimated, sometimes leaving us in the counterintuitive position of claiming for such sophisticated and highly financed modern institutions that their interests were best served by a sudden transformation of existing—profitable and easily regulated—practices.

Reinforcing this problem, the emphasis of overarching archaeologies of cinema upon the formal and technological lineages of large-scale, moving, and projected images has shown less interest in investigating the economic and social existence of nineteenth- and early twentieth-century media. Nor has the widespread acknowledgment of the intermediality of the late nineteenth-century cultural environment and of the significant transformation of visuality that this occasioned, sufficiently explained the way that early cinema and other media actually functioned for the institutions that utilised them. But if the aesthetic and mechanical origins of the cinema are to be recovered in a manner that fully accredits the independent significance of earlier media and, therefore, also details the complexity and diversity of their piecemeal influences on cinema, this will most surely be accomplished by demonstrating that they were inseparable from the social and institutional, as well as visual, practices that had occasioned them. For it is the continu-

2

ities and changes in these practices, interacting within equally dynamic commercial environments, which established the kinds of uses to which new and existing media might, most usefully and profitably, be put.

Responding to these concerns, one of the principle claims of this book is that the functions of early cinema were most directly derived from earlier entertainment traditions, and that we therefore need to understand not just film's intermedial prehistory, but also its longstanding institutional heritage. This claim potentially initiates a massive research enquiry, since patterns of institutional development never lead from one set of practices and conventions to another in a straightforward, linear manner. Rather, they progress in multiple directions at the same time time, sometimes becoming reified in relatively stable configurations that become more obviously significant. It is not the case that any one of these configurations—say, that of the late century magic lantern industry—had an overwhelming or exclusive influence upon the early cinema. Neither is it true that lantern and other practices were somehow consumed by the moving pictures: they have survived in varied (commercial, educational, and other professional) formats throughout the twentieth century and have fed into many institutions besides those associated with moving pictures. Rather, it becomes obvious that uneven and branching developments such as these belong to a far greater pattern of cultural, social and commercial change, which has most often been described in terms of the conditions of industrial modernity. It does not seem contentious to say, in this light, that the early cinema was produced by and contributed to the massively productive (but uncontrollable) complex of institutional forces with which we have all, in industrially developed nations, been more or less complicit.

But such a grand perspective might appear wildly out of step with the historicising trend of early film studies, perhaps because it has the savour of so-called Grand Theories, whose rejection as unhistorical and dogmatic, 'but the outer sign of those who are blind to any application of that theory,' is now familiar enough to have become a largely implicit premise of revisionist histories.[5] Still more suspiciously, this book contends that charting the relationships between spectators and institutional practices (a concern upon which Grand Theories expended considerable effort) should actually be central to an inclusive archaeology of cinema. However, it also contends that these relations have always been both multiple and dynamic, and that it is impossible to come to a meaningful understanding of either spectatorship or the nature of film institutions without grasping, in full historical detail, the material conditions in which they actually functioned. Indeed, far from wishing to abstract institutional imperatives from the individuals who

3

enacted them, whether these were entrepreneurs, filmmakers, exhibitors, or spectators, I wish to emphasise the active role such individuals had in formulating and amending, as well as obeying, these imperatives. Rather than hapless consumers, awash amid a sea of images, these individuals were capable of exercising a degree of control and even mastery over their apparently bewildering, media-saturated environment.

Therefore, this book seeks to recover early film institutions—by which I mean film producers and exhibitors, as well as their audiences and all of the practices and discourses that connected them—as sophisticated interpreters of an immense textual, intertextual, and contextual range of information. But this expertise was seldom practised in a self-conscious or openly theorised manner; rather it had been accumulated through decades of shared experience of earlier media, popular entertainments and educational presentations. Describing some of the key dimensions of this institutional prehistory is therefore essential to any further interpretation of the activities of early film producers, exhibitors, and spectators. For without this knowledge of longstanding practices associated with earlier entertainments and other institutions—knowledge that the audiences themselves possessed—we are left to account for such complex processes as early film spectatorship with, at best, a partial understanding of the existing capacities and likely interests of spectators. This is only to say that, before we attempt to interpret the significance of early film texts for their first audiences, we should acknowledge and define the popular frames of understanding that determined what they were likely to regard as 'significant' in the first place.

This book will therefore describe a representative selection of earlier entertainments, with an especial emphasis on performance and business practices in the variety theatre, lecture theatre, fairground and other touring or temporary shows in the years after 1850. This selection and chronology by no means represents an exhaustive survey of the range of possible institutions that might be said to have had a significant impact upon the cinema: such a survey would arguably need to include, at the very least, a detailed account of the activities of the popular press, the commerce of photography and print illustration, to say nothing of the circulation of optical toys and of remarkably diverse public and private entertainments during the latter half of the nineteenth century. But it does provide a focus on those sites that most often housed the moving pictures in the years before 1908, giving us a strong indication of the expectations of audiences when these sites began to exhibit moving pictures, and of the business and performance regimes which governed them. It also enables us to give further shape to Hopwood's 'generalisation' concerning the origins of the cinema, and allows us to examine, in

4

the light of this information, the continuities as well as the transformations of earlier and later cinematic practices. And, as we might expect given the capacity of modern leisure institutions to capitalise, repeatedly, upon the same set of attractions by means of graduated change and variation, the similarities across even this period of sixty years are at least as compelling as the changes.

Among these continuities, Hopwood's comments, made during the first wave of the moving picture's industrial consolidation, also give us an indication of one factor that would remain especially significant throughout this period. Offering us one account of the way the film industry saw itself, or had come to present itself, at an early point of substantial commercial development, moving pictures were to be seen as more than a technological artefact or a function of a marketplace with a growing obsession for images. They were the 'work of nineteenth-century civilized man', a prominent part of the enlightenment principles that were credited with revolutionising professional and personal lives in the wake of industrial modernisation. Hopwood clarified to his readers, many of whom presumably had an interest in entering the growing industry, that moving pictures were no mere novelty but were part of a grand developmental process within Western cultures, that the new century offered unlimited scope for further developments, and that all of this had resulted from human endeavour. In other words, he articulates some of the key tenets that would continue to inform the manner of the film industry's self-mythologisation, exaggerating utopian impulses associated with the emergent mass media and giving those institutions which developed and exploited these media a distinct and recognisable human profile.

A second key claim of this book is that comments such as Hopwood's concerning qualities of human invention associated with film typify an especially important institutional strategy that film entrepreneurs borrowed from earlier entertainment industries. Though the growth of increasingly distant, centralised institutions, such as those associated with film production, were part of the process wherein individuals were becoming increasingly divorced from the means and methods of production, this paradigmatically modern industry thrived because it successfully personalised certain aspects of its products. In this light, discourses of invention played a similar role to the later celebration of other creatives, such as stars, screenwriters, or directors, within the industry: they played up human qualities of individuality and originality, promising that the patterns of light projected on-screen carried authentic expressions of personality to their distant audiences. Thus, though dependent upon continued technological advance, tied to abstract commercial imperatives that bore little relation to the content of the films, and thriving on the medium's capacity to exploit the distance between the creation and consumption of the moving image, the film industry was inaugurated primarily as a means of generating personal and social reassurance. Film was to be seen as part of the expanded expressive repertoire of modern life. It was a mechanism that responded to the perceived disjunction between the growing consumerist culture of the late nineteenth century and the need to preserve or regenerate value-laden ideals of community and communication, and it did so by embedding idealised patterns of expression in an easily consumable form.

The early film industry was certainly not the first to capitalise upon this significant cultural motive: it had long been associated with a broad array of highly institutionalised entertainments in the latter half of the nineteenth century. The following lengthy explorations of earlier entertainment institutions that had a relatively direct impact on the film industry will therefore emphasise the performative and representational strategies that enabled them to capitalise upon this desire for reassurance. They will show that popular constructions of such pervasive figures as lecturers, showmen, performers, and various media producers had a substantial impact both upon the reception of these entertainments and upon the manner in which these institutions organised and promoted themselves. However, perhaps because the moving pictures appeared to embody so clearly the propensity of modern institutions to disembed and displace forms of personal, face-to-face contact, they also worked especially hard to provide multiple opportunities for the reinsertion of such contacts. In various ways, filmmakers and exhibitors were professionally engaged in the creative task of designing such significant relationships for their audiences, bringing to the technology of the moving pictures a series of interpersonal mechanisms, some associated with the use of live performers alongside the screen and others with the image track itself. Such mechanisms enabled spectators to attribute intentional content to the moving picture, often identifying this with particular individuals or at least with certain well-known stock caricatures.

This flux of competing human agencies introduced fundamental questions concerning the interpretation of moving images:

> How much can the pictures tell? How much shall the monologue tell?
> What shall be told twice—that is to say in the pictures and in the mono-
> logue at the same time? How shall the interplay of pictures and text best
> secure for each its necessary share of attention, and avoid the loss to
> auditor and spectator of points communicated by either?[6]

Alexander Black is speaking here about his idiosyncratic moving image 'picture plays', which predated the Lumière projector by several years and which negotiated questions that would remain fundamental to the reception of the projected image. He aptly expresses these questions as a playoff between alternative communicative possibilities in relation to the development of a competent spectator. The questions he raised would only become sharper as the modes of address associated with moving pictures rapidly diversified in the few years following the introduction of film.

A typical film programme in this period is very difficult to identify, and it has therefore often been defined in terms of its variability, but it is certainly the case that, as in Black's picture plays, they exploited multiple modes of address, often all at once. The exhibition of numerous short films, each with its own signifying modes of address and each perhaps drawn from radically different earlier institutional contexts, would often be accompanied by live performances, again probably drawn from varied traditions, so that early film shows potentially offered to their audiences a bewildering array of communications and references to earlier institutional configurations. However, though such material was diverse, bringing all manner of subjects to the screen, it was persistently unified by its capacity to foster some sense of meaningful contact for its audiences. Indeed, I am suggesting that this function coherently explains both the proliferation of modes of address associated with early film shows and the generally comfortable and benign experiences audiences appear to have taken from the majority of these shows. It also accredits the competence of early spectators to interpret the material they were shown in a manner consistent with existing interpretive regimes. Early films arrived within entertainments that already had fully developed exhibition and performance practices, and which had carefully cultivated the nuanced expertise audiences now habitually brought to their interpretation of moving pictures.

The evidence for these assertions is drawn in the following chapters primarily from the context of nineteenth- and twentieth-century shows in Britain, but I believe that the institutional model that emerges from this study shares certain equivalencies with the institutional configurations existing in the USA, France, and other countries, which were also undergoing similar processes of industrial modernisation at this time. As several commentators have shown, anxieties concerning the alienation effect popularly associated with such factors as the rationalisation and professionalisation of the workplace, the redevelopment of the modern city according to capitalist principles of investment and flow, and the development of mechanised transportation and communications technologies (including the cinema) were internationally pervasive at the *fin de siècle*.[7] It is not surprising to find that the institutional responses to such anxieties, at least insofar as these were reflected in the film industry and in earlier entertainment institutions, also shared a number of key principles across international borders, a factor which became immensely productive when early filmmakers successfully marketed their productions overseas.

The dominant response of early film institutions to popularly expressed anxieties concerning modernity was therefore to capitalise upon them, just as popular entertainments had done for decades. It is this type of relationship, in which institutions of film, for sound commercial reasons, encouraged audiences to negotiate and accommodate such anxieties, that this book describes as the marketing of modernity. Thus, early film institutions were able to market modernity successfully not because they passively mirrored the well-known idea that modern sensoria thrived on speed, distraction, and a passion for images; rather, they actively created an opportunity for spectators to exercise their capacity to read such images according to familiar communicative and performative regimes. In particular, such features as the international prominence of lecturers to describe the content of many early films; the success of early films depicting well-known public personalities or stock personae; and the subsequent development of new modes of acting, narration, and authorship directly associated with the screen can all be seen as strategies intended to retain aspects of communication, performance, and personality that would be both affectively engaging and comfortably familiar for transatlantic, if not global, audiences.

However, it may well be objected that, as in a long critical tradition in film studies, this line of enquiry simply commits the methodological error of attempting to create something like authorial personae within a medium that actually does not possess such figures. David Bordwell has criticised movements such as *auteur* criticism as extreme and untenable applications of the person schemata upon which people customarily depend in everyday life.[8] Bordwell has argued that the spectator's ascription of real human bodies, perceptions, thoughts, emotions, and motivations to abstract narrators and filmmakers is a kind of 'anthropomorphic fiction' repeated by critics at their peril.[9] In response to this, I contend that film is an anthropo*centric* medium, as indeed are all media which participate in and contribute to the practices of everyday life. More specifically, I argue that spectators' abilities to reconstruct agency from the flow of images on-screen bespeak a degree of expertise consistent with the democratic possibilities Benjamin saw at the heart of mechanical reproduction, and that, if this positive and constructive attitude of the spectator is to be understood in its own terms, it must also be an object of reflection for the critic.[10] Still more importantly, the institutional functioning of such anthropocentric world views associated with the early film show may only be approached from this supposedly naïve perspective. As early as 1923, Béla Balázs recognised that this configuration of intimacy with film audiences, which he believed 'makes us see a human physiognomy in every phenomenon', was primarily attributable to economic causes.[11] This general insight persistently informs my study of the earliest experiences of the film-going public and of the institutions of film that produced and were the product of it.

The emphasis on the institutional configuration of the early industry also explains the significance attributed by this study to artefacts associated with the publicity and marketing of early films. Although working on a wide range of sources, this book has especially utilised those materials intended to disseminate the account early film institutions gave of themselves. Most significant, here, have been resources such as the trade presses associated with the industries of fairground, magic lantern, music hall, and film, which played a strong role in circulating and promoting examples of institutional 'good practice' to filmmakers and exhibitors alike, and which often described themselves explicitly as guardians of their relevant professions; the catalogues of early filmmakers, which were intended to instruct exhibitors on matters of exhibition as well as to advertise new productions; the group of guide books such as Hopwood's, which might potentially reach a wider public interested in the development or commercial possibilities of the new medium; and the remarkably varied anecdotes detailed in numerous sources concerning early film production and exhibition, which, though factually unreliable, probably represent the early industry's most compelling and widely-disseminated mythologisation of itself to the general public. Clearly, such sources varied considerably in tone, audience, intention, and accuracy but they all embody significant institutional imperatives, and they all seek to share, promote or enculture these among filmmakers, exhibitors, and potential audiences. In particular, as the following chapters will show, drawing from a variety of social and cultural theorists as well as from evidence of this kind, discourses concerned with personality and performance were consistently prevalent throughout such material, suggesting the significance of constructions of 'authentic' personhood within an industry which otherwise appeared to be founded upon technological and industrial premises.

The following chapters approach the archaeology of the early industry from a variety of interrelated perspectives. Chapter 1 seeks to contextualise early film in the broader context of institutional modernity, suggesting that

9

an inclusive account must describe the regulatory, self-reflexive practices initiated by modern industrial practices, which closely tied the agendas of increasingly centralised commercial institutions to the everyday lives of their consumers. Drawing from the sociology of Anthony Giddens, the chapter thus seeks to expand upon the application of models of modernity to early film, which have often drawn strongly from the critical tradition inaugurated by writers such as Georg Simmel in the late nineteenth and early twentieth centuries. Working through a series of case studies, the chapter suggests that the experience of speed and fragmentation described by such writers had often entered explicitly into debates concerning the nature of modern life at the beginning of the twentieth century, and that this knowing attitude to a culturally recognisable problem was therefore ripe for exploitation by contemporary media producers, including filmmakers and exhibitors. It also argues that calling upon relatively familiar, comfortable, and already highly institutionalised models of personality and performance provided an obvious, accessible and instantly marketable means for the early industry to capitalise upon such anxieties.

The subsequent chapters seek to evidence and analyse this idea in two principle ways. In Chapters 2 and 3, dealing respectively with the traditions of performance associated with the film lecturer and the showman, routines of live performance derived from these distinct entertainment traditions are traced in some detail back into the nineteenth century in order to contextualise fully the sophisticated interplay between live performers and audiences that early film shows might potentially call upon. Investigating the business and performance practices of such individuals, these chapters suggest that the relatively direct, face-to-face relationship they might entertain with audiences was remarkably productive for the early industry, not only bringing fully developed and stable commercial practices to film institutions, but also adapting tried and tested methods of generating personal and social reassurance for audiences. Chapters 4 and 5 seek to recover the range of more distant and abstract agencies associated with the image track: the performers on-screen, and the personae credited with responsibility for the expressiveness of the film itself. Working through a representative selection of early film genres and performance styles, these chapters demonstrate that, though the early film industry certainly underwent a rapid process of institutional change matched by the formal development of longer, narrative films, it was consistently underpinned by more pervasive constructions of personality and performance, which link the early film industry backwards to nineteenth-century entertainment traditions and forwards to the development of the so-called institutional or classical cinema in the years that followed. The early film industry thus mobilised models of communication and expression that audiences already recognised, and passed them on, though not without change, to future generations of media industries.

Intimacy with such distant personae has been enjoyed by media audiences ever since and thus far has proved to be both an institutionally coherent and an infinitely flexible configuration of expressive energies. As Giddens has explained, it has also brought about a radical transformation of our manner of 'going on' in the first world.[12] The roots of this transformation need to be traced back into the nineteenth century in order to understand how, around the beginning of the twentieth, film effected a conjunction of cultural and institutional forces that would have a substantial impact on the practices of everyday life. This book contributes to our understanding of this intersection and, in doing so, reflects upon the significance of popular models of personality and performance at the beginning of the era of technological mass media communication.

Performing Intimacy
An Institutional Account of Early Film

During the first decade of cinema, filmmakers, exhibitors and audiences participated in a thorough and self-reflexive examination of the properties of the new medium and of the uses to which it had been put by existing entertainment venues. Screened at music halls, fairgrounds, lecture theatres, bazaars, and even within street shows, film both reflected and influenced existing practices of performance and spectatorship, initiating changes within these institutions that would cumulatively come to redefine them and would lead to the development of new institutions dedicated specifically to cinema. This process was not planned or co-ordinated in any systematic manner. Although it was certainly the case that, from the Lumières onwards, influential film producers, exhibitors and others sought to predict the direction the industry would take (with some limited success), or made attempts to control key aspects of the business (with almost universal failure), early institutions associated with film were too fragmented, and their interests in the new medium too dispersed, to permit any explicit co-ordination of their business practices. To a limited extent, this type of planning would become more feasible in the years after 1908, when the development of picture theatres and of films intended primarily for screening within them contributed to a degree of centralisation within the industry and consequently to the capacity for more effective practices of monitoring and self-regulation.[1] But even at this later point, when consensus concerning the future direction of the industry appeared to have been reached, at least in the pages of the British trade press, film institutions remained characterised by their openness to new influences, their willingness to develop and exploit new markets, and their sensitivity to the untapped potentialities of their audiences.[2]

The business histories of early film institutions are therefore only partially accounted for by existing records of their commercial practices and financial dealings, or by accounts of the decisions reached by key personnel. The commercial conditions of the early film industry were the product of an intense series of negotiations between audiences, exhibitors, producers, and external agencies such as local authorities and trade bodies. Some of these took place openly, as in the public debates initiated by certain producers, exhibitors and public bodies concerning the status of film as an educational tool, dedicated to the moral and intellectual improvement of audiences.[3] More often, however, they were dictated by the customary transactions upon which the industry was founded: the day-to-day interactions of film producers with exhibitors, of exhibitors with their audiences, and of audiences with the screen. This complex network of relationships, sometimes invisible to those at the heart of them, allowed the stabilisation and consolidation of the industry in the years before 1910 because it enabled each of the interested parties to respond to the needs of the others. The industry grew, that is to say, because highly sophisticated and institutionalised routines were already in place by 1895 that enabled spectators to fulfil the commercial ambitions of varied filmmakers and exhibitors, and filmmakers and exhibitors to enact valued functions for their varied audiences.

This series of relationships, established by negotiation, agreement and, occasionally, by force, was not unique to the film industry or to business practices at the *fin de siècle*, but had been and would remain characteristic of commercial institutions in general under conditions of industrial modernity. Borrowing from the sociology of Anthony Giddens and a number of other social theorists, this chapter will argue that early film should therefore be seen as part of this broader logic, in which commercial imperatives are stitched into the everyday lives of consumers and producers, and the changing needs of these individuals are written back into institutional routines in a perpetual interplay of structure and agency. It will also investigate some of the most effective strategies employed by film producers and exhibitors to captivate their audiences, and will suggest that the potential of film to reinforce increasingly troubled constructions of self-identity in this period initiated the cinema primarily as a mechanism of personal and social reassurance. Among several new technologies at the *fin de siècle*, the medium of film most successfully enabled audiences to recover a comforting sense of intimacy that otherwise appeared threatened by the alienation effect popularly associated with conditions of industrial capitalism and particularly with modern media. One of the principal reasons early film institutions thrived was that they encouraged spectators to identify and interact with performers and personalities on-screen and on the platform in front of it. Further, they did so in conventional and repeatable ways, thus enabling them to develop interpretational strategies consonant with the consolidation of a stable marketplace for moving pictures.

Debating Modernity

However, an institutional account of the early film industry runs significantly against the grain of some established methodologies within early film studies, which have sometimes emphasised the perceptual and experiential discontinuities encountered by spectators. Often seeking to account for discrete phenomena, such as the emergence of particular genres or models of spectatorship, it has been possible to draw an analogy between the rapid pace, disjointedness and spectacular impact of performance and exhibition conventions of many early film shows, especially those that depended upon a variety aesthetic, and a general rendering of the experience of modernity as characterised by speed and distraction. According to Ben Singer, for example, the exhibition of early film was closely connected with the everyday experiences of audiences because 'both are characterized by the prominence of fleeting, forceful visual attractions and contra-contemplative spectatorial distraction'.[4]

Work concerning the development of the modern metropolis and new technologies of transportation and communication have proven especially significant for scholars seeking to account for sensational aspects of early twentieth-century representations. The mental and physical dangers posed by cultural and technological trends in the city seem to offer some kind of explanation for the anxieties registered at this time within representations on the screen, within literature and, perhaps most powerfully, in the periodical press. This aspect of early film studies has therefore pursued the spectator of early film from the penny gaff and music hall into the urban landscapes of the *fin de siècle*, describing early film as a manifestation of much broader cultural anxieties.[5] Work such as this has tended to emphasise selected social and cultural rather than institutional aspects of modernity, uncovering the disjointedness experienced by urban dwellers and film spectators. Before proceeding with my account of institutional modernity in relation to the early film industry, and of the experiential continuities experienced by spectators, it is therefore instructive to reconsider this type of reasoning and some of the evidence that has supported it.

As Singer and Tom Gunning have shown, anxieties concerning modernity were international and regularly expressed, reflecting commonalities in experience across Europe, North America and other areas of the world affected by urbanisation and mass industrialisation.[6] The reasons for these anxieties were very varied, reflecting the range of individuals and groups who shared an interest in contrasting what they took to be the fundamental characteristics of modern life, especially in the city, against opposed (and often rather outdated) versions of traditional or alternative modes of life. Participants of the modernity debate included, but were not limited to, supporters and opponents of certain aspects of industrial modernisation; urban explorers and reformers keen to analyse the nature of modern mass publics and consumerism, or interested in the development and planning of the modern metropolis; writers such as Georg Simmel, who have come to be seen to represent the first wave of modern sociologists; medical experts who sought to explain what they believed to be a plague of nervous diseases affecting the modern citizen; and an eclectic group of artists, novelists, critics and intellectuals including Charles Baudelaire, who in 1863 famously defined 'modernity' in relation to art as 'the ephemeral, the fugitive, the contingent'.[7] As might be expected, however, a group this diverse defined modernity in a host of interrelated and often contradictory ways.[8] For example, the range of perspectives offered concerning the nature of the modern city and the conditions of existence within it extended from celebratory accounts of the diversity of the modern metropolis, such as George R Simm's lavishly illustrated, three-volume account of *Living London*, to the grim exploration narratives offered by texts such as William Booth's *In Darkest England and the Way Out*.[9] Dealing with many of the same areas of London, the presentation of the metropolis within such texts was coloured by alternative understandings of modernity, presenting unseen areas of the city to a wide readership as being simultaneously familiar, vibrant and progressive, yet hidden, indolent and absolutely corrupt.

Such writings, it is important to realise, were not neutral or natural renderings of the material conditions of everyday life; however, they did familiarise readers with a variety of perspectives concerning modernity and furnished them with a partial understanding of it. According to one anonymous writer's 'Reflections on Modernity' in 1911, an article which focused especially on the cinematograph and gramophone, the important point was not simply to reproduce or describe the conditions of modernity, but to afford 'all thinking men and women' an opportunity 'to discern what it all means'.[10] However, it is those traditions of writing that sought to emphasise the disempowering and alienating aspects of modernity which have thus far had most influence in early film studies, and these have sometimes been taken as accurate representations of the actual conditions of existence at the *fin de siècle*. Among these sources, Simmel's 1903 essay 'The Metropolis and Mental Life' has occupied an eminent position, one further elevated by its powerful influence on Walter Benjamin's subsequent works concerning urban modernity.[11] In one regularly cited part of Simmel's carefully nuanced essay, the substance of modernity is articulated as a series of attractions that accost the urban subject on every street, in every arcade, at every shop window:[12]

> Lasting impressions, impressions which differ only slightly from one another, impressions which take a regular and habitual course and show regular and habitual contrasts—all these use up, so to speak, less consciousness than does the rapid crowding of changing images, the sharp discontinuity in the grasp of a single glance, and the unexpectedness of onrushing impressions. These are the psychological conditions which the metropolis creates. With each crossing of the street, with the tempo and multiplicity of economic, occupational, and social life, the city sets up a deep contrast with small town and rural life.[13]

This prognosis for the city-dweller has proven exceptionally productive for historians and theorists of early film, especially those with an interest in the distractive qualities of early film texts. Among several celebrated contemporary pieces that have been identified by film historians, it goes some way to explain the early film's predilection for bizarre, exotic and risqué material, and also its fascination with the hustle of street-level *actualité* footage and with phenomena such as Hale's Tours, which offered 'phantom rides' to spectators within theatres designed like train carriages.[14] On such occasions, the cinematograph seems to have responded to the appetite of audiences for novelty, which, if arguably a little jaded, did not seem substantially diminished in the first years of the twentieth century. The attractions of a typical variety film show might include scenic views of foreign landscapes, exotic views of other cultures, all manner of representations of bodily otherness, the regular transgression of bodily boundaries, or the exoticised view of local places, personae and events.[15] Reports of shows and films such as these, which are quite common among the many and varied styles of early film exhibition, thus support the proposition that early film prioritised visual pleasure, spectacle and exhibitionism at the expense of the diegetic, the familiar and the intimate. The 'latest cinematograph freak,' as one fairground journal described an unnamed 1906 trick film in which a baby was eaten, piece by piece, by a horse, promised potential audiences unfamiliar, shocking, humorous, outrageous excess.[16]

17

One problem that has been identified in such views of modernity by writers such as David Bordwell and Charlie Keil is that they pay less attention to alternative styles of film, and that they therefore offer a restricted version of what the highly complex term, modernity, might mean in the context of early film.[17] The analogy between city-dwelling and film leaves a surplus on both sides that has been inconsistently acknowledged. For some commentators, it has led some readings to exaggerate urbanism at the expense of a wide diversity of definitively modern experiences associated with all kinds of human landscapes, and all kinds of representations of these landscapes, at the turn of the century. Early film also demonstrated a fascination with bucolic rural life, with exotic locations, and with the wildernesses that were so often the destinations of late Victorian and Edwardian adventurers. On the other hand, the description of distractive, heterogeneous modernity as a kind of master paradigm for both urban experience and film spectatorship has tended to focus attention away from the familiar and partly traditional routines that typified the reception of early film texts. It has therefore also downplayed the significance of entertainment forms such as magic lantern and dioramic shows, which sometimes provided models for early varieties of film spectatorship.

In response to criticisms such as these, Singer has robustly argued that discontinuity, distraction and speed may not be the only pertinent qualities of experience associated with modernity, but they are certainly important enough to warrant study. 'It is fair to say,' he has explained, 'that proponents of the modernity thesis think it is worthwhile to explore the possibility that the emergence of urban modernity—arguably the most momentous social transformation in human history—had some degree of impact on an art form that developed within this context.'[18] However, the nature of urban modernity is itself a point of sharp critical contention. In response to Bordwell's critique of the modernity thesis, Singer has also acknowledged what he calls the 'habits-and-skills' interpretation of perceptual modernity, agreeing that, in response to the urban environment, a degree of habituation certainly took place among city-dwellers.[19] To some extent, the ability of individuals to cope within the city, to perceive the city as a familiar and comfortable space rather than a site of sensory overload, also goes some way toward explaining the fascination with 'cinematic dynamism'.[20] Gunning has subsequently clarified that a thorough understanding of modernity in relation to cinema must take into account the varied dimensions of this term, a perspective thoroughly evidenced in much of his own work: 'Only by focusing on its various aspects (as well as on the systematic way in which they interrelate, this being a definitive aspect of modernity) can we seriously discuss its impact in history or its impact on film.'[21]

This emphasis on the varied experiential qualities associated with modernity has also begun to inform work concerning late nineteenth-century city life. Borrowing from Henri Lefebvre's *Rhythmanalysis*, Ben Highmore has convincingly argued that the everyday experience of citizens in London at the turn of the century was not characterised uniquely or principally by speeding up, or by a sense of physical and mental danger at large within the city, but by varied rhythmic experiences, most of which were more comfortable than Simmel suggested.[22] Support for this position can be found within the periodical press of the 1890s, which occasionally offered reflections on what French literary critic René Doumic called in 1898 the popular 'craze for modernity'.[23] For writers such as the celebrated British inventor and medical man, Thomas Clifford Allbutt, the much publicised connection between nervous diseases and 'the fretfulness, the melancholy, the unrest due to living at high pressure . . . the whirl of the railway, the pelting of telegrams, the strife of business,' had in large part been manufactured by 'fashionable doctors' on behalf of an increasingly self-conscious and impressionable public.[24] According to Allbutt, the rapid pace of the urban environment had not produced genuine neurasthenic symptoms in patients, only a deluge of discourses concerning neurasthenia in the medical and popular press. Indeed, the tempo of life had actually been responsible for bringing into existence an unprecedentedly healthy young generation, whose experience of such frantic rhythms was leisured and calm:

> It is not then by impressions which are fleeting, but by those which penetrate and endure, that we measure the degrees of excitability and perfection of our nervous systems. As we become more and more able to subordinate the impressions of the moment, and compare them with our stores of previous impressions, we learn that momentary realities, keen as they are, must take their places in the larger sequences of that beautiful instrument which harmonises our joys and resolves our discords.[25]

Allbutt thus distinguished between the speed with which modern life was conducted, particularly within the professions, and the cool, unhurried reflection that potentially allowed individuals to make sense of all of this. For Lefebvre, too, metropolitan experience is characterised by the simultaneous existence of multiple rhythms, some of which reflect the development of faster modes of life, some of which are associated with the linear, progressive rhythms of institutions, and some of which correspond with the more familiar, cyclical, even-paced routines of individuals. Importantly,

19

Lefebvre's work also suggests that these different modes of experience are directly interlaced in the course of day-to-day living, so it becomes problematic to isolate one variety of urban rhythm at the expense of others, or to address cultural, institutional and personal aspects of modernity as if they had ever existed independently.[26] The undoubted increase in the speed with which certain aspects of everyday life was conducted in late nineteenth-century cities produced a complex series of responses from individuals, many of which were co-ordinated by the increasingly pervasive, regular and comfortable rhythmic experiences generated by institutions. Indeed, one of the most significant features of modernity was its incremental tendency to stitch institutional structures and personal and cultural identity ever more closely together—a relationship that was palpably enacted in the course of the early film shows.

This perspective inevitably places emphasis on the conditions in which films were exhibited, and suggests that in order to come to a comprehensive understanding of these conditions we must take account of the long institutional *durée* of their development. Spectatorship is thus contextualised in its dynamic relationship with longstanding institutional sanctions. The explanatory power of this position resides in its ability both to describe the continuities experienced by spectators, and to associate these continuities with the financial stability of the institutions that first adapted film. For example, as distractive as some aspects of the shows undoubtedly were, it has remained hard to imagine how it was that institutions, which habitually publicised as widely as possible their ability to shock audiences, were ever able to achieve this effect. Moreover, even if they did manage—repeatedly—to generate a sensationalist charge of shock for audiences, what was the persistent attraction for audiences of material that was intended to make them uncomfortable? One suggestion has been that sensationalist content roused spectators from the torpidity induced by the routine overstimulation of their everyday lives, and that their desire for it therefore had something of the nature of a compulsion. A closely related version of the same argument has suggested that spectacular novelties served the cultural function of inoculating audiences against the neurasthenic *mêlée* of the city street, the workplace, and their increasingly busy lives.

But, significant as these social roles may have been, these answers do not altogether explain the overwhelmingly easy and nostalgic tone of most first hand accounts of variety shows. As was the case under conditions of urban modernity in general, according to Lefebvre, the speed at which film shows were conducted and their occasional emphasis on unsettling features of modern life did not only produce a distractive, ephemeral or fretful experience for spectators. After all, many of the cinema's first audiences were exposed on a daily basis to a great deal of the same publicity material concerning film that now fascinates film historians, and they were certainly much more familiar with the experience of the variety aesthetic, so it should not be surprising that they quickly developed some degree of 'habits and skills' mastery over cinematic sensationalism. As one 1907 recollection of the first film show to be screened in an English village recorded: 'to the ignorant country mind there was a touch of the uncanny about it all . . . But as the evening wore on and picture after picture followed in quick succession enjoyment began to take the place of wonderment.'[27]

In this context, it is possible to identify yet another productive application of Tom Gunning's influential account of the early 'cinema of attractions'.[28] In addition to enacting 'surprise, shock, and trauma', as Gunning suggests, the early cinema enabled audiences to read these qualities of the new medium knowingly, and in a manner which probably sat quite comfortably with their presuppositions concerning the subjects of the films or expectations of the show. Thus, as Charles Musser has also argued, directly citing Gunning's work on early attractionism, 'early film spectators performed significant intellectual activity involving comparison, evaluation, and judgment—as opposed to (or simultaneously with) either the enraptured spectator passively contemplating a beautiful picture or the "gawker . . . held for the moment by curiosity and amazement"'.[29] I would add to this assessment that the provision of novelty was a highly institutionalised affair, and we can look to the analysis of key institutions under conditions of modernity to explain why this particular format, among several others, became so popular within early film. Furthermore, doing so is far from inconsistent with Gunning's own position on these issues: 'I have written,' Gunning has confirmed, 'that aspects of the cinema of attractions . . . corresponded to the new modern environment of shocks as described by Benjamin and others. But I have never claimed that these social and environmental factors on their own constitute a sufficient explanation of all formal aspects of early motion pictures.'[30] Placing emphasis on the institutional dimensions of modernity allows us to consider in more detail the complex functioning of attractions for the audiences who encountered them, and also to focus on the creative role these audiences might play in relation to such materials.

There were a number of institutional strategies for presenting attractions to audiences, some of which have remained enduringly significant throughout the nineteenth and twentieth centuries. For example, in separate studies, Tony Bennett and Timothy Mitchell have described the

21

capacity of even the most heterogeneous nineteenth-century exhibition spaces to tutor audiences in the organisation of knowledge about the world, making it comfortably visible and knowable within conventional spectatorial regimes.[31] 'By the end of the century,' in Bennett's words, 'the fair, no longer a symbol of chaos, had become the ultimate spectacle of an ordered totality.'[32] Closely related work concerning exhibition environments such as freak shows, travelogues and ethnological shows has demonstrated the significance of the spectacular exhibition of otherness in the reassertion and consolidation of normative models of national, racial, sexual and gender identity.[33] As Simmel also understood, it was only in the possibility of stepping into otherness that the borders of the human being acquired what he called, in a less celebrated essay, their 'significance and dignity'.[34]

When film first appeared, often exhibited by showmen with a long history of working the shows, many of the same strategies would be adopted.[35] This understanding of alterity was one of the primary logics underpinning variety styles of film show, in which cultural oddities were presented by filmmakers and showmen in order to confirm their audiences' comfortable acquiescence with a respectable or familiar norm. The marketing of otherness facilitated this process directly and deliberately, becoming, as might be expected, most intense in periods such as that at the turn of the century, when constructions of personal identity appeared most under duress. This was one of the ways in which early film institutions began to stitch themselves into the everyday lives of their consumers. They thrived on the sense of crisis circulated so pervasively by popular and professional discourses during this period because they were able to offer some measure of reassurance to audiences. In fact, they had inherited a long tradition of doing just this: as we have seen, modernity had been persistently represented by many commentators as a perpetual sense of ongoing crisis, so it is not surprising to find that popular entertainments had long ago evolved to capitalise on this fact. In this light, early cinema can be regarded as an environment that not only reproduced some of the most widely disseminated perspectives on modernity, including those associated with the speeding up of certain aspects of everyday life, but also allowed them to be registered, deliberated, and worked through, thus fulfilling invaluable cultural functions for knowing audiences in addition to the residual appeal of novelty, spectacle and the ephemeral.

Space, Time, and the Problem of Empathy

An understanding of the value of alterity in film shows thus leads us directly into consideration of intimate questions of personality and self-identity, which appear to have borne a heightened significance at the turn of the century, as commentators on literature of the period have done much to establish.[36] Such questions are not to be addressed lightly, for they touch upon complex and constantly evolving relationships between modern institutions and individuals that are not only central to a history of early film and of its reception, but also lie at the heart of conditions of industrial modernity. However, film, among several media technologies at the turn of the century, arguably has a doubled significance in terms of the analysis of personal and institutional dimensions of modernity. As Giddens explains, such media are 'as much an expression of the disembedding, globalising tendencies of modernity as they are the instruments of such tendencies'.[37] On the one hand they were part of the general process of 'disembedding' in which social relationships were lifted out from local contexts and reorganised into new relationships with distant and centralised institutions. On the other, because such media often sought to represent distant realities to mass audiences, and because they enabled the storage of such representations across long stretches of time, they were a direct and material enactment of this same process of disembedding, distancing and dialogue. They therefore offered a unique opportunity for reflection upon these effects of modernity.

The *fin de siècle* concern with space and time, expressed widely within philosophical, professional, popular and commercial discourses—though seldom in exactly these terms—was therefore an important part of the snowballing dialogue between institutions of early film and their audiences, and can be read as part of the process of coming to terms with the technological and representational properties of the medium. Additionally, because film appeared to enact so clearly the general conditions of time/space distanciation upon which modern institutions depended, it even became the focus of a series of reflections on the general conditions of modern life. Within this debate, issues of intimacy, communication and empathy became particularly significant. The film's distant personae embodied perfectly the widespread cultural anxiety that the relationships between humans were degenerating, becoming increasingly distant and abstract, with potentially disastrous consequences for individuals and the societies they composed.

Such varied and well-known discourses of entropy and degeneration in the 1890s and 1900s would afford proponents and critics of the cinematograph fertile grounds for an appraisal of its mechanical, populist representations of human identity. As writers such as Allbutt knew only too well, there was already an established symptomatology of modernity upon which all manner of pessimistic commentators could draw. The 'Modernity Hospital', as one writer for *Atlantic Monthly* called it in 1895, was filled with

23

young 'new women' and 'yellow men' unsure about their gender roles and faced with a disorientating urban, professional or domestic environment that appeared to endanger the construction of a healthy personal identity and to compromise personal and sexual relationships at every step.[38] Equally, however, the cinematograph could be represented as a positive response to these same anxieties, promising to bridge the gaps between individuals, to project *living* pictures of real individuals—somehow more than mere images—onto the screen, or to shore up constructions of normative personal identity with representations of personal and social 'good practice'. Both perspectives tended to interpret the cinematograph, its representations, and the form of attention it demanded from audiences as symptoms of a broader transformation of experience whose implications, positive or negative, were yet to be fully played out.

Frequently, critics found in the cinematograph a perfect realisation as well as an apt metaphor for the growing value of abstraction and alterity within modern life. Indeed, an emphasis on the alienating, distancing features of modernity appeared in some of the first reviews of the Lumière Cinématograph, which sometimes described the moving pictures as further evidence of the dominance of a debilitating and increasingly hysterical consumerist urban culture. Critics such as O. Winter, writing in the *New Review*, and (most famously) Maxim Gorky explicitly opposed themselves to the prevailing accounts of the extraordinary realism of the Lumière productions, variously emphasising the artificial, mechanical and inhuman qualities of the new medium.[39] Describing the 'fatuity of a near approach to "life"' in all art forms, Winter attributed the wonderment inspired by the cinematograph to the profound ignorance of its audiences concerning the work of authentic artistic creation.[40] Believing themselves to be brought closer than ever to reality by the apparently lifelike representations projected on-screen, Winter argued that these audiences had never before been so distant from the only form of contact that the artwork could genuinely deliver: the communication between artist and viewer. The experience of watching the films was therefore peculiarly empty, being little more than a fascination with abstract figures, hollowed of significance, flitting across the screen in an absurd parody of life. 'It seems,' Gorky evocatively claimed of Lumière's *Jeux de Cartes* (1895), 'as if these people have died and their shadows have been condemned to play cards in silence unto eternity.'[41] From these accounts onwards, distrustful commentators on the early moving image were often far from convinced that the apparatus could evoke an empathetic response in its viewers and began to see it as symptomatic of the dehumanising propensities of society in general and of modern technologies in particular.

In doing so, of course, these commentators gave little credence to the experiences of most early film audiences, which were more likely to emphasise a sense of emotional proximity to the screen. Denigrating popular tastes for realism and sentimentalism that now seemed typified by moving pictures, critics such as Winter suggested instead that these experiences were probably harmful for audiences, and especially for those groups deemed most impressionable, or vulnerable to habitual models of thinking, such as women, children, and the working classes. This perspective also enabled them to defend the increasingly permeable boundaries between high and low cultural forms. For example, the graphic artist Joseph Pennell, writing in 1897, found that the arrival of moving pictures had merely extended the long-standing debate concerning the potential status of photography as a fine art. In order to secure images of the Jubilee procession that were of 'artistic importance', the article argued, it would have been necessary to secure the services of 'half a dozen accomplished artists' in place of the 'senseless lens' of the camera.[42] The mechanical reproduction of images, such accounts often assumed, would inevitably lead to a degree of automatism in their viewers, and would therefore be likely to contribute to the anaesthetising effects popularly associated with modernity. The moving pictures, as another cultural commentator was still arguing almost twenty years after Winter's piece, typified this trend, having 'an enervating influence on the imagination, and for this crime there could be no forgiveness'.[43]

In his 1907 work, *Creative Evolution*, published in English in 1911, Henri Bergson considered the cinematic apparatus not only as a symptom of these features of modernity, but also as an elaborate metaphor for the damaging and alienating features of modern life, which he had begun to describe in the late 1880s. The cinematograph, he claimed, merely imitated reality, 'extracting from all the movements peculiar to all the figures an impersonal movement', and was therefore an apt model for an abstract, spatialising form of thought that prevented each individual from understanding their own unique positions in the world or those of others.[44] In everyday life, Bergson complained, individuals had acquired a pragmatic but psychologically disastrous ability to place themselves outside the 'inner becoming of things' and beyond the possibility of comprehending the *durée* of existence.[45] The problem for the modern individual was that it had become impossible to escape from subtractive processes of consciousness, and that he or she therefore only attempted to comprehend those aspects of life from which some identifiable material gain was to be had, bracketing out other aspects as irrelevancies or distractions. It had become impossible to remain open to an authentic experience of existence. Gilles Deleuze has re-read these passages in order to argue that the cinema would eventually realise aspects of Bergsonian *durée*, but Bergson's initial condemnation of the apparatus was consistent with the thinking of other critics of film in this period and, considered in this context, remains a highly developed and pertinent response to the early film.

The impersonality of the medium, accounts such as these suggested, was representative of a broad trend within modern life, wherein individuals had become adept at objectifying others and detaching themselves from the responsibilities of genuine intimacy and empathy. For such critics, the mechanism of the cinema, which introduced a fundamental distance between the film's performers and audiences, could also exemplify the threat that individuals were becoming divorced from the possibility of genuine empathy or self-knowledge. The social and personal problems credited to this analogy were various, so that the film show became an important contributor to popular conceptions of the modernity hospital, with a symptomatology all its own. In addition to the anticipated deadening of imaginative powers that was predicted for the new generation of moving picture audiences, certain physical symptoms, comparable to those that had been diagnosed in neurasthenics and other supposed victims of the modern sensorium, were also ascribed to film spectators.[46] Initially, these emerged as a consequence of the flickering effect created by the earliest projectors and the disorientation sometimes induced by operation of the apparatus. Indeed, criticism of 'the whizzing and whirling and twittering of nerves, and blinkings and winkings that it causes in not a few of the spectators', in which it is possible to discern echoes of certain contemporary medical discourses, are common amongst early reviews of film shows.[47] But problems associated with frequent attendance at cinematograph shows were soon to be discussed much more directly as issues requiring professional medical attention. Injuries caused to the eyes and nerves attributed to the early apparatus were of concern to film societies, and were sometimes debated in the British film trade press.[48] A familiar Victorian pathology of hysteria in early film spectators and in certain key films has been described by Lynne Kirby, who has also associated this response with contemporary writing concerning neurasthenia in the urbanising, technologising world of the 1890s.[49]

The film show was thus criticised or condemned by a range of commentators. But though the cinematograph seemed to typify the tendency of modern media to alienate their audiences from authentic interpersonal communication, other commentators, such as the writer of 'Reflections on Modernity', emphasised that it could also connect them across great distances of space and time:

In the darkness of one of London's innumerable Electric Palaces that have sprung up like mushrooms almost in a night let us try to shake ourselves free from the rather apathetic mesmerism of the performance, and detach ourselves with an effort from the fascinating adventures, and quietly think what is happening. We are listening to an impersonal voice, and we are looking at an impersonal play, both *almost* to the life, but without the living presence of actor or singer. What has done this?— primarily, powers of thought. Where our forefathers saw fleshly personalities we stand on the threshold of a new era; we are beginning to see thought-people and hear thought-voices.

The world seems to be rising from its apparently established fetters in every direction, mind is overcoming limitations of time and space in ways that have never been even faintly imagined possible to man.[50]

Accounts such as this, which emphasised the potential of the apparatus to enhance communication or to educate audiences were also very common in this period, though they seldom adopted such a contemplative approach to this phenomenon. In the first thirty years of the film, the positive possibilities for filmic communication were more often celebrated within universal language metaphors of mutual understanding. As Miriam Hansen has indicated, metaphors connoting 'egalitarianism, internationalism, and the progress of civilization through technology' proliferated from the Lumières' first screenings.[51] These internationalist ideals of film language can be traced back to long-established educational impulses among earlier visual media, such as those associated with photography and magic lantern culture. 'Pictures are paramount at the present time,' wrote one observer of educational entertainments by 1900, 'and the world at large is greatly benefited thereby.'[52]

Borrowing from such discourses, early film institutions countered accusations that they functioned by cheapening and over-exciting the popular imagination with positive images of mutual enlightenment, and enthusiastically promoted the democratic opportunity the device extended to audiences for virtual travel and other means of self-betterment. From 1903, the Charles Urban Trading Company logo proudly announced the capacity of their films to 'put the world before you', and Montagu Pyke, owner of Pyke's theatre chain, claimed in 1912 that the Cinematograph had 'annihilated space . . . with the result that sympathy is excited, different races begin to understand one another and to feel that though the colour of their skin, or the articulate sounds by which they convey their thoughts may differ, they are, nevertheless, bound together by the firm cord of humanity'.[53] Urban and

Pyke, both masters of self-publicity, had a direct commercial interest in exploiting discourses of self-improvement and self-help, which had become increasingly common from the mid-nineteenth century. For such writers, the moving pictures were to be celebrated, either because they afforded audiences the opportunity to expand their horizons, making hitherto impossible contact with the screen's distant personae, or because they educated audiences concerning models of social good practice, or simply because the spectacle of otherness was deemed to have value in and of itself. From this point of view, film was to be associated with the most utopian impulses of modernity, helping to shrink, harmonise, and rationalise the world.

The fundamental properties of the medium were thus intensely scrutinised within varied popular, professional, and philosophical discourses at the turn of the century, with particular attention paid to the contested relationship between audience and medium. Whether the cinematograph was regarded as a technology that distanced or alienated spectators from its subjects or that connected them with scenes and peoples otherwise unavailable to them, it was persistently linked within the public imagination to fundamental questions of space, time, presence and communication, all of which had a much broader resonance within *fin de siècle* culture. Such debate was not simply an effect of the arrival of the new technology, and cannot be taken only as evidence of an analogy between the cinematograph and the conditions of modernity. It was a key feature of early film culture from the beginning, understood by many parties with an interest in moving pictures, including producers, exhibitors and audiences, and was therefore instrumental to the development of the industry. The debate can be seen most profitably as part of the context that enabled audiences to make sense of film shows, and also as part of the process of rapid institutional development undergone by producers and exhibitors of film, suggesting some of the ways in which all of these parties were interconnected.

For the institutions that first adopted film and for their audiences, the quality of human presence during the show was a shared preoccupation, one that linked them in a manner that proved absolutely compelling for both. However, in order to engage more extensively with these processes of institutional definition at work in the early film industry, it is now necessary to offer one further description of the conditions of modernity, intended to take account of the constitutive activities of modern institutions, and of media institutions in particular. In doing so, we will continually return to the questions of empathy, presence and personality with which so many contemporaries were concerned. For, in a culture increasingly co-ordinated by the actions of highly centralised institutions whose success was founded upon a capacity to remove consumers from the means and conditions of production, the surrogate forms of contact and intimacy offered by moving pictures became uniquely valuable.

An Institutional Account of Early Film

Institutional theories of film have been most widely associated with the American classical filmmaking tradition of the period between approximately 1912 and 1950. This tradition has been approached from several widely diverging theoretical perspectives, some now regularly discredited, but most accounts have agreed upon the basic formal characteristics of classical film. According to David Bordwell, Janet Staiger and Kristin Thompson, classical film relied on 'notions of decorum, proportion, formal harmony, respect for tradition, mimesis, self-effacing craftsmanship, and cool control of the perceiver's response' for its effects.[54] Arguably, an inclusive account of this period of filmmaking would also include heterogeneous and incongruous elements largely bracketed out by this definition, perhaps, to adopt the terms introduced by Rick Altman, emphasising the performance of each film screening in terms of its unique status as an event.[55] However, the tendency has remained for early film studies to define pre-classical cinema in antithesis to this list of characteristics, emphasising its apparently low levels of institutional coherence. Indeed, relationships have been suggested between early film and examples of avant-garde film partially on this basis.[56] Other studies have demonstrated the significance of local contexts of production, exhibition, and reception and have suggested that in some instances it is possible to read local practices in terms of deliberate resistance to centralised institutional control.[57] A great deal of evidence underwrites such claims, but in relation to the development of commercial institutions such as those associated with the film industry, it is important to see paradigms of dominance and resistance, which appear to have emerged only fitfully and under particular social pressures in the first years of cinema, as only one part of a broader series of transactions connecting film producers and exhibitors with their audiences.[58] That is to say, we should regard them as features of institutional transactions.

As we might expect, given the continuity of practices most often experienced by their users, institutions associated with film did all they could to avoid sudden paradigm shifts and seldom experienced periods of rapid change as crises. In most circumstances, they underwent developmental processes that led smoothly between early and later traditions and their associated, highly institutionalised, patterns of spectatorship. Recent research concerning the business strategies of key British early film institutions confirms that, from the beginning, they sought to establish market stability and that they maintained consistent strategies of production and exhibition in order to achieve this. For example, Richard Brown and Barry Anthony's extensive work on the British Mutoscope and Biograph Company has shown that this company's films were perfectly crafted to satisfy the expectations of audiences in British music hall and that they established a close relationship with exhibitors at these sites in order to protect this market.[59] It also shows that the style of the films and the manner in which they were marketed were subject to gradual transitions which, without depending upon developmental teleologies or upon antithetical models of later cinemas, cumulatively led to what I believe might legitimately still be called an 'evolution' of film in response to this dynamic exhibition environment.[60] Similarly, Luke McKernan's study of the various companies led by Charles Urban from the 1890s to the 1920s has revealed a persistent, though not wholly successful, agenda to establish a marketplace for educational moving pictures, and has uncovered evidence of repeated efforts to stabilise this business, making further contacts with entertainment venues, education boards and potential audiences internationally.[61] Broader studies of early shop-front exhibitions in London (the counterpart of the US nickelodeons) and of British fairground Bioscope shows have also shown that these venues were operative for much longer than had been previously assumed.[62] These exhibitors have been characterised as facing a crisis from about 1910, and most certainly their numbers did eventually fall away in response to a number of factors, not least the development of the picture theatre. But it has also become clear that both of these sites had also originated exhibition practices that would have a lasting influence on spectatorship in the picture theatres during the 1910s and 1920s, and that their institutional structures are therefore of great interest in relation to the study of subsequent cinemas.

Such accounts suggest that the 'transitional phase' of cinema dated approximately from 1907 to 1915, which has described formal aspects of film in transformation between the early and classical periods, becomes rather empty and arbitrary in relation to patterns of institutional development.[63] These processes were incremental and continuous, and were carried out across long time periods by many different institutions, any of which might potentially impact upon the others. Ben Brewster has cautioned, in the context of US filmmaking, that the definitions of early, transitional and classical cinema, though descriptively useful, are therefore always likely to be problematic: 'periodization is a dubious enterprise; everything is always changing into something else'.[64] Given that institutions are notable for their stability, for their capacity to weather all kinds of challenges within a commercial environment, and given also that they customarily present themselves as unchanging and secure, this dynamism is sometimes rather difficult to see. From the first film screenings, spectators, exhibitors and producers called upon an inherited and highly institutionalised repertoire, whose continuities were—and are—apparent. But these groups were each also able to initiate changes to this repertoire, even if they were not always conscious of doing so. It is this fundamental interaction between dynamic institutional structures and creative agency that we must account for within any model of institutional change.

This kind of relationship, in which creative agency and institutional structures become interdependent and their interaction is the motor driving institutional change, has been described by Anthony Giddens in terms of the principle of *duality of structure*.[65] Giddens's influential account of this idea emphasises the centrality of institutions under conditions of modernity, but offers a corrective to pessimistic assessments of a culture industry as entirely dominated by hegemonic institutional forces.[66] For Giddens, the term 'institution' describes the reification of structural continuities within social systems across broad stretches of space and time. Modern institutions are relatively stable clusters of conventions and resources which do not merely impose constraints on the practices of individual agents (although this is certainly one of the things they do) but are 'both constraining and enabling', offering to agents a range of choices which are in fact the condition of institutional change.[67] At the same time, the situated actions of agents have the effect of reproducing the conditions for the existence of the institution, though this effect is not usually the guiding motivation for these actions. This is why, under conditions of modernity, the structures of modern institutions and of personal identity become so closely interlaced: institutional structures are woven into the most routine everyday practices of individuals, but the enactment of such practices always carries with it the possibility of rewriting them. This kind of potential is most often held within practical consciousness, enacted in the course of everyday life rather than theorised or openly debated, and this means that under normal circumstances institutions are never essentially under any individual mechanism of control. They roll forward, often in a manner unintended and unanticipated, as an accumulation of decisions made by a variety of agents. Once the action of institutions enters into consideration, it becomes clear that modernity is, to adopt Giddens's most famous metaphor, an out-of-control juggernaut, one that somehow hurtles in multiple directions. It also becomes clear that, though this metaphor describes a nightmare scenario of powerlessness, institutional continuities ensure that we seldom experience our lives as disempowered, alienated or numbed. 'It has become commonplace to claim that modernity fragments, dissociates,' writes Giddens, 'yet the unifying features of modern institutions are just as central to modernity—especially in the phase of high modernity—as the disaggregating ones.'[68]

The potential impact of this theory upon our understanding of the early film industry is perhaps easiest to discern in relation to relatively familiar debates concerning spectatorship and film institutions.[69] In relation to audiences, exhibition is shown to be a central point of mediation in the duality of structure: the screening of a film participates in the creation of the spectator at the same time as the conventions for film exhibition and styles of filmmaking are reassessed and reproduced by the spectator. In doing so, of course, the spectator reacts to a much wider range of influences than could ever be foreseen by producers or exhibitors, not least the responses of other members of the audience. It is therefore not useful to speak of an ideal film spectator whose relationship with the screen was straightforwardly dictated by a dominant or conventional institutionalised relationship. Rather, the early film spectator creatively responded to a variety of competing social, cultural and institutional stimuli, sometimes conforming to institutional expectations and sometimes, perhaps less often, calling these expectations into question or reorienting them altogether. This confirms commonsense assumptions concerning each spectator's position within an audience—often in sympathy with the responses of the others, but sometimes in less comfortable positions of incomprehension, disagreement or conflict. As the hotly contested history of the 'train effect' has testified, even the responses of the first film audiences to the threatening spectacle of an oncoming train on-screen evoked heterogeneous and competing responses between and within audiences.[70]

However, in the empirical field of this study—and it is important to note that Giddens is not seeking to write a history of institutions, let alone a history of early film institutions—three amendments to the idea of duality of structure are especially pertinent, and it will be productive to pursue these in some depth.

First, given the concrete and strongly determinative form of institutions, it seems unlikely that the degree of freedom that Giddens accords to the agent in his or her encounter with them could ever be achieved. John B. Thompson, in a powerful critique of Giddens's account of structural constraints to agency, imagines a situation in which the range of feasible options available to an agent is limited to one—a situation wherein the institution and the powerful social groups associated with it indeed possess unlimited control.[71] Returning to the example of film spectatorship, I do not believe that this was the position of audiences at any historical moment; the structural conditions of early film in particular offered a proliferation of choice, not least in the variety of exhibition venues that were available.[72] However, in the specific institutional context of, say, a music hall cinematograph show, the behaviour and receptive activities of the spectator were likely to be very strongly constrained by their environment. Institutional sanctions were habitually put into force here by staff and live performers; by the convention-ridden community of the audience; by the representational style and subjects of the images on-screen; and even by the design, layout, and lighting of the exhibition site. All such factors introduced aspects of what Lefebvre has called 'dressage': a kind of personal and social training that most often takes place within practical consciousness, though it also occurs overtly in a range of educational environments. In the context of a film screening, dressage certainly constrained the range of activities that spectators were able to pursue, but its capacity to enable creative responses was likely to be much more limited. In the first years of early film, when exhibitors and filmmakers were policing very intently the range of possibilities of audience response in order to safeguard existing profitable practices, dressage was especially important.

Second, Giddens's underestimation of the role of constraints upon agency has led to a parallel neglect of what he calls 'material constraints', consideration of which is especially vital in relation to the modern mass media.[73] In the first place this term refers to the limits placed upon agency by the physical capacities of the human body within its environment, but it also refers to the enabling and constraining capacities of the media that agents encounter—from verbal conversation to film. According to Thompson's description of twentieth-century mass media in general, early film offered 'a structured situation in which some individuals are engaged primarily in producing symbolic forms for others who are not physically present, while others are involved primarily in receiving symbolic forms produced by others to whom they cannot respond, but with whom they can form bonds of friendship, affection, or loyalty'.[74] As the contemporary debate concerning space, time and communication in relation to the cinematograph has already demonstrated, the material capacity of the film apparatus to make some form of contact across large distances was especially important to its first users.

As in the case of all modern mass media, material constraints were tied very closely to the patterns of dressage that connected a film's producers with its exhibitors and viewers. Thus, films not only generated a one-way communication between distant places and peoples: unlike most of the products of modern institutions, films were also able to train consumers in the 'correct' methods of exhibiting and interpreting them. The large number of films before 1910 that portray film shows being interrupted by 'deviant' examples of spectatorship testifies to such producer-led attempts to contain and control the manner in which films were watched. But the most significant feature of this form of dressage, as Thompson suggests, was the consistent presentation of familiar models of personality and performance to audiences. The appearance of performers such as comedians and acrobats or of recognisable public personalities on-screen, of live performers alongside the screen, and also the implied presence of narrative and authorial agencies 'behind' the screen, all encouraged audiences to interpret the exhibition of film in a manner consistent with existing performative regimes, and therefore superimposed these regimes onto the medium's actual material constraints. Thus, early films performed an experience of intimacy for and with their audiences, effectively guiding audience responses by enabling them to recover a cherished sense of contact with the screen's distant personae.

At the same time, the material capacities of the early film show also enabled exhibitors and audiences to respond, directly or indirectly, to the decisions made by film producers on issues such as these. Exhibitors might pass on to producers some of the concerns and desires expressed by their customers, either directly or through the pages of the trade press, and filmmakers were, of course, always sensitive to popular reactions to earlier productions and to general trends in the market. Ultimately, the style and content of films and the qualities of intimacy that they reproduced were generated by an uneven process of negotiation between all of these interested parties. This process was central to the institutional development of film. Understanding it allows us to describe the evolving relationships that institutions of film production and exhibition had with audiences as the industry developed. For example, it demonstrates that, as filmmakers gradually took responsibility during the 1900s for the narrative and thematic content of the shows from exhibitors, they also adapted and repackaged models of personality that had been important to audiences for decades.

My third variation on Giddens's work concerning institutional duality of structure is simply that it maintains a degree of abstraction and generality that is incommensurable with the universe of social phenomena he hopes to account for. In order to engage more specifically with detailed empirical material that can contextualise and explain developmental trends in early film, it is therefore also useful to distinguish between what Thompson has called 'specific institutions', such as individual exhibition venues or production companies, and 'generic or sedimented institutions', which can describe the institutionalised structures and conventions shared by specific institutions.[75] This distinction adds specific institutions as a third term to Giddens's duality, introducing individual, concrete organisations as the bodies responsible for negotiating between abstract institutional imperatives and individual agency. In actual practice, specific and generic institutions are very difficult to separate, but an understanding of their close interaction allows us to describe developmental processes for both.

The arrival of film in the British entertainment marketplace offers an obvious case study of this process of interaction between specific and generic institutions, largely because this was the first moment in which specific exhibitors, producers and spectators, all of whom were constrained by earlier generic institutional structures, encountered and responded to the material constraints of the new medium. In particular, it enables us to investigate the redeployment of the highly institutionalised Victorian market for personality by varied specific institutions associated with early film, as becomes clear when we address each of these interest groups in turn. For exhibitors, as is well known, there was a tendency to adopt the cinematograph into all manner of exhibition venues, or, indeed, anywhere that large crowds might gather, and to adapt existing performance practices so that moving pictures might integrate seamlessly within existing routines. Within the first few years of its appearance in Britain, film appeared most regularly in variety theatres, magic lantern entertainments, fairground shows, and shop-front shows: established entertainment venues, each with a dynamic but secure set of generic performance conventions firmly in place. In each case, as specific institutions assimilated the new medium within existing practices, they contributed to broader changes made to generic institutional conventions. For example, as Richard Crangle has noted, in order to accommodate moving pictures, the highly institutionalised routines of lantern lecturing were considerably altered between 1895 and 1910, with lecturers embracing, resisting, or compromising with a medium that could substantially 'speak' for itself.[76] The success of moving pictures meant that each lecturer had to find some kind of performative response in order to survive within their substantially altered market, and such changes also introduced changes to the range of generic conventions lecturers shared.

Similar relationships were also at work for film's first producers, though these relationships are not always so clearly understood. Filmmakers emerged from a wide variety of generic institutional contexts: many, like Frank Mottershaw's Sheffield Photographic Company, were specialists in the photographic trade; Bamforth and Co. already had a well developed business in magic lantern slides; William Haggar had been a travelling showman in Wales for decades before he purchased his Animatograph apparatus from Robert Paul, another early producer, who had been working on the technology of moving pictures for some years. Each of the specific institutions led by these individuals adapted earlier technologies, representational styles, and performance practices in their production of film in a complex series of interactions, most recently theorised in terms of the idea of intermediality.[77] Of course, they were open to all manner of influences, not all of which relate obviously to other media, but in the first instance they were certainly most likely to seek to satisfy the markets they knew best. Bamforth, for example, sought to exploit the existing lantern market, and their films often directly reproduced the narratives of their own slide sequences, including character stereotypes with which their audiences were likely to be familiar. William Haggar initially produced films intended to satisfy the audiences of his own travelling Bioscope show, and, as David Berry has noted, his characters and narratives are consequently designed to appeal primarily to working-class tastes.[78] In doing this, these producers introduced stylistic, narrative and performative features into their own film-making that fed into the generic institutional development of film style as a whole, and which consequently have come to be seen as innovations.

Audiences, too, drew upon a set of shared generic conventions that had informed earlier practices of spectatorship, but also upon a wide variety of textual, contextual and intertextual knowledge. Especially significant, once again, was the expectation that films and live performers would present recognisable and comfortable models of personality and performance. On the fairground, for example, audiences of the Great Shows, such as large menageries and ghost illusion shows, had traditionally been confronted by an array of live performers, including acrobats, freaks, comics, dancers and musicians, not to mention the showmen themselves, all of whom might address the crowd both outside and within the canvas. These distinct performance traditions each tended to initiate a dialogue with audiences whose open and interactive quality was a significant attraction of the fair. When film was widely adopted on the fairground during 1897 and 1898, audiences therefore brought certain expectations, which were met by the showmen, that similar practices would be reproduced by the Bioscope shows. However, the actual practice of Bioscope spectatorship also inevitably introduced changes to these shared conventions and, consequently, directly influenced the practices of exhibitors. Within the shows, though practices varied, live variety performances often appeared only between films, or perhaps were replaced by the relatively transparent performance of a lecturer, and so the quality of dialogue associated with exhibition at the fair also underwent a subtle, uneven transformation.

In relation to the early film industry we must therefore take account of a wide range of interactions between generic institutional structures and specific individual institutions. As duality of structure explains, although concrete acts of film production, exhibition and spectatorship were co-ordinated by familiar institutional sanctions, these acts could also profoundly influence and alter such sanctions, potentially introducing changes to the entire industry that were more or less unpredictable from their point of origin. The industry can be characterised as developing simultaneously on many separate fronts, with each individual change intrinsically connected to other, apparently distant activities. This supports Giddens's notion that, under conditions of modernity, institutions successfully connect local contexts of action with distant imperatives, often across large spans of time and space. In relation to early film, it also enables us to take into account the massive variations in the actions of specific institutions, without sacrificing the idea that they each contributed to the much wider institutional frameworks that co-ordinated the industry as a whole.

The well-known international 'crisis' in film legibility initiated by the growth of longer narrative films during 1908–09 offers a second relatively clear example of this kind of multi-layered interaction at work. As I will show in Chapter 2, some commentators did not, in fact, believe that there was any such problem for the average spectator but for those exhibitors who felt that audiences were befuddled by complex visual narratives a number of solutions were possible. For some, the reintroduction of a film lecturer—a very familiar figure for most audiences—was the appropriate response, but others self-consciously promoted longer, more difficult films, a strategy associated with attempts to intellectualise and legitimise the cinema. Still others decided to continue exhibiting shorter, formally simpler movies, so that the problem did not arise. Of course, such decisions depended in part upon the responses of existing audiences, and had a considerable impact on the way different exhibition venues came to describe themselves to these audiences. Consequently, generic institutions of film exhibition gradually changed. For film producers, faced with the same problem of narrative clarity and also with the responses of exhibitors, there was a parallel set of options. Some concentrated on film genres that supported traditional lecturing practices and formats, such as travelogues and current event films. Others introduced more extensive and frequent intertitling in order to support longer narrative formats, or developed editing practices that were more easily internalised, because they fostered voyeuristic tendencies within audiences, or specialised in comic genres that created fewer legibility problems. Once again, each decision had lasting generic institutional consequences, contributing to distinct and heterogeneous filmmaking practices within later cinemas, from the production of features or comic shorts to newsreels and travel films. For spectators, these possible decisions of exhibitors and filmmakers among countless others, impacted upon the choices they made in their selection of entertainment venue and informed their viewing of the films, ultimately introducing changes to practices of spectatorship in general and, therefore, to the entire industry. In this context, the development of a 'narrator system' within fictional narrative film, in which 'the spectator can identify with the camera's power to unmask and penetrate into the hidden feelings of the figure on the screen', can be seen as just one among many developments in spectatorial conventions—though certainly a very significant one in terms of the subsequent growth of feature filmmaking.[79]

As the two foregoing case studies concerning the appearance of the new medium and the supposed crisis of narrative legibility have suggested, processes of institutional change are never as straightforward as consumer or producer command models imply and are very rarely the responsibility of only one decision-making agency. It is important to remember that producers, exhibitors and spectators in these transactions were each capable of directing the responses of the others, that their varied imperatives were sometimes in conflict, and that they were each, at various points, subject to external industrial, cultural and legislative forces that could be partially determining for all. For example, where it occurred, the issue of legibility in the 1908–09 period appears to have arisen out of a conflict between those film producers who were persuaded by a broader external agenda to legitimise cinema, and those audiences who were resistant to this change or comfortable with existing practices of film exhibition. But even where this conflict was at its sharpest, the interests of all parties were best served by many and varied compromises and negotiations, of which the reappearance of the lecturer and the development of longer narrative films are only the best known examples, and it is these multiple processes rather than individual moments of crisis that come to the fore in considerations of institutional change. The model that remains does not describe early or transitional cinemas continually poised, always in the process of becoming classical, or 'institutional,' but emphasises the constancy and coherence of several generic institutions that were cumulatively able to accommodate any number of small changes and that had been consistently unifying for their users (producers, exhibitors and spectators) from the beginning. Furthermore, because it does not privilege any one pattern of institutional development, this model fulfils Miriam Hansen's stipulation that early film studies should 'take away some of the *inevitability* the classical paradigm has acquired both in Hollywood self-promotion and in functionalist film histories'.[80] We are left to account for consistently varied film production, exhibition and spectatorial practices, though the focus of this diversity partly shifted from film exhibitors to producers before 1910.[81]

Thus, it is certainly true that early film shows underwent a great deal of change in the period before 1910 and were characterised by heterogeneous and often contradictory experiences. However, this instability was played out by institutions that required cultural continuity and economic security and that developed systematic routines of production, exhibition and reception in order to achieve it. The early film industry therefore exhibited a surprisingly high degree of complicity both with existing models of hegemonic, post-1910 classical cinema, and with the various paradigms of competing Victorian and Edwardian cinemas as catalogued and theorised in recent early film work. This is because early and later cinemas were both highly institutionalised, seeking to develop consistently profitable relationships with audiences, and because they both traded on heterogeneity, seeking to fulfil the diverse and gradually changing requirements of these audiences.

Institutional analysis of this kind allows us to see that early films were connected to prevailing contemporary ideas concerning the distractive nature of modernity, not because they unwittingly reproduced them, but because early film institutions found that this was an effective way of securing the interest of audiences. In particular, because films appeared to exemplify the alienation effect popularly associated with modern life and especially with technological mass media, film shows were designed to foster a surrogate sense of intimacy for spectators, generating cherished qualities of presence on and off the screen. Exhibitors and producers exploited familiar models of personality partly because this enabled them to overcome resistances within audiences to new uses of a new medium. Of course, the relationships established between audiences and live performers, performers on the screen, and with narrative, authorial, and other personae were by no means equivalent. However, their establishment during film shows served one similar function, ensuring that moving pictures created new opportunities to re-embed social relations that had been lifted out of familiar conditions of co-presence.[82] Understanding how this was accomplished allows us to describe the weaving together of modern institutions and self-identity that was achieved by early film shows. It demonstrates that early film institutions thrived partly because they preserved, adapted and reproduced for audiences experiential qualities of intimacy that otherwise appeared under threat.

39

Film Personae: Presence, Performance, and Personality

The sheer number and diversity of performers, personalities, and other personae that addressed early British film audiences perhaps illustrates most strikingly the significance of the sense of human presence that pervaded early film shows. Potentially confronted by live performances of all kinds, including those of showmen and lecturers, not to mention projectionists, musicians and sound effects men, when audiences turned their attention to the screen they found that this too opened up onto remarkably varied models of personality and performance, some derived from earlier popular entertainments, some delivering the spectacle of exotic individuals or actions, and some simply presenting the familiar and everyday business of work, leisure and street life. The existence of these multiple possibilities for fostering empathy and communication within the moving pictures raises further questions concerned with the material constraints of the medium. How did the qualities of live performances differ materially, socially and psychologically from those delivered in various ways by the medium of film? Where two or more lines of communication were open at once, as in the case of a screening accompanied by a live lecture, how were they organised and structured? What purposes did such forms of mixed communication serve? Spectators resolved such questions during early film exhibitions with a great deal of fluency, because they were thoroughly conversant with relevant patterns of institutional dressage—even though it is unlikely that they often did so self-consciously. Recovering these patterns of dressage therefore allows us to approach some of the key determinants of the experience of the early film show.

These performative aspects of early film shows have not been neglected by the modern discipline of early film studies, especially insofar as they have detailed the influence of live performance traditions. In a movement initiated by commentators such as Martin Sopocy in Britain and Charles Musser in the US, critics have consistently emphasised elements of live performance that sometimes dominated film shows before 1907, especially insofar as they introduced sound to the image track.[83] Such histories have emphasised that film shows often included a lecturer to describe or narrate the action on the screen, dialogue provided by actors behind the screen, live music or mechanical synchronised sound, varied methods for producing sound effects, and variety entertainments or the patter of showmen.[84] Rather than placing responsibility for the piecemeal invention of cinema in the hands of a selection of prescient filmmakers, the exhibitors are instead seen as the most important creative and experimental agents of film development. Musser's early and definitive proposal that 'early cinema be examined within the context of a history of the screen, of the projected image and its sound accompaniment' may thus be taken to characterise a powerful paradigm shift within early film studies more generally, one that has proved enduringly productive in relation to the sounds of so-called silent cinema.[85] Such studies have often emphasised that it was the exhibitor who selected and arranged the components of a film show, perhaps drawing a succession of short films into a contiguous narrative or descriptive lecture. Even if films were screened in silence, the show's arrangement on-site still imparted a strong sense of the liveness of the performed event.[86]

However, although the exhibitionist quality of live performance strategies in early film shows is now comparatively well-known, the coherence of the institutional traditions these performances called upon, and the continuities of experience this brought to audiences, have been unevenly considered. For example, the roles performed by lecturers or showmen at film shows depended substantially upon an inherited repertoire of performance strategies with which filmmakers and audiences were very familiar, but these are still only partially understood. It is therefore difficult to discern the complex ways in which film producers and spectators reacted to this inherited social repertoire, and to see how the development of models of personality associated with the image track corresponded with parallel developments in exhibition practices.

Other work has focused on the roles of filmmakers in developing conventions of screen acting performance, especially in the years after 1908.[87] This has demonstrated that performance and staging traditions associated with the legitimate theatre had a lasting impact upon the cinema when it too was a seeking a degree of cultural legitimacy. But the bulk of earlier film production did not call upon acting skills derived from theatrical institutions, very often presenting performance conventions from other institutional contexts, from magic theatre to music hall to freak show, or bringing the most mundane of activities to the screen. With the exception of work on local filmmaking, studies concerning the performative and communicative work conducted by on-screen figures such as these are still very scarce. However, perhaps the most poorly understood of the film's personae were those agencies implicitly 'behind' the film, which film studies has customarily sought to describe as narrators or authors. In his narratological work concerning early cinema, André Gaudreault has greatly expanded upon this vocabulary of personality, and has shown that in these films it is very often more appropriate to speak of a 'monstrator', an agency responsible for showing audiences a world, than of a narrator, who, under the conditions initiated by the development of the narrator system in film, might be said to tell us about that world.[88] From an institutional perspective, abstract figures such as these can be identified with specific traditions of performance and representation, such as those associated with lecturers, showmen, conjurors, and other performers, some of which had a very powerful impact upon the interpretive activities of audiences.

All of these film personae, from live performers to individuals represented on-screen to monstrators, narrators and cameramen, played a significant role in co-ordinating the elaborate dressage between audience and screen, and were therefore intrinsic to the dynamic interactions between institutions of film production and exhibition and their customers. Their 'presence' was likely to be reassuring not only because they contested the apparently inhuman qualities of mechanical reproduction, but also because they guided audiences, with great representational economy, through the nuanced and gradually changing perspectives adopted by the screen.[89] Consciously or unconsciously, explicitly or implicitly, early film producers and exhibitors thus designed the experience of the film show to ensure that it reproduced desired qualities of intimacy for audiences, and that it did so in such a way that it might redeploy the cultural functions served by earlier entertainment forms. Furthermore, because they had a remarkable diversity of entertainment forms to choose from, they could also respond with great rapidity to the changing conditions of the marketplace and to the new or newly discovered demands of audiences.

For Giddens, reflecting upon similar issues in relation to the modern mass media in general, the provision of exemplary models of personality within the media has had a profound impact upon fundamental notions of self-identity, enabling individuals actively to construct a coherent but dynamic narrative for themselves, in a world that otherwise threatens to slip out of their grasp. Calling upon such personae, each individual continually reflects upon and reviews his or her own integrated sense of self. Although the modern mediascape is distracting, invasive and utterly pervasive, Giddens thus demonstrates that mass media forms have materially contributed to what he calls the 'reflexive project of the self', enabling individuals to reflect upon the social world, and, therefore, to some extent, to position themselves within it, ultimately contributing to its shape.[90] This description of the activities of media consumers fully credits their capacity to process the potentially bewildering array of information with which the modern world presents them, and seems to me an especially apt description of the competence demonstrated by the early film spectator. At the turn of the century, the mechanically-reproduced moving image distorted parameters of space/time orientation, bringing exotic locations, impossible actions, and grotesque personae to spectators who occasionally reported the disturbing effects of these definitively modern perceptions. But these disturbances quickly became familiar to their knowing audiences and indeed were soon commodified as such by early institutions of film production. Confronted with a technologically advanced medium, spectators were still able to rehearse their considerable expertise in interpreting conventional performance and communicative practices. Early film institutions set in motion a reconfiguration of everyday life that would become the trademark of media technologies throughout the twentieth century, confronting the distance implicit to mechanical reproduction with the possibility for intimacy with a mass public.

2

Expertise and Trust
Popular Lecturing Traditions and Early Film

Live performance was fundamental to the success of early film entertainments in Britain. Drawn from a variety of earlier entertainment traditions, these performances tended to frame the new medium, placing it within institutional frameworks that were understood by audiences because they had already gone through decades of development. The physical presence of performers enacting conventional routines could also represent a reassuring landmark for audiences confronted by unfamiliar images and exotic scenes. Whether they interacted with a lecturer on a platform by the screen, with the showman or 'barker' within or outside the show, or with variety performers before, after or during screenings, early film shows were characterised by a flux of human activities with a range of attractions for audiences. This chapter and the next will explore some of these activities and will argue that, though live performances were heavily constrained by the institutional conditions under which they took place, such constraints were quickly modified under the circumstances initiated by the film show, enabling new performance strategies and new institutional structures to emerge. In this way, live performances participated fully in the process of institutional change described in the previous chapter in terms of Anthony Giddens's principle of duality of structure; tracking their development through the nineteenth century allows us to consider both the stabilities and the dynamism of institutional practice and of audience experience within early film shows.

These chapters will concentrate upon two performance traditions that had a particularly direct and pervasive influence on the early British film show, namely those associated with the figures of the lecturer and the showman. Of course, these were not the only live performers who might have played a significant role in early film shows. For example, in shop-shows and the smaller halls or fairground shows, the operator of the projector would often be visible during screening, perhaps positioned somewhere amongst or in front of the audience.[1] Elsewhere, variety performers would appear before the show or in the gaps between films. But the lecturer and the showman played especially significant roles in developing the institutional sanctions that governed each show, generating continuities of experience for film audiences derived from entertainment traditions that had always defined themselves in opposition to the practices of the other. According to these definitions, which were highly productive for both professions, the lecturer and the showman had popularly come to represent a distinction between knowledge and knowingness. Whereas the lecturer was typically associated with the adoption of a position of authority within the tradition of the rational amusement, the showman was considered to be less concerned with the dissemination of knowledge than in sharing a sense of knowingness with audiences. Working under the aegis of the conspiratorial wink, the popular image of the showmen emphasised their dependence upon their audiences' well-humoured complicity in the tricks and cons apparently played out upon them. During the nineteenth and early twentieth centuries, these two figures inherited and adapted longstanding patterns of dressage from earlier entertainment institutions, such as those associated with fairground, music hall, sideshow and lecture theatre, and played these out creatively in relation to the moving picture.

In practice, almost all of the examples I will present across the next two chapters will suggest that performers typically adopted aspects of both styles of performance. Indeed, play with these distinctions was extremely productive for both professions, allowing them to capitalise fluidly on all of the performative resources that were on offer in the market for popular entertainments. Therefore, the lecturer often sought to reproduce the knowing irony and fresh-talking familiarity with audiences that was popularly associated with showmanship; and the showman frequently aped the didactic tone most often associated with the tradition of the illustrated lecture. In doing so, they were exploiting broader public discourses concerning their professions, linked with ideals of popular education and self-help on the one hand and with a more earthy commitment to the practices and realities of everyday life on the other. These figures were therefore connected by much more than their association with popular entertainments: they can be seen as class-inflected embodiments of a much broader, discursive distinction between bourgeois improvement and popular 'commonsense'. Each of these positions was copied and caricatured by the other, so assuming aspects of both enabled most lecturers and showmen, following a dominantly economic imperative, to call upon the aspirational inclinations of spectators but also upon their self-reflexive capacity for irony.

The relationship between these two positions had been played out for decades within Victorian entertainment institutions and, in order to understand the accretion of performance practices that would subsequently come to inform the film show, it will be necessary to address the development of both.[2] Whereas the archaeology of optical technologies and entertainments has become much better understood in the last decade, the elaborate dressage associated with these shows has remained comparatively neglected. As a consequence, our understanding of the social practices of early film shows has been considerably impoverished, since a full account of the varied, highly institutionalised traditions that such shows drew upon has not been available. For this reason, this chapter will dedicate a great deal of attention to the illustrated lecture's development during the nineteenth century, focussing initially upon large-scale dioramic and panoramic shows, and then upon the substantial growth of magic lantern lecturing that took place from the 1870s. The levels of investment required by dioramas and panoramas in the late nineteenth century were much higher than those typically associated with magic lantern shows, and this had a substantial impact on the lecturing styles associated with them. The chapter will then examine the uneven inheritance of both traditions after the arrival of film and the resulting alterations made to lecture routines.

Tom Gunning noted in 1999 that the film lecturer had been rediscovered regularly over the previous twenty years.[3] However, coming to an understanding of the institutional authority and coherence of longstanding lecturing traditions also enables us to address the continuities of experience this brought to audiences, which would be played out in a complex manner during the 1900s and 1910s. Throughout its history, the figure of the lecturer was instrumental in fostering a faith in expert culture, though it did this inconsistently, and not without a concurrent self-reflexive critique of this position. Whatever his exact function during a show, the lecturer's presence, the long-institutionalised routines he drew upon, and his ability to anchor safely the audience's interpretation of the moving image was a highly significant factor in the fundamental ideology of reassurance that underpinned *fin de siècle* entertainments.

Spectacular Entertainments and the Development of the Illustrated Lecture

The illustrated lecturing tradition, which thrived throughout the Victorian and Edwardian periods, was strongly influenced by spectacular entertainments, such as stationary and moving panoramas and dioramas, in the first decades of the nineteenth century. These depended principally upon a spectacular effect of realism to achieve their effects. Picturesque views of cities or landscapes, both foreign and domestic, and later, images of great battles and historical scenes were offered up to the British public for consumption. As several critics have shown, working largely from press accounts (which were themselves highly stylised), expressions of astonishment and wonder were considered to be the most characteristic responses of audiences to these exhibitions.[4] However, in spite of the absence of a lecturer to explain and contextualise the view for spectators, aspects of personality and narrative also tended to mitigate the overwhelming impact of such grand exhibition spaces, anchoring the experience of spectacle within safely bounded interpretative frames.

By the 1850s a great number of these spectacular visual entertainments were available to a British public that appeared, at least in large cities, to be tiring of them.[5] A second wave of interest in panoramas swept Europe during the 1870s and 1880s, and touring panoramic entertainments remained popular into the early 1900s, coexisting for a while with film shows. Each entertainment sought to claim for itself a distinctive novelty, but all offered to audiences a visual illusion including spectacular perspectival effects.[6] 'The whole thing is nature itself,' reported the *Times* of Daguerre's Diorama in 1823, emphasising the illusion of being-there that appeared to bring the exotic and spectacular view under every individual's command.[7] Recent critics have strongly echoed this perspective, and have suggested that, as well as reproducing the experience of being in the landscape, spectators were led to ideologically conservative readings of these spaces. At the same time, the spectator also stepped into an economic order that brought the landscape view increasingly into the sphere of marketable objects.[8] As Nicholas Green has suggested of Parisian entertainments in this period, such easily consumed views were therefore designed to confer upon audiences a sense of security and control.[9] Drawing upon recent work concerning the experience of anxiety in the nineteenth-century metropolis, Andrew E. Hershberger has even suggested that L.J.M. Daguerre's massive Diorama images, which 'displayed an exceptionally high degree of inflowing excitations', tended to act 'like a vaccine, or inoculation', ultimately protecting audiences from the overstimulation of the city street.[10]

However, though such studies have suggested that the visual regimes of these entertainments tended to reinforce a composed and centred sense of self for their audiences, these audiences were also exposed to a great deal of printed publicity in relation to the exhibits, and this often encouraged them to adopt more active, even critical, interpretive strategies. For example, from the beginning of the nineteenth century, leaflets for Robert Barker's Leicester Square Panorama frequently included fully labelled circular diagrams and brief descriptions, which offered their audiences a straightforward means of dissecting the spectacle before them.[11] Other panoramic entertainments followed suit, creating a wealth of printed material for publicity and sale, and reports in newspapers and journals tended to support their approach by including details of each entertainment's design, explanations of the view, or anecdotes concerning the artists involved.[12] Sometimes the adventures and hardships of panoramic artists, such as Robert Barker and Robert Burford of the Leicester Square Panorama, were advertised within pamphlets accompanying the show, and this information was also likely to inform the experience popularly associated with their visual spectacle.[13] Such accounts gave spectators of the panorama one possible means for anchoring the significance of the spectacle: they could identify with or feel empathy for the artist-adventurer. They stepped from the street into the denouement of the adventure, albeit without undergoing the laborious and often frustrating duration of the journey, and with the proprietor's assurance that the view would not disappoint.

Another strategy was to encourage spectators to interrogate experiences that so obviously coupled realism with artifice. According to one first-hand account, Daguerre's experimental 1832 diorama *View of Mont Blanc Taken from the Valley of Chamonix* was viewed 'under the eaves of a Swiss chalet', and included a live goat, the noise of the herd in the distance, and farm tools scattered about 'as if our unannounced arrival had driven away the shy owners'.[14] During the performance, girls dressed in peasant costumes served breakfast to the audience. As usual, the entire image was scrupulously arranged so as to conceal its process of mediation, but Daguerre also openly solicited attention to this process: 'I wanted to rob nature,' he told one audience, 'and therefore had to become a thief.'[15] Such moments of authorial mastery are relatively unusual within these entertainments, but they eloquently acknowledged what spectators of the panorama already knew: that the illusion of being there had been designed by someone, someone, in Daguerre's case, with a firmly established reputation for illusionism. The presence, on this occasion, of live animals within the Diorama building presumably only reinforced this idea. Indeed, the idea that such spectacles were so realistic that they actually conflated art and reality was regularly satirised and would be further exploited by humorous illustrated lectures later in the century.

This argument is an important one because it addresses the ability of audiences up to and including the introduction of film to consider artistic, commercial and other motivations that might lie behind spectacular productions. The capacity for informed reflection on these issues was not only the province of those elitist discourses that recurrently sought to condemn such productions as markers of vulgar, middle-class tastes for realism. It was implicit to the commonplace acknowledgement that somebody had designed them for reasons that were always very much open to debate. Such figures enabled spectators to order a massive visual field according to the knowledge they brought with them into the exhibition space, and this placed them in a rather more authoritative position than reports of their responses are inclined to suggest. Paying close attention to surviving written elements of the exhibitions allows us to identify and analyse some of these figures, and suggests that audiences were likely to entertain a surprisingly knowledgeable understanding of the shows.

For obvious reasons, the verbal aspects of the shows were especially significant in the case of illustrated lectures.[16] Within lectured entertainments, it was possible to enact the interpretative frames that static dioramas and panoramas had always implied, making the lecturer himself a distinct attraction of the exhibition space. Illustrated lecturing traditions had a substantial but mixed heritage, from the longstanding eighteenth- and nineteenth-century popular tradition of travelling peepshow exhibition to the development of lectured moving panoramas, chiefly intended for relatively genteel audiences, in the 1820s. But, following a vigorous revival of moving panoramas in the 1840s and 1850s, the celebrity lecturer began to take centre stage in the landscape of popular entertainments, a position he would maintain until the beginning of the twentieth century.[17]

In the moving panorama, a wide strip of canvas, sometimes hundreds of metres long, would roll between two giant spools on either side of a proscenium. The canvas was portable, and itinerant showmen adapted their performances for any proscenium of sufficient width. Often, this canvas was backlit, enhanced by musical accompaniment, or by special effects involving mechanical devices. In many cases, a perspectival *trompe l'œil* effect was maintained but, most significantly, the moving canvas also permitted a complex and coherent storyline to evolve. In this way, the moving panorama in its various forms compressed the sensory reality-effect back into a more familiar brand of narrative realism than the stationary entertainments. It brought an experience of 'apparitional space and time' to audiences, which enabled them not only to step into the pictorial denouement of the adventure, but also to identify or empathise with its chief protagonists in the course of the journey.[18] Within many shows a journey would unfold, in which a continually rolling canvas presented a scenic view of the landscape as it passed by. In this way the principle sights of the world's most spectacular journeys were brought to the lecture theatre traveller, all condensed into an hour's comfortable viewing. Within others, the canvas would roll sequentially from one static scene to the next, enabling lecturers to foster some degree of narrative engagement with any individuals depicted.

It was also possible to present these exhibits in a manner that directly enabled instruction rather than fostering contemplation. Lecturers in this period were frequently expected to disseminate knowledge which had been discovered through their own intellectual enquiries or adventures, and because these shows tended to tour widely, they brought enlightenment discourses to far-flung locations across Britain.[19] By the 1850s, moving panoramas were most commonly accompanied by lectures, whose publicity most frequently promised an educational experience, though the shows might also engage audiences with music and popular songs.[20] For example, *The Diorama of the Ganges*, which was performed in London during 1850, was accompanied by Sylvester Walsh's 'instructive lecture', and took the spectator in a principled way from an overview of Calcutta, along the Ganges into 'jungles of tropical vegetation', finishing at the Taj Mahal.[21] Reviews of the entertainment regularly credited Walsh, who described these scenes 'in a manner that proves him to be a scholar and a gentleman'.[22] In 1853, J.R. Smith's *Tour of Europe: The Largest Moving Panorama in the World* was exhibited in Leicester Square, lectured by Charles Alexander Hartkopff, and rather grandly claimed to join 'the telegraph, the railway, and the Steam-Boat' as a means 'to bring about a Brotherhood of nations'.[23] But even the most didactic of lectures ensured that a powerful charge of spectacle, and something of the spice of the sideshow, was also present in the show. For example, The *Grand Moving Panorama Illustrative of the Great African and American Slave Trade* lectured, in 1857, by the missionary W.H. Irwin, was designed to instruct audiences on the evils of the slave trade, but included spectacular scenes such as 'Family surprised and captured' and 'Slaves cast overboard in their chains'. The lecture explicitly described 'the sufferings, sales, and various hardships to which Slaves are subject' and introduced a 'fugitive slave', whose adventures informed audiences directly of the conditions in which slaves survived in the USA, while also capitalising on the spectacle of his racial identity.[24]

A similar commitment to educational and moral improvement, coupled with the showman's eye for a sensational attraction, often informed scientific lectures which, since at least the mid-eighteenth century, had adopted magic lanterns to illustrate educative material.[25] Although, from the 1850s, the laboratory often disavowed the lecture room, lecturers continued to capitalise on a widely-held presumption that science was a matter for open public entertainment. For example, astronomical lectures remained particularly popular with itinerant lecturers, sometimes illustrated with illuminated diagrams of the stars reproduced by lantern.[26] Most famously, from 1838, the Royal Polytechnic Institution in Regent Street had aimed to distribute expert scientific knowledge, including astronomical entertainments and other lectures illustrated by magic lantern, to a much broader audience.[27] The Royal Panopticon of Science and Art in Leicester Square was specifically designed with a utilitarian compromise between instruction and amusement in mind, and was launched in 1853 with a pamphlet for potential audiences (and shareholders) that reads like a manifesto for the rational amusement:[28]

> A pleasing feature of the present age is a disposition on the part of a large portion of the community to seek such recreations as are calculated to assist by moral and educational agencies the best interests of society. To promote the application of science to the useful arts—to instruct, by courses of lectures, to be demonstrated by instruments, apparatus, and other appliances, in the various departments of science and literature . . . to illustrate history, science, and literature by pictorial views and representations, accompanied by music . . .[29]

These discourses of moral and educational uplift were not new in the 1850s, but the substantial investment in institutions such as the Royal Panopticon and the Polytechnic, which was completely renovated in 1854, exemplifies their growing institutionalisation. Wyld's Great Globe, established in 1851, also in Leicester Square, was equally committed to the educational lecture format. The design of this building, which featured a globe 60 metres in diameter on its interior surface viewed from four viewing platforms within it, is relatively well known. However, the exhibition itself did not substantially depend upon this spectacular image. Rather, as reviews testify, 'interesting descriptive lectures, historical as well as geographical', which took place between 10 a.m. and 10 p.m. each day, were the chief attractions. These were to be distinguished from other entertainments because they were 'obviously the result of much careful study and acquaintance with subjects of which they treat'.[30] Although Wyld's and the Panopticon were relatively short-lived, the illustrated lecture remained until the end of the century the most obvious and most commercially successful means for ensuring that public entertainments were improving for their audiences, playing an important part in a pervasive and increasingly prominent culture of self-help.[31] At the same time, playing upon such discourses of improvement also allowed these entertainments to continue to deliver sensational materials to these audiences, in a manner not so far divorced from less respectable shows.

In order to achieve this, it was necessary that the lecturer be regarded as a trustworthy expert in a relevant field, and great care was taken to convince audiences of this. The Royal Panopticon clearly advised customers that 'the Lectures in this institution shall be of the best character, and the services of men of the highest ability and eminence will be secured'.[32] Publicity for illustrated lectures had a number of ways to allude to the lecturer's qualifications: relatively scholarly lecturers claimed affiliations with professional organisations or advertised books they had authored; others gave details of practical experiences that qualified them for the platform.[33] This hierarchy between lecturer and audience enabled the lecture's dissemination of knowledge to take place because it set in place a simple relationship of trust. Listeners trusted in the veracity of the lecture and required its content to take precedence over the evidences offered by their own senses or by communal forms of folk wisdom. Of course, sometimes it was the case that the lecturer knew very little about the subject at hand, and sometimes a lecturer would call upon the knowledge possessed by members of his audience, but this type of play tended to leave the fundamental relationship between lecturers and audience firmly in place. The form of the lecture therefore participated in the broader development of an expert culture during the nineteenth century in which the proliferation of disciplinary knowledge led to the specialisation of experts and expert discourses in each field. Anthony Giddens explains that this is a key part of the development of self-identity under conditions of modernity:

> Specialisation is actually the key to the character of modern abstract systems. The knowledge incorporated in modern forms of expertise is in principle available to everyone, had they but the available resources, time and energy to acquire it. The fact that to be an expert in one or two small corners of modern knowledge systems is all that anyone can achieve means that abstract systems are opaque to the majority. Their opaque quality . . . comes from the very intensity of specialisation that abstract systems both demand and foster.[34]

The rapid diversification of genres of illustrated lectures from the 1850s testifies to this movement, and indicates that specialisation also led, apparently paradoxically, to the wide dissemination and popularisation of expert knowledge. Lectures concerning travel and popular science were consistently fashionable, but vogues for current events, adventure and exploration, popular anthropology, zoology, military history, medicine, astronomy and anatomy were fostered from the lecturing platform as much as from the newspapers and periodical press.

Although successful lecturers were in this way credited with privileged knowledge, they were also subjected directly to the demands of their audiences, tending to adopt perspectives that courted popular opinion. The authority and respect extended to them, therefore, was partly conditional upon their fulfilment of certain cultural functions for audiences. For example, Crimean War lectures inevitably described British troops in a favourable light, and colonial exhibitions tended to bring a familiar imperial perspective to the exotic scene. In the *New Oriental Diorama* exhibited at Willis's Rooms in St James during 1850, the spectator was even 'to suppose an officer to leave Calcutta in order to join his regiment in Lahore, in the Punjaub' in order 'to render the connection between the various pictures in the Diorama clear and intelligible'.[35] This strategy typifies the tendency of lecturers to bring imperialist narratives to such scenes, allowing audiences to identify with colonial and military adventurers. Such techniques were likely to offer reassurance to audiences, particularly during periods when British colonial supremacy appeared under military or ethical threat.

Uniquely positioned as representatives for an expert culture, yet also claiming to represent the interests of the general public, lecturers were therefore in a powerful but precarious position. They were required to negotiate between popular tastes for instruction and spectacle, between imperatives to educate and distract, and this was played out primarily in the skilled combination of word and image. From this relationship too came the opportunity to engineer a public personality somewhere between the audience and the screen. As Erving Goffman has explained of academic lectures, the manner in which lecturers deal with such materials enables them to create 'an audience-usable self to do the speaking' while actually at the podium.[36] Doing so also enabled lecturers to outgrow their marginal position, and this opened up fascinating possibilities for an internal questioning of the didactic tone of illustrated lectures. Even when the relationship between lecturer and audience was formally structured like that between expert and initiate, the lecturer openly and visibly embodied this pedagogic imperative and in doing so also gave audiences the opportunity to call it and the assumptions that came with it into question. In this respect, according to Goffman, lecturers can also resemble theatrical performers, whose performances were played

out in the course of an interactive and often humorous or digressive relationship to their audiences.[37] Their performances in illustrated lectures were
sometimes the central attraction of the show and sometimes merely contextualised the images, but they were always to an extent limited by the forms
of dressage associated with the show, directly answerable to audiences. Some
lecturers encouraged their audiences to be cynical.

In the case of the biggest celebrity lecturers, there was a tendency for the
public personality to acquire an institutional legitimacy of its own, which
often kept an ironic distance from dry disciplinary allegiances or popular
discourses of self-help. Such personalities were aggressively marketed,
becoming available to a much wider public and also informing the content
and style of other performances. *Banvard's Geographical Panorama of the
Mississippi and Missouri Rivers* was particularly successful. It had first visited
England in 1848 when Dickens saw it at the Egyptian Hall, and it was still
touring through America and Europe during the 1850s. 'The panorama is
not,' Dickens confirmed for the art purists, 'a refined work of art,' nor, he
added for devotees of the stationary panorama, was it 'remarkable for accuracy of drawing, or for brilliancy of colour, or for subtle effects of light and
shade':

> But it is a picture three miles long, which occupies two hours in its
> passage before the audience. It is a picture of one of the greatest streams
> in the known world, whose course it follows for upwards of three thou-
> sand miles. It is a picture irresistibly impressing the spectator with a
> conviction of its plain and simple truthfulness, even though that were
> not guaranteed by the best testimonials.[38]

Dickens collaborates with Banvard's hyperbole, finding 'plain and simple
truthfulness' in this blatantly exaggerated representation of the lecturer's
adventures. Banvard's performance permeated the show, drawing audiences
not only into vicarious participation in the adventure, but also into a relationship with the adventurer himself. Banvard promised expert knowledge
of the American landscape to his audiences, but he also exaggerated his
struggles *en route* and made the completion of the panorama (whose length
was also grossly exaggerated) a matter of personal triumph over accident and
misfortune. More informed spectators, such as Dickens, found in the canvas
a revelation of showmanship and sheer personality, and this was where the
truth of the matter was to be had. 'These three miles of canvas have been
painted by one man,' Dickens grandly proclaimed, 'and there he is, present,
pointing out what he deems most worthy of notice. This is history.'[39]

Of course, some personalities were more successful than others. Undoubtedly the most influential and best known of illustrated lectures at the mid-century was Albert Smith's *Ascent of Mont Blanc*, a show which ran for over 2,000 performances, securing an estimated £30,000 of profit and an enviable reputation for both efficiency and bonhomie amongst the London literary elite.[40] Smith's performance in this show was far from a simple descriptive account of Alpine scenes; Smith sold himself as the well-informed and observant traveller, as the seasoned adventurer, as raconteur and society wit, and as showman and satirist.[41] This remarkable elocutionary range allowed him to vary the inflection of his performance and to deliver it with an 'air of spontaneity', according to one regular patron, as though 'the lecturer had apparently only just thought of saying the things he was relating'.[42] It also enabled him to adopt a strongly satirical tone that was apparently at odds with the straight-talking expertise and objectification of foreign scenes popularly associated with the rational amusement. Above all, it was this flexibility in performance style that made Smith such an important influence on late-nineteenth-century lecturing, up to and including traditions of film lecturing. Sometimes allowing the images to dominate and sometimes using them as simple illustrations for his discourse, Smith cleverly varied the relationships he entertained with audiences, making of the lecture a remarkably adaptable and fluid expressive resource.

The show itself was equally varied, including the spectacle of William Beverly's brilliantly backlit illustrative views; Smith's impersonation of numerous characters, whose adventures would be updated from year to year (a comic form known as the 'monopolylogue'); and the participation of audiences in topical songs. In the most celebrated part of the entertainment, spectators followed Smith through the highlights of his climb and brought this extraordinary experience into an everyday register by means of an identification with, or empathy for, the adventurer before them.[43] Smith's bravado thus extended further than the summit, encapsulating his mastery over audiences as well as over the landscape. At the same time, Smith's sharpest satire was chiefly directed at himself and at the growing class of English mountaineers and travellers he confessedly epitomised, whose age, fitness, and good intentions were easily called into question. Even if he was keen to conquer exotic landscapes, Smith did not often extend this territorial objectification into parody of foreign races and cultures but levelled a remarkably self-reflexive gaze back upon the English, whose presence in an increasingly accessible Europe was not a wholly welcome phenomenon.[44] This gesture added one further performative dimension to Smith's show, flattering the bourgeois sensibilities of audiences by sharing a knowing and rather lofty appreciation of the vogue for mountain climbing, the growth of popular tourism, and even the tastes for spectacular entertainments that had contributed to these phenomena.

The wide range of relationships between word, image and audience engineered by Smith would continue to influence dioramic and magic lantern shows until the beginning of the twentieth century, and many sought to repeat his winning formula. In the wake of *Mont Blanc*, Richard Altick notes that there was a sense of 'uninspired imitation', but this did not lead to a substantial decline in moving panorama entertainments from the 1860s.[45] Smith's show appears to have survived him, following his death in 1858, when, as one pamphlet suggests, his adventures were narrated by another lecturer, still accompanied by Beverly's original scenes.[46] Direct transcriptions, such as Mr T. Lawrence's touring 'Popular Entertainment' of 1858, *A Climb to the Highest Point in Europe: Ascent of Mont Blanc*, were not uncommon.[47] More generally, the adventures encountered by the world traveller reappeared regularly within British popular entertainments. Sometimes, itinerant lecturers who had perhaps acquired canvasses from grander entertainments, or used the magic lantern in order to illustrate their lectures, brought them to temperance halls, schools and lecture rooms across the country.[48] Other entertainments openly adopted Smith's fresh-talking performance style or talent for impersonation. As late as 1894, the singer, raconteur and impressionist Snazelle was still proudly proclaiming himself 'the Albert Smith of today'.[49]

The celebrated American burlesque lecturer, Charles Farrar Browne—better known by his pen-name, Artemus Ward—openly acknowledged the institutional significance of the *Mont Blanc* format, but sought to undercut it at every turn. 'What sort of a man was Albert Smith?' asked Ward of an English friend, 'And do you think that the Mormons would be as good a subject for Londoners as Mont Blanc was?'[50] On his arrival in London in 1866, Ward chose to perform his comic lecture on the Mormons at the Egyptian Hall, using a moving panorama much like Smith's. However, Ward's lecturing style persistently undermined his own authority at every turn, and the sequence of illustrations was similarly jumbled, misleading, or simply absurd. Adopting a Barnumesque persona that called neatly upon the class prejudices of middle-class British audiences, Ward could master neither the images on-screen nor even the flow of his own narrative. 'His intention was merely to amuse,' recalled one admirer, 'and if possible, send his audience home well pleased with the lecturer and with themselves, without their having any clear idea of that which they had been listening to, and not one jot wiser than when they came.'[51] For example, his mock educative lecture, *Sixty Minutes in Africa*, had nothing whatever to do with Africa. Exaggerating existing caricatures of the didactic lecture into absurdity, Ward careered haplessly between a series of humorous digressions, returning apologetically to the topic at hand with his concluding sentence. Thus, Ward openly elicited the audience's cynicism and laughter, exposing to ridicule the idea of a dissemination of knowledge.

Such parody was far from unprecedented in Britain where showmen and lecturers had long satirised a stock figure called 'Dryasdust'—an unflattering caricature of tedious and pretentious didactic lecturers who, in the course of their rational amusements, did not amuse.[52] However, Ward's ramblings perhaps confirmed too openly the peculiarly modern form of risk brought about by an unreliable expert culture.[53] According to T.W. Robertson, many 'stupid people' at the Egyptian Hall were genuinely expecting a travel lecture on the Mormons and simply 'did not see the fun of Artemus Ward's lecture'.[54] In fact, by turning the objectifying gaze of the audience sharply around, Ward had brought to them an uncomfortable parody of their own habits of trust and intimacy with the well-dressed stranger on-stage. Ward simply brought a modern form of paranoia to the fore of his show and demonstrated, much more openly than Smith and other performers, that audiences shared a trusting relationship during lectures with intrinsically flawed and often mendacious personalities. Even pamphlets for the show carefully undermined the kinds of reassurances customarily extended by lecturers to their middle-class audiences: 'During the vacation the Hall has been carefully swept out and a new Door Knob has been added to the Door,' boasted one, directly referring to the precise publicity Smith had produced for each new season of Mont Blanc at the Hall.[55] One contributor to *Chambers's Journal* sought to explain this knowing brand of humour: 'the grin is broader, under the mask of which lies, if not the deepest wisdom, most sterling common-sense'.[56] Like generations of showmen, Ward encouraged audiences to develop their own expertise and bring a critical attitude to the illustrated lecture. Though he died only a year later, his entertainment was fondly remembered for decades, and inspired a series of editions of his most popular lectures.

Shows that attempted to reproduce the scale, expense and variety of Smith's entertainment delivered a much higher charge of spectacle, tending to be less idiosyncratic and more enduring. Like Ward, they sought to avoid dry or overly descriptive material, but they did so as Smith and other showmen had done, by engaging audiences with stories and personal anecdotes, songs and impersonations, or by punctuating the show with spectacular visual effects or violent action. Alexander Lamb's *Royal Diorama of Scotland*, which had already been exhibited for several years in cities throughout Britain, appeared at the Egyptian Hall in 1873, and included a massive moving panorama with 'mechanical and dioramic effects never before attempted', a 'historical and descriptive lecture' led by two lecturers, Maclagan's monopolylogue of 'Scottish character', and music from the 'Original Scottish Minstrels' and the 'Champion Strathspey and Reel Players'.[57] Other entertainments delivered a changing roster of travel-based entertainment, including moving dioramas and magic lantern effects. Hamilton's Excursions toured major British cities regularly until William Hamilton's death in 1907, with entertainments such as *Across the Atlantic* in 1874 and *The New Overland Route to India via Paris, Mont Cenis, Brindisi* in 1876. The show was eventually incorporated by the Poole family, whose remarkable careers as moving panorama and cinematograph showmen in cities and on fairground has been charted by Hudson John Powell.[58] During the 1870s Poole's Myriorama included a descriptive lecture, character imper-sonation, and musical accompaniment on piano. Later, the entertainment introduced variety performances and a clown who interrupted the lecture in a parodic 'cross-talk' act that tended to jeopardise its capacity for instruc-tion, rather more in the manner of Ward. As Fred Poole explained in an interview in 1889, 'a panorama is not self-supporting, and it must be supple-mented by a variety entertainment', since this was the only way to ensure that 'the audience don't get too bored by too much canvas'.[59]

The line between instruction and entertainment is equally difficult to draw within shows dealing with conflict and current events. During 1885, Poole's Myriorama toured their moving panorama of the *Egyptian and Soudan Wars*, lectured by Mr Oscar Hartwell, but also including the usual music, songs and impersonations. In 1900, this moving panorama was reprised, now bulking out the scenes from the Boer War, which were exhib-ited as soon as completed, in a show that also included the performances of acrobats, comedians, singers and ventriloquists. Even the 360-degree panorama, when it appeared, was not often the contemplative experience of earlier shows. For example, the *Panorama of the Defence of Paris against the German Armies*, which was exhibited in London during the 1870s and 1880s, shortly after the event itself, included both an extensive circular panoramic view and a moving panorama (on this occasion, called a 'diorama'). 'If the Panorama exhibits what Paris was outside the walls during the bombard-ment,' claimed an explanatory booklet for the show, 'the Diorama shows what was passing within'.[60] The static panorama gave spectators a detailed insight into the military stratagems of the invading forces, and was intro-duced with an instructive 'historical notice' delivered by a lecturer, but the moving panorama focused more intimately upon the violent, desperate action within the city:

> At that moment, a shell strikes the corner of the butcher's house and shatters the wall to pieces by which several persons are killed or wounded; the people nearest to the wounded are rushing to their assistance; others are looking at the spot where the shell has burst and trying to get out of the way of the slivers of stone which have been impelled in every direction. The emotion is general and reflected in every face.[61]

Printed descriptions such as these sought to emulate the sense of immediacy generated by a lecture which, during this part of the show was less concerned with instruction than with the emotive, personal narrative of the siege. The lecturer's primary role, here, was to amplify the dramatic content of the images, performing an additional role as master of ceremonies in order to connect the different parts of the show.

Shows such as these, which brought elements of variety to the spectacular exhibition, typify the diversification of lectured panoramic entertainments during the second half of the nineteenth century. Whereas most lectures still required their audiences to trust in the expertise of the lecturer or at least to support his or her interpretation of the images, others deliberately undermined this position, or were intended simply to heighten emotive reactions to spectacular or violent visual materials. However, whether they placed emphasis upon instruction and information, spectacular effects, sensational scenes of current events, or offered an ironic critique of one or all of these positions, the presence of the professional lecturer regularly anchored interpretations of the shows. Placed between audience and image, lecturers skillfully negotiated the show's content depending upon the demands of the audience, the expectations of the exhibition site, and the subject matter being treated. Most sought to avoid comparison with dry-as-dust caricatures, instead adopting a fresh-talking attitude more likely to engage with varied audiences and thus able to support the high levels of investment required by the massive infrastructure of such shows. It was thus very important for professional lecturers that they retained aspects of the showman persona, just as Dickens had suggested of Banvard, because this enabled them to respond reliably to varied audiences, while making the most of the visual and other attractions on offer.

The size and expense of dioramic and panoramic shows of the mid to late Victorian period and the varied styles of performance that accompanied them, suggest direct comparisons with many early film shows, which brought similar economies of scale into play and a similar style of variety format during exhibition. As Laurent Mannoni has shown of early French film exhibition, in Britain it was the same travelling and fairground showmen who had exhibited panoramas, dioramas, magic lanterns and peepshows that would do most to promote and popularise the cinematograph in its first years.[62] For example, by the beginning of the twentieth century, Poole's was operating seven separate shows, which toured for forty weeks during the year and now included the cinematograph in a starring role alongside other variety attractions. According to one account, just one of these shows employed 35 people and included three or more separate diorama canvases, each of which might cost up to £2,000.[63] The new medium of film was quickly mobilized within such shows to serve much the same functions as had moving panoramas and effects-driven lantern shows for decades. They required large, regular audiences and adopted an exhibition style that had always been designed to accommodate as many as possible, carefully negotiating between imperatives to entertain and instruct. The lecturer remained a stock figure in these negotiations, as he had been for the past sixty years. Members of both the Hamilton and Poole families, following the audiences, soon entered the film business more seriously, and by 1908 both had attempted to make the transition to the rapidly developing film business.[64]

These lectures can be distinguished from the growing number of magic lantern lectures taking place from the 1870s, which customarily required much lower levels of investment, were often targeted at niche audiences or on behalf of specific interest groups, and frequently were delivered by nonprofessionals. However, the frequency of lantern lectures in the final decades of the nineteenth century, the technological resemblance of the lantern and cinematograph, and the existing repertoire of lantern narratives and photographic styles that could be easily adapted to the moving image, made it inevitable that many lanternists would also seek to adopt the cinematograph.

Lantern Lectures and Lantern Culture

The magic lantern show of the late nineteenth century has long been considered the central and predominating influence upon early film entertainments in Britain. Deac Rossell has written that the magic lantern was 'the environment into which the cinema was born', and more specifically 'the institution which provided its early business practices'.[65] However, it was not the only environment to which the new medium adapted, and not the primary influence upon its commercial strategies so far as exhibition was concerned. In an important essay emphasising discontinuities between lantern and early film lecturing practices, Richard Crangle has suggested that 'moving pictures proceeded as a bricolage of narrative, technical, economic, presentational, and audience practices taken from here, there, and everywhere,' and that the presence of the lecturer 'borrowed from the magic lantern trades' represented only a part of this complex pattern of inheritance and adaptation.[66] Crangle's observation characterises much broader debates concerning new media technologies, which have suggested that the so-called invention of a medium is always characterised by a 'remediation' of earlier media forms and earlier presentational formats.[67] The weight of revisionist historical work concerning early film, which has consistently sought to broaden the range of relevant contexts and influences to be considered, has done a great deal to evidence this suggestion. However, although it has been important to qualify earlier understandings of the magic lantern show as the dominant precursor of early film, and although I would agree with Crangle that even the influence of the lantern lecturer was perhaps no greater than that of the panorama lecturer or fairground spieler, a growing body of work concerning nineteenth-century lantern shows has suggested a series of material connections between the two trades.[68]

The popularity of the magic lantern in the late nineteenth century depended upon the wide range of cultural functions it was able to serve. The apparatus had always assisted the conjuror as much as the popular entertainer or educator and now found a place within diverse public institutions, from the fairground ghost show to the classroom, but the balance of these entertainments shifted as the century progressed. Prior to the 1860s, in spite of its regular educational application within institutions such as the Royal Polytechnic, the lantern's primary use was as an entertainment medium. Itinerant shows were illustrated by hand-painted slides, some of which moved in a variety of ingenious ways, or which were used within 'dissolving views', in which changes were gradually introduced to a scene or one scene might fluidly merge into another.[69] Such shows persisted, especially within children's entertainments or as a part of the variety bills upon which the cinematograph would also subsequently appear.[70] But, while the panoramic show after the 1860s became increasingly concerned with entertainment and spectacular effects, the instructive lecture began to dominate the magic lantern show. As Jens Ruchatz and Crangle have independently shown, 'for the bulk of the second half of the nineteenth century the factual or documentary, especially as rendered by photography, was the most important mode in the medium of public entertainment image projection'.[71] Even in the case of variety lantern shows, which might introduce a wide range of short lectured topics to their audiences, instructive sections of the show were likely to be longer and more numerous than other genres. Photographic slides were popularised during the 1870s and depicted a wide range of scientific, travel, religious, temperance, and other themes. These appeared to guarantee the veridicality of the lecture in a manner quite different to the artistry of hand-painted slides, lending further authority to the lecturer whether he or she intended to entertain, teach or preach. 'On looking at a photograph,' concluded one lantern slide manual, 'we feel sure that we have a faithful representation of the subject, for the photographer has neither the power to add nor to detract from his subject.'[72]

These discourses had a powerful impact upon the magic lantern marketplace, even after the manipulability of the photographic image became public knowledge. For a few lecturers, particularly those with a connection to the celebrated lectures at the Polytechnic, they lent enough authority to generate the kind of publicity that had been enjoyed by Albert Smith earlier in the century. Like panoramic entertainments at the end of the Victorian period, these shows were able to tour as independent concerns, making their own bookings and relying upon visual material that had usually been generated by the lecturers themselves. But most professional lantern lecturers worked on a much smaller scale, depending upon bookings from varied exhibition venues. Equally, many venues depended upon local and amateur lecturers, who often acquired their slides and readings from large commercial outlets, and whose qualifications and experiences were perhaps more easily called into question by audiences. Shows such as these had a less obvious but more pervasive influence on the general public. The thousands of rank and file lecturers of this kind, and the rapidly growing class of amateurs from the 1880s, reached audiences of all classes and in all parts of Britain, so that it is not fanciful to talk of a 'magic lantern culture' in this period. In an 1897 interview in *Titbits* with 'one of our largest lantern slide-makers', the interviewee emphasised the significance of this movement:

> No one who is not in the midst of it has the slightest idea (and you cannot convey an idea) of the enormous development in the use of pictures in education. You may take it roughly, multiplying the parishes by the number of lantern exhibitions given and by the pictures presented at each, that this process of conveying instruction and amusement presents to the eye of the British public millions of pictures in a single season.[73]

Recent studies by Terry and Debbie Borton in the USA and by Stephen Herbert and Damer Waddington in Britain have confirmed the quantity and diversity of lantern exhibitions taking place in even small urban centres, suggesting that the overall scale of lantern culture was, indeed, very significant.[74]

The influence of instructive lantern shows in this period should not be underestimated. Lanterns and lantern slides, alongside other photographic technologies and a new generation of illustrated periodicals, contributed to the apparent democratisation of expert culture in this period. The vibrant market for such expertise made the cheap industrial manufacture of slide series and accompanying lectures inevitable, and brought the instructive lecture easily within the grasp of the home, schoolroom, church, and town hall, not to mention the hundreds of lecture societies and missionary or temperance societies that formed the backbone of the lantern industry from the 1880s. By the mid-1880s the practice of lantern lecturing itself had been commodified in a relatively stable and popular form, and the largest British slide manufacturers, Riley Brothers of Bradford, and York and Sons of London, claimed annual slide production in hundreds of thousands.[75] Trade catalogues indicate that by the 1890s slide sets and accompanying lectures were available for topics from fairy tales, to scientific study, to comedy, to illustrated songs, but instructive and educational material tended to dominate.[76]

This range of genres remained stable between 1880 and 1910, though Crangle has shown that life model series, which used photographic slides to illustrate a fictional narrative, and illustrated song slides, which enabled audiences to sing along with the verses projected on-screen, became more popular in the last years of the nineteenth century.[77] The roles of the lecturer also remained stable during this period, though, of course, performance styles varied considerably depending upon the material depicted, genre, audience, and the personal disposition of the lecturer. Lecturers were usually (but not always) male, and their authority was marked by their position on the platform, the silence they usually demanded from audiences, the specialised discourses they offered and the confidence with which they offered them, the inevitable evening suit they wore, and, on some occasions, by a pointer, which gave them the physical means to interpret images to their audiences. Audiences entertained a degree of complicity with these easily recognisable experts whose culture they were encouraged to share and whose perspective, like theirs, tended to objectify both the screen and the material projected upon it.

As in panoramic entertainments, this hierarchical relationship became especially obvious in the case of travel lectures, which were an extremely popular part of the lantern repertoire and, subsequently, of the cinematograph show. Lectures describing the landscapes and customs of European nations inevitably brought a touristic view to bear upon these locations. But lectures on the colonies and other exotic locations depended more obviously upon anthropological and ethnocentric discourses, which also brought with them the savour of the freak show. A typical travel lantern script, entitled *A Thousand Miles Up the Congo River* (and bearing a striking resemblance at points to Conrad's *Heart of Darkness*), includes descriptions of scenery and wildlife, but most of the photographic slides exhibited were of native people, their strange customs and lives.[78] As was most often the case, the text of the lecture was not original, but substantially borrowed from previously published sources. On this occasion, the lecture derived partly from *Life on the Congo*, a tract written on behalf of the Religious Tract Society, and partly from a lecture series originally devised and performed in the USA by the missionary, Revd J.M. Lewis. In such cases, the dissemination of knowledge from expert to initiate was founded upon an identification of lecturer and audience as the civilised, the touristic, the British—as precisely the antithesis of the objectified alien.

Most other genres of lantern lecture also reproduced this relationship, objectifying the images on-screen in order to instigate some form of cultural commonality between lecturer and audience. The unquestioning attitude that such shows seemed to require of audiences goes some way toward explaining the remarkable formal stability of the didactic lantern lecture. Certainly there was room for spontaneity, interaction and even disagreement in such shows—most shows did not require silence from audiences, and music was not uncommon—but even for the genres of life model and comic lantern lectures, a shared but unspoken agreement upon a series of cultural presuppositions opened out onto the narrative and made sense of the images on-screen. In Riley Brothers' *The Little Match Girl*, the pathetic story of a young girl left to die of hunger and cold by her abusive parents, several popular motifs support bourgeois assumptions concerning the urban working classes.[79] While the girl's parents are represented as inebriates or monsters, their condemnation is not matched by any commitment to improve the conditions of such children. Rather, the impoverished scene is replaced, as was customary, by the girl's vision of heaven—presumably her reward for suffering so quietly. The twin motifs of children and death, which Mervyn Heard and Crangle have found recurring regularly within temperance propaganda, are here used by the Methodist-run Riley Brothers to convey a message that both condemns poverty and celebrates faith as the only positive response to it.[80] As the script of another popular lecture observed, 'Working men, the moral is soon told;—It is not how much money a week you earn, but what you do with it when you get it.'[81]

Of course, the lantern was not an inherently conservative medium. Lantern lectures were also applied for more radical purposes and became a useful tool across the political spectrum within the labour movement. Groups such as the National Liberal Federation were enthusiastic about the potential of the lantern 'to advance the cause of liberalism' across the country, and willingly supplied lantern slides and readings to local constituencies.[82] It was also always possible for lecturers to produce scripts that undermined the conservative tone of mainstream lantern culture. Adventurous lecturers sometimes combined elements from different slide sets so that a curious form of variety lantern lecture was produced. The fascinating artefacts of this practice are the cut-and-paste lecture scripts sometimes used, which evidently served the more idiosyncratic purposes of these performers.[83] It was equally possible for audiences to disagree, perhaps vocally, with messages conveyed by the lecturer.

However, lantern culture faced a greater threat than ideological resistance to the messages it typically conveyed, namely the possibility that instructive lectures might simply not be taken seriously. This was because the market depended upon contradictory premises: while it was commercially important to the industry that novices could be converted into expert lecturers simply by virtue of purchasing a script, it was also socially and aesthetically crucial that the knowledge hierarchy between lecturer and audience was maintained. If this hierarchy could be shown to be fictional, the relationship of trust between lecturer and audience might also break down. Whereas lecturers like Smith had openly satirised the Dryasdust tradition, but did not challenge the desirability of an active didactic lecturing tradition as such, the democratisation and commercial distribution of lantern lectures threatened the very expert culture it claimed to enshrine. The survival of this type of lantern culture depended upon an ability to monitor, police or defuse this threat, and this responsibility fell most directly upon the lecturer, whose role consequently became more and more prescriptively defined toward the end of the century.

The circulation of scathing anecdotes poking fun at amateur lecturers and part-time professionals who were willing to accept lower fees had traditionally accomplished much of this work.[84] But the growing range of publications targeted at the lantern lecturing industry from the mid-1880s regularly repeated key elements of advice to lantern lecturers that reinforced the fundamental relationship between audience, lecturer and image in the instructive lecture. Several late-nineteenth-century books on the lantern included sections dedicated to 'hints to lantern lecturers', and slide catalogues and commercial lecture scripts sometimes offered useful advice for any novices.[85] Similar articles appeared in the *Optical Magic Lantern Journal and Photographic Enlarger*, after it was established in 1889. These were primarily intended for professional lantern lecturers, whose prospects were jeopardised by the growing numbers of amateur lanternists.

By the turn of the century, the lecturer's function within the show was repeated with such regularity that it is possible to characterise an ideal lecture at this time from the point of view of lantern culture itself. The following points represent the most frequently repeated instructions gathered from a wide survey of books and journals published between 1888 and 1905:[86]

1)   The lecturer should appear to have an understanding of his subject more thorough than that of his audience. He may gain this by experience, study or subterfuge. He should take it for granted that they know nothing about it.

2)   He should not explain the slides, the slides should explain him. Instruction should emanate from the lecturer, so he must not allow the spectacle of the images themselves to predominate.

3)   He should have a sufficiently loud voice to be heard without effort or discomfort in any part of the room.

4)   He should always work from a written lecture, but never read from the script. He should know the lecture by heart and should practise adapting it to unfavourable circumstances.

5)   He should not dwell for too long on each slide, nor should there be too many slides (one slide per minute for approximately one hour seems to be the consensus).

6)   He should have an easy, natural and professional manner. The lecture should not be recited too quickly, nor in a monotonous sing-song manner, nor in a staccato, discontinuous manner; it should make good use of pauses, inflection, and emphasis, and every word should be clearly articulated.

7)   He should not move unnecessarily while describing a slide and should not turn away from the audience, but should demonstrate his mastery of the material by an occasional acknowledgement of the screen (a convex mirror placed on the lectern should inform him which image is on-screen). Pointers should only be used to direct audiences toward important details of the slides.

8)   He should never acknowledge the existence of the operator or of the lantern, and the use of ostentatious verbal and visual effects should be prohibited.

9)   He may use an occasional joke, but a bad joke is disastrous. He must never be coarse or vulgar.

10)   He should never panic, nor lose his temper, especially when his apparatus breaks down.

These regularly repeated principles for a successful show assisted the lecturer in devising an entertainment founded on the audience's perception of the lecturer as a professional: educative, but informal; fluent and eloquent; and thoroughly in control of every element of the performance. Ideally, the lecturer would have personal or professional experience of the subject at hand, though some—invariably anonymous—commentators claimed that their own knowledge of many subjects had come primarily from the periodical press. 'I have been greatly amused,' wrote one such lecturer, 'when in reading certain newspapers I have been spoken of as an authority on certain subjects whereas a day or so before I practically new nothing or little about them.'[87] Accounts such as these confirm Goffman's proposition that the impression given by the lecturer depends less upon what they know, than upon the presentation of self upon the podium. Memorisation of lantern scripts was most often recommended, but the success of the lecturer's self-management depended upon the illusion of fresh talk. Any distractions from his authoritative, free-flowing discourse were carefully avoided. Even the acknowledgement of his own physical presence, or the presence of the lantern, was an unnecessary distraction for audiences. According to celebrated caricaturist, lantern lecturer and film scenarist Harry Furniss, 'the people have their eyes fixed upon my quickly changing pictures, and the strong light on the screen, in the centre of the platform, makes the darkness at either side, seem more intense'.[88] In ideal circumstances all would be conducted so that audiences would attend unquestioningly to the text of the lecture and its illustration.

The second point listed above is repeated with particular regularity in the articles surveyed. The idea that the verbal content of the lantern lecture should frame the slides was at the heart of a debate that took place within lantern culture throughout this period. 'There are two kinds of lantern lectures,' confirmed lanternist George E. Brown: 'In one the lecturer's part is the same as the "literary" matter in some of our illustrated magazines— merely a convenient and agreeable background for the pictures. In the other the lecture is the thing; the pictures take second place.'[89] On almost every occasion that this distinction was made within the *Optical Magic Lantern Journal*, the writer clarified that the second type of lecture was preferred: 'the pictures for the lecture, and not the lecture for the pictures'.[90] When, instead, the variety of images exhibited became the organising principle around which the lecturer's discourse was arranged, as in popular panoramic entertainments of the same period, this tended to undermine the highly institutionalised practices of lantern culture. It also endangered the businesses of slide manufacturers, whose massive catalogues of slides were arranged as coherent series, usually with accompanying lectures. This unusually stable relationship between pictorial and verbal aspects of the entertainment would also come to inform the way the cinematograph was viewed by lanternists.

Lecturing Traditions in the Early Film Show

The varied lecturing practices inherited by the early British film show were certainly familiar to audiences, and offered them a comfortable reference point within the flow of moving images. While such shows practised an annihilation of space and time that could be disconcerting for spectators, they could also evoke a close and trusting relationship between lecturer and audience. Tom Gunning has suggested that 'the attraction of being addressed by a fully present human being' was important to audiences and that the lecturer therefore 'responded to [an] anxiety or sense of lack within the film image'.[91] This argument has been extended by Germain Lacasse, who has recently suggested that the lecturer can therefore be profitably regarded as a kind of 'mediator of modernity'.[92] This reassuring presence depended upon the ability of lecturers to continue to fill the roles with which they had long been associated. As in earlier entertainments, film lecturers were most often male performers with the specific tasks of either providing a running commentary on the images exhibited or making introductory remarks between them.[93] They mediated the images appearing on the screen and crucially, their own performances made a substantial contribution to spectatorship. They were usually answerable to audiences during perform-ance and consequently were in a unique position of responsibility for the success or failure of the show.

But if lecturers could be a comforting, familiar presence, the styles and applications of their lectures were as inconsistent and contradictory as they had always been. The relationship with audiences could be played out prima-rily as a dissemination of knowledge, as in the case of most lantern lectures, or as a straightforward presentation of spectacular images, as in most panoramic shows. Many of the most successful film lecturers also brought a strongly satirical self-consciousness to the entertainment, which seemed to hark back to the tradition of Albert Smith and Artemus Ward. Thus, the various highly institutionalised lecturing traditions that had developed during the nineteenth century each had an impact upon distinct sections of the early film market. In particular, the complex compromises traditionally made by lecturers between entertainment and instruction, and their rela-tionship to the idea of expert culture, had a powerful impact upon film exhibition. Like the photographic lantern slide, the moving picture apparently offered audiences a faithful representation of the world, supporting the authoritative discourses of the lecturer. But like the moving panorama or dissolving view, it also promised audiences emotive action and spectacular effects, whose impact did not necessarily rest upon the spoken word. Lantern lecturers had always been in a precarious professional position, negotiating word and image, but now they also encountered a moving image that brought a substantial discourse of its own to the show. If they were to retain their customary authority, the performances of film lecturers had to co-exist with the performative content of the film, of its actors, narrators and filmmakers. Thus, as the institutional constraints levied by existing entertainment institutions shifted with the introduction of moving pictures, so too did the relationship between lecturer and audience.

Film lecturing was very common in Britain in the pre-1907 period, and again during a 1909 resurgence of the practice much heralded in the trade press, which parallels that often described in the United States at this time.[94] The crisis and brief return of the lecturer in this latter period seems to have generated far more prolonged discussion of lecturing practices than had been customary in the industry. In the poorly documented pre-1907 period, film lecturers have left behind few traces of their discursive livelihoods. Unlike lantern shows, lectures were rarely printed, but vanished as they were spoken, and the lecturers themselves died long before any serious historical attention was paid to them. Within the trade press, references to lectures tend to describe them as a customary and wholly unremarkable activity. Indeed, throughout records of film exhibition, live performance was an essential element most often taken for granted within a culture for which it had long been a founding premise. André Gaudreault and Jean-Pierre Sirois-Trahan have also noted that the lecturer is mostly absent from classic histories of the origins of the movies.[95] Even as due respect and attention has returned to this figure, work on the British context has often attempted to trace it through the apparently confusing, lacunic narratives of early films, but this perspective serves largely to expose a substantial gap in our knowledge of the subject.[96]

In the most thorough account of international film lecturing practices to date, Germain Lacasse has usefully distinguished the range of titles given to the lecturer internationally, and finds in the French language especially a precedent for a classification of the different roles of the lecturer.[97] Similarly, Gaudreault and Sirois-Trahan, speaking of exhibition practices in Montreal, find in the French terms, 'bonimenteur' and 'conférencier', a precedent also for a formal distinction between alternative institutional practices.[98] The *conférencier* is best compared to the British lantern lecturer, connoting educative discourses illustrated by projected images. The *bonimenteur* has no British counterpart in wide critical usage, but in the sense that Gaudreault intends here, it might usefully be compared to those speakers within panoramic or lantern shows whose primary role was to direct attention toward a relatively self-sufficient image.

However, in Britain the word 'lecturer' is almost always used by contemporary sources on any occasion that live commentary accompanies a visual attraction, suggesting that popular perception of this figure was relatively consistent across a wide range of practices. Furthermore, the practices of the *conférencier* and *bonimenteur* were very difficult to separate in practice. Lecturers familiar with either approach creatively exploited different techniques of speaking and self-management as they saw fit, but would certainly seek to gratify the conventional expectations of a specific audience entering a specific type of show. Thus, the association of film lecturing with different traditions of magic lantern and panorama lecturing does not necessarily suggest a simple institutional inheritance in either case. Magic lantern culture, in particular, had a mixed response to the moving picture, but certainly saw it primarily as a threat. As James Parkes acknowledged in 1901, from the institutional perspective of the lecturing profession itself, there were clear discontinuities between the two practices:

> It is well known that hundreds of cinematograph exhibitions are given daily by as many exhibitors, who, until the introduction of the fascination, had not given the lantern business a thought, and as no special gift or talent is wanted to become efficient in the line, a reasonable capital spells success to the men possessing business tact. And as the ordinary user of the lantern lacks capital to place before the public anything so elaborate as the above, or the lecturer any inclination to mutilate his teaching by such an introduction, both have to be satisfied with fewer bookings.[99]

For Parkes, the profitable exhibition of film differed from lantern exhibition principally because it required 'no special gift or talent' from its live performers. Three months earlier, the same point had been made in *The Showman*, which complained that during a film show 'the public are not so much interested in the history of the subject, for there is no story attached and no ability displayed'.[100] By 1902, T. Perkins was encouraging lecturers to resist the encroachment of the cinematograph upon lantern culture:

> The kinematograph appeals to the eye chiefly, if not entirely. It is a rival

to the 'effect' slides shown by means of double and triple lanterns, but does not lend itself very fully to the illustration of lectures, the object of which is rather to instruct than amuse. But, undoubtedly, the new departure has been, and still is, a rival of the illustrated lecture, and it behoves all lecturers to do their best to hold their own in popular esteem.[101]

Perkins's call to arms suggests that the cinematograph's appeal was best compared with spectacular visual effects, such as dissolving view slides, and had very little to do with the lantern lecture. Parkes and Perkins also record the distaste felt by many for a medium that might 'mutilate' the instructive impulse that had always governed lantern lectures. As we have seen, instruction had traditionally co-ordinated lecturer and audience in their relationship toward the projected image. Film introduced a new element to the spectatorial regime of the entertainment that resisted the objectification of still images.

The rarity of published lecture scripts for moving pictures, a few of which were, however, available by request from manufacturers, also suggests a substantial reorientation of the role of the lecturer within film shows.[102] Trade journal *The Bioscope* reported that a few printed film lectures did exist for travel entertainments, though even here these were principally regarded as 'reading matter' for lecturers rather than scripts, as such.[103] Even the catalogue descriptions of films, which have often been understood as basic scripts for film lecturers, were, with some pertinent exceptions, little more than basic summaries of the action on-screen and seem to have been designed to supplement the image, rather than to structure or interpret it. One lantern manufacturer, which distributed films alongside their extensive back catalogues of educative slides, explained that, for schools, the cinematograph was 'too costly and the working too troublesome and expensive for frequent use, besides which lecturing and teaching are more difficult and less effective with moving pictures'.[104]

The educational value of the cinematograph would remain a bone of contention among producers and exhibitors for decades to come, but, as these commentators also suggested, the economics of film exhibition were still more problematic. Most lanternists had been facing difficult economic circumstances for some time and simply could not afford to adopt the new apparatus. An important 1900 article entitled 'Lecturer's Profits' in the *Optical Magic Lantern Journal* distinguishes in particular between the profession of celebrity lecturers like Professor Benjamin J. Malden—a dominant figure at this time—who booked his own theatres and could expect considerable financial returns, and that of the great majority of lecturers, who toured the circuit of local lecture societies for smaller returns.[105] The writer claimed that £300 per annum was an extremely good (and unlikely) profit for the latter class of performer, who faced an increasingly competitive market among the lecturing societies.[106] Furthermore, lecturers frequently complained that exhibition sites had become increasingly unwilling even to pay their considerable travelling expenses.[107] Such low levels of remuneration effectively prevented many lanternists from entering the moving picture business, even if they wished to do so, because the cost of purchasing and maintaining equipment was too high. A more substantial problem was the regular cost of buying up-to-date films and replacing those that had become worn through use—a problem much more severe than that associated with the relatively inexpensive and durable lantern slide, and which was exacerbated by public tastes for footage of current events.

The cost of lectured cinematograph shows, if they were to be attempted, were also usually too much for the lecture societies upon which the lanternists' careers had depended. A good idea of the relative costs of lantern and film shows can be gained from the catalogues of manufacturing and distributing companies such as Newton and Co's, who had a team of professional lecturers and operators available for hire, in addition to the slides and films they had for sale.[108] Shortly after the turn of the century, the cost of a lantern, screen, and operator, not including costs for slides or travel expenses, was £1 17s. 6d. If amateur exhibitors wished to put on a show themselves, costs were dramatically reduced: slides cost 2 shillings per dozen for the first night and the average lecture was only sixpence. At the same time, a cinematograph and operator cost a minimum of £4 10s., and the films themselves were likely to add a good deal more to this sum. Under these conditions, all but the largest lecture societies wishing to respond to the popularity of the moving picture were likely to feel the squeeze.

The mode of operation of the cinematograph thus seemed to favour large and centralised institutions of production and exhibition, such as those associated with panoramic entertainments, variety theatres, and fairground shows, and this presented a substantial problem for lantern culture in general, which had been largely constituted by a great number of small-scale enterprises. From independent and itinerant lecturers to parish associations, small charities, schools, and lecture societies, there is no doubt that the moving picture represented an aesthetic, financial and moral challenge. But it also presented a few eminent lecturers and relatively wealthy organisations with fresh opportunities. If they could afford the cinematograph and could find a way to incorporate it seamlessly into their shows, they would simply be continuing the long tradition of the rational amusement: allowing popular spectacle and instructive discourse to interact in a constructive manner. Importantly, the dress code, position, and elocutionary style of the lecturer on the platform persisted in such cases, even if his discourse was substantially altered.[109]

In the first year or two of film exhibition, instructive lectures that sought to showcase and explain the film apparatus were especially influenced by traditions of scientific public lecturing, especially in the fields of optics and photographic technology, in which information passed almost exclusively in one direction from educator to listener, from expert to initiate.[110] Similarly, travel cinematograph shows, like panoramic and lantern shows before them, continued to offer audiences the opportunity to view foreign lands and customs in the physically and ideologically safe environment of the lecture theatre. Once again, because they played so effectively upon long-established discourses of improvement, these shows also gave audiences the opportunity to speculate upon material that might have been taboo, or at least inappropriate in other exhibition contexts, because it had been framed by the well-dressed representative of expert culture on the podium.

The most enduring genre of lantern lecturing practices within the film show was the 'travelogue'—a term coined in 1904 in order to describe the celebrated lantern and cinematograph shows of American lecturer Burton Holmes. These shows remained popular into the 1920s, and are relatively well documented within recent US-based studies.[111] It was predominantly the personality lecturers at the apex of the lantern industry, men who, like Albert Smith and many others, had developed a reputation for gathering their own images, films and anecdotes for use during the winter lecturing season, who made a financial success of the travelogue. For example, the Yorkshire-based lecturer, Henry Hibbert, toured his Boer War and Paris entertainments in the first years of the twentieth century, lecturing both to lantern sequences and to films with his own, highly personalised commentary.[112] Arthur B. Malden, son of celebrity lecturer Professor Benjamin J. Malden, also delivered travel shows illustrated with photographic slides and films of his subjects, his lectures adding historical details intended to contextualise the images.[113] Lectures such as these perpetuated the dynamics of the rational amusement in the context of film exhibition and were lauded by those who saw the future of the profession in this development. According to the *Optical Lantern and Cinematograph Journal* (which had previously been titled *The Optical Magic Lantern Journal*), Malden's audiences were 'delighted with the interesting and at the same time educational feast he has provided', and suggested that such performances 'should revive interest in the optical lantern as entertainer'.[114] The journal reviewed Holmes's 1905 tour of Britain extremely positively, suggesting a new opportunity for the beleaguered profession of lantern lecturing:[115]

> In his description of the scenes there is nothing pretentious; no hard and dry-as-dust lecture, but a calm and interesting statement of facts which appeal to the audience, and give them a ready grasp of the subject and a large interest in the views portrayed. We have time after time advocated moving picture lectures, and if Mr. Holmes' Travelogues are taken as a pattern, the revival of the optical lantern would quickly be at hand.[116]

In the context of American travelogue entertainments, Charles Musser has described this relationship between lecturer, audience and screen as part of a 'cinema of reassurance', from which bourgeois assumptions concerning foreign lands and peoples took succour.[117] The espousal of reassurance within early film, derived in this instance from generations of ethnographic entertainments, was certainly central to these film shows, as the printed volumes of Holmes' lectures tend to demonstrate. Meanwhile, the persuasive value of film was being developed more directly by some lecturers, according to Alan Burton, who has detailed the role of film from 1898 within the British Co-operative Society movement.[118] Film was regularly used by pressure groups and partisans who cleverly exploited the affective power of such shows for financial and political gain. By 1905, one correspondent to the *Optical and Magic Lantern Journal* was keen to promote the political use of film more widely:

> For the past five years I have used the cinematograph (Walturdaw Bioscope) in connection with my political meetings in different parts of the country, and have proved it of great value, not only in the way of entertainment, but also for imparting instruction on political questions of the day. I am thoroughly convinced that there is a wide opening for the cinematograph in the political world.[119]

Of course this show was not intended as a rational amusement, as such, in the same way as the travelogue show, but the emphasis on 'imparting instruction' via film in conjunction with lectured discourse indicates that a similar relationship was in place. At a meeting of the politically conservative Primrose League in 1906, a movie was screened in which 'Starving men and women were depicted stretching out their hands to the "large loaf", for which they have no money to pay'.[120] The affecting images on-screen were accompanied by sharply persuasive political commentary from filmmaker Lewin Fitzhamon. In fact, throughout the General Election of 1906, the political parties made much use of both magic lantern and cinematograph, hoping to exploit the pull and the power of the projected image:

> In many instances politicians have experienced the greatest difficulty in getting electors to their meetings. Dry speeches from more or less able orators are not the class of entertainment the present working man desires after his days' task, but give him living pictures, or even common place slides, and he takes his political medicine with spoonfuls of jam, and, what is more, the truths depicted on the screen have more effect than much of the platform twaddle.[121]

The success of such shows can largely be measured in the degree to which audiences were convinced by their political content. They suggest the potential power which the combination of the lecturer's address and the moving image could wield over spectators.

Scientific, travel and political lectures were among several lantern genres that successfully incorporated the cinematograph. But such expensive and specialised shows did not reach audiences, parish to parish, in the way that the lantern did, and they did not wholly undermine this diffuse market during the 1900s and 1910s. In this period, lantern lecturing continued to find a powerful foothold among educational and charitable institutions.[122] The success of instructive cinematograph lectures such as Holmes's travelogues depended upon a very different commercial logic, in which the authority of the expert lecture was strongly supported both by the show's scale of investment and by the discourses of celebrity these performers generated. Holmes, like Artemus Ward before him, imported his fame from the USA, where it had been earned over many years on the lecturing circuit. Arthur Malden inherited his celebrity from his father, who had remained a significant figure within British lantern culture after his retirement in 1900, and was sometimes present among his son's audiences. Politicians also depended upon aspects of the burgeoning personality culture in this period in order to make a success of their film shows. As Peter Cherches has argued of the performance of 'star lecturers' in nineteenth-century America, 'what was ultimately consumed by audiences was not a demonstration of competence for which a celebrity's recognition had been earned, but rather a display of personality or the projection of an image'.[123] Furthermore, this relationship was already in place before the entertainment began. Famous lecturers brought an institutional momentum of their own, and audiences anticipated the appearance of key structures of performance and personality that would help them interpret the show.

This marketing of personality owed as much to the panoramic lecturing tradition as it did to the lantern show. Celebrity film lecturers worked on a smaller scale than large organisations like Poole's Myriorama, but they had much in common with shows of this kind, bringing high quality images to the public that could not be seen elsewhere, and placing greater emphasis on spectacular action. Other early film shows adopted similar strategies in order to attract a public large enough to support their commercial ambitions. Famously, Alfred West established from 1898 a popular entertainment entitled 'Our Navy', shortly followed by a second entitled 'Our Army'.[124] By December 1899, in the wake of British military involvement in South Africa, the show was two hours long, contained magic lantern slides, jingoistic sing-alongs, forty films with novel sound-effects, and was lectured by West himself.[125] West even acquired copyright for the show, consolidating its dominant institutional position, and hoping to prevent others from replicating its enormous success.[126] The strength of patriotic sentiment evoked by the entertainment was such that, according to one review, 'there were forty at Newcastle and eighteen at Sheffield applied to join the navy after having seen it', a trend that was recognised by the navy in the support and patronage it gave to West.[127] In 1901 West was exhibiting 'realistic pictures of Army life shown two or three times a day,' and the show had proven so successful a recruiting agent for the armed forces that the projector had been renamed the 'Recruitograph'.[128]

Smaller variety entertainments also made limited use of lecturers, some of whom had begun their careers firmly entrenched within lantern culture. Following the growth in amateur lecturing since the mid-1880s, some professional lanternists had adopted practices apparently at odds with the educational lecture tradition, attempting to bring the lantern to new markets, such as music halls, or tent shows during the summer months.[129] Sideshow and fairground showmen were also willing to adapt aspects of the illustrated lecture, derived, in part, from the tradition of the peepshow as well as from larger scale entertainments, provided they believed the show had novelty enough to attract audiences. *The Showman* regularly advocated 'the showman's method of combining entertainment with instruction' to a readership largely composed of fairground, shop-front, and music hall exhibitors.[130] These entertainments appeared at unexpected locations and in a variety of bizarre hybrid forms. For example, the showman Harry Addison developed a show called 'Barnumania' during the 1890s, which included a lantern lecture that enabled him to describe the life and history of sixty famous freaks within twenty minutes.[131]

Following the introduction of film to hybrid entertainments such as these, the lantern and cinematograph often alternated, and the discursive weight of the show therefore also alternated between lecture and projected image. In order to accommodate this trend, several early film projectors were specifically designed to handle both film and slide.[132] There are many examples of such shows and also considerable variety in the methods of conjunction of the two media. Most frequently, lantern slides were used simply to occupy the pause during the exchange of film reels, a practice recommended by the first generation of film exhibition manuals. According to Henry V. Hopwood, writing in 1899, this use of the lantern was to be especially recommended because it had the effect of 'heightening the effect of Living Pictures by contrast with a motionless one'.[133] Cecil Hepworth, whose father was a celebrated professional lanternist, added that shows of this kind also had the key advantage of maintaining the kind of continuity associated with the lecturing tradition:

> Undoubtedly the best plan is to show one or two lantern slides between each animated photograph. The still picture is a great relief to the eyes and a thorough rest after the always more or less tiring living photograph . . . And further, and most important of all, it gives the entertainer the opportunity of stringing his pictures together, to a certain extent; of making one follow another with an attempt at natural eloquence, which, if properly carried out, will do more to create a good impression in the minds of the audience than the most excellent photographs in the world shown higgledy-piggledy.[134]

Hepworth's own shows in this period usually applied this technique of maintaining a running commentary in order to connect the still and moving pictures projected. However, many shows took a different approach to the combination of these media, testifying to their adaptability within all kinds of exhibition contexts. At London's Egyptian Hall, for example, the films were accompanied by the commentary of Nevil Maskelyne, who introduced each one, 'occasionally pointing out some celebrity who might otherwise have escaped our notice'.[135] Between each, famous lanternist C.W. Locke introduced intricate lantern effects, though these were not usually lectured.[136] By contrast, one contributor to *The Showman* proposed that the film portion of the entertainment might be improved by merely announcing the titles (either by a title slide, or via the lecturer) or 'by introducing a jest or short anecdote' now and then.[137] Another exhibitor described the lantern lecture as 'an admirable means to stir up enthusiasm' only when his customary film entertainment had 'failed to give satisfaction' to more demanding audiences.[138]

The variety of lectured film shows available to the public during the first ten years of cinema eloquently demonstrates that, even if it was unusual for lectures to follow the very precise guidelines dictated by lantern culture, the flexible combination of lecturer and image had remained a remarkably productive arrangement. The showmen's trade press, in particular, regularly advocated new methods for managing this relationship, or suggested new novelties to which it might be applied.[139] But within this fragmented and apparently unpredictable market, the demand for travel, science, military, and current events subjects, even on variety bills, suggests that aspects of the rational amusement remained as popular as they had been within panoramic and lantern shows for the previous thirty years. Film producers moved to meet this demand, just as they met the demand of other pre-existing entertainment institutions, and some came to specialise in educational films intended for the popular market.

The film entrepreneur Charles Urban, who worked for the Warwick Trading Company before leaving in 1902 to form the Charles Urban Trading Company, would be instrumental in this trend up to the 1920s, as Luke McKernan has extensively demonstrated.[140] A brilliant publicist, Urban made very few fictional films in his career but, as had been the case for earlier institutions associated with the rational amusement, took every opportunity to advance the cause of the educational and topical productions in which his companies specialised. These films were marketed internationally, though their success as educative rather than spectacular productions was likely to depend on the presence and quality of the lecturer who described them. In order to mitigate the problem of the lecturer, Charles Urban Trading Company catalogues included particularly detailed and entertaining descriptions of new educational series, sometimes running to several pages, though they did not do so for the comic sketches sold on behalf of other filmmakers. Additionally, from 1903, Urban also managed a flagship entertainment at the London Alhambra music hall, in which a series of educational subjects were screened to audiences, usually accompanied by a high-quality lecture.[141] In fact, such discourses of uplift were not uncommon among early film exhibitors more generally, especially those who wished to try their hand at travelogue entertainments.[142]

Thus, although spoken commentary was a very pervasive part of the nascent film industry in Britain, this did not always extend to lecturing in the sense cherished by the lantern industry. However, by bringing continuity and stylistic coherence to such variety shows, the lecturer remained partly responsible for maintaining a degree of stability within these early institutions of film exhibition. The attractions of a film show might be very fragmented and its audiences varied, but the lecturer remained a visible, human point of reference, anchoring the interpretation of the films and sometimes coming to embody the characteristics of the exhibition site at which he worked. This function was highly valued across the spectrum of early film shows. Even on the fairground, film lecturers (often known as 'describers' at this site), such as James Styles, were well respected for the easy and entertaining manner in which they accompanied the films.[143] Nonetheless, film lecturers in Britain continued to work within a fragile profession, their existence dependent upon the uncertain demands of audiences and the goodwill and tastes of exhibitors. Furthermore, they had to accommodate an extremely unstable and rapidly developing medium whose appeal to audiences diversified while the range of exhibition sites narrowed. The lecturer's worth to exhibitors and audiences was a question continually under review.

This unstable and dynamic position has been theorised by Lacasse, who has emphasised the film lecturer's negotiation between different social groups, cultural imperatives and tastes. For Lacasse, the lecturer was first and foremost an instrument of mediation between representation and spectatorship: 'He is like a surface where opposed forces meet, a surface where these forces will combine in a dynamic process of attraction and repulsion.'[144] However, the lecturer's task of mediation under such circumstances was neither so purely instrumental nor so effortless and invisible as the metaphor of the interactive surface would suggest. Indeed, if we can speak of an interactive surface of any kind, this was a visible surface with a definitively human profile, one which not only negotiated the multiple forces to which it responded, but also sought to carve out a legitimate professional space between them. Lecturers worked within local institutional structures that inevitably placed certain constraints upon them, but they might also initiate changes to these structures.

The profession of lecturing thus developed flexibly alongside the institutions in which it took place, but this form of work also exerted an influence on these institutions and, as the example of the Charles Urban Trading Company suggests, even impacted upon the kinds of films that were produced for them. Since lecturers worked in the direct presence of customers, they also became the medium across which spectatorial feedback concerning the film shows returned to managers of exhibition sites and production companies. This, of course, was especially the case for exhibitor/producers such as Cecil Hepworth and James Williamson, whose regular contact with the public strongly influenced the types of films they began producing. However, even when film producers grew more powerful and the gap between production and exhibition widened, the lecturer remained a commercial and aesthetic touchstone for the early film industry. This became most obvious in the debate that sprang up from the end of 1908 concerning the uncertain value of the lecturer to the new generation of picture theatres. In Britain, this debate was sparked by the advice offered especially by *The Bioscope* to managers and operators, which gave a series of commentators an opportunity to speculate upon the kind of audiences picture theatres could attract and the relationship these audiences ought to entertain with the screen when they got there. For some, the ideal was simply to interpret the action on-screen on the behalf of audiences who might not be able to make such connections alone:

> I have come to the conclusion that a bioscopic representation of a play, or a historical event, or a voyage of discovery is not half so good unexplained as when accompanied by a good graphic lecture, and people who have watched the pictures under the latter conditions are very chary at going to a hall where no lecture or next door to none is given. Managers will be furthering their own interests as well as adding to the enjoyment of their patrons if they will engage a man who is really capable to tell people what the films really represent.[145]

In particular, the increasing complexity and popularity of story films dictated the growing importance of lecturers who could contribute to narrative comprehension of the image. To a limited extent, the lecturer was now needed 'to solve the crisis in narrative form as filmmakers were caught between new ambitions and older forms', as studies of post-1908 lecturing in the USA have suggested.[146] This was not a new phenomenon, however, and does not seem to have been experienced as a crisis, probably because narration had always been part of the film lecturer's most conventional duties, borrowing substantially from storytelling practices within the panoramic and lantern traditions. Nor was it the only function for lecturers in this period. Indeed, for one British 'speaker on pictures' in January 1909, 'to even a half-intelligent audience the picture explains itself', the real need being only 'to give an audience some idea of what the characters on screen are saying'.[147] Furthermore the lecture understood as narrative voice-over was often supplanted at this time by other forms of verbal commentary. Another correspondent to *The Bioscope* suggested that this role of the lecturer might also be fulfilled by 'some small booklets giving a story of the plot which could be sold to the audience', or by the more extensive use of inter-titling.[148]

For other writers, the explanatory practices of lecturers were only useful in conjunction with other educational genres. A 1913 review of a social welfare show, which ran for an entire week as part of a grand 'kinemato-graph exhibition' at London's Olympia Hall, bemoans the absence of the lecturer, who happened to be ill.[149] Spectators had far more interest in the other nine 'projection theatres' in the Hall, drifting away from this instruc-tive show because it gave 'no previous announcement of what was going to be shown, and no explanation of it while it was going on'.[150] A section of the show dedicated to travel seemed similarly disorganised, presenting 'a jumble of pictures from all over the world' with no apparent logic. The lecturer clearly still had a vital role to play in such shows. The *Motion Picture Hand-book* (an American publication also copyrighted at London's Stationers Hall in 1910) offered advice on the successful lecturing of travelogues:

> The lecturer *absolutely must speak clearly and distinctly*. Reading the lecture impairs the effect very much. Naturally four-fifths of the effect as a whole depends on the lecturer himself, or herself. The sing-song talker, or the talker who speaks so fast or so low that the words cannot be followed except by an effort, spoils it all. Properly done, the illustrated lecture is excellent. Wrongly done, it is worse than nothing at all.[151]

In terms of the lecturer's appearance and performance style, these instruc-tions are virtually identical to those given in earlier generations of handbooks on lantern operating and lecturing. Most of all, an easy and unpretentious manner is demanded of the lecturer—a fresh-talking communicability which must not appear scripted or practised, but which must be intellectu-ally informative for audiences. However, as another contributor to *The Bioscope* suggested, the film lecturer should also avoid becoming excessively 'academical', since doing so will cause 'his listeners [to] accuse him of looking down on them':

> The lecturer's key to success is 'to tell the tale'. It should be told simply, clearly and intellectually. The lecturer should know the picture well before he attempts to explain it to others. He should keep perfect pace with the projecting machine, should quietly indicate the inner cause when the outer is taking place. He should indulge in no stock phrases, no personal reminiscences which the picture may recall, no opaque

phrases, no drawn-out, windy sentences; in fact, nothing which could possibly lower his description in the estimation of any single member of his audience. [152]

According to this writer, the lecturer should not flaunt his expertise, nor elicit his audience's inclusion within exclusive highbrow discourses, but should speak familiarly, conversationally, and in a manner inclusive of as wide a public as possible. Nor should he seek to dominate the pictures, but should carefully synchronise his words with a dominant image track. Responding to one manager who confessed himself ill-equipped to deliver such a lecture, the editor of *The Bioscope* even suggested that professional lectures tended to get in the way of 'real narrative', and that 'the real man to give the lecture is the manager himself'.[153]

The recommendation of such practices suggests that the lecture in the picture theatre primarily served the discourses of the image track. But it also demonstrates that the presence of the right personality in the right place remained extremely valuable to audiences. The important point for manager-lecturers wishing to sustain their businesses within developing institutional contexts was that they nurture and promote their own particular mode of agency, expressing confidence in their personality and attitude to the films, whatever that might be:

> Confidence in [the lecture's] worth must be exhibited by the lecturer or the audience will never come to see that the idea is good at all. For a lecturer to be telling himself all the time that he is no good, that he is only a mere super, a glorified fill-up, is to court failure. We hope the manager of D___ Picture Palace will read again our words of advice on this subject.[154]

Such advice testifies to some of the difficulties experienced by speakers to pictures in this period. Film lectures had always been threatened by the moving picture, but films now accommodated a wealth of competing personalities, and within this environment the lecturer courted professional failure whenever he began to accept a supplementary role to the bodies associated with the image track. As discourses of acting and stardom developed during the late 1900s, the lecturer inevitably moved to support these, and this made preserving a meaningful sense of his own performance extremely difficult. Once again, *The Bioscope* offered an optimistic prognosis for would-be lecturers: 'verbal explanation is necessary,' it explained, 'because it is impossible to place on the screen real pathos, and real humanness—these must be preserved from the full glare of people's eyes or the effect is lost'.[155] The lecturer's actual presence on the stage therefore offered the only opportunity to bring such intimate relationships to light: 'spectators will not trouble to look for these latent qualities unless the search is suggested to them'.[156]

In fact, there is a good deal of evidence to support the idea that pathos and humanity were very much the business of the screen in this period.[157] It is hard to see what the lecturer could contribute to the publicity already attendant upon a new generation of picture personalities. Opportunities for lecturers to explain the action on-screen or to place the films into an overarching verbal context had become increasingly scarce as audiences became more adept at reading longer, self-sufficient narratives. Still more significantly, as actors and filmic narrators became more prominent, it became almost impossible for lecturers to preserve their own personalities in the space between screen and audience. Part of the logic of encouraging managers to lecture, after all, was that these individuals, having the most direct connection with the modern cinema industry, seemed most likely to blend seamlessly into its institutional fabric, becoming representatives for a centralised movie culture that was increasingly being defined in continental Europe and the USA. Although the film lecturer continued to perform for a surprisingly long period in Britain, particularly during travelogue entertainments, his professional position became less stable and his influence upon institutions less potent during the early 1910s.

At this stage, the lecture remained only one, largely overlooked, option in theatres which might also exploit ciné-variety in the style of music hall; illustrated songs, which encouraged the audience to sing along with the pictures; local topicals, which recorded local events at which members of the audience had most likely been present; feature films and spectaculars; and screenings involving either live or recorded music.[158] However, as the profession became fragmented, the powerful influence wielded by the lecturer did not disappear. Although lecturing practices were significantly weakened in Britain by 1909, the roles that lecturers had traditionally sought to fulfil effectively moved backwards through the industry, from institutions of exhibition to distribution and production. Here, they would reappear in the developing profession of screenwriting, not to mention in the newsreel, the cinema travelogue, and other genres of factual filmmaking. The centralisation of cinema institutions did not mean that audiences were dislocated from the reassuring presence of the public personality. Rather, as was also the case in live performance practices associated with showmanship, this would be productively displaced onto screen practices.

3

Knowing Better
Traditions of Showmanship and Early Film

The significance of the diverse group of entrepreneurs, public speakers and entertainers known collectively as showmen within the early film industry has only been exposed comparatively recently by the work of revisionist historians. Such writers have emphasised especially the importance of exhibition practices in the fairground bioscope show, demonstrating that these travelling showmen were largely responsible for popularising the new medium across the UK, and for opening up a large market for film within institutions that functioned very differently to those dominantly associated with the illustrated lecture.[1] Deac Rossell has usefully distinguished between alternative classes of itinerant showman, and has shown that the practices and commercial ambitions of the fairground bioscope showman, the itinerant film exhibitor who screened films in church or town halls, and the amateur film exhibitor were very different, and require the marshalling together of varied forms of evidence.[2] Jon Burrows has also demonstrated that the commercial infrastructure of London's shop-front film shows in the years after 1906 was very substantial, and that traditions of showmanship thrived within these venues, in spite of the hostile interference of the authorities.[3] Similarly, Vanessa Toulmin has argued that the role of town hall showmen was far more significant to the development of the early British film industry than has been assumed.[4] Showman-led practices associated with the variety format of film shows that occurred at exhibition sites such as the music hall have also attracted academic attention, particularly on those occasions that live performances, such as the provision of dialogue, music or sound-effects contributed in some way to the screening of the film.[5]

Such work is cumulatively beginning to show that the practices associated with showmanship were at least as varied as the venues the showmen worked within. However, the coherence of the centuries-old tradition of showmanship, and the continuities of experience this brought to audiences across these exhibition sites have not been the primary focus of these studies. Most often associated with working-class entertainments, showmanship had for decades—and especially since the arrival of Barnum in the UK in the 1840s—described any practices that combined a highly articulate and fresh-talking performance with a capacity for exaggeration or outright deception. By the 1850s the term 'showman' was more widely dispersed, and was applied to eminent popular lecturers such as Albert Smith, Artemus Ward and Burton Holmes, all of whom adopted recognisable aspects of the showman persona on the behalf of middle-class audiences. As these examples have suggested in the previous chapter, principles of good showmanship were certainly not limited to those who explicitly identified themselves as showmen, and were adopted across the entertainment marketplace. Moreover, the association of showmanship with principles of entrepreneurial commonsense made the showman a significant iconic component of the commercial landscape more generally, a figure whose supposed capacity to sell anything to anybody resonated powerfully with the diversifying commodity culture of the late nineteenth century.

The popular figure of the showman was therefore widely recognised, having a discursive existence at least as influential, and as widely imitated and caricatured, as that of the dry-as-dust 'improving' lecturer. Indeed, these two stock figures were frequently opposed to one another across the spectrum of popular entertainments, with most performers finding it productive to adopt aspects of both personae in order to reach large, diverse audiences. However, although the fuzzy line between lecturing and showmanship was always likely to be traversed during the course of most performances, it was also the case that this distinction was underpinned by material differences in actual institutional practices. Whereas the illustrated lecture was most often associated with the panoramic and lantern industries, showmanship was directly tied to practices on the fairground, shop show, and street show. This chapter will focus primarily on exhibition strategies at these latter sites, arguing that the infrastructure of this marketplace was just as advanced as that associated, for example, with the late lantern industry. Moreover, at these sites the image of the popular showman as a fresh-talking, shrewd, shameless entrepreneur had a direct commercial application; after all, it was partly these features, in addition to the provision of a good show, that enabled the showmen to create paying audiences from the crowds of the fairground and city street.

According to popular definitions, what showmen of all classes shared was an ability to convert even unpromising materials into highly consumable public spectacles, calling upon an intimate and, most likely, intuitive knowledge of the value of particular exhibits to paying customers. This process was by no means simple. The public understood and cherished the showman's skills of exaggeration, duplicity, and 'bunkum', and this reflexive knowledge was a key part of their appreciation of the shows. Moreover, this complex exchange between showmen and audiences was usually experienced seamlessly, without self-conscious theorising. Indeed, the relationship between showman and audience closely resembled communications that took place within everyday practices of social exchange, being an uneven blend of information delivery, formal dialogue, and banter. It was neither necessary to trust the showman's discourse, nor to accept him or her as an authority, and most audiences adopted a more open, interrogative attitude. Audiences were not ordinarily required to be silent: in fact the noisy exchange of opinions before, during and after a show generated the type of word-of-mouth publicity upon which the showmen depended. In order to achieve this kind of impact, the showmen customarily placed the exhibit at the centre of the show—whether this was the body of a corporeal freak, the performance of the showman himself, or the screening of films—exaggerating the attractions of such items so that they came, in some way, to possess consumable value. At the same time, audiences were able to challenge this mode of presentation without compromising their relationship with the showman: it was all just part of the show.

The showmen's livelihood depended upon an ability to gain an audience's confidence, encouraging them to hand over their pennies before they had any clear idea of the actual substance of the entertainment – though, most often, the shows did exactly what was promised. According to popular accounts of showmanship, it mattered little to the showmen whether they actually delivered the promised attraction, exploited the gullibility of audiences, or played upon the participation of audiences within the openly duplicitous conditions of the show. However, showmanship certainly gave audiences the opportunity to share in the showman's worldly perspective, to count themselves among those privileged confidants who were 'in on' the joke. For such spectators the value of authoritative knowledge and truthful reference was supplanted by a more enigmatic quality, which Peter Bailey has termed 'knowingness'.[6] Within this relationship, the strict referentiality symbolised by the lecturer's pointer was undermined by the artful and conspiratorial wink. This is why anecdotes concerning these shows so often take such pleasure in recounting the showman's ingenuity in duping the crowds. As the first section of this chapter will show, the wide circulation of such stories didn't just reproduce the myth of the resourceful showman and naïve audience, they helped to foster a knowing attitude amongst audiences, who were understandably unwilling to feature in the punch line of the next anecdote.

Explaining this reflexive quality of mid to late nineteenth-century popular culture, Bailey has aptly described knowingness within British music hall as 'what everybody knows, but some know better than others'.[7] Explicitly or implicitly opposed to officially sanctioned discourses, knowingness was 'a countervailing dialogue that sets experience against prescription, and lays claim to an independent competence in the business and enjoyment of living'.[8] Bailey also shows that this resistant practice was part of the institutional structure of music hall, and that knowingness here was enacted specifically within 'a distinctive if slippery form of comic pragmatism' performed onstage.[9] Such performance styles allowed the halls to define themselves productively in terms of resistance to dominant high-culture institutions such as the legitimate theatre. Their success, at least until the gentrification of the halls during the 1880s and 1890s, depended strongly upon the provision of a boisterous, inclusive, interactive environment wherein authoritative discourses could be safely caricatured and parodied, without bringing the commercial foundations of the show itself into question. In parallel with this account of music hall performance, the second part of this chapter will show that street, shop-front, town hall, and fairground shows from the 1880s also adopted specialised performance regimes intended to foster a reassuring sense that each spectator 'knew better' the actual conditions of the show. It will also demonstrate that far from the spontaneous, improvisatory affair suggested by anecdote, the business of knowingness was underpinned by a substantial commercial infrastructure, whose flexibility allowed the showmen to take full advantage of the novelty of moving pictures.

These sites do not represent the full range of showman-led institutional practices associated with early British film, but during the 1890s and 1900s, as the confrontational style of music hall performance continued to shift in favour of the more highly regulated practices of variety theatre, they were the most numerous and successful venues for the interactive practices of the showmen.[10] Upon entering such shows, one of the key strategies of the knowing spectator was to demonstrate some understanding of the exaggerated or duplicitous discourses of the showmen. Gaining this measure of control within such an unpredictable environment was likely to be extremely valuable. In a modern world where responsibility for selfhood and personal identity seemed to be slipping from the grasp of the individuals themselves, becoming the province of large financial, administrative and industrial institutions, the showmen offered spectators an opportunity to regain a sense of mastery, always provided they were prepared to pay for the privilege.

This description bears instructive comparison with certain sociological and cultural studies that have described the modern city in terms of the everyday experiences of its inhabitants. The figures variously named the *flâneur* (Baudelaire, Benjamin), the *stranger* (Simmel), the walker in *dérive* (Debord), and the *Wandersmänner* (de Certeau) have all embodied the perspective of a competent and knowing wanderer through the city streets (though the terms are by no means equivalent).[11] This bottom-up reading of the city is usefully described by de Certeau as a poetics of practice through which 'the weak must continually turn to their own ends forces alien to them', knowingly opening up spaces in official discourses and structures which are beyond the ken of these authorities.[12] The showmen worked within institutions that mirrored these resistant practices, giving their customers an environment in which they could assert themselves as active and intelligent agents, but without taking substantial personal or social risks. Though preserving its connection with the confidence and savvy of the modern citizen, connoting native cunning, worldliness and street-sense, knowingness therefore describes a mode of communication that was highly institutionalised.

Showmanship should be seen in this light as a reliable professional practice calculated, like all good advertising, to appeal to the rapidly changing psychological or social needs of spectators. In this sense it mirrors commercial practices more often associated with the development of twentieth-century media industries, offering consumers carefully regulated opportunities to practise a degree of mastery in relation to the chaotic world around them. Unsurprisingly, perhaps, the professional practices of the street showmen typify this institutional structure, but it was also fundamental to other more complex showman-controlled organisations. As late as 1908, advice to aspiring picture theatre managers emphasised the significance of predicting the audience's needs:

> The man who wants to make money out of amusing the public with moving pictures must, among other qualifications, possess tact, knowledge of the business, judgement, and he must understand the public in general and his own little public in particular. His personality must count for something with the patrons.[13]

The showmen's practices were flexible and adaptable, being adopted by a wide range of performers in very different institutional contexts. As the third section of this chapter will show, it was the ability of these performers to capitalise upon the strengths of any new exhibit, or to frame old exhibits in such a way that they still appeared charged with novelty, which allowed the showmen to make an early commercial success of the cinematograph. Their performance practices were simply less restrictive than those associated with many illustrated lectures, and this allowed them to rethink and reframe the new medium in order to match the varied requirements audiences had of it. In order to achieve this, the showmen had a great many strategies at their disposal. Among these, they could reproduce certain aspects of the illustrated lecture, perhaps laying claim to expert knowledge not available to audiences; they could allow the exhibits to speak for themselves, leaving audiences to make up their own minds about the quality of the show; or they could aggressively market the otherness of the exhibits, encouraging audiences to experience shock and wonderment, much in the manner suggested by the idea of a cinema of attractions. But good showmanship was not merely a talent for managing and promoting the effects of novelty, alterity and shock within a variety format; it was also characterised by an unfailing ability to represent exhibits in a manner that did valuable cultural work for audiences.

Anecdote and Institution

The names of eminent showmen were well known to the public, and were often as widely mythologised as picture personalities were to become. This self-mythologising tendency presents both methodological problems and opportunities for film historians. Anecdotes, in particular, were recorded principally by performers who did not want to divulge the real conditions of their performance, or by spectators whose reports tended to be coloured by their own varied sentiments concerning such shows, and they have proven notoriously unreliable as empirical evidence.[14] Sometimes all that remains of the highly institutionalised practices of showmanship is the myth itself: the naturalised model of performance and personality the showmen wanted their audiences to see. However, the parodic, community-oriented functioning of anecdote is very closely associated with the performance styles of the showmen, and close attention to it can tell us a great deal about the way this section of the film industry functioned.

The trade journal *The Showman*, for example, frequently devoted much of its column space to stories that chronicled the legendary ingenuity of showpeople, or the gullibility of their audiences. The circulation of these anecdotes to a readership largely composed of the showmen themselves suggests something of their significance to the industry. Detailing tricks of

89

the trade, or ridiculing shows that failed to attract custom, anecdotes provided readers with suggestions for good commercial practice in an industry that depended upon responsiveness to local or temporary conditions. On such occasions, the anecdote's punch line documents a moment of institutional consolidation in which inappropriate practices of performance and spectatorship are set aside. Furthermore, it does so without laying out prescriptive and inflexible rules, like those that typified advice for lecturers in the magic lantern trade press during the 1890s. Anecdote can therefore be read as a specialised form of discourse, easily passed from showman to showman as they passed between fairgrounds and other temporary venues, which co-ordinated the performance practices of this diverse group and unified them as a professional community.

Anecdotes aphoristically told the stories the industry wished to tell about itself at any given moment, so it is not surprising to find that they also dominated written reports of the shows. Of course, it was not necessarily the case that the anecdote-teller was actually aware of these deep institutional motivations, but the close correspondence between anecdote and the showman's self-interest is nevertheless compelling. For the audience, too, anecdotes were an informative resource. Above all, they gave spectators good reason to adopt the knowing attitude upon which the shows depended, suggesting to each spectator that trying to uncover the tricks of the trade was all part of the fun. They also generated invaluable word-of-mouth publicity for showmen and women, who consequently delivered plenty of them within the shows.

The story is frequently repeated, for example, of the cinematograph 'Professor' (a generic title amongst professional showmen) in the awkward position of presenting a film of a popular female dance artiste to a church hall audience. The name given to the film varies between tellings; however, a number of dance films were made during the late 1890s in the style of the popular experimental dancer, Loïe Fuller. Among these, the *Annabelle Serpentine Dance* (Edison, 1895), performed by Annabelle Moore, seems a likely contender. In spite of the pastor's objection to the *risqué* dance, the lecturer had no wish to omit the coloured film that was the highlight of his show. The earliest account I have come across, from an 1898 article in *Photographic News*, continues the story of the anonymous lecturer:

> And when the time came for showing the tabooed *Skirt Dance*, the resourceful professor announced it as *Salome Dancing before Herod*. To say that this particular item of the programme was enthusiastically received, is to give but a faint idea of the *furore* it created. None of the

audience thought of taking the least exception to it, and the pastor himself failed altogether to identify it with the picture which he had prohibited. The only comment upon [*sic*] which reached the professor's ear was that of an old lady, who thought it quite the best thing shown that evening, adding: 'Well, we live and learn; I never knew until tonight that they took photographs in the time of Herod.'[15]

This anecdote is repeated with minor variations from preamble to punch-line on several subsequent occasions. Lily May Richards identifies the resourceful professor as her father, the travelling showman William Haggar.[16] Celine Williams claims that the showman was her great grandfather, the showman Randall Williams.[17] Most famously, lecture-room film exhibitor and filmmaker Cecil Hepworth resurrects the story of the '*Serpentine Dance*' at least twice, ascribing this showman-like adaptability to himself.[18] However, there is no direct evidence to support the assumption that the Salome anecdote derived from Hepworth, rather than Haggar, Williams, or some other showman.[19]

The significance of such anecdotes so far as the early industry was concerned was that they circulated very widely, making light of difficult issues for the trade. Although the Salome anecdote does not allow us to draw any direct conclusions concerning the shows of Hepworth, Williams or Haggar, its regular repetition among so many sources does tell us a great deal about how such men presented themselves to the public. Most obviously, the aesthetic and commercial import of the showman's ability to transform his entertainment for new audiences is firmly established. The showman had to respond to the feedback of his audience, whether this was the objection of the pastor or the subsequent approval of the audience. More specifically, the principle is established that, as a 1900 article in *The Showman* also explained, 'in connection with churches, chapels and other religious institutions' the cinematograph showman should 'be careful to adapt his lecture and views to his audience'.[20] This was crucial for showmen such as Haggar, who spent weekdays performing variety programmes at the fairground and on the road, and Sundays catering for the important church and temperance markets for film exhibition with 'sacred concerts' of hymns, lantern slides, and films.[21] The showmen's fortunes depended upon those of their audiences, and they simply could not afford an unfavourable reception in the areas where they did most trade. In general, it paid to be adaptable, and the showmen tended to conform flexibly to the requirements of audiences .

The responsiveness of the showmen did not just allow them to adapt their performance styles; it was implicit to the very texture of each performance.

The Salome anecdote suggests something of the cultural and financial value of the showman's improvisational skills, a theme that the showmen emphasised more strongly than any other. In each of the written versions of the anecdote, the most celebrated element of the story is the showman's entrepreneurial ability to turn to his advantage an awkward situation that might otherwise threaten his livelihood. Indeed, this is a quality of entertainment and entertainer that often seems to contribute more strongly to perceptions of the showman's capital wealth than does the ownership of films, equipment, staff, or even an exhibition site. Good showmanship had long been associated with the successful self-management implied by natural-seeming fresh talk. The anecdote takes the further step of asserting that the showman's fresh talk truly was improvised moment to moment, and that its freshness extended into an ingenious ability to reimagine the material conditions of the show. The showmen, such anecdotes claimed, could convert almost any exhibit into a show because they possessed the ability to read their audiences, telling spectators what they wanted to hear rather than allowing them to trust the evidence of their eyes.

Of course, these representations of the ingenuity of the showmen were matched by the (rather unlikely) naïveté attributed to their audiences. The Salome anecdote ridiculed the prudish pastor and gullible audience of the church hall, both of whom were taken entirely into the showman's confidence. Old ladies were among the most popular victims of anecdotes of this kind in the UK, but rural or rustic communities were also often represented as easy marks for the showmen. It was simple to stereotype such individuals as representatives of an imagined innocent age, and therefore to imply that the showmen belonged, with the cinematograph, to a modern culture in which entrepreneurial street-sense had become a universally desirable quality. At the same time, the anecdote flattered the sensibilities of the majority of audiences, assuring them that they, too, were not to be so easily fooled. In these circumstances, the old lady's comic misunderstanding of the conditions under which the skirt dance had been staged clarified the basic relationship between showman, screen and audience. The anecdote showed that the performances depicted on-screen were no more to be trusted than the discourses of the showman. They, too, were elaborately staged, and therefore required their audiences to demonstrate an active and knowing interpretation, or at least to be more knowing than this particular old lady. The showman had played upon his audience's trust in expert culture, and demonstrated that a better policy for up-to-date, knowing audiences was a healthy degree of cynicism.

Importantly, however, given that the showmen wished to present themselves as part of a benign, if crafty, industry, audiences were rarely represented as substantially the worse for their deception. Popular representations of the showmen usually suggested that they were friendly, community-minded individuals, whose mischievous insights could play a valuable social role. On the stage prior to the 1860s the showman was sometimes represented as a traditional stock character called 'Puff' whose gibberish discourse parodied the showman's patter and hustle.[22] Dickens offered numerous representations of street, circus, and pub showmen, and such figures were still appearing regularly in fiction at the end of the century.[23] Children's literature often represented them as romanticised versions of earlier generations of 'galantee' showmen, who would carry their magic lantern or peep show entertainments with them from village to village, hoping to give performances in homes, churches or town halls. One 1871 collection of sequential art entitled *Walk Up! Walk Up! and see the Fool's Paradise* was modelled explicitly upon the street peep-show, with 'Professor Wolley Cobble's' patter running underneath the series of panoramic images. The volume described the Professor as one of the 'old school of showmen; voluble in small talk, ever ready with answers to countrymen and others, and with a never-ending supply of Bartholomew Fair trumpet-jokes'.[24]

Even those anecdotes that focused upon the showman's duplicity tended to suggest that he or she had merely played upon some of the less attractive features of their audiences. As in a confidence trick, the point was to exploit the audience's weaknesses, but within the shows the price of admission was usually all that audiences had to lose. One anecdote that, according to *The Showman*, was 'going the rounds' during the first months of 1902, suggested that playing a trick upon paying customers could be the only attraction a show had to offer:

> A certain showman touring Lancaster, recently invited the public to 'walk up and see the most wonderful baby on earth!' Such an invitation, as might be expected, brought forth a good response. Soon the show was full, and the worthy proprietor carried forward a very ordinary looking child. 'What is there wonderful about it?' asked one of the disgusted audience. 'We can see babies like that every day'. 'Well,' remarked the showman, getting as near the aperture in the booth as possible, 'all I can say, is that its mother assured me that it was the most wonderful kid that ever happened, and if she don't know, who does? You'll have to take the lady's word for it!' he yelled, as he dodged an empty bottle and disappeared from view.[25]

This simple anecdote took advantage of the discourses of the freak show, an entertainment in which audiences were already accustomed to the absurd exaggeration of the attractions within. The casual disgust of audiences presented with a disappointingly 'ordinary' baby arguably spoke volumes about their questionable desire to consume other bodies in general.

There are many anecdotes such as these, all offering the spectacle of a well-judged trick played upon a public that deserved little better. Collectively, they consolidated a particular vision of the showmen with important implications for early film shows. If anecdotes taught audiences that showmen were cunning and untrustworthy, they did so in such a way that this ingenuity came to seem an essential and entirely natural description of showmanship. By 1900, the phrase 'good showmen are born, not made' was regularly heard, suggesting that these skills were not acquired over time, nor learned from others within the industry, but were simply part of a universal order that did not require further justification.[26] It is not, therefore, that anecdotes actively denied the truth about the real conditions and techniques of the showman's performance; rather, they made of duplicitous showmanship an image of the natural order of things. Showmanship had effects, but did not seem to have any causes—it just *was*. The punchline, which always revealed how the trick had been played, enjoined anecdote confidants to share uncritically in the humour of the episode but still served to remind them that if they wished to visit the shows, they should keep their wits about them.

Anecdotes therefore recorded the definition of a guiding myth of showmanship, naturalising the commercial interests of the showmen. This myth also characterised the way in which audiences experienced film shows, and was carefully cultured by the institutions on fairgrounds and in shop shows that depended on those audiences. Within these institutional structures, spectators understood that, as in their everyday lives, they needed to scrutinise the attractions they were exposed to, particularly when those attractions appeared too good to be true. This knowing response to the shows, carried principally by word of mouth, would subsequently come to inform traditions of classical filmmaking, which also sought to naturalise institutional imperatives, for example, when movie publicity generated exaggerated representations of stars or special effects, leaving for audiences the private pleasures of picking their way through such material. But within early film, the fascination generated by confessedly unreliable publicity was closely related to the way in which showmen presented themselves to audiences during the shows, and this was far from a private affair. The myth of showmanship overcame all scruples and proprieties, enabling spectators to become productively engaged in the discourse of the showman, always sensitive to the institutional conditions in which they found themselves, and able to respond actively to them. This made the relationship between showman, screen, and audience seem more like a dialogue, in which the provenance and status of the films, the tales the showman told about them, or the expectations the audience had upon entering the show were all, potentially, up for negotiation. At the heart of it all, however, as audiences knew very well, was a set of performance conventions and commercial strategies that reliably served the showmen wherever they set up shop.

The Business of Showmanship

Whereas recent work concerning the lantern industry has begun to establish the commercial principles upon which it depended, it has been far more difficult to gain a clear impression of the showman's business practices, which were consistently profitable during this period. In part, this is because the caricatures and stereotypes generated by the anecdotes that remain to us were intended, precisely, to distract audiences from the real, material conditions under which the shows took place. These frequently suggested that the showmen possessed remarkable freedoms of expression, poking fun at authority figures or duping their audiences, and that they were easily able to overcome the regulatory practices of local authorities or the police. Associated especially with working-class audiences, rural communities, or children, such representations implied that showmen had a continuing role to play in a popular tradition of satire and social renewal, overturning authoritative hierarchies in favour of potentially subversive insights generated from below. However, although this image usefully suggested to audiences that the showmen were a valuable part of the communities they performed in, and though the showmen certainly encouraged knowing spectators to assert some limited measure of control over the exhibition space, their survival depended upon an institutional framework that was highly self-regulated, and which preferred, whenever possible, to compromise with external regulatory pressures rather than challenge them. It is therefore essential that the guiding myths of showmanship be fully contextualised in relation to both the stable business practices and adaptable performance practices that governed the shows.

During the 1880s and 1890s the establishment of national and regional trade bodies who could speak on the behalf of their showman constituents consolidated this machinery of self-regulation. The United Kingdom Van Dweller's and Showmen's Protection Association was inaugurated in 1889, becoming known more simply as the Showman's Guild by the turn of the century.[27] With the large investments made during this period by some showmen-entrepreneurs in shows such as circuses, merry-go-rounds, and cinematograph shows, and the increasing tendency of local authorities to interfere with these businesses, the development of organisations intended to defend their interests is not surprising. The president of the Showman's Guild in 1900 was 'Lord' George Sanger, the proprietor of the most successful of Victorian circuses, and a man whose wealth, celebrity and status were more likely to carry weight during negotiations with the authorities. The size of the Guild's constituency, though spread thinly across the UK and largely composed of itinerant families, was another significant factor. Addressing a group of eminent showmen during the Guild annual meeting in 1901, Sanger cited a census that had been compiled during the Easter, Whitsun, and August bank holidays of the previous year, days when all active showmen were certain to be performing, claiming that 'he should like to make it known that the actual number of showmen and van dwellers in the British Empire was 485,300'.[28] This number is difficult to verify, and it was certainly in the interests of the Guild (and of *The Showman*, which reported it) to exaggerate the size of the industry, here including showmen outside Britain and many van-dwellers who did not perform in the shows. According to Toulmin, a more likely estimate places the number of professional showmen and circus-class variety performers in excess of 15,000[29]. Another suggestive figure derives from Charles Booth's massive 1891 survey, *Life and Labour of the People in London*, which conservatively estimated that there were 2,099 showmen working in the capital alone, and this figure did not take into account the travelling showmen.[30]

The remainder of the business of the 1901 meeting of the Guild was largely perfunctory, being designed to support the objectives of the Guild, which it usefully outlined. In particular, its fourth and final resolution congratulated the success of the Guild's 'Parliamentary Agent', Mr. F. Millar, in defeating 'the opposition offered by various corporate bodies last season', and proposed that 'the meeting, in view of the serious nature of Private Bill proposals to restrict and harass open-air entertainers, pledges itself to use all legitimate means to defeat the same'.[31] The showman, Major Wilson, also took the opportunity to make a rallying call to beleaguered showmen:

> He said that the less showmen were interfered with, the better; laws should not be passed if they in any way hampered people who were engaged in a legitimate calling. If there was any need to improve the entertainment, he felt sure that showmen would gladly respond to it, for

he believed that there was no body of men or women in this country who followed their calling more honourably or respectably than the show people.[32]

Such accounts of the showmen were starkly at odds with the image often generated for the public by anecdotes concerning the shows. As in any mature industry, it had become important that appropriate representation was made at all administrative and legal levels in order to support the commercial basis of the trade. Although the Guild did not begin functioning effectively as a legal body defending the fairs at a local level until 1906, much of the actual work of negotiation with local authorities had been conducted by regional unions such as the Yorkshire Union of Showmen, which was formed in 1902.[33] Such organisations might also seek to settle issues such as the rents charged by the owners of show-grounds in the provinces, or disputes between individual showmen.[34] The decision to close fairs, such as that at Saffron Walden in 1902, which was one of the oldest in the country, meant the agreement of the Watch Committee, the Town Council, and the Home Secretary, and it was important that the showmen protested such measures with each of these authorities.[35]

Representative bodies such as these were often created in response to an increasingly hostile regulatory environment, but they also gave a recognisable institutional profile to a large community, whose unique culture and proud family traditions did not otherwise have a substantial influence upon prevailing legislative conditions. Especially important in this regard was the trade journal *The Era*, which remained strongly associated with fairground and other showman-led professions during the 1890s and 1900s. During its brief run as an independent journal between 1900 and 1902, *The Showman* also sought to give the trade an autonomous voice. Though it did not supplant *The Era* as the principal forum and source of information for the showmen, *The Showman* provides a unique source of materials relating to the business and performance practices of showman-led institutions during the period when the Bioscope shows were becoming increasingly dominant. Such publications lent unity and continuity to the business of showmanship at the turn of the century, even though the trade appeared to outsiders to be characterised by instability and risk. *The Showman* naturally presented itself as a forum monitoring good business practices amongst its readership, even proposing to establish a Bureau intended 'to obtain engagements at the best price possible for every entertainer or amusement provider'.[36] In fact, the demand for shows on fairgrounds and in city streets had remained reasonably stable throughout the nineteenth century, but the shows themselves depended for their survival upon the continual adoption of new novelties and attractions to entice the public and were therefore frequently obliged to undergo change. The showmen also faced the possibility that fires or other disasters could rob them of their most prized capital. It was essential, therefore, for trade bodies to protect show-grounds and the rights of individuals to perform on them, since, without this certainty, the showmen could not guarantee any long-term return on the large investments they were continually obliged to make in new exhibits and infrastructure. At the turn of the century, according to *The Showman*, 'the travelling showman thinks nothing of spending two or three thousand pounds on his apparatus', and many shows cost a good deal more than this.[37] The careers of showmen were often founded upon such speculative investments set against the likelihood of strong returns, a modern commercial practice that also enabled the most successful showmen to move flexibly between very different types of shows as demand dictated. This set in place the conditions for a vibrant and secure marketplace, which tended to reward entrepreneurial common sense and the ability to read public tastes and sensibilities, keeping abreast of the latest novelties and finding ingenious methods of keeping them fresh.

For example, the showman James Chipperfield's career lasted throughout much of the nineteenth century, a period in which the fairground itself changed dramatically.[38] Born into the family business in 1824, by the mid-1830s he was appearing within Chipperfield's Show as a 'hanky merchant', performing simple illusions, then as a 'shadow pantomimist'. He subsequently introduced his own children, James and Mary, into the show as the 'Lilliputian Circus', where he also performed as a clown alongside an educated pony. Family businesses such as this appear to have been both efficient and stable, allowing the showmen to manage their shows flexibly, sure in the knowledge that their itinerant trade had a permanent, trustworthy and professional staff. The Chipperfields became best known in the latter half of the nineteenth century as exhibitors of freaks, including a tribe of Zulus, a giant, a fat boy, and most famously, the living skeleton, Robert Tipney. Tipney toured throughout England and France, and proved so successful an exhibit that upon his death Chipperfield was able to open his 'Glypthothea', a substantial entertainment which included numerous automata and a ghost illusion. When this burned down in 1892, destroying both the infrastructure of the show and its exhibits, Chipperfield gradually began to acquire wild animals. By the turn of the century (with Chipperfield now aged seventy-six), the family was touring with a fully stocked menagerie.

Such varied and eventful careers were not unusual for showmen at all levels of the trade, though, naturally, the showmen had an interest in exaggerating the risks to which their businesses were exposed. For performers within the shows, it was equally important that they could market their talents competitively, finding new and more lucrative locations at which to perform. Few felt committed to only one type of show. Even freaks, customarily thought to be the most objectified and powerless of all performers, sometimes fully understood the very high value that their unique bodies possessed for the showmen and marketed themselves accordingly.[39] It was equally important that showmen could move up the scale of exhibitions, perhaps beginning on the street or performing within other shows, before progressing to ownership of larger venues, or adopting more expansive exhibition practices. At the bottom of the scale were the numerous temporary shop-front shows, often known as 'sideshows' and more occasionally—and pejoratively—as 'penny gaffs', and the smaller stall-holders at the fairgrounds. Among the highest class of exhibition sites were the circuses, the 'Great Shows' on the fairground, such as ghost illusions and cinematograph shows, and large permanent venues such as the Royal Aquarium or the 'Ark of Exhibitions', the Egyptian Hall, which had hosted such luminaries as P.T. Barnum and Albert Smith, and which would go on to exhibit its own idiosyncratic film shows. This remarkably diverse market grew substantially from the mid-nineteenth century and offered opportunities for investment to those who wished to enlarge or gentrify their exhibitions, bringing them to audiences with more spending power.

Among the best known of British rags-to-riches stories was that of 'Lord' George Sanger, whose career prior to his presidency of the Guild had begun in his father's peep show in the 1830s, but who progressed to owning ten circus 'ampitheatres' across the UK in the 1850s, a tale enthusiastically retold in his 1908 autobiography.[40] But the model for this kind of aggressive career-making (and for creative practices of autobiography-writing) was Barnum, whose brilliant marketing skills became widely known in Britain following his tours with the dwarf, General Tom Thumb, and the original Siamese twins, Chang and Eng, during the 1840s.[41] In 1872, he established the 'Greatest Show on Earth', a massive menagerie, freak show and circus combination, which toured throughout the USA and Europe for decades to come, subsequently amalgamating with James Bailey's circus, and cornering the market in freak and animal exhibition. By 1902, ten years after Barnum's death, Barnum and Bailey's Limited was listing profits in the hundreds of thousands and boasted a buoyant share price.[42]

Barnum remained synonymous with the idea of entrepreneurial showmanship in the UK, but other showmen at the end of the nineteenth century also began to expand their assets aggressively, establishing small entertainment empires that operated with a different commercial logic. Rather than developing economies of scale within grand entertainments such as Barnum and Bailey's Greatest Show on Earth, Poole's Myriorama, or Sanger's circuses, showmen such as Tom Norman, George Kemp and Thomas Howard diversified their holdings, progressing from street showmanship to management of large numbers of entertainments, which might offer a wide variety of attractions.[43] The growing trend toward expansion within the penny sector, which Jon Burrows has identified in London's film trade between 1906 and 1914, was therefore part of long established commercial practice intended to capitalise upon the showmens' limited resources and to mitigate the risk of bad business or regulatory interference in any one property.[44] In addition, it meant that the day-to-day running of the shop shows could be left in the hands of others, usually street showmen, who were usually culpable in case of any infringement of minor by-laws.[45] During the mid-1880s Norman ran five shops in Nottingham, three in Stratford-upon-Avon, and thirteen in London (if his own account is to be believed), and he quickly expanded into fairground exhibition. Exhibits were circulated regularly among these properties, varying from freaks to the cinematograph, and it was common practice for some of the more successful items to be hired or exchanged between the showmen.[46] Later, Norman's skills would serve him equally well as an auctioneer of sideshow exhibits, a position that enabled him to capitalise further on the infrastructure of the trade.[47]

As Toulmin has shown, Norman was among the most successful of British showmen at the turn of the century, partly because he was able to generate income from several different types of shows.[48] Ownership of fairground shows made it possible to capitalise on the business of the rural, urban and provincial communities, particularly during the summer. On bank holidays, crowds of all kinds would pour into the fairgrounds, making these the most profitable days of the year. Shop shows drew more substantially upon metropolitan crowds, and their business was not dependant upon the fairground calendar (or the weather), being conducted more steadily throughout the year. Some showmen also performed in bazaars, which were sometimes run in public buildings such as schools, with a show allocated to each classroom, or at much larger exhibitions, which might be organised in city parks or at the larger public halls.[49] Among the larger exhibitions, Toulmin has described the important roles of 'museums of curiosity', which contained a series of attractions in individual booths.[50] This variety of exhibition venues was useful for smaller, independent showmen, too, some of whom spent their summers touring their shows at fairgrounds and their winters doing business within the city. The rent charged for these venues varied considerably depending upon such factors as the status of the space, its accessibility for the public, the potential for high returns, and the type of show being exhibited. Those shows, like the larger waxwork exhibitions, which required a good deal of room, or those, like shooting galleries or cinematograph shows, for which the management might need appropriate insurance, tended to pay more. In consequence, as with any other commercial outlets, the best positions in city streets, bazaars, museums, or on the fairgrounds were usually secured by the more prestigious shows, with smaller holdings relegated to quieter or less propitious quarters.

The management practices associated with the shows varied considerably depending upon their environment. Fairs were usually located on traditional show grounds, with the shows clustered manageably together and present only for a brief, scheduled period in which the public would be attracted in great numbers. Although fairs did not contribute to local taxation, and extracted a good deal of money from the towns, they also drew visitors from surrounding areas and usually worked to the benefit of local traders. By contrast, shop shows often appeared and disappeared apparently at random, were difficult to monitor and police, usually depended upon passing trade, and were often blamed for distracting potential customers from their business in town. Whereas the fairgrounds faced growing regulatory pressures during the 1890s, the presence of shop shows on city streets, rubbing shoulders with 'legitimate' shops, accommodation areas and, sometimes, with powerful institutions such as schools and hospitals meant that, at the end of the century, they were even more liable to attract unwelcome attention from the authorities.[51] Surviving accounts of shop shows are scarce, and are often provided by writers who wished to close them down, or by the late century generation of urban ethnographers, who saw them primarily as evidence of the city's degeneration. However, if these are read alongside accounts in the showman's trade press, occasional descriptions derived from the showmen themselves, and articles appearing in the popular illustrated press in the 1890s, which sometimes mined the more respectable and enduring shows for novelties, it is possible to gain a reasonably clear picture of the performance practices within.

At the lower end of the market, shop shows were usually housed in little more than a portable booth or in city shops that opened directly onto the busy thoroughfares from which their custom was drawn. These shops could be acquired relatively cheaply, the owners, according to one contemporary estimate, asking for approximately one third of the takings in rent.[52] Since they were usually available on short-term leases, they could be abandoned at short notice if the show did not prove profitable or if the authorities took exception to it. The showmen would also need to pay a salary to performers or functionaries working within, and there would usually be initial and maintenance costs associated with the exhibit, but overall, the relatively low outlay and potentially high profits meant that, in those areas where they were tolerated, shop shows proliferated:

> In most of the principal streets of our metropolis, the monotony of endless rows of shops is occasionally broken by some grandly painted, and brightly postered side-show, whose only mission seems to be to cheer, mystify, and satisfy the morbid curiosity of the passers by, who, attracted by the strains of delightful music (otherwise barrel organ), become auditors of the outside lecturer, who, in turn, can generally manage by his eloquence to induce his listeners to willingly part with their humble penny to see the fun.[53]

Some thoroughfares became crowded with shows touting for custom, an environment in which it became essential to bring the attractions of each forcibly to the attention of the passing crowds. Consequently, according to Tom Norman's *Memoirs* the paintings covering the façades were 'large, and often repulsive in the extreme', tending to exaggerate greatly the appeal of attractions within.[54] The outside lecturer, sometimes known as a spieler, or barker, was 'generally a man with a voice like that of a roaring lion', and he would shout into the crowd 'all the most absured [*sic*] things, or barefaced truths imaginable, and in all sorts of languages', to attract their attention.[55] Sometimes he would wear a uniform or oriental costume, perhaps reflecting upon the nature of the exhibition within.[56] He might also hand out pamphlets to potential customers, usually including images and a brief description of the exhibit, and perhaps press reports testifying to its authenticity. Montagu Williams QC, who took a leading role in the closure of London shop shows during the 1880s and 1890s, imprisoning a number of showmen on grounds of obstruction to a public thoroughfare, recorded that 'to those who had the misfortune to live near these places, the noise they occasioned must have been a great curse. Organs were played, drums were beaten, bells were rung, and it was in stentorian tones that the public was invited to enter.'[57] However, it was not necessarily the case, as reformers such as Williams and generations of historians subsequently assumed, that the shows were messy, unsanitary or dangerous places to visit. Indeed, according to one showman, writing in 1900, 'nothing can compensate for a dirty show', and the provision of a reasonable carpet, drapings and bunting, or perhaps a few pot plants or plaster statuettes, could make all the difference to the showman's trade:

Be smart in the appearance of your show, and any reasonable expense you may incur in attaining this object will soon come back. 'Where can I take my children for an afternoon's entertainment?' asks one lady of another. 'Oh! Mr So-and-So's show is just what you want,' is the reply; 'It is such a superior place'. A visit is paid to your show, and the recommendation passed on to someone else.[58]

As in other entertainments, the better appointed the exhibition space, the more likely it was to attract the custom of families and of higher spending middle-class audiences.[59] Much depended, too, upon the quality and nature of the exhibits, which varied considerably according to the prestige of location, prevailing fashions for novelty, and time of day. Some businesses opened during the day in order to attract passing trade, but others only opened in the evening between about eight until half-past eleven, perhaps because the exhibits within were considered too risqué for exposure any earlier.[60] Among the most respectable late Victorian exhibitions were conjurors and illusionists, magic lantern shows and boxing entertainments. Many, by 1900, also included at least a few 'automatics', such as mutoscopes, kinetoscopes, phonographs, or mechanical models and automata, each of which, according to one observer, 'appears to coax itself into the favour of many patrons, and undoubtedly they materially increase the Showman's revenue by their takings'.[61] Mutoscope parlours might include many such devices, offering customers the opportunity to consume in relative privacy moving pictures on subjects from practical jokes to erotic scenes, without the obligation of openly interacting with showmen or other spectators (**Fig. 1**).[62]

During 1901, according to *The Showman*, the shop show exhibits available to the public were 'many and varied . . . but probably fat women, skinny men, living novelties, freaks, illusions, and waxworks form the most appreciated items that Londoners delight in viewing'.[63] The attraction of these exhibits tended to fall considerably short of the promises made to paying audiences, as the bulk of those seeking admittance presumably already knew. 'It is true,' reflected A. St John Adcock in 1902, '[that] you may even yet be startled by seeing in a shop window a presentment of an elephant-headed man larger than life, with one leg elephantine and the other human, and a writhing trunk of the first water; but inside you discover that he dwindles to a leathery-looking object pickled in a glass jar, and having the appearance of a fossilised small boy playing a flageolet'.[64] The showman's performance under such conditions meant weaving these unremarkable exhibits into narratives that recreated them as spectacles, worth a penny to see. In doing so, it mattered little to the showman whether he played upon the naïveté of

THE MUTOSCOPES.

Fig. 1 Private pleasures. Comic cartoon featuring the use of an erotic scene on the Mutoscope (*The Showman* (1 March 1901), p. 144). Image courtesy of the National Fairground Archive, Sheffield.

audiences or upon their knowing participation within the openly untrustworthy conditions of the show. However, widely distributed accounts from men such as Adcock, which clearly took great pleasure in uncovering the exaggerated bunkum of the show, are most likely typical expressions of the sideshow experience for most audiences.

Fairground exhibitions also depended upon the construction of knowingness between audience and showman. However, at the turn of the century, these shows were often conducted on a grand scale, thriving upon the quality of their exhibits and upon reputations for spectacle that had sometimes been built over decades. Fairgrounds were characterised by excess, both in terms of the quantity and scale of the attractions on offer and the spendthrift extravagance they encouraged from the crowds, this latter feature leading to some of the most vicious denunciations of working-class leisure pursuits in the late nineteenth century.[65] This popular image of the fairground, which drew further upon ideas of holiday license, served the best commercial interests of the showmen, and was, in fact, set in place by the highly institutionalised managerial and performance practices upon which the shows' survival depended. This was especially important from the 1880s, as the commercial conditions of fairground showmanship became increasingly competitive and the regulatory restrictions they faced more severe.

Partly as a consequence of these changes, costs were on the rise. In addition to the outlay and overheads on exhibits and infrastructure, payment for paraffin to light the shows, salaries for performers and staff, as well as the losses that could always be incurred during periods of bad business, the fairground showmen often complained that ground rent had become abnormally expensive, with prices reaching up to £1 per square foot in the best fairs by 1901.[66] Often these changes were accompanied by the introduction of more stringent restrictions on the fairs' mode of operation, means of transportation, or opening hours, suggesting that the price hikes were not wholly driven by economic concerns.[67] However, in spite of these difficulties, the fairs were at their peak at the turn of the century, and continued to attract massive crowds, many of which now had more leisure time and more money to spend than ever before. For example, on just one day at the 1900 Hull Fair, the trams had brought an estimated 92,000 people to the fairground, and many others, of course, had come from outside Hull by other means.[68] On busy days, the only problems the showmen had was managing what one commentator called the 'stream of humanity' that passed through the fairs, keeping the crowd back 'to prevent any of the advance party from carrying the place by storm'.[69] Within this chaotic environment it became possible to conceive of showmanship as a mature professional praxis known by the showland community to secure custom wherever they set up shop. Toulmin has described the 'new hierarchy of businessmen and entrepreneurs' who thrived in the fairground from the 1880s and 'the increase . . . in the range and size of shows' which they brought.[70] At the top of the hierarchy were the circus and merry-go-round proprietors whose shows often formed the hub of the showgrounds and who sometimes rented out the surrounding space to the smaller shows. The showman, Pat Collins, owned cinematograph shows, menageries, gondolas, gallopers and switchbacks, and could sometimes dominate the

105

prime positions on the showground. In spite of the difficult administrative climate in some areas, such entrepreneurs were able to establish new fairs, even as the old ones were legislated out of existence.[71] Others brought 'miniature fairs' to town centres around the UK, particularly during the winter, where they might remain for several months at a time.[72]

Modern commercial practices such as these contributed to the growing centralisation of the fairground trade, which paralleled that occurring within the music halls in the same period, in which relatively few individuals took a growing share of the industry. Understandably, the scale of these enterprises meant that showmen such as these were especially unwilling to risk upsetting customers or the authorities, and their shows therefore delivered an increasingly sensational charge of variety and spectacle, but tended to steer clear of subjects that might create friction with local authorities. They were continually obliged to stay one step ahead of competitors, and this meant that levels of investment in the shows soared from the 1880s. The electric organs alone, which often appeared on the façades of larger shows, could cost up to £1,000 by 1902, and as the decade progressed, they became more ornate. However, unlike the music hall, the inclusive environment of the fairground continued to support a much broader range of shows than this, and from all classes of showmen.

In the 1890s the range of entertainments available at large fairs rivalled the shop shows, but also included rides such as steam swings, gondolas and switchback railways, alongside other Grand Shows such as menageries, ghost shows and, by 1897, the bioscope shows—the name usually given to the cinematograph on the fairground. At the lower end of the spectrum were the smaller stallholders, whose business varied from waxworks, peep shows, boxing booths, freak shows, shooting stalls, conjuring shows, Punch and Judy shows, and tents filled with automatics, to coconut shies, Aunt Sallies, and food stalls. Others managed curious combinations of these exhibits, sometimes adding popular new attractions, like the cinematograph, to existing shows. Shows such as these were relatively easy to transplant into shop or fairground exhibitions, requiring little more than an appropriately sized, covered space, and a showman able to recycle his discursive performance for different audiences.

For example, waxwork exhibitions in shop shows, bazaars, museums and on the fairground allowed showmen to give material form to some of their exaggerated discourses, many including effigies of celebrities such as freaks, actresses, sportsmen, statesmen, or members of the royal family, and, during the Boer War, soldiers engaged in acts of heroism.[73] As in most types of show in this period, one of the showman's most successful strategies was to

106

'harmonise with some particular event that is exciting the public mind, and exhibit in realistic fashion, things that are attracting general attention'.[74] Edifying spectacles derived from recent conflicts did not, however, attract as much attention from critics as the chamber of horrors, which included waxworks of particularly gruesome murders, often reproduced shortly after they had been committed.[75] Stewart's Waxwork Exhibition at 108 Upper Street, London, consisted of 150 figures, on several floors, and was, according to one writer for *The Showman*, 'one of the finest buildings of this description extant', including an especially gory chamber:

> Frederick Deeming is represented in the act of packing his crowds of victims into the kitchen floor, stamping down the cement that was to have hid his awful deed from the police; but this is nothing, as far as the spectacular is concerned, compared with the Bakehouse Murder. John Schneider, a German baker, has just been battering the head of his friend Berndt, with a life preserver until he is rendered unconscious. Then the bleeding mass of humanity is bodily thrust into a red-hot oven, there to be literally burnt alive, and in the act of frizzling up we are permitted to gaze at the scene. Blood is pouring from the oven cracks like gravy, and Schneider is gloatingly watching the effects of the heat.[76]

Accounts such as these certainly testified to the shocking and spectacular content many of these shows wished to offer, but they are perhaps best understood as approximations of the hyperbolic discourses and theatrical presentational style of the tales told by the showmen to potential audiences. *The Showman* frequently repeated these tales to a readership largely composed of shop-front and fairground exhibitors, even dedicating a regular column to 'Entertainers' Patter', intended to instruct these showmen in the elocutionary tools of the trade.[77] Later, *The World's Fair* regularly reinforced the importance of telling the tale to successful showmen.[78] For these journals, tale-telling was a skilled discursive practice fundamental to the professional identity of the showmen, so it made perfect sense to circulate examples of good practice.

The tales were delivered by the barkers outside the shows, by other showmen waiting within, and sometimes by those exhibits waiting in booths who were capable of telling the tale for themselves. They were a mixture of well-known tricks, puns, anecdotes and histories nominally intended to introduce particular exhibits, but actually designed to secure the attention of audiences fresh from street, marketplace, or fairground, to part them from further pennies after they had entered the show, and then to encourage them to pass on positive reports of the show to friends and relatives. The telling of the tale was clearly distinguished by the showmen from the practices of professional lecturers, who sometimes also appeared within the shows, largely because it predisposed audiences to a noisy and collaborative spectatorship and required showmen to respond to this with further dialogue. It was also designed to attract the attention of potential spectators who had not, like the audience at a lecture theatre, already committed themselves to the show, but perhaps had been distracted momentarily by the noise and colour of the sideshow façade. Customarily dressed in a top hat and tails, the showmen were easily picked out, and this assisted them in generating this unique relationship with city and fairground crowds.

Interrupting the circulatory patterns of the thoroughfare, the showmen appeared to create what Gustave Le Bon had called a 'psychological crowd': a group of individuals apparently no longer led by their own volition and inclined to fall instinctively under the control of a 'chief'.[79] Le Bon's work reflected late-nineteenth-century bourgeois anxieties concerning the possible acquisition of political and class identity among crowds, a concern relevant, too, when the practices of the showmen were considered. The showmen appeared to depend upon the crowd's threatening capacity to 'attain to identity', becoming engaged with a single event or speaker at the cost of individuality, intellection, or the everyday social rituals of the street.[80] However, the actual practices of tale-telling depended less upon this hypnotic fascination than upon the creation of dialogue between showman and crowd. The showmen did not require passivity; they depended upon their potential audiences' desire to penetrate the shows' façades, and upon a knowing appreciation for the telling of the tale.

This relationship had also been recorded by Henry Mayhew, who claimed that showmen survived the unpredictable environment of the street because they possessed 'that quickness of perception which is commonly called "cunning", a readiness of expression, and a familiarity (more or less) with the topics of the day'.[81] Mayhew was also one of the first to record the codification of this highly professionalised form of street-sense within the various forms of secret language employed by the showmen.[82] Although widely associated with London street culture earlier in the century, *Backslang* or *parlyaree*, as used by the showmen, was intended, according to Toulmin, 'as a form of communication that outsiders do not understand'.[83] Less a grammatically complete language than a glossary of words used by the showmen, backslang prevented outsiders or 'flatties' from understanding those elements of the conversation that might prejudice them against the shows. The street showmen could discuss with impunity which pitches were the most profitable or which customers were most generous with their pennies. Parlyaree thus presupposed a structure of knowledge about the world that was not shared with audiences. However, as David Birch has pointed out in work on the possible anti-societal motivation for secret languages, that although 'the secret code depends for its effectiveness upon the presence of an uninitiated audience, that audience may well have the same moral and political views'.[84] There was no reason for the knowledge concealed from potential customers by the showmen to inhibit the construction of know-ingness between them. In fact, one contemporary visitor to the fairground was 'much impressed' with the manner of the showman's speech: 'eloquence before the public and slang among his own class of people'.[85] Use of parl-yaree clearly marked the apparent secretiveness of showland culture so that the visible strategising of the street showmen simply fed the curiosity of the knowing spectator.

Tale-telling and the relationships this generated were also often central to the showmen's written accounts of the shows, and it is informative to read these as recollections of the showman's patter. Tom Norman claimed that his first experience of showmanship came in 1878, when he was tempted into an Islington shop-front show one Saturday afternoon, an episode which sets the tone for the performance practices revealed in his *Memoirs*.[86] The exhibit was a 'rather scantily robed' young lady named Electra who, the showman claimed, was 'born deaf and dumb, also full of electricity, in all parts of her body'.[87] Customers were invited to touch her, but as they did so they unknowingly completed an electrical circuit conducted by zinc plating under a damp carpet on stage. The popular 'Electric Lady Stunt' was successfully achieved when the predominantly male customers received an unpleasant shock for each licentious touch. But, of course, as Norman says of the stunt, 'you must have a showman or tale teller proper or its [*sic*] no use'.[88] The tale told on this occasion followed a quasi-scientific pattern very popular in the freak show, where the deformities of the exhibit were traced back to pre-natal trauma. 'The only cause for this remarkable phenomenon we can come to,' explained the showman, 'is, that several months previous to her birth, her mother received a very servere [*sic*] shock by lightning'.[89] But, Norman continued, the reaction to the tale was far from unanimous:

> The audiance [*sic*] swallowed the tale, some sympathised with her, some stood with their mouths open, whilst at least one exclaimed, Ah; poor thing, A few of the more scientific, and knowing ones who saw the joke, laughed and were about to be thrown out by the sympathisers, when the showman quietened them.[90]

According to Norman, the tale was met by a variety of noisy and conflicting reactions from the audience, some of whom appeared to be taken in by it, perhaps because electricity still appeared to many to possess mysterious qualities, while others, better informed, displayed a more knowing reaction. Another likely reaction was the emergence of a principled cynicism concerning the show, perhaps born of long exposure to tale-tellers rather the application of scientific knowledge. However, it did not matter to Norman what, if anything, audiences learned concerning the condition of the unfortunate Electra so long as they were profitably engaged in the telling of the tale in some way. The 'sympathisers' among the crowd were an important group, since the showmen found that they could often tempt these individuals to part with extra pennies within the show, perhaps for a printed version of the showman's tale, particularly if it was suggested that this money formed part of the salary of the performer.[91] But the construction of 'knowing ones' amongst the public was not problematic; it simply gave Norman a different kind of purchase on all those who tried to see through the trick. This relationship was quite different to that dominantly associated with the didactic lecture: it was more important for spectators to understand *how* to read the relationship between the showman's discourse and the exhibit than it was to understand *what* he had to say about the exhibit. As in the understanding of anecdote, it was not necessary that they entertained trust in what the showman had to say, only that they be able to demonstrate a fundamental competence in their apprehension of the showman's motives for saying it.

Although many showmen at the end of the century thrived principally on the quality and reputation of their exhibitions, for others the knowing relationship with audiences made it possible to present almost anything to the public as an attraction, if appropriately dressed up. Most importantly, this gave showmen the opportunity to reinvigorate old tricks, provided they were accompanied by a new tale. For example, in the wake of the Boer War, a conflict that most accepted had come as a boon to the business, the celebrated showman, Harry Addison, reinvented the electric lady stunt with 'Kin Kon, The Electric Boy'.[92] According to Addison's tale, Kin Kon had been a despatch bearer at Ladysmith during the infamous siege of 1899, when his loyalty to General Buller had obliged him to run through a river poisoned by the 'bad, wicked Boers'. Though his life had been saved by a passing doctor, 'it was found that the poisoned water had deposited into his system an enormous amount of electricity', with the consequence that, for those who wished to congratulate the young man's heroism, shaking his hand inevitably led to the discharge of the shock.

In shows such as this, the showmen inventively capitalised upon issues of contemporary public interest, accentuating current events that brought forth patriotic or nationalist sentiments but also mining cultural issues that had a more enduring significance for the public. Whereas Norman's Electra had played upon sexuality, Addison's Kin Kon also raised issues concerning race, a lively question once it had become clear that British troops had depended upon the support of black South Africans during their campaign. Both entertainments had offered highly sensationalised discourses to their audiences and both depended upon their audiences' licentious desire to touch the exhibit, but both ultimately reassured them that, under ordinary circumstances, these objectifying practices were fully justified—could even be quite funny—and were part of the cultural values that the general public shared in common. As several commentators have remarked in relation to freak shows, the consequence of presenting such potentially challenging or shocking materials was more likely to be laughter or the generation of community spirit, at least for target audiences, than the provocation of anxious introspection.[93]

As in other narrative traditions, tale-telling thus served broad institutional imperatives, structurally mapping the needs of audiences onto exhibits or events that fulfilled particular cultural functions for them. In doing so, the showmen merely capitalised upon fears concerning constructions of gender, nationality and race that were routinely expressed at the turn of the century. This explains why it was possible for some showmen to make a living from presenting apparently bizarre or innocuous exhibits to audiences: these individuals depended upon large sections of the public to share similar social or psychological needs, and modified the tales in order to capitalise upon them. Furthermore, the tales were delivered in a manner that was long familiar to audiences, and which fostered a conventional, but unrehearsed, form of dialogue with them. This could be a reactive and surprisingly intimate experience. Whether the tales were delivered within or outside the shows, at fairgrounds, shop shows, or elsewhere, they called upon each spectator to interrogate their relationship with the showmen even as they gazed upon the exhibits within. Faced with the most sensational and shocking exhibits that contemporary culture could muster, spectators were also committed to a face-to-face, verbal relationship with performers, the terms of which were well-known; not so distinct, in fact, from the principled scepticism—or common sense—that informed relationships in everyday life.

The reciprocal and reflexive nature of this relationship also enabled institutions led by the showmen to be highly responsive to the demands of popular culture. Routinely exposed to the feedback of audiences, the shows offer an excellent example of the capacity of modern institutions to monitor

111

their own practices, always able to revisit old strategies in order to initiate changes when purposeful or profitable to do so. At the turn of the century, secondary organisations such as the Showman's Guild or trade journals such as *The Showman* were able very quickly to reflect upon, promote, and circulate such changes, partially superseding the word-of-mouth communication network that had always connected this itinerant trade. Borrowing from John B. Thompson's discussion of media institutions, it becomes possible to conceive of showmanship under these circumstances as a generic institutional structure, a set of resources and conventions at least as coherent and highly regulated as that associated with lantern culture at the turn of the century. However, the specific nature of showmanship and the substantial machinery that had grown up around it in the latter decades of the nineteenth century made the showmen uniquely placed to exploit new attractions such as the cinematograph—a technology whose own capacity for tale-telling would respond immediately to the demands of this ready-made market.

Showmen and the Cinematograph

Whereas the lantern trade struggled to accommodate moving pictures, the institutional stability and performative flexibility of showmanship made it ideally suited to adopt the cinematograph at an early stage. Within early film shows the face-to-face relationship between showman and audience persisted for some time, and would subsequently come to influence the performance practices of cinema managers during the 1910s, including procedures for arranging film programmes. As in earlier showland entertainments, film shows thrived on the generation of chat before, during and after the show, reminding us that moving pictures, too, were subjected to the everyday scepticism which audiences brought with them from work, street and home. So far as film producers were concerned, it was, of course, vital that they satisfy the substantial marketplace represented by the showmen, and so they tailored films that were likely to serve existing showman-led practices, significantly influencing public tastes. Thus, the development of a substantial publicity apparatus within the early industry tended to emulate some aspects of the sideshow experience, encouraging audiences to apply their own expertise in interpreting the tales they were told. In fact, wherever discourses of showmanship survived in the production and exhibition practices of the industry, so too might the audience's proficiency in decrypting them.

The showmen brought film quickly to every part of the UK, and their style of performance largely determined national public opinions concerning the moving picture. Although reliable figures are not available concerning the numbers of individuals who used films, E.H. Montagu of the Selig Poly-scope Company recalled that 'our best customers were probably travelling showmen, of whom there were hundreds, who used to tour the country with their own machines'.[94] In June 1907, the *Kinematograph and Lantern Weekly* grudgingly recorded that 'lacking as he does a really good market for films among what one might call "kinematograph theatres" the English manu-facturer is forced to pay particular attention to the wants of the showman, who goes from fair to fair with a tent fit-up and gives a show at 2d. or 3d. a time'.[95] This was an unusual admission for a film trade press that was largely dedicated from 1907 to the expansion of the new breed of picture theatre. Journals such as *Kinematograph and Lantern Weekly* and *The Bioscope* tended to represent the fairground bioscope show as a remnant of a bygone age, and were explicitly opposed to the business of penny shows common in large cities at this time.[96] Following these examples, standard histories of early cinema have also tended to marginalise the showmen, recalling them only in the anecdotal manner the showmen themselves had first adopted. More recent work has addressed this imbalance by retrieving other sources of evidence concerning the shows, often derived from the regulatory bodies most resented by the showmen, or has emphasised the significance of jour-nals sympathetic to them, such as *The Era*, *The Showman*, and *The World's Fair*.[97] These latter sources make clear that, although the cinematograph proved the greatest exhibit the showmen had encountered, it too had a specific place in a remarkably diverse, showman-centred intermedial envi-ronment.

To some extent, the first generation of cinematograph showmen found that the new medium bore direct comparison with a range of existing attrac-tions, allowing them to persist in tried and tested exhibition practices. As in most variety shows, the cinematograph presented living, moving individuals who were able to bring a discourse of their own to the show. Unlike the lantern lecturers, therefore, the showmen were well practised at allowing exhibits to speak for themselves when it paid to do so, and had already devel-oped tale-telling practices that need not infringe upon the tales told by the cinematograph. The cinematograph show also gave showmen the opportu-nity to capitalise upon current events and popular celebrities in much the same way as moving panoramas, waxworks, and other spectacular represen-tations had done.[98] As in the waxwork shows, royals and actresses proved to be enduringly popular subjects for the screen, as did the re-enactment of notorious murders that were exciting the public imagination. For example, waxwork figures of the notorious Sheffield murderer, Charles Peace, tended to display the actual murders themselves, or emphasised the grotesque physiognomy of the villain.[99] But the two films made of *The Life of Charles Peace* in 1905, one by the showman, William Haggar, pursue the killer from crime to execution, capitalising fully on the narrative of the chase in much the same way that the waxwork showman's tale might have done. The ghost illusion show, which had used various means to convey to audiences the impression that a phantom presence was interacting with live actors on the stage, was relatively easily aped by early filmmakers, who quickly learned that superimposition could be used to achieve similar effects. Even at the shooting stall, owners found in the cinematograph a novel means for exploiting the growing public interest in big game hunting; by presenting audiences with projected images of live animals, they could now offer the opportunity to shoot at moving targets from sub-Saharan Africa to the poles.[100]

Within such shows, the responsiveness and reflexivity of the profession of showmanship made it relatively easy to incorporate the cinematograph into a range of existing practices. The showmen were also uniquely qualified to answer the more unpredictable demands that arose when audiences were confronted with a new medium. Whereas, for film lecturers, the criticism that their commentary appeared unreliable or untrustworthy was potentially disastrous, for the showmen it could all be part of the fun. Under these conditions, even the photographic basis of the medium, which seemed, at least, to guarantee the veridicality of the film's representations, might be the subject of well-humoured scrutiny. This relationship, too, had a long professional heritage, derived principally from those showmen who exhibited magic lantern slides, panoramic views, waxworks, or other media that made strong claims to representational fidelity.[101] Early film anecdotes regularly made play with the widely publicised capacity of the medium to represent the world. According to one of these, William Haggar came unstuck when he screened his version of the '*Russo-Japanese War*' too close to Treharris, where he had also filmed it. A member of the cast was recognised by the audience, and as Haggar's daughter recalled, 'it took us some time to live this one down'.[102] In the Salome anecdote, too, the showman's tale is radically able to alter the audience's interpretation of the celebrated erotic spectacle of the skirt dance. Informed by such tales, the knowing customer approached film shows with a practised appreciation for the unreliability of photographic representation, or at least of its potential for manipulation in the hands of the showmen.

The existence of such anecdotes suggests that the dialogue between showman and audience that had always characterised the shows persisted when the cinematograph was adopted. However, the showmen's professional practices did not integrate moving pictures entirely without difficulties. In particular, the expense of running a show could be as problematic to smaller showmen as it was to the lantern lecturing trade, as one contributor to *The Showman* reported:

> As a well known owner and exhibitor of cinematograph and lime-light illustrations, I speak with knowledge from practical experience, and I affirm that the present system of exhibiting animated pictures (to be up-to-date and appreciative) is a most expensive one, and to a small showman these heavy expenses, in many instances, make the whole concern unprofitable.
>
> The real question at issue, and one that is agitating many minds, is how to attain that high standard of efficiency that will produce the maximum of public interest and enthusiasm at a minimum cost.[103]

That question, of course, had always confronted the showmen in their considerations of the cost of apparatus, staff, transportation and infrastructure, but the use of the cinematograph tended to exacerbate the problem. One substantial teething problem for small exhibitors was that they often had little expertise in the use and maintenance of a projector, and were obliged to hire experienced operators in order to avoid the setbacks that damaged films, equipment, and reputations could create.[104] A more persistent difficulty was that the showman's customary reliance on the latest novelties or current events to intrigue the public. Although these were supplied by the cinematograph in a reliable and constant flow that was largely to the showman's advantage, this also made the showmen strongly dependent upon the shrewd business practices of film producers and distributors. To an extent this reproduced the conditions of the existing market for novelties, which priced exhibits principally according to their sensation value. However, because film permitted unique spectacles to be reproduced any number of times, they were, in principle, available to any showman prepared to pay for them, meaning that those who chose not to do so risked being seen as out of date. 'So long as there is a continuous flow of new subjects being imparted into an exhibition,' continued the writer for *The Showman*, 'the interest is unbounding and the show will be patronised, but to keep up a stock of films of the latest subjects is no small item.'[105] Showmen either had to obey the logic of the new market and set aside a substantial amount of money, week by week, to acquire new subjects, or they needed to find an altogether different strategy for securing customers.

Additional costs were incurred because of the increasingly heavy regulatory burden that was sometimes heaped upon cinematograph operators, notably in London, though other local councils appear to have been even more restrictive. The showmen regularly complained that the authorities scrutinised film shows in an unprecedented and excessive manner, making it difficult for them to maintain a regular trade. The regulations imposed by the London County Council in January 1898 have been summarised elsewhere.[106] However, the showmen themselves were particularly aggrieved by the LCC's stipulations that an inspector should always be able to see the apparatus at work at least three days before any public exhibition, that the apparatus should be placed in a fireproof room or a closed sheet-iron box, and that two or three operators should always be present within that box during the exhibition.[107] The regularity and quality of these inspections also came under attack, with the showmen claiming that the inspectors had a rather poor understanding of fire safety issues associated with the apparatus (**Fig. 2**).[108] The controversy over the inspections emerged because precise obedience to LCC regulations effectively prevented the lower class of sideshows from adopting the cinematograph. These had always depended for their survival upon responsiveness to local circumstances and on relatively low levels of investment and staffing, but this mode of operation had now become all but impossible. Similarly, the cinematograph was accommodated only with considerable difficulty within bazaars, with one piece of advice to managers suggesting that, at the very least, 'County Council regulations . . . should be studied before making arrangements to hire one.'[109]

However, according to Burrows, the existence of an unknown number of unlicensed London shop shows in the 'infancy of the cinema', which appear to have escaped the LCC's notice, is an 'established fact', though these exhibitions had 'no real continuity with later developments' in the period after 1906.[110] Tony Fletcher has corroborated this position, showing that during the 1896-1906 period, in spite of the LCC's public-safety drive, an ever-decreasing but significant number of small exhibitors were working the London circuit, including some whose services could be hired by bazaars, pubs, and other public venues.[111] Outside London, similar local council regulations were unevenly applied and there is some evidence to suggest that permanent shop-front cinematograph shows were present in other cities for a longer period.[112] Professor Thomas Howard claimed in 1901 to have 'exhibited nearly every novelty, from the "spotted girl", to a cinematograph', within the penny shows that formed a large proportion of his business.[113] Writing in 1912, Frederic A. Talbot recalled that 'empty shops in permanent thoroughfares, railway arches, even sheds, available at nominal rents, were acquired and converted into darkened halls' in order to exhibit the cinematograph.[114] George Pearson's recollection of these shows, first published in 1938 and then reproduced by Rachel Low, is typical of subsequent accounts in that it romanticises the primitivity of the apparatus and its operation, and is vague in terms of dates and details. However, read as an impressionistic reminiscence on the conditions of early showmanship, his account of tale-telling outside the shows remains instructive, reproducing closely the accounts the showmen had always given of their own practices:

> It was outside a derelict greengrocer's shop. The hawk-eyed gentleman on a fruit crate was bewildering a sceptical crowd. In that shuttered shop there was a miracle to be seen for a penny, but only twenty-four could enter at a time; there wasn't room for more. His peroration was magnificent; 'You've seen pictures of people in books, all frozen stiff. You've

Cinematograph Show under the new L.C.C. Rules.

Oh! have the audience all assembled?   Are the firemen standing steady?   Is the fellow there who has to
  Have you put the barriers round?   Bring the blankets right up here!   Watch the films come out and in!
Have you got the hydrant ready?   Have you got the pails handy?   Have you put the fire-proof box on—
  Laid asbestos on the ground?   Is the special exit clear!   Right!—Then let the show begin!
                                            ALPHONSE COURLANDER.

Fig. 2 Regulatory interference. Cartoon satirising the enforcement of the London County Council's safety regulations for cinematograph shows (*The Showman* (8 March 1901), p. 159). Image courtesy of the Houdini Collection of the Rare Book Division of the Library of Congress.

never seen people come alive in pictures, moving about natural like you and me. Well, go inside and see for yourself living pictures for a penny. Then tell me if I'm a liar.'[115]

Within Pearson's anecdote it was the telling of the tale and the open and compelling acknowledgement that the showman might be a 'liar' that proved irresistible to audiences. Although there are ample grounds for distrusting its substance, the anecdote does go some way to suggest that the knowing dialogue that existed between showman and audiences had persisted within the earliest shop-front film shows; indeed, this was the impression of the showmen that survived when all other aspects of their business seemed to have been forgotten. In such cases, the popular image the showmen had generated concerning their business was easily adopted by the later industry, which, after all, had a closely related propensity to mythologise its own history in the service of a good yarn.

The costs and inconveniences incurred by shop cinematograph shows led many showmen to exploit other means of bringing moving pictures to town. From 1894, kinetoscope and mutoscope devices appeared in shop-front shows throughout the UK, but, as I have suggested, these were most often supplementary to the main attractions, and established a private relationship between image and spectator in which the showman need play little part.[116] The development of other optical projection devices, some arranged in an ad hoc fashion by the showmen themselves, predicated a much more familiar relationship with city crowds. In 1901, one writer for *The Optical Magic Lantern and Photographic Enlarger* reported that in an unnamed Northern city a crowd of several hundred had been attracted to a single wagon, covered in black tarpaulin, in which a series of humorous slides were being screened.[117] Following the collection of money, the show had simply moved on to another location, where the performance was repeated. Cinematographic buskers were reported as early as 1899, when the showmen A. Jones and S. Gold were charged with 'causing a crowd to assemble' and with 'exhibiting indecent pictures' including films, from a barrow in Southwark Park Road, London.[118] While the extent of these shows seems limited, they can perhaps be seen as part of the response of the showmen to repressive safety regulations, since they recaptured some of the adaptabilty and mobility that had made the shop-front shows so successful (and so slippery) in the first place. They neatly evaded the troublesome implications of building regulations by disposing of the necessity of a building, but, by the same virtue, became especially prone to charges of obstructing the public thoroughfare.

Another great difficulty for street cinematograph showmen, of course, was that the successful projection of films required darkness. Those showmen who did screen moving pictures outdoors tended to do so on warm summer nights, and at sites more predictable than the street, like public parks, or at fêtes and galas. Professor Stone, a marionette and Punch and Judy showman by day, whose favoured pitch during the summer months was at Scarborough, performed cinematograph shows at night, which he believed were better off outdoors: 'I wonder there aren't a few more doing the animated photographs in the open air,' he reportedly claimed, 'it's a lot more pleasant.'[119] Mr Dove Patterson was recorded to have had record attendances at his open air 'Graphic Kinematograph and Pictorial Reviews', which took place in a public park in 1907.[120] Although held in open spaces, such exhibitions were cordoned off, allowing the showmen to charge gate money rather than taking collections.

However, the problems associated with open-air cinematography were probably answered most comprehensively by the brief vogue at the turn of the century for the Street Cinematograph, the device that was most obviously tailored to the specific requirements of the smaller cinematograph showmen. This apparatus revived an ancient tradition of street peepshow entertainments, already in decline by the 1850s, but which had traditionally allowed the showmen to follow the crowds and to present their exhibits regardless of weather, season, location or time of day. It was essentially a film projector and screen completely enclosed within a large box, with ten peepholes along each side of the enclosure offering individual customers a perspective on the projected image.[121] An 1898 advertisement explained that the outfit produced 'Fine Results in the Open Streets in Broad Daylight', and that it therefore enabled showmen to transform crowds into paying audiences without requiring them even to pass through a gate.[122] According to *The Art of Projection and Complete Magic Lantern Manual*, the apparatus could be extremely effective in the right hands: 'The financial result . . . depends upon the showman and a suitable position, these attained, success is ensured'.[123] G.R. Baker, writing for the *British Journal of Photography* as early as October 1898, had already shown that 'cinematographs in the streets and public places, such as market squares, seem to be quite the rage, and . . . are paying well'. Baker also confirmed that the appeal of such devices still depended principally on the abilities of the seasoned showman:

> But those films! One ought not to expect much for one penny, I suppose, but the splashes of light and defects due to the films being damaged neutralised the attractiveness of the exterior of the machine . . . The titles given to the films by the showman were such as to bring up

waverers and rouse their curiosity, so as to cause them to part with the humble penny without reluctance. How many were satisfied with what they saw it was difficult to judge.[124]

Baker was most likely fully justified in his account of the quality of the films. There was little reason for the street showmen, who did not depend substantially upon repeat trade, to renew their stock of films regularly. Such showmen might also rely upon inexpensive second hand films, which could be acquired relatively cheaply from classified pages in the trade press or from entertainment agents, but were often out of date or damaged by frequent use.[125] Again, it was the showman's discourse rather than the exhibit itself that brought in the pennies. From the announcement that 'these were the finest animated photographs ever exhibited', no doubt taken by the majority of customers with an appropriate degree of scepticism, it was the showman's personal engagement with customers that won them over. Showmen had long been understood to embody a tradition of duplicitous fresh talking and to manipulate all resources at their disposal in order to maximise profits, so it is not surprising to find that this ingenious variant of the street peep show might also encourage a knowing response from potential customers, a response not so different, in fact, from Baker's commentary.

Other showmen adopted different strategies. For those who were unable to keep their own stock of the most up-to-date films, but who also did not wish to enter the increasingly marginalized business of shop-front and street shows, it was possible to rent films for short periods from professional cinematograph bureaux. This was particularly significant for those independent operators, like one correspondent to *The Showman* in February 1901, 'who do not show every night, and yet wish to have up-to-date subjects'.[126] By the end of the same year, substantial developments were already taking place in film rental businesses such as Walker, Turner, and Dawson (later Walturdaw). According to Walker, 'all [the cinematograph] wants now to bring it even more to the front is better facilities for the hire of films, for some of them are much too dear for any ordinary showman to purchase right out on account of their so soon getting stale'.[127] Businesses such as these enabled the development of film shows that depended upon the regular turnaround of films rather than the mobility of their exhibitors, and also set in place the conditions for a certain degree of standardisation within such shows:[128]

> Their method of doing business is very simple. They buy a quantity of each film that is any good from almost every maker in the trade. On their

books they have a large number of customers who each week require an entire change of films, so that they can give a different entertainment every seven days. There is no compulsion to have what Messrs. Walker and Co. choose to send you, for the showman can select his own. Most of the customers, however, prefer to leave the selection to the firm, just instructing them to send comical, trick, war, or other pictures, just as may be wanted. For this, their charge is very moderate. In fact, Mr. Walker assured our representative that for one guinea a week a splendid show of films could be hired.[129]

This simple rental system, which had, in fact, already been in operation for a while, was designed to assure showmen that, even if they did not themselves possess an up-to-date knowledge of recent film releases, they could depend upon an expert selection to be made on their behalf.[130] The faculty to request particular genres also enabled the company to supply the remarkably varied requirements of different shows in this period, without increasing administrative burdens. However, it also meant that such companies could supply complete film exhibitions on the behalf of almost any institutions and interest groups, but with the considerable advantage over the showmen of an extensive film library. Walker and Co. boasted that a typical one-hour show from one of their operators included an average of £450 worth of films and equipment, but cost only a 'few guineas'. Shows such as this could feasibly compete with even the most successful of major town hall exhibitors, whose cinematograph shows in large urban venues were an extremely important factor in the development of the early industry.[131]

Practices such as these suggest that, even at this stage of the film industry's development, the institution of showmanship experienced some frictions with increasingly centralised production and distribution companies. Not only could these bodies infringe upon the business of exhibitors, they could also monitor the types of films that the showmen were using, and this could have implications too for the style and delivery of the shows. The showmen were skilled at building narratives around the exhibits they had on offer, but it was now possible to leave some responsibility for the arrangement of the films in the hands of third parties. However, the largest showman-led cinematograph shows usually did not require the help of external agencies to secure the best films or to arrange them effectively. On the fairground, the new generation of showman-entrepreneurs brought levels of investment to the moving pictures that would remain unprecedented until the arrival of the picture theatre chains in the late 1900s, and this tended to secure for these showmen a greater degree of autonomy than smaller exhibitors. The popularity of the bioscopes was such that, only five years after their introduction in 1897, they were widely regarded as 'the main attraction at all the fairs'.[132] Reviews typically recorded the presence of at least three or four at every fair, and it was not unusual to find many more than this. At the 1900 Hull Fair, one observer counted no less than nine, all 'crowded to the covers', and there were typically more than a dozen at this site in the following decade, often lined up in a row.[133] Business was so reliable in the first years of the century that a showman like Pat Collins was able to gamble an estimated £3,000 of venture capital on the success of just one of his shows, with levels of investment soaring during the next decade.[134]

The competition among such establishments was intense, with the showmen themselves laying particular emphasis on the quality of the films they screened. 'We all do our best,' wrote one bioscope proprietor, 'to get better, or at least, more interesting and up-to-date films than the man who pitches just beside and all around us . . . For obvious reasons, none of us dare breathe a word as to the particular fair we shall visit a week or two hence, in order to avoid unfair competition.'[135] Securing such films in advance of their competitors enabled the shows to gain a small advantage, which, in the context of the spendthrift fairground environment, could translate into a great deal of money. Equally significant in attracting the attention of audiences were the intricately carved façades of the shows, whose grand scale and detailed ornamentation far outstripped anything earlier shows on the fairground had offered. Within, some shows could accommodate over a thousand customers and promised them comfortable, clean seating, ornate decoration, and increasingly high-quality entertainments.

Typically, customers were enticed into the show by the popular tune played on the organ, by the variety performances known as the parades which occupied the front stage, and by a doorsman in dress coat and top hat who would announce the show's opening by telling the tale at the front. As in the shop shows, the doorsman sometimes continued to tell the tale within the show, where, if he was suitably qualified, he might perform the role of the lecturer or even of the pianist. The parades were extremely varied and included performances that might previously have appeared within independent booths, including musicians, dancers, comics, freaks or topical revues. Mitchell and Kenyon's fascinating film of the *Whitsun Fair at Preston: 1906*, almost certainly commissioned from this company by Sedgwick's Bioscope show for screening at the same fair, depicts one of these parades. In the first scene of this film, the camera pans across the fairground and shows a dense crowd milling between carousels, bioscope shows, and other entertainments (though, clearly, many individuals are more interested in the spectacle of the camera than in the fair). In the distance, Green's Cinematograph is visible with its engines running. But most attention is reserved for the second scene, which depicts a comic turn on Sedgwick's parade wherein a clown is lathered up for a shave by an unnecessarily forceful barber. Glancing excitedly at the camera, the crowds gather to watch the free performance and listen to the doorsman before pouring with exaggerated vigour into the show itself. They are marshalled inside by the uniformed step men who were responsible in these shows for maintaining the crucial boundary between the performances inside and outside: the pay box. The film thus reproduced the passage of spectators from the competing attractions of the fairground, to the parade of Sedgwick's show and finally, inside, where the film was also most likely screened later in the same week.

A great number of performance regimes were exploited within the shows, depending upon the greater structure of the show and the expectations of audiences. Some shows were structured thematically, with lecturers carrying these themes between and during films. One observer recalled a 1902 show with a 'short, but highly instructive lecture'; 'Colonel' William Clark employed both a 'qualified lecturer' and a 'skilled musician' in his show; and William Haggar hired a lecturer 'to describe the various films' during the screening.[136] Those anecdotal accounts that detail the failure of the apparatus make this supplementary, descriptive role of the lecturer clear. 'Ladies and Gentlemen,' began Haggar's troubled lecturer according to one story, 'if you could see this film it would be a picture of a train emerging from a tunnel.'[137] Another lecturer was 'hooted off' the platform in a 1906 bioscope show when he 'could not tell what the views represented', and so was unable to describe them.[138] Other shows exploited a form of ciné-variety that owed more to practices in the music hall. Combined shows often introduced moving pictures as a novelty amongst other tried and tested attractions, such as menageries, circuses or waxwork shows. One correspondent wrote glowingly in 1901 of 'Houpla's Grand Continental Circus and Cinematograph Entertainment'.[139] Another recalled an early mechanical waxwork and cinematograph show on the fairground, half of which was divided into a number of alcoves, like earlier Museums of Curiosity. Within the alcoves were a series of gory historical reconstructions including the 'dying struggles of the Emperor [Napoleon] represented in vivid fashion', an effect heightened by 'the pungent comments of the lecturer'.[140] For twenty minutes the lecturer told the tale before 'the kinematograph show proper was begun' on the other side of the tent. In other shows it was only the gap between films, when the next reel was wound on to the projector, which was filled by a turn. This was usually performed by the paraders and may have had little to do with the films

123

themselves.[141] Sometimes the quality of the variety was more strongly emphasised, and one fictional representation, written by Reverend T. Horne, who was a highly influential figure in the Showman's Guild, described 'the present ideal of the portable theatre of varieties, with the pictures as the great draw, and varieties to give turns inside and to parade in the front'.[142]

Filmmakers quickly learned which films were most likely to satisfy the showman market in the long term. The Warwick Trading Company made an especially strong bid for the business of the showmen, issuing a series of full page advertisements in *The Showman*, one of which depicted their customers, invariably marked out by their top hats, disposing of the outdated apparatus and films provided by other companies (**Fig. 3**). The pages of the trade press were littered with prominent advertisements for films concerning current events, from the funeral of Queen Victoria, to war subjects, to sporting events. The appeal of such films was short-lived and required immediate turnaround, being especially well suited for exhibition by the showmen. Magic trick films, or films of acrobatic or comic performance also remained popular on the fairground and these, too, tended to reproduce the attractions of earlier entertainments within the new medium. Perhaps the greatest attractions, however, as a great deal of recent scholarship has shown, were the local subjects that the showmen sometimes produced themselves, or which they could commission from a wide variety of manufacturers, including Mitchell and Kenyon, Hepworth, and The Warwick Trading Company.[143]

By 1907 *The Kinematograph and Lantern Weekly* was still in no doubt that the influence of the fairground showmen was 'one of the most important factors in determining the class of picture to be put out', and that 'the impression taken away from fair pictures very often determines the manner in which members of the audience will regard any future living picture shows desiring their support'.[144] The journal probably made this case in preference to acknowledging the large numbers of unlicensed penny shows that proliferated in London after 1906. In fact, both the shop-front and fairground bioscopes would remain extremely important exhibition sites until 1914.[145] However, in spite of the pejorative representation of showmanship that dominated the dedicated film press from the late 1900s, the permanent cinemas in fact adopted many of their regular performance routines primarily from the town-hall and fairground showmen. Indeed, while the most successful of theatre chains ran along practised business models, being led and financed by a variety of businessmen and entrepreneurs, the industry necessarily had to come to terms with the demands of existing audiences, and this meant adopting the most successful of existing exhibition practices. This became most apparent on the relatively rare occasions when cine-

Fig. 3 Reeling in the showmen. Advertisement for the Warwick Trading Company, depicting showmen disposing of outdated or low quality films procured from other companies. (*The Showman* (6 December 1901), p. 4). Image courtesy of the National Fairground Archive, Sheffield.

matograph showmen attempted to set up their own theatres, but the practices of showmanship had a more pervasive influence than the biographies of such individuals suggest.

For example, during December 1908 a lively debate appeared in the pages of *The Bioscope* concerning the status of ciné-variety within the new picture theatres, which suggested that some of the performance regimes most strongly associated with cinematograph showmen on the fairs had survived. In response to an exhibitor who wished to open a 'permanent picture show' in a small town, *The Bioscope* made the case that the correspondent 'would do better to pay more for film hire, rather than put on mediocre variety turns'.[146] In the next few weeks, a selection of travelling showmen and permanent theatre managers entered the debate. Some believed that 'the shows which draw the most money are those that engage variety artistes', and that a two-hour show composed only of films was likely to be 'wearying' for audiences.[147] Others suggested that the problem for ciné-variety was that the films tended to be of a substantially higher quality than the turns and that, 'if the show were run well, as the average picture show is run, the patrons would not hanker after variety'.[148] The debate demonstrates that longstanding variety routines survived within some picture theatres at this time, but that others were now purely dedicated to pictures, often accompanied by music. It also suggests that, although the first fifteen years of the film industry were turbulent, and ultimately saw control begin to pass from substantial institutions associated with the lanternists, showmen and music halls to film-dedicated institutions such as the picture theatres, there remained basic continuities in the experiences of audiences visiting the shows.

The showman's adaptability to circumstance and practices of tale-telling also found a place within the picture theatres. For John B. Rathbun, writing in 1914, the salient point for cinema managers was 'to pay attention to the comments of the audience as they leave the theatre', so that appropriate programming could be selected for a particular neighbourhood.[149] Such sensitivity to the customer's demands should then prevail over the manager's preconceptions of the marketplace and ambitions for his theatre. Addressing both showmen and theatre managers, one 1908 article also advised exhibitors to 'gain public confidence', and suggested that the successful manager should 'go among his people, and talk to them personally'.[150] The 1911 guide, *How To Run a Picture Theatre*, strongly recommended to managers of the new purpose-built cinemas a lecturing practice closely related to the telling of the tale:

> Do not hesitate to boom a picture well ahead of its showing, both by announcement on the screen and, if your manager has a good presence,

as he should have, by the delivery of a well thought out little speech. Some theatres owe all their success to the fact that the managers make a point of showing themselves between the pictures and detailing the coming features. This personal appeal is worth volumes of printing. Lecture your film before it comes and when you get it, the seed you have sown will bear fruit.[151]

This was a lecturing practice whose founding premise, like that of the showman, was one of salesmanship: managers exploited a dynamic of personal appeal to potential customers, seeking to convert them into future audiences. Not only were customers tempted by forthcoming movies, but the persuasive address of a familiar public speaker who construed customer loyalty as a matter of personal concern suggests an appeal to patrons in excess of written advertisements. The difference, of course, is that the static show could not, like the itinerant show, move on to fresh markets, and this made it especially important that, as in the case of town hall showmen who had long depended upon regular local trade, the pictures boomed by the manager should live up to expectations and were exchanged for others on a regular basis. Once the public's confidence had been gained it was essential for static theatres that it should not be lost in the short-term profitability of the confidence trick. The picture theatre did all in its power to meet its promises. One observer optimistically recommended that the manager should even 'write a good honest description of his chief film each week for the local weekly paper . . . praising where praise is possible, and faithfully pointing out the parts which certain people will like better than others'.[152]

Most significantly, however, the appeal of a knowing reaction to the shows also persisted, regardless of the picture theatre's gradual displacement of the showman's verbal performances. The influence of showmanship had taught the public that uncritical appreciation of the shows could leave them at the mercy of its illusions and confidence tricks, and this relationship did not disappear simply because there were no showmen within the picture theatre. As the burgeoning popular film press of the 1910s continued to mythologise filmmakers' tricks of the trade, the spectator's active application of critical commonsense expanded from the exhibition site, taking into consideration as well the practices of picture personalities and other well-publicised aspects of the filmmaking process. During the nineteenth century, the showmen had perfected the ability to tell tales that audiences needed to hear, presenting spectacular exhibits that were ultimately most likely to generate reassurance for them. Given that, in the first decades of the twentieth century, the cultural and social conditions initiated by industrial modernity seemed, if anything, to be becoming increasingly unstable, it made perfect commercial sense for film producers to meet the demand for reassurance by replicating it. Spectators confronted a moving image that also told tales of uncertain reliability, wherein, at some level of enunciation, the showman was still at work, seeking his audiences' complicity in the tricks played upon them. Of course, emerging within the media-saturated environment of the 1890s and 1900s, even this type of relationship between image and spectator was nothing new. The business of the next two chapters will be to investigate the development of such dialogue between spectators and the distant personae associated with the screen.

4

'Oh, there's our Mary!'
Performance On-screen

In the first months of 1898, following the initial wave of interest in the moving pictures, two reviews, one appearing in the UK and one in the USA, described entertainments that seemed to bring the technological basis and representational capacities of film directly into question.[1] The longer of these reviews, in Charles Francis Jenkins' 1898 book, *Animated Pictures*, recorded what he called 'an animated picture show which was entirely without shakiness':

> I had been invited to witness what purported to be the latest develop-
> ment in moving pictures. When the cue for this part of the
> entertainment was given, the usual white screen was rolled down at the
> back of the stage, and the lights turned down. The familiar whirr could
> be heard and when the light was thrown upon the canvas it revealed three
> dancing girls. Even from the first glance it did not seem quite right, and
> presently the whole scheme was distinguishable. The stage was a real
> stage, the girls were real flesh and blood specimens, and the whole was
> illuminated with an intermittently projected light in such a realistic
> fashion that the illusion was almost perfect.[2]

The word 'illusion' seems especially heavily loaded in this context, since it reverses the already widely disseminated idea of film's imitation of life. Here, life was imitating the animated pictures' imitation of life, and audiences were seemingly left to decipher the spectacle of an illusion of an illusion. However, the purpose of the show was not to deceive audiences, nor to set before them an elaborate perceptual and cognitive puzzle, and there is no evidence to suggest that discomfort or disorientation characterised their experience of it. Instead, as the anonymous reporter from *The Photographic*

129

News explained, audiences were able 'instantly to see the point of the joke, and indulge in a hearty laugh at the very newest "take-off".[3]

We might speculate about their enjoyment of this novelty: perhaps it derived from the show's implicit contention that little was added to live performances, such as the spectacle of dancing girls, by their reproduction on film; or perhaps from its play upon the publicity that tended to herald the arrival of new film projectors on the market, which frequently declared a marked technological advance on predecessors; or perhaps simply from a well-humoured appreciation of the ingenious and painstaking effort that had been taken to stage a single joke. Regardless of the exact motivation for and force of the trick, however, spectators appear to have been keen to count themselves among those who appreciated its wit and playfulness. The joke therefore depended for its success on the self-conscious sophistication of early film audiences, their ability and willingness to participate in a knowing, showman-like relationship to the representations on-screen and the conditions of exhibition. As the previous chapter has shown, this type of relationship was far from unusual in the early years of film, but here it focussed the attention of audiences directly onto the film apparatus and on the grandiose claims made for it by filmmakers, showmen and the popular press. The show openly burlesqued the premise of liveness upon which so much of the appeal of living pictures had thus far depended. In doing so it made implicit play of the contemporary debate concerning the ontological value of mediated forms of presence, allowing audiences to negotiate, calmly and with humour, the substantial changes technologies such as cinema were introducing into social and communicative aspects of their everyday lives.

Such moments of purposeful introspection are not uncommon in the earliest film shows, where consideration of the medium was encouraged by the exhibitionist qualities of its presentation, and sometimes by the visible or audible operation of the projector. In addition, the films themselves regularly thematised the conditions of recording and screening, presenting the cinematograph camera, its operator, and even the audience as viable objects of representation. As Noël Burch has remarked, British 'gentleman filmmakers' such as Cecil Hepworth, George Albert Smith and James Williamson seem to have specialised in now relatively well-known 'experimental gag films', such as *The Big Swallow* (Williamson 1901), which directly represented the use of the camera, and *As Seen through a Telescope* (GAS, 1900), which thematised the act of viewing.[4] Similarly, Robert Paul's *The Countryman and the Cinematograph* (1901) presented the naïve reaction of a filmgoer terrified by the on-screen approach of a train, and three years earlier his *Difficulties of an Animated Photographer* (1898) had focused on an actuality filmmaker who, 'having posed his subject, is pestered by passers-by and small boys'.[5]

These parodic productions of early filmmakers represent a creative response to pre-existing conventions and institutional constraints and may be understood as part of the process wherein these constraints were productively reoriented. For example, occasional parodies of educational films levelled a sophisticated internal critique at the pervasive contemporary cultural imperative to disseminate knowledge and to inform, and this generated new relationships with audiences. The Hepwix film *The Unclean World* (1903) clearly parodied Urban's *Unseen World* series of the same year (whose publicity promised a microscopic revelation of 'nature's closest secrets', including titles such as *Circulation of Blood in the Frog's Foot*).[6] The Hepwix catalogue was keen to advertise—with customary exaggeration—their film's innovative relationship to Urban's widely publicised series, suggesting that, 'for the first time in the history of the Cinematograph, that instrument has been used to burlesque a popular application of itself'.[7]

Such parody borrowed loosely from a tradition of illustrated burlesque derived principally from lecturers such as Artemus Ward, who had also ridiculed the enlightenment mission of rational amusements, sometimes illustrating their performances with absurdly unrealistic or exaggerated images. However, the formal implications of this tradition within films such as *The Unclean World* also proved to be highly productive for developing film institutions. The novelty of the Urban Micro-Bioscope series rested upon the very specific form of viewpoint it had sought to reproduce, but *The Unclean World* transformed this analogy into the butt of a sophisticated joke. The privileged site of vision, representational authority, and dissemination of knowledge promised by educational films were thus undermined by the empowering laughter of the audience. But the crucial point was that in destabilising an earlier productive alignment of the audience with the apparatus, the film also helped to sophisticate the kinds of communication the cinematograph was capable of achieving. Within such films it is possible to identify the dialogic potential, always associated with parody and satire, to ridicule authoritative discourses and hence generate new forms and genres of expression. From this perspective, the case of *The Unclean World* illustrates in an unusually obvious way the active promotion of new forms of spectatorial expertise: the nurturing of an ever wider variety of scopic and cognitive regimes for the expert interpretation of film. Such expertise might then be habitually or automatically practised by spectators, becoming part of their practical consciousness during film viewing and evolving into more enduring generic conventions.

131

Thus, while writers such as Maxim Gorky were directly enquiring into the 'soundless spectre' produced by the cinematograph image, the films themselves opened up an arena wherein questions concerning the nature of the medium might be seamlessly negotiated.[8] Whereas live performances associated with early film shows most often tended to reproduce familiar patterns of audience address, performance on film inevitably began by stretching existing forms of dressage, reorienting relationships with spectators in a manner that would quickly generate a bewildering diversity of film genres and styles. In this light, the marked heterogeneity of performance styles in early film shows can be seen, not only as a continuation of the variety tradition, but also as a feature of an evolving institutional relationship between audience and screen, in which film producers, exhibitors and spectators—unwittingly obeying the institutional imperative to roll forwards inexorably—explored and tested the communicational capacities of the medium. This chapter and the next will track the development of these relationships, concentrating respectively on the changing qualities of on-screen performances and the more abstract agencies associated by audiences with the production, authoring and narration of films. They will show that, even after the novelty of moving pictures had worn off for most audiences, the technological and representational flexibility of the apparatus meant that the medium continually went through such moments of invention and innovation, and these cumulatively led the young industry through rapid institutional change.

Early Genres and Other Distinctions

An account of the processes of genre definition and diversification at work in early film offers a good point of departure for this analysis. Though little theorised, genres were at least as important to early filmmakers, exhibitors and audiences as they were to later cinemas since they formalised and structured the apparently chaotic, unstable possibilities for communication between audience and screen. Indeed, the precise use made by early film producers of words such as 'subjects', 'scenes', 'views', or 'series', in place of what we might now simply term, 'genres', suggests that the business of distinguishing between film types in this period was a relatively nuanced affair. From as early as 1897, increasingly complex generic distinctions began to emerge as filmmakers, in the organisation of their catalogues, and exhibitors, in their programmes, distinguished between different classes of view, performance and potential audience.[9] The Warwick Trading Company, who distributed the work of several early filmmakers in addition to their own productions, were already in this year classifying numerous discrete subgenres, making fine distinctions, for example, between scenic views such as 'Railroad and Steamship Subjects', and 'Panoramas taken from a moving boat or train'.[10] As the popularity of these and other subjects waxed and waned, the publication of the annual catalogue and frequent catalogue supplements reflected these changes. By 1902, perhaps registering the growing interest in travelogue entertainments at this time, as well as some weariness with the novelty of a moving camera, Warwick's list of scenics distinguished between the countries or regions they represented rather than the vehicle from which they had been cinematographed, even though the use of trains to generate spectacular, mobile views had remained very popular.[11] In the same period, however, there was little change to some other genre classifications. For example, recognising the continued popularity of childhood scenes, and perhaps also the likely presence of children within many audiences, the 1897 Warwick catalogue subheading, 'Juvenile Subjects', remained in place in 1902 as 'Juvenile Series'.

Though some of the earliest genre classifications had disappeared by the early 1900s, the general trend in the years before 1905 was one of rapid genre diversification, matching the proliferation of subjects for the cinematograph. This process was registered within early film catalogues, which became increasingly sophisticated during this period. For example, Hepworth and Co.'s 1903 catalogue included a three-page 'Classified Index of Film Subjects', intended to point exhibitors to the ever more specialised genres and subgenres their audiences potentially desired. Each new sub-genre, from 'Jokes on Policemen' to 'Pillow Fights', implied the establishment of subtly different relationships between on-screen performers and audiences, and therefore added further to the potential heterogeneity experienced during early film shows.[12] Tracking changes and continuities such as these can offer useful insights into the shifting configuration of the market for film, and therefore into the types of relationship with the screen the public most cherished. However, genre was only one of the factors that determined such relationships. Even the most precise of sub-genres could generate an array of performance styles, and tracking these can be extremely difficult: specific modes of screen performance appeared and disappeared rapidly, were often highly localised, seeking to address audiences with disparate requirements, and were seldom formalised as such by film producers, exhibitors or critics.

In spite of these difficulties, several accounts have sought to demonstrate continuities of performance practices with earlier entertainments, finding in different ways that early film accomplished a remediation of existing forms, and therefore reproduced familiar pleasures for their audiences. Such studies

133

have necessarily focused on discrete traditions, such as sequential art, varied panoramic and dioramic entertainments, music hall performance styles, and the staging of photographic lantern slide sequences, but they have tended to demonstrate that the impact of such images, performances and discourses could be very far reaching indeed. For example, Frank Scheide has traced the tradition of direct audience address associated with British music hall performers through into Chaplin's comedies of the 1940s and 1950s.[13] However, the prevailing critical response to the slippery notion of early screen performance has been to isolate the development of the specific labour of acting that would become dominant within feature films, especially insofar as this derived from legitimate theatrical traditions.[14] This has initiated a project sketching continuities between formal nineteenth-century theories of theatrical gesture and popular acting styles associated with stage melodrama, through the development of idioms of characterisation on-screen, to formal theories of film acting.[15] Partly in response to such writing, Ben Brewster and Lea Jacobs have suggested that the tradition of stage pictorialism, rather than the concept of a gestural lexicon as such, provides an inclusive means of accounting for the diverse 'visual repertoire' of fictional early film.[16] Within this repertoire a variety of performance styles found a place during and after the 1910s.

Following Brewster and Jacobs, I also believe that early film fluidly exploited a range of performative repertoires, and that many of these remained active long after the feature film had become the dominant commercial product of the film industry. However, because most studies of acting performance have tended to focus on the industry's developments after 1908, the heterogeneity of earlier film styles has not been their primary concern. Although they first appeared quite early, techniques of dramatic characterisation, in which a performer's identity is subordinated in some way to that of a fictional character, are only sporadically present or, at least, very difficult to unpick from other modes of performance, in the first ten years of British filmmaking. Indeed, as a series of studies have now shown, much early film production disavowed theatrical and fictional conventions altogether in favour of a scenario of the everyday that brought the most mundane of activities to the screen. This enabled filmmakers to market familiar constructions of personhood, which had a value quite different from those promised by theatrical institutions. In place of an emphasis on acting performance, then, a generic notion of self-presentation in relation to the screen promises a more inclusive consideration of screen performance in the years before 1908.

Furthermore, productive as it has been for writers such as Scheide to identify precedents for selected screen practices in earlier entertainment industries, the common functions that these and other modes of self-presentation provided for the film industry have not been widely considered. In particular, the prevalent tendency of early films to experiment with the relationship between screen and audience, regularly bringing new formulations of personality and performance to the screen, requires further explanation. Faced with a new technology of mechanical reproduction, filmmakers and performers quickly brought into being on-screen personae and performance styles that portrayed varied relationships to potential audiences, and these relationships help to explain both the heterogeneity of early film shows and the experience of reassurance that spectators took from them. Attendant on an anxiety that the medium carried only inauthentic shadows of personhood, these intimate communications offered bonds of sympathy and empathy to audiences and proliferated long before discourses on screen acting and stardom were initiated as such. Filmmakers, like exhibitors, understood the value of presence and personality to early audiences, and they therefore adopted the pragmatic commercial strategy of diversifying and formalising the performance styles they brought to the screen.

Performing Presence: Strategies of Self-Presentation in Selected Early Genres

At stake in the moving pictures, as in any primarily visual representational medium, was the possibility of apprehending the world and its people as images, a possibility that depended upon an analogy between the technologically mediated pictures on-screen and the spatial and temporal practices of everyday life. In many respects the success of film was therefore dependent upon its ability to mimic these everyday practices, typically allowing audiences to apply customary cognitive strategies comfortably to their understanding of the individuals and actions depicted upon the screen. A number of characteristic mechanisms for rendering human presence and personality on the screen were adopted—an objective that did not go unobserved even in the earliest notices and catalogue descriptions for the moving pictures, where it was sometimes expressed in admiration for the ingenuity of the medium's inventors, camera operators, or performers. Such descriptions suggest that this new technological mass medium was already at work reconfiguring basic qualities of selfhood and identity. Although its mechanism appeared to guarantee the estrangement of performers and audiences, it also offered valuable opportunities for both parties to manage and regulate their relationship, securing fresh forms of intimacy in place of those

135

guaranteed by their proximity. Thus, as Jonathan Crary has noted, the introduction of visual technologies such as cinema during the late 1890s did not result in a widespread public rejection of such apparently inhuman mechanisms of seeing. Regardless of the fears expressed by some writers, cinema was most often 'hailed as an extension of existing forms of verisimilitude, with its own particular structures of empathy'.[17]

The genre of 'animated portraits' of famous people depended explicitly on the establishment of such intimate relationships, as in another way did the screening of local views and other genres of non-fiction to audiences. When George Albert Smith devoted three films to the actress *Miss Ellen Terry* (1897), he captured her 'at her country cottage window', 'gathering flowers in her garden', and taking 'afternoon tea with a lady friend in the garden'.[18] These scenes were staged for the camera, but Terry's celebrated acting performances were not foregrounded by the catalogue description. Rather, the films were an attempt to reconstruct her personality, or at least an authentic-seeming image of her personality, for distant others. Her pursuit of mundane and domestic normalcy within what the catalogue called 'very characteristic' films staged a model of respectable middle-class behaviour for audiences.[19] On such occasions, the cinematographic apparatus proved as useful for performers as it was entertaining for spectators. Terry did not proffer the still disreputable associations of the woman on the stage, nor did she emphasise her unconventional family life.[20] Instead, an unlikely idyll of untroubled domesticity is represented.

The successful management of the self on-screen was one condition for the emergence of picture personalities in the years following 1908, but the skilful conversion of individuals into filmic personae (and symbolic commodities) had begun much earlier, as the example of Ellen Terry demonstrates. The moving image offered for the first time an ideal vantage point on performance and the opportunity for individuals to adjust—as if in a mirror—the representation of self. It was an opportunity for regulated publicity embraced by no less a personage than Queen Victoria, who appeared in numerous scrupulously staged films in the final years of her reign.[21] In *Scenes at Balmoral*, an unattributed film of 1896, the royal carriage approaches from the background of the gardens before pausing directly before the camera, where the Queen casts a technologically mediated sovereign glance over her subjects. As Richard Brown and Barry Anthony have noted of the British Mutoscope and Biograph Company's royal productions, such films 'conferred on royalty the gift of being both accessible and artificially humanised'.[22] *Scenes at Balmoral* thus reproduces the carefully managed publicity that had characterised the later decades of Victoria's reign, on this occasion also evoking an intriguing sense of an intrusion into her everyday business.

Filmmakers also conspired in this consolidation of the solemn pomp and ceremony of royalty. A series of surviving letters from Charles Urban to varied local authorities and representatives of the royal family testifies to the substantial effort that was involved in securing permission to film them.[23] Although footage could usually only be taken at the discretion of this substantial and bureaucratic publicity apparatus, the rewards could be substantial, and film companies were therefore prepared to invest time and money into securing the best views of major royal events.[24] Victoria's Diamond Jubilee in 1897 and funeral in 1901 were among the most popular of all early film attractions, as the bulk of advertising in these years testifies.[25] Her funeral, in particular, provoked a period of intense competition between major film producers and distributors, including Hepworth and Co., Mitchell and Kenyon, L. Gaumont and Co., Walter Gibbons, and the Prestwich Manufacturing Co., with each promising exhibitors the largest number of views of the procession, the closest shots of the principal mourners, or the coverage of unique scenes, perhaps from outside London (**Fig. 4**).

Most of these companies also took pains to capitalise on the unprecedented public gathering of European royalty and other celebrities at the procession, a strategy that had developed substantially during 1896 and 1897 at events such as Gladstone's funeral and the Coronation of the Queen of Holland.[26] In their six-film series, collectively titled *Funeral of Queen Victoria* (1901), Hepwix claimed that 'in most cases there are portraits of all the important personages who took part in the proceedings and so life-like and well-defined are they that they are easily recognisable'.[27] Notices for Gaumont's *London—Victoria Station* (1901), the third of a five-film series, promised 'the most excellent portraits of considerable duration on the screen' and, like advertising for other companies, emphasised the especially clear views that had been obtained of King Edward, Queen Alexandra and the German Emperor.[28] In addition to bringing the grand scale of the ceremony and the public spectacle of mourning to audiences across the UK, this repeated emphasis on 'life-like and life-size portraits' indicates something of the growing fascination with celebrity in this period.[29] Although, to judge from catalogue listings, royals were by far the most popular of these subjects, animated portraits of celebrated soldiers also became successful during conflicts such as the Boer War, with numerous films of men such as Field Marshall Lord Roberts addressing or presenting decorations to the troops.[30] In *Buller's Last Appearance at Aldershot* (Gaumont, 1901), 'the popular

Funeral of The Queen.

IMPRESSIVE AND SOLEMN SPECTACLE.

SUCCESSFUL AT EVERY POINT.

Absolutely the Finest Pictures of this all-important Event have been secured by me at the following points during the Two Day's Ceremonies:—

THE ISLE OF WIGHT.
ON THE
ROAD FROM OSBORNE.

STARTLING PORTRAITS OF

KING EDWARD VII.,
THE GERMAN EMPEROR,
QUEEN ALEXANDRA,

as every one of these followed Her late Majesty's Body on Foot.

LIFE-LIKE AND LIFE-SIZE PORTRAITS

have in all cases been secured, making a most Valuable Film for Exhibiting Purposes.

THE COFFIN,

covered with a Beautiful White Silk Pall, is a

NOTABLE FEATURE.

Length 105 ft.

The Passage of the Solent

Several Notable Incidents have been secured of this Interesting Spectacle, which are more valuable on account of their being

THE ONLY ONES SECURED.

ROYAL YACHT "ALBERTA,"

with the Queen's Body under the Awning, and the

ROYAL MOURNERS ON BOARD.

Length, 75 ft. to 250 ft.

AT THE MARBLE ARCH.

Favoured by the sunshine here, I have secured a Splendid Picture of the Funeral Cortège, about 350 feet long, practically without a break.

The EIGHT CELEBRATED CREAM HORSES

drawing the

GUN CARRIAGE WITH THE BODY

come slowly into the Middle of the Picture, forming an absolutely perfect photographic record.

Preceded by the Draped Royal Standard.

King Edward VII.
WITH
The German Emperor

by his side, follow as Chief Mourners.   Length 175 ft.

The two parts can be joined without the loss of a single picture.

Then follow:—

Her Majesty
Queen Alexandra

and other Members of the Royal Family in the

FIRST STATE CARRIAGE,

the other Five State Carriages following at intervals.

Length 125 ft.

25/- per 50 ft., or 6d. per foot net.

Look out for Pictures of the King Opening Parliament in State
ON THURSDAY NEXT.

Write or apply immediately, or a Golden Opportunity is lost.   First Come, First Receive!

WALTER GIBBONS, 60 Chandos St., Strand, W.C.

Telegrams: "RANDVOLL!"   Telephone No. 3828 (Gerrard).

Fig. 4 Coverage of unique scenes at the funeral of Queen Victoria. Advertisement for Walter Gibbons' films targeted at the showmen. (*The Showman* (15 February 1901), p. 4). Image courtesy of the National Fairground Archive, Sheffield.

138

General' Sir Redvers Buller was viewed 'while he is standing among a group of officers, and being life like, kindle [*sic.*] much enthusiasm among his many admirers'.[31] Similarly patriotic sentiments were evoked by films of national sporting heroes, such as *Dr. W.G. Grace, Batting* and *Dr W.G. Grace, Bowling* (WTC, 1901). Other sportsmen were presented by filmmakers who specialised in local productions, such as Mitchell and Kenyon, who regularly filmed football matches for exhibition to fans of regional teams.[32]

Like the traditions of portraiture and biographical writing that were proving so popular in contemporary illustrated magazines such as *The Strand* and *The Harmsworth Magazine*, animated portraits such as these promised audiences privileged access to famous individuals. In part, the attraction of these films rested upon the proximity of the camera to its subjects, and catalogue descriptions of films such as *The German Emperor Reviewing his Troops at Fall Manœuvres* (WTC, 1902) indicate the careful staging that was sometimes employed to emphasise this effect:

> In this picture a long line of German troops are seen standing at 'attention'. In the distance and gradually approaching the camera one can see the German Emperor, accompanied by members of his Staff, closely inspecting each man as he passes him. He gradually approaches closer and closer, until finally a most magnificent portrait is obtained. The value of the film is greatly enhanced by the fact that the Kaiser is in the field of the camera for such a long time, thus giving the audience an excellent opportunity of scanning his features. Photographically perfect.[33]

Once permissions had been obtained, films such as these could depict such individuals in intimate detail, even in the course of their most crowded public engagements at home and abroad, on this occasion even dramatising the Kaiser's approach to the camera. But they could also suggest the possibility of bridging other kinds of distance. Regardless of the careful staging of public engagements by filmmakers and their famous subjects, films such as *Miss Ellen Terry* and *Scenes at Balmoral* presented themselves as open invitations into private, often class-restricted, spaces.

In the era of the new King and Queen, the apparent democratising of such spaces and faces continued. The Biograph Company for France's *Their Majesties, Edward VII and Queen Alexandra Starting for a Motor Ride* (1901) reportedly depicted the Queen chatting informally to friends at Fredensburg Castle, then the King appeared in similarly relaxed fashion, pausing to light his cigar. Finally, the two set off in the automobile, whose presence was perhaps intended to mark their embrace of the new century.[34] The chief attraction of Hepworth's *Visit of the King and Queen to Dartmouth to lay the Foundation Stone of the New Naval College* (1902), as one reviewer noted, lay in the performance of the Queen, who 'on entering the carriage turns toward the camera and smiles, as indeed she does on several other occasions'.[35] But, though fostering a sense of inclusion, such films also continued to replicate and reinforce the deference that had been routinely paid to Victorian royals. The Biograph Company affirmed that their film had been taken 'by special permission of their Majesties', and the Hepworth catalogue description suggested that the unique access they had been granted had allowed them to capture 'the finest portraits of their Majesties ever produced'.[36] In doing so, both companies, like Charles Urban, sought to associate themselves with their elevated subjects, and therefore remained complicit with the techniques of self-management and self-presentation that underpinned the market for celebrity.

Subjects of this kind, which were usually advantageous for all concerned, remained popular throughout the early period, into the 1910s and beyond, when the tradition survived on feature programmes in the form of newsreels and other actuality genres.[37] However, the opportunities for good publicity these films afforded did not come without some measure of risk. One observer recalled of the first audiences of royal films in an isolated village that 'it took them some time to recover from the knowledge that their Queen was apparently like any other old lady'.[38] Equally, although the animated portrait genre tended to show off celebrities to their best advantage (thus guaranteeing continued access to them), the industry quickly learned that capturing public figures at inopportune moments, or gently poking fun, could also prove a powerful attraction. For example, the 1897–98 Warwick Trading Company catalogue description of *Russian Officers Attached to the President* emphasised the indulgence of its jovial subjects 'in something stronger than Russian Tea'.[39]

Other genres capitalised directly on the unpredictability of their subjects. We might think here of the antics of individuals, especially children, who played up to the camera within the street, city and industrial scenes typical of local genres: 'there is generally some comical feature that causes much merriment', insinuated one advertisement for local films.[40] In *Boy's Cricket Match and Fight* (Bamforth, c.1900), a supposed actuality scene descends into a fight, but, as in numerous films involving children, several of them forget the roles they have been instructed to play, turning to stare instead at the camera. Similarly, in *Feeding the Pigeons in St Mark's Square* (BMBC, 1898), a young family are caught, supposedly unawares, in the course of their trip to Venice, but the film is enlivened by their little girl who repeatedly stares at the camera, then runs directly towards it. Both films introduce children, whose performances are conventionally coded as 'innocent' and 'authentic', and who are therefore able to expose and exaggerate the artificiality of other modes of role-playing.

Alternatively, the behaviour of individuals unaware of the presence of the camera could contribute to a sense of authenticity, as in many early crowd scenes in local subjects. In 'factory gate' films such as *Workforce of Ormerod's Mill, Great Moor Street, Bolton* (M&K, 1900) or *20,000 Employees Entering Lord Armstrong's Elswick Works* (M&K, 1902), the numerous employees passing before the camera adopt all kinds of attitudes towards it, from fascination, to irritation, to ignorance. Indeed, as Tom Gunning has commented, the sheer variety of strategies of self-presentation in factory gate films represented (and still represents) a key part of their attraction to audiences:

> While frank engagement of the camera is characteristic, this engagement runs a full gamut of styles and attitudes. While these films abound with broad smiles, necks craned to see the camera better, flirtatious poses, waves of hands and caps, bits of performances and attempts to attract attention, we also find their opposites. People hide their faces behind hands or shawls, ignore the camera, regard it sullenly if at all, or stare at it without delivering a quiver of recognition.[41]

Other sub-genres of local filmmaking could deliver still more intimate portraits of certain individuals, picked out by the camera operator perhaps because they typified something about the event or locale of which they were a part. For instance, in the provisionally titled *Children's Sports No. 3* (M&K, 1902), following an example of a childhood rough-and-tumble scene, there is a surprisingly intimate, but powerfully representative, portrait of one little boy, tensely waiting to begin a race. In the fascinating film *Ralph Pringle Interviewing Private Ward, V.C., Leeds Hero* (M&K, 1901), a kind of local Boer War subject, an interview takes place in which the gestures and expressions of the soldier and interviewer are emphatically telegraphed for the camera, as if they were somehow trying to overcome the silence of the image track. Whether or not the substance of this conversation was ever made clear to local audiences during screening, the film certainly exploited Ward's celebrity as a recipient of the Victoria Cross, and thus strained to close the distance between on-screen persona and audience, exaggerating the regional, as well as the patriotic, aspects of self identity that linked them.

Locals thus offered those filmmakers who specialised in this type of production another clear opportunity to capitalise on the capacity of the cinematograph to foster varied bonds of recognition and empathy with their audiences, and to generate relationships that were characterised by intimacy as well as exhibitionism. Some exhibitors purchased camera equipment specifically to produce such shows, whereas others in the boom for these subjects that began in the summer of 1900 depended on hiring operators and equipment, at relatively little expense, from producers like L. Gaumont, Hepworth and Co., The Sheffield Photo Co., or Mitchell and Kenyon.[42] In fact, this type of practice had begun as early as 1897, when Warwick first advertised the availability of travelling operators, who for a little over £3, plus the costs of film and developing, would produce films of what they called 'Special Subjects' for their clients.[43] However, once the distinct attractions of the locals genre had been formally identified within catalogues and reviews, this type of activity became especially profitable for the showmen. During the summer of 1901, *The Showman* reported that A.D. Thomas' show at the Curson Hall, Birmingham, which included 'living pictures of principal thoroughfares on a busy day; workers leaving factories; and interesting movements of sport, military, and social activity as carried on in everyday life within the city', had already attracted over 275,000 people, and was likely to continue its run.[44] This degree of popularity fell away in the UK after 1902, and though the *The Kinematograph and Lantern Weekly* promoted their use to exhibitors quite frequently during 1907 and 1908, the journal also bemoaned the fact that 'local subjects are not sufficiently utilised'.[45] Nonetheless, Stephen Bottomore has demonstrated that local films persisted in some travelling shows, then picture palaces, until at least 1912.[46]

In part, this degree of early success is explained by the unique and novel manner in which these films brought the faces of friends and neighbours to local screens. As the Hepworth Company advertised, exhibitors were virtually guaranteed the custom of those captured on film and 'all their friends and relatives', and in turn these spectators were guaranteed a fleeting glimpse of themselves under conditions partially of their own making.[47] This scenario was regularly dramatised in reviews and advertisements for local films and film shows, which therefore tended to emphasise the highly personal investments their audiences had in these scenes. According to *The Showman*, 'the big draw' of 'Lawrence's World-famed Electrograph' at the 1900 Belper annual fair 'was a local film of the Belper mill hands leaving work; and I must say it was rather amusing to be inside when they were showing this one, as you kept hearing the refrain (*ad lib.*), "Oh, there's our Mary!" "Oh, that's little Sally Smith!" etc'.[48] In 1902, a review in *The Music*

Hall and Theatre Review of Professor Ball's Bioscope Show at Reading Fair also described a loud public reaction to locals, concluding that, 'the shouts of the audience on recognising familiar scenes and faces testified to the popularity of such experiments'.[49] As we have seen, this type of interactive response to moving pictures was far from unprecedented in fairground shows, and, in fact, had traditionally been one of the key attractions of a visit to one. Responding primarily to this market, the Warwick Trading Company therefore suggested to exhibitors that audiences would 'flock to your exhibit in order to see themselves and their friends reproduced on the screen'.[50] Similarly, the Hepworth Company's *The Strikers at Grimsby* (1901), which showed the crowds surging during the strike, was presented by one reviewer as a specialised form of local rather than a news item of national interest: 'To those who are acquainted with the actors in the dispute, it will be of interest to recognise them, or some of them, in the crowds which pass by, and faces are distinctly seen, rendering them easily recognizable.'[51]

The repeated dramatisation of this kind of scenario by various representatives of the early industry suggests that, as in animated portraiture, the ability to recognise the screen's subjects was an important feature of the spectator's enjoyment of locals. But this relationship between audience and screen was also clearly distinguished from that fostered by other actuality genres, since it suggested that the technology of moving pictures served specific communities, families and individuals. As the showmen, who had long experience of addressing local crowds, knew best, this could be invaluable for the developing industry, because it allowed audiences to claim a degree of ownership over at least some of the cinematograph's productions. In particular, because local films gave all of their subjects limited opportunities to manage their appearance on-screen, it also allowed them to feel that, though they could not share in the growing media expertise associated with *fin de siècle* celebrity culture, they might yet exercise some small measure of control over supposedly runaway technologies such as the cinematograph. The films seem to have offered to anonymous spectators a glimpse of the inclusive, interactive, even democratic possibilities for film spectatorship, which Walter Benjamin would later identify as the key opportunity afforded by mechanical reproduction.[52]

For a brief period at the beginning of the twentieth century, this kind of relationship between audience and screen possessed considerable institutional value. These productions, which were a substantial part of the growing marketplace for moving pictures, exemplified the general tendency for early film institutions to foster a degree of showman-like expertise in their audiences, flattering them that they too could make important contributions to

143

the rapid development of this new mass medium. A similar function was served by allowing spectators to take a degree of control over the cinematographic apparatus itself, bringing moving pictures directly into the home. Between 1899 and 1903, companies such as Gaumont, the British Mutoscope and Biograph Company, the Warwick Trading Company, and the Charles Urban Trading Company made substantial investments in domestic devices such as the Kinora and the Biokam, intended primarily for sale to the growing, increasingly leisured middle class.[53] By 1902, Warwick was selling Biokam projectors at £2 and a wide selection of minute-long versions of their own films, including a number of celebrity animated portraits, were available at six shillings apiece. For amateurs who wished to produce their own moving pictures, the Biokam 'combined Cinematograph and Snap-shot Camera, Printer, Projector, Enlarger and Reverser' was available for just over £3.[54] Meanwhile, Londoners could already obtain short animated portraits of themselves and their families from Biograph's specially equipped Kinora studio on Regent Street, and by 1903, they could bring home flickbook versions of these scenes.[55]

Highly customised films like locals and Kinora portraits enabled early producers to exploit regional and domestic markets, in spite of the industrial centralisation that underpinned their businesses. They also provided audiences with further reassurance that the cinematograph afforded new opportunities for them to reinsert themselves into familiar relationships with the individuals on-screen. As in the case of animated portraits, they tended to reinforce constructions of self-identity and personality with which spectators were already familiar, and were therefore complicit with the institutional imperative to generate stable, predictable relationships with consumers. Other genres of early film accomplished much the same effect by drawing upon the existing, stable performance regimes associated with earlier entertainment institutions, such as music hall, magic theatre and fairground. This was a substantial resource for the early film industry, which was quick to capitalise on the existing diversity of professional performers by bringing them to the attention of national and international audiences. Sometimes the attraction of these films rested on a simple demonstration of skill: jugglers, acrobats, athletes, strongmen and boxers made regular appearances in early film programmes. More frequently, filmmakers took big name performers from the variety theatres and other entertainment venues, fully exploiting their celebrity status as well as their talent.

Variety artists were among the first subjects to become popular on the screen, appearing widely from early 1896 in the music halls.[56] Though the novelty of such films fell away quickly in many of the halls—perhaps because they seemed redundant in shows that already substantially depended on live variety performances—their appeal remained across the full range of early exhibition venues.[57] By 1902, Warwick listed a wide variety of the most famous of them under the subheading, 'Dramatic and professional person-ages, music hall turns &c'.[58] Favourite subjects included the strongman, Eugene Sandow, and comedians such as Dan Leno, Herbert Campbell, Will Evans, Little Tich and Harry Tate, all of whom had a national or interna-tional reputation that proved extremely valuable to filmmakers. In most of these films, the performer would re-enact short, highly physical, set pieces, drawing from their most characteristic sketches: Sandow lifted a horse; Will Evans performed an unlikely tumbling routine as the 'Living Catherine Wheel'; Harry Tate delivered impersonations of other famous music hall artists. Furthermore, the relatively close framing of these films ensured that it would also be possible to reproduce the tradition of direct address that characterised many forms of music hall performance. In *Amann, The Great Impersonator* (BMBC, 1899), the protean entertainer Ludwig Amann, pauses between his impressions of Dreyfuss and Emile Zola, in order to deliver a series of bows directly to the camera. Similarly, the remarkable, energetic tumbling performance of *Will Evans, the Musical Eccentric* (WTC, 1899) is punctuated with smiles clearly intended for distant audiences. In *Little Tich and his Big Boots* (Gaumont, 1902), the diminutive comedian (real name, Harry Relph) runs rapidly through a series of his most popular routines, including a burlesque skirt dance and an ingenious balancing act involving his trademark extra-long boots. Although the film presented a varied series of attractions to audiences, continuities were marked, once again, by Relph's repeated looks to camera, which here emphasised his playful attitude to his own performance.

To audiences today, the formal simplicity of this device is a self-evident part of the appeal of these films; Scheide notes that performers such as Relph are 'able to cross the decades and *confront* the contemporary viewer'.[59] But its significance for early viewers, who had most likely experienced at first hand the subtle permutations of music hall traditions of direct address, was likely to be rather more nuanced than this. According to Harry Randall, another variety star at the turn of the century, the point of this exhibitionist, self-aggrandising style in music hall had been to engender a focused, convivial relationship with audiences, but one which might be clearly differ-entiated from that of other performers on the programme:

> Many theatrical critics have admitted that it takes a clever man to be a 'solus' performer, as music hall artists are—or were. He was not like the

145

actor in a play where, perhaps, he was talked of long before he entered, or as the Irishman said: 'He was there before he arrived'. Personality and individuality played a prominent part in a 'single turn'. He had to create his own 'atmosphere', and work to gain the attention of his audience— and keep it![60]

The business of variety depended substantially on the abilities of performers to foster, in only a short space of time, a sense of familiarity and ease among the socially diverse members of a music hall audience: a practice aptly described by Peter Bailey as 'the friendly exploitation of mutuality'.[61] This type of relationship had traditionally depended upon the potential for direct interaction between the audience and the stage, which made of music hall shows a highly improvisatory, potentially noisy affair. But, as theatre historians have pointed out, the marked gentrification of the halls that took place from the mid-1880s would also occasion the prohibition—by consensus or force—of many of these interactive practices, and a new tendency to emphasise visual aspects of performance.[62] Conditioned to an increasingly silent, passive form of spectatorship in the grand new theatres of variety in the 1890s, it became increasingly important to audiences that alternative means were found to entertain equally convivial, rewarding relationships with performers. In a variety of ways, the big stars of music hall in the late 1890s accomplished just this: they instantly established what Randall called an 'atmosphere' within the theatres, somehow generating distinctive, personalised forms of intimacy with a mass public, in spite of the professional distance that had grown between them. Dan Leno, the greatest star of the variety theatre at the turn of the century, was a talented dancer, burlesque artist, and 'gagger', but according to Randall his greatest skill lay in his free flowing repartee, and especially his ability 'to convulse an audience with a look'.[63]

The specific institutional configuration of late century variety theatre therefore offers us one more explanation for the success of variety performers on the early screen. Unlike performers in the legitimate theatre, stars of the halls had developed a number of eloquent mechanisms for projecting personality, individuality and charm directly to their silent audiences. This proved uniquely valuable in moving pictures, in which the separation of performer and audience was an unavoidable attribute of the medium's operation and in which, for a few years at least, it was equally necessary to foster a productive relationship with audiences in only a short span of time. While capitalising fully on the spell cast by these celebrities, films of their performances also sought to echo the richness of the performative regimes they drew from, emphasising especially the most distinctive and expressive comic routines. For example, the physicality and self-deprecating playfulness of Dan Leno's comedy is strongly emphasised in catalogue descriptions of his films, leading the Warwick catalogue to advise potential exhibitors that 'no matter what Dan Leno does, it is funny'.[64] Furthermore, because the cinematograph could follow performers such as Leno beyond the proscenium of the variety stage, it could potentially add a new resonance to old routines. In *Mr Dan Leno, Assisted by Mr. Herbert Campbell, Editing the 'Sun'* (BMBC, 1902), the famous music hall partnership was pictured on the day the newspaper had reportedly handed them the editorship.[65] As the catalogue explained, the film replicated one of their celebrated comedy punch-ups, thus reinforcing the self-deprecatory nature of their slapstick while gently poking fun at the authority of the office they had been foolishly allowed to occupy.

The attractions of films such as these were likely to be as varied as the performers that were their subjects, but, as in animated portraits and local films, variety turns on-screen also shared a capacity to foster a very specific sense of inclusion among their audiences. Thus, even films featuring the apparently straightforward 'skirt dances' of Loie Fuller and her imitators— films which emerged from the US vaudeville tradition and represented a single body in motion on the screen—engendered a surprising variety of interpretive responses, including those that found such performances exemplary of New Womanhood, or of a newly technologised human body.[66] Such possibilities for inclusion, if not interactivity, during early film shows were only reinforced by the development of various technologies for synchronising sound and image. Although most of these systems did not become practicable for the marketplace, from 1896, sound-on-disc systems like Edison's Kinetophone had accompanied the screening of silent films to British audiences.[67] Descriptions of such devices in the trade press regularly emphasised the enhanced realism of the films.[68] In November 1900, the prominent music hall film exhibitor, Walter Gibbons, introduced his Phono Bio-Tableaux at the London Hippodrome, and met with considerable success.[69] As one reviewer recorded, the show included scenes of the fire brigade turning out, a perennial favourite of early programmes, and further actuality scenes of the opening of a railway station, in which, 'one *hears* as well as sees the lusty welcome accorded to the gallant C.I.V's by the crowds'.[70] However, the review continued, 'perhaps the best examples of the new machine . . . are the representations of the American Comedy Four in two of their most popular songs, "Sally in our Alley" and the "Cornfields Quartette", in which it is difficult to believe that one is not really enjoying the performance of these talented artists'.

As in conventional films depicting music hall performances, the performance of presence was a vital aspect of these early sound films, and advertisements and reviews for them repeatedly strained to express this abstract idea. From 1902, the Gaumont Chronophone, would also produce a high proportion of song titles drawn directly from the halls, and these again attracted flattering reviews for the device.[71] On the competitive fairground circuit, where the exhibition of singing and talking pictures proved, as one commentator put it, 'a feature of immense pulling power', William Taylor's show was one of the first to exploit the Chronophone.[72] Pat Collins' and William Haggar's Bioscope shows, among others, employed an improved Chronophone from about 1907.[73] In 1907, the singing pictures at the London Hippodrome, now furnished by the Gaumont Chronomegaphone (a louder version of the apparatus), were drawing flattering notices in *The Kinematograph and Lantern Weekly*, which also regularly promoted the use of sound effects or the provision of live dialogue—techniques that had been sporadically popular among some exhibitors for a number of years.[74] As the journal advised in its account of one cinematograph show, the use of such techniques had 'added verisimilitude to the scene to an almost incredible degree'.[75]

Such notices evidence the contradictory status of most new cinematic technologies, which have routinely promised to deliver a more convincing impression of presence on the screen while actually supplementing the process of mediation.[76] In early film, this re-embedding of face-to-face social relations into conditions that were outside the social context of dialogue took numerous forms, which have often appeared experimental or primitive with teleological hindsight. But films of celebrities, local characters, or music hall stars were, in fact, exemplary of the capacity of the cinematograph to reproduce sophisticated modes of address that audiences already understood and cherished. Such relationships diversified rapidly and, arguably, the multiple genres of early film developed a social space more complex and varied than any offered by the cinemas that were to follow. The significance of such relationships is neatly summed up by Bailey, whose conclusions concerning early twentieth-century British music hall could, with equal felicity, be applied to the early film industry:

> People fashion affective relationships within the most depersonalised social systems; conversely, the appeal of amiable inclusion is likely to be a necessary interpellation or hook in any scheme that seeks to make a business out of pleasure. This was certainly true for Billy Holland and the other big men of London music hall who made friendship a powerful engine of a new form of capitalism—capitalism with a beaming human face.[77]

But the cinematograph's mechanism of 'amiable inclusion' had other resources to call upon than the skilled presentation of selfhood on-screen. Although models of theatrical performance were only popularised on the screen in the years after 1908, early films had exploited the interpellative potential of dramatic characterisation from the beginning, seeking to stitch spectators into relationships with characters that rested on a quite different set of premises.

Dramatic Characterisation and Performance Styles in Early Fiction Films

As the foregoing discussion has argued, strategies of self-presentation before the camera had a pervasive influence on the styles and genres of early film. However, while each of these genres thrived on the notion that they were somehow capturing an authentic model of selfhood for distant audiences, they were each also exploiting a series of relatively stable performative regimes. This was readily apparent in the case of the variety genre, in which a self-reflexive attitude to the performance of selfhood had always been a key attraction. In celebrity and local films the staging of personality, whether delivering an intimate portrait of royalty or a simple smile to camera as a worker left a factory, was much more difficult to discern because it was more closely tied to practices of self-presentation in which audiences were already complicit. However, role-playing, as sociologists such as Erving Goffmann and theorists of performativity such as Judith Butler have regularly pointed out, is an intrinsic part of the constitution of the self and the conduct of social life, and in this sense all early film productions can be characterised in terms of their implicit or explicit theatricality. In this broad sense, even those individuals in local films who chose to ignore or hide from the camera were actually adopting a performative attitude directed towards it and the film's potential spectators.

This diversity and fluidity of role-playing practices was a highly productive resource for the fledgling industry. Indeed, the unstable generic constitution of the early industry ensured that, as genres hybridised and diversified, the presentation of selfhood in films such as celebrity or local subjects quickly became entangled in more self-consciously theatrical regimes. Thus, when music hall stars entered actuality scenes, as in Warwick's *One Mile Champion Belt Race* (c.1900), audiences were presumably left to unpick the star personae of these performers from their earnest attempts to win the race.[78] However, although the industry thrived on the continual intermixing of styles and genres of performance, traditions of dramatic characterisation, in which the individuals on-screen openly played fictional roles for the camera, were also routinely distinguished from those genres which presented supposedly authentic versions of selfhood to audiences. The dominant convention of genres described in the catalogues as 'comic', 'humorous', 'dramatic' or 'trick' subjects was to interpose the fourth wall between performer and camera, partially enclosing the films' performers in a self-contained world only indirectly connected to that inhabited by spectators. The explicit acknowledgment of the conditions of filming and screening, most obviously delivered by the look at the camera, was utilised more sporadically and indirectly in such films, perhaps to foster a heightened degree of empathy for a particular character, to punctuate a key narrative point, or to emphasise a spectacular aspect of the film's staging. Such glances still held the possibility of closing the distance between the instances of filming and screening, but here they generated the audience's sense of inclusion within an explicitly fictional landscape.

Although styles of dramatic characterisation in these genres now sometimes appear relatively simple, untheorised and spontaneous, quite unlike the traditions of acting performance in legitimate theatre, they still required audiences to apply considerable expertise concerning earlier entertainment forms, such as variety sketches and magic lantern shows. Even in films such as *King John* (BMBC, 1899), which brought the death scene famously played at Her Majesty's Theatre by Herbert Beerbohm Tree to British and American audiences, the tradition of legitimate theatre is not the only relevant performative context to consider. In fact, the performance of similar sensational theatrical scenes had been widely practised in variety theatres in the USA for some time, and this arguably had at least an indirect influence on filmed versions of scenes, like those produced by the international Mutoscope and Biograph group, that were marketed overseas.[79] Equally, Burrows has argued that the British Mutoscope and Biograph Company's prolific 1898–1902 film productions featuring theatrical scenes, of which *King John* was a part, might be experienced by audiences in much the same way as news reports or as trailers concerning the stage production.[80] They could also be regarded as 'Animated Picture Postcards', complementing British Biograph's own sideline business in portrait shots and postcards by presenting elaborate animated portraits of celebrity actors in performance to audiences.[81]

Therefore, the comparative absence of discourses concerned specifically with legitimate theatrical performance in the period before 1908 does not imply, as Richard deCordova has suggested, that the 'economy' of spectatorial engagement with early forms of screen performance 'precluded . . . an attention to the human labour involved in the production of film'.[82] In fact, the wide variety of performance styles associated with different entertainments in the 1890s was another substantial resource for filmmakers, who fully understood the significance of translating these sophisticated, highly institutionalised routines into recognisable screen practices. For example, the staging, costuming, and gestural language of life model lantern slides could deliver a great deal of information to audiences, and early filmmakers familiar with these techniques tended to translate these to moving pictures.

Defined by Richard Crangle as 'a photographic representation of human figures in a fictional context, usually in costume and poses representing characters of an extended fictional narrative', life model sequences were used both within general entertainments and by specific interest groups such as religious, political and temperance organisations, who found these visual fictions to be an eloquent method of persuasion.[83] Unsurprisingly, early film producers were equally keen to develop these markets, and they exploited existing styles of lantern presentation in order to accomplish this. The two major producers of life model slides, Bamforth and Co. and York and Son, had already developed diverse genres to suit all such requirements, categorising them in their lists in a manner that prefigured the catalogues of early film producers. As *The Optician and Photographic Trades Review* suggested in 1899 of Bamforth's catalogue of life model slides (which it also supplemented in the same issue), these genre productions could establish an excellent rapport with varied audiences:

> We expect thousands of hungry little street urchins will be gazing open-mouthed at the wonders unfolded by these works of art, for such they are. And not only the urchins of the street, but the pampered pets of happier homes will also receive enlightenment, enjoyment and pleasure from these slides. Even the oldest of us will become rejuvenated when we gaze at the antics of the various clowns, animals, etc., etc. And even the hardest of us with wills as stubborn as a mule, and hearts as stubborn as lead will be touched by the portrayal through Mr. Bamforth's slides of the wife or the lover, the working man and the drunkard.[84]

This description, designed to advertise the key attractions of a Bamforth slide show to a readership of potential amateur and professional lecturers, emphasised the quality of the slides and especially the ability of their models to move distant audiences. Thus, although Bamforth's slides were almost always sold with a highly expressive reading or song and, in fact, were usually staged in order to capitalise on existing verbal material of this kind, their

a   b

Fig. 5a-d Pictured unawares. Undemonstrative performance styles and artificial settings in the life model lantern sequence, 'Sarah's Christmas Pudding.' Various annotations to be found on the slides themselves indicate that these have been reordered several times, and were part of a longer sequence, suggesting that they

capacity to establish affective relationships, which special interest groups so prized in the lantern, was most strongly associated with the staging of emotionally nuanced attitudes and interactions on the screen.

As *The Photogram* reported in two articles in 1899, this effect was not accomplished without the skilled and creative management of lantern scenes by men such as James Bamforth.[85] The models themselves, who were amateurs drawn almost entirely from the small town of Holmfirth where Bamforth and Co. were based, coupled with the skilled arrangement of these individuals on-screen, helped to ensure that these scenes appeared familiar, relevant and realistic to the audiences they sought to address:

> To most genre photographers the task of making pictures from such models would seem hopeless, yet a great deal of James Bamforth's success depends upon his skill in adapting himself to untrained material. The very personality of his sitters forced him to choose homely stories as his themes, and the very nature of the stories with the unaffected naturalness of the figures in the illustrations has endeared his life model sets to millions of children and of 'the masses'. These critics are strong realists with no great amount of 'art' prejudice, hence they at once

152

c

d

may have accompanied alternative narratives for successive lanternists. Images courtesy of the Bill Douglas Centre for the History of Cinema and Popular Culture, Exeter.

recognise a 'real' policeman, and like him much better than the policeman of the opera stage or the artist's studio.[86]

Leaving aside the characterisation of 'children' and of 'the masses' here, whose tastes appear to have been exercised just as liberally by less mundane representations, this does seem an accurate description of the staging of much life model lantern production, in which the necessity of telegraphing strong emotional content was tempered by the use of models untrained in dramatic gestural techniques. For example, the brief, unattributed life model sequence, *Sarah's Christmas Pudding*, simply depicts the return of a father to his working-class home with good news for his wife and daughter. The postures adopted throughout are undemonstrative, and successfully give the impression—in spite of the self-evident artificiality of the lodgings—that this idealised working-class family have been pictured unawares in their own domestic space (**Fig. 5**). In the spectacular 1890s Bamforth sequence, *How Jane Conquest Rang the Bell*, a woman must decide between staying at home to nurse her sick child and heading into a blizzard to save a burning ship. Such scenes frequently made liberal use of special effects, but the posing of the figures does just enough to convey the melodramatic potential of the plot, again doing little to suggest a pantomimic display that might openly acknowledge camera or audience.

Life model slide sequences therefore negotiated a tricky balancing act, staging apparently naturalistic performances from models within productions that depended explicitly upon artificial aspects of staging, framing, and effects. This style of representation, which enabled audiences to recognise and identify with qualities of experience depicted on-screen, was also characteristic of some modes of fictional early film production. For example, films such as *Wedding Ceremony in a Church* (GAS, 1900) and *Santa Claus* (GAS, 1898) also coupled rather inexpensive looking backdrops with an undemonstrative performance style that obeyed the 'fourth wall' convention. *Wedding Ceremony in a Church*, which simply depicted a wedding ceremony (conducted, however, in about thirty seconds), reproduced a sense of everydayness with which varied audiences could potentially identify. It is possible to discern here possibilities for naturalistic forms of characterisation—a style of performance usually associated with the legitimate theatre and with the moving picture in its post-1908 developments.[87] *Santa Claus* also capitalises on this relationship, but like more spectacular life model sequences, it also introduces a trick effect when Santa's supernatural appearance on a rooftop is depicted in a matte, while two children sleep on the other side of the frame. It is likely that contemporary audiences would initially have read the matte as a dream image, as was the convention in lantern productions (the Warwick catalogue described it as a 'dream vision'), so the implication was that the film simply represented a treasured moment of childhood experience.[88] Such films were likely to engender a knowing appreciation of familiar scenes in their audiences, based upon the recognition of common, if rather idealised, models of everyday experience.

The attraction of this type of performance style and mundane subject matter was not lost on filmmakers and distributors, who sometimes emphasised in their catalogues that such films did not depend upon overblown or pantomimic acting performances. For example, this was a feature of R.W. Paul's early fiction productions that the Warwick Trading Company repeatedly emphasised in an 1898 catalogue supplement, describing a series of these films as 'perfectly acted and natural', 'naturally acted', 'comic, but natural', and so forth.[89] Paul's *Come Along Do!* (1898), which was listed among these, exemplifies this type of performance style. In the opening scene, an old couple outside an exhibition building quietly settle down for lunch, but their performances are so undemonstrative that they attract little more attention from spectators than do other passers-by. Only in the second scene, when they enter the exhibition, does the subject become clear: the old man is led away by his wife when he catches a glimpse of a statue of Venus.[90] Thus, though the film enacts a fairly routine gag, the overwhelming tendency of its performances is to suggest a simple, humorous episode extracted from everyday life. As in the case of life model sequences, although this film developed an openly fictional scenario, it also called upon the audience's recognition of models of 'authentic' selfhood, reflecting qualities of everyday experience which they felt they already understood. This powerful sentiment could also be exploited by films that drew on social themes, such as Paul's *Buy Your Own Cherries* (1904), which was directly adapted from a lantern entertainment regularly produced by temperance groups, in which a miserable young family finds happiness once its head renounces the bottle. As in Paul's earlier productions, its performance style seems largely restrained and naturalistic, perhaps seeking to foster identification in working-class audiences. However, on this occasion, as in earlier versions of the story, this affective relationship with audiences was mobilised in order to further promote a social agenda.

Significant as life model production seems to have been, other types of lantern slide production had a quite different influence on performance styles in early film. For example, the fast and furious action of the 1899 Bamforth and Co. film, *Women's Rights*, in which two gossips (played by men) have their skirts nailed to a fence by two men, was adapted directly from a drawn lantern slide sequence of the same name, first published by Bamforth in 1888. As is well known, the slide sequence and the film played out a straightforward joke on the women's movement, a routine gag which apparently required little more from the chief protagonists than the ability to strike a series of conventional poses.[91] But the poses and costumes in the film were drawn from a longstanding and complex system of caricature and typage, which the lantern had done much to popularise and disseminate, and which clearly signalled to audiences that they were supposed to read stereotypical gender characteristics, such as feminine fickleness or hysteria, into the film's performances. Equally, the hysterical movements of the two women upon discovering their predicament, in which they wrench frantically at their dresses and make beseeching gestures directed at the audience as much as at their tormentors, seems to borrow more obviously from the overblown theatrics of variety comedy sketches. This film therefore carried a quite different set of associations for audiences than the tradition of life model lantern recitations would suggest. Its value, for much of the audience, at least, did not depend on identifying with these self-reflexively theatrical performances, but in recognising and approving the popularly held prejudices and stereotypes the film played out.

155

Although performances in films such as this did not routinely include the look at the camera, as Frank Kessler and Sabine Lenk have demonstrated, the pantomimic traditions of gesture they exploited often verged on direct acknowledgement of the audience.[92] In pre-1908 British film this highly telegraphed performance style is regularly found within comic genres, where pantomimic ability often fostered the collusion of audiences with gags or practical jokes. In the Hepworth Manufacturing Company's comedy, *Poison or Whiskey?* (1904), a spurned lover drinks from a bottle and collapses in apparent pain, thus regaining the attentions of his paramour. Unfortunately, the surviving copy of this film is incomplete, so the punchline suggested by the title remains implicit. However, in the sequence that remains, the comically exaggerated pantomime of the 'death scene' is compromised by a smile, visible to spectators, playing across the lips of the trickster. The convention of dramatic irony was therefore enacted in such a way that the trick practiced upon the lady victim of the ruse might be conspiratorially shared with audiences. As in *Women's Rights*, and numerous other early British films, spectators were included as confidants of a sexist joke played out between male and female characters. Similar relationships were also implied by George Albert Smith's *Hanging out the Clothes* (1897), *The Old Maid's Valentine* (1900), and *Let Me Dream Again* (1900). The 1913 film, *Milling the Militants; A Comical Absurdity* (Clarendon Film Company), in which a husband dreams of putting a stop to the suffragette movement, suggests that such attitudes remained significant in some genre productions. Other films reversed the direction of this gender-based humour. In Haydon and Urry's *The Bride's First Night* (1898), for example, a young bride undresses, unaware that her husband is watching from behind a screen. The voyeuristic identification with the husband, itself a characteristic convention typified by keyhole films at this time, is disturbed when the bride turns over to sleep, leaving her husband to kneel beside the bed in a gesture of frantic supplication. On such occasions we might agree with Miriam Hansen that 'even when the woman is reduced to an object of prurient anticipation' the female performer may yet 'add a twist to an otherwise sad joke'.[93] Similarly, at the end of *Milling the Militants; A Comical Absurdity*, the wife responds to her husband's dream by tipping a bucket of water over him.

Performances of this kind were thus complicit with a set of deeply engrained social and class distinctions, which were not likely to challenge the attitudes and prejudices of their audiences, but did occasionally offer an opportunity to play with such distinctions. Other stock characters in early film elicited further, highly conventional, relationships with audiences, and these could also playfully reinforce prevalent social constructions of gender, race, age and class identity. Drawing from the pervasive mid- to late-nineteenth-century tradition of comic typage, which was a common feature of popular literary traditions, the periodical press and music hall, as well as magic lantern entertainments, early filmmakers had a wide range of such well-known personae to choose from. From the caricatures of 'new men' and 'new women' taken from the pages of *Punch* to the Champagne Charlies of the music hall stage, the audience's existing stock of knowledge about these figures meant they could be flexibly inserted into old and new narratives.

For example, the mischievous child proved as popular a subject in fictional filmmaking as it did in locals and other actuality genres. In Smith's *The House that Jack Built* (1900), a boy knocks over his little sister's toy house piece by piece, before the film reverses and he appears to rebuild it. In *When Daddy Comes Home* (Hepworth, 1902), two boys create a human figure from a punchball, fooling their drunken father into attempting to make conversation with it. Practical jokes were also the subject of *Our New Errand Boy* (Williamson, 1905), which represented a series of pranks played upon a policeman, a curate and other representatives of authority, concluding with a close up of the boy laughing. By the end of the 1900s, films such as *When Mamma's Out* (Precision Film Company, 1909), in which children create chaos in the kitchen, and *The New Baby* (Walturdaw, 1910), in which a young girl makes a comic attempt to dispose of her new brother, illustrate that this type of character had remained popular.

Criminal or tramp personae also proved to have an enduring appeal. In Bamforth's *Weary Willie* (1898), an occupied park bench is cleared by the eponymous tramp; Willie leers intrusively at its occupants and breathes smoke into their faces before sprawling full length across it with an exaggerated show of fainéancy.[94] More often, such figures operate as simple plot devices, as in *Rescued by Rover* (Hepworth, 1905) and *Oh! That Cat* (Gaumont, 1907) in which the vagabonds kidnap a baby and steal a cat, respectively. *Winky and the Dwarf* (Bamforth, 1914), one of a series of films starring the playful Winky character, played further on the convention of the criminal vagrant, subjecting an innocent tramp to a number of pranks, but ultimately allowing him to take revenge on some of his tormentors.

As such examples indicate, stock characters, whose performances could be reduced to a few persistent signifiers (the child's exaggerated laughter; the tramp's bottle), coexisted with less demonstrative performance styles intended to chime with popular constructions of naturalness or everydayness. The two versions of *The Kiss in the Tunnel* made in 1899, films which have more often been celebrated for their use of techniques suggestive of continuity editing, exemplify this distinction between naturalistic and pantomimic modes of address to audiences.[95] In George Albert Smith's version, thought likely to have been the first, the faltering, uncertain, stolen kiss suggests the nervousness of the couple: perhaps this is the end of several months of anxious courtship, or perhaps this is part of some coy marital ritual played out by the lovers. In Riley Brothers' version, the kiss is more demonstrative and lengthy, offering to spectators a coded suggestion of promiscuous sexuality. Smith's film thus interposes the fourth wall and seems to open a perspective onto an everyday, but private, moment, whereas the later film communicates taboo but stereotypical actions in a pantomimic style that undercuts the possibility for naturalistic characterisation. Although representing the same subject, carrying an identical title, appearing in the same year, and composed by the same shot structure, these films therefore differed crucially in terms of the performance regimes they drew from. One might imagine the different approaches a film lecturer would be obliged to adopt when presenting them. As well as exploiting strategies of self-presentation on the screen, filmmakers such as Smith and Riley Brothers therefore drew flexibly from a mixed set of repertoires associated with earlier traditions of dramatic characterisation.

This mixed repertoire persisted during the early period and through into the 1910s. By 1908, however, *The Bioscope* reported that for 'large manufacturers' at least, a new generation of professional screen actors had largely displaced the use of amateurs, and that this professionalisation of the industry had contributed to the growing consolidation of genre definitions according to performance style:

> It is true that pantomimic ability is a necessary requirement for the successful portrayal of parts in moving picture productions, but strictly speaking this applies to comedy parts. There are a number of pantomimists who have contributed largely to the production of comedy films, but the percentage of these who have also figured with success in dramatic subjects is very small. The same rule applies to the moving picture stage as that relating to regular theatrical performers. Those who can fill roles from comedy to drama can be counted on the fingers of one hand. So it is when work is required before the camera. Certain people are selected for comedy roles and others for the more serious and heavy work, and the same care and attention is given to the selection of these people as that devoted by those who assign the parts for the regular stage productions.[96]

The pantomimic acknowledgement of the audience often played out by stock characters and stereotypes would remain a significant feature of many comedy films throughout the 1910s and beyond. Conversely, the growing dominance and public visibility of feature filmmaking during the 1910s generated a new body of advice for would-be screen actors, openly advocating a naturalistic playing style that permitted more intimate scrutiny of individual faces and gestures.[97] Though this advice began appearing regularly from the mid-1910s, the industry itself had already acknowledged and conceptualised this approach to performance. In a fascinating 1911 account of a film rehearsal at the British Production Department of Pathé Frères, *The World's Fair* was already explaining that, as opposed to acting on the stage, 'for picture purposes, it has been discovered that the fewer and the more deliberate the gestures the better'.[98]

In many early fiction films, the resolution of the mixed repertoire of performance styles and modes of self-presentation remained dependent (as it always must) upon the instance of exhibition and spectatorship, but we may minimally conclude that it predicated multiple possibilities for establishing connections of empathy and identification in audiences. From moment to moment, spectators fluidly adjusted and readjusted to competing and slippery personae, whose attractions were both varied and compelling. Such films exemplify the capacity of the early industry to generate a sense of inclusion for their varied audiences, because they do not hinge upon the symmetry of any single performance, but seek instead to elicit a range of possible effects for these audiences. By contrast, those films that focussed especially upon the facial expressions of performers, perhaps offering only the intimate expressions of a single human face, did appear to extend such symmetry. However, they also tended to undermine the straightforward model of communication they seemed to propose.

Representation of the Face in Early British Film

The face was at once the most communicative and intangible of objects to be captured by the cinematograph. This is because its interpretation is not usually conducted in a conscious or openly theorised manner: in fact, under normal communicative circumstances, this process is not experienced as a form of work at all.[99] Nonetheless, the ability to produce or read facial expressions is an acquired skill that invisibly generates complex possibilities for the communication of selfhood. Furthermore, if this communication is conducted effectively, it articulates a version of selfhood that somehow appears more genuine than that associated with verbal and other languages. 'The face is the mirror of the mind', declared one 1896 physiognomic work, and 'the eyes of men converse as much as their tongues, with the advantage that the ocular dialect needs no dictionary, but is understood all the world over'.[100] For early filmmakers, the face was therefore an extremely important resource. Without the establishment of an elaborate narrative or the development of an extensive and consistent set of editing and staging conventions, the face promised the ability to express eloquently to an international audience a wide range of emotional and psychological content, and to do so without stretching well-practised, everyday or theatrical conventions of face-to-face communication. Indeed, representation of the face in early film exemplified the tendency of the apparatus to confirm, interrogate and challenge constructions of identity that audiences so cherished.

Although it was not always easy to pick out individual faces from the many that might appear on the screen, and though these individuals often had to compete with live performers, facework in film promised qualities of intimacy quite unlike those associated with other media and performance traditions. Unlike static media such as photography, film articulated the connections between physical and emotional movement, enabling viewers to interpret the transitions between gestures and expressions. Unlike performances on the stage, the apparatus permitted a much closer scrutiny of facial features, and early filmmakers tended to exploit and play upon this characteristic across a full range of genres, from comic to local subjects. For these reasons, according to one writer for *Kinematograph and Lantern Weekly* in 1907, the moving pictures even promised to supersede artistic portraiture, whose expressive power had always depended on its capacity to produce intimate, if not faithful, representations:

> The painter seeks to embody his subject's expression in the portrait, but expression is an ever changing thing, and the utmost genius cannot transfer its modifications to canvas. It can, at the utmost, suggest. The kinematograph film can show each subtle change of feature and expression, and as a consequence can present a portrait beyond the power of the most gifted painter, so far as fidelity to the original goes.[101]

Of course, by now facial recognition was a well-established and well-advertised facility of the medium. In addition to celebrity and local subjects, the Warwick Trading Company also produced what we might call class or regional portraits, capitalising upon the capacity of spectators to identify social distinctions from facial expression. Seeking to capitalise further on the success of their local subjects by marketing them to new audiences, Warwick's 1901 series of 'Provincial and Miscellaneous Scenes' promised a 'study of humanity as we find it in the smaller towns'.[102] The description of *Sunday in a Provincial Town* emphasised, presumably for the benefit of potential urban exhibitors, that 'the surprise with which some villagers regard the camera as they pass before it is plainly depicted in the countenances, and is of a most amusing character'.[103] *One Sort of Sunday Crowd at Hyde Park* presented a study of a different social group: 'Here's where you get expression of countenances and can study human nature as you will find nowhere on earth.'[104]

Equally, catalogue descriptions of several genres of early fictional production often accentuated the realism and comic effect of facial expression. For example, the 1897–98 Warwick catalogue described several of Robert Paul's films, such as *The Twins' Tea Party* (1898), in terms of their 'amusing and realistic' facial expressions, even though these films most often did not provide close ups of their performers.[105] Other fictional films seem to have introduced facial expressions in order to guide audience responses to the frequently bizarre action depicted on-screen. In *The Cheese Mites; or, Lilliputians in a London Restaurant* (Paul, 1901), the chief attraction was the magical appearance of three six-inch-tall 'little people' on a restaurant table.[106] However, the R.W. Paul catalogue description also emphasised 'the evident delight and enjoyment of the diner, as shown by his animated expression and movements', perhaps implying that the audience might share his satisfaction with this 'novel effect in cinematography'.[107]

Early filmmakers were certainly concerned with the human body, and especially with the communicative abilities of the human face. The early film thus brought into sharp aesthetic focus a wider concern with the transparency of facial expression in the late nineteenth century, which had also been subject to a good deal of debate among physiognomists and theorists of performance.[108] By the early twentieth century, writers such as Theodor Lipps and Georg Simmel were openly exploring the significance of facial aesthetics to general structures of empathy.[109] The work of both writers epitomises the general imperative in this period to justify the faith placed in facial expression as an authentic site of selfhood. The argument was a significant one, because it enabled such writers to counter the popular idea that the capacity of individuals to communicate meaningfully had been eroded by conditions of modernity. 'Whenever I see a laughing face,' wrote Lipps, 'whenever I see just these spatial changes in a face, I experience a stimulus to grasp them.'[110] Many early films and their catalogue descriptions seem designed to give audiences new opportunities to experience such basic, communicative impulses, suggesting that film functioned to connect individuals in a manner that defied not only the supposedly alienating conditions of everyday life, but also the technological properties of the medium. [111]

Arguably, for similar reasons, the first generation of film theorists in the 1910s would also be especially keen to offer explanations for the communicative potential of the face within a supposedly dehumanising, populist medium. From 1916, Vachel Lindsay described the anthropomorphic tendencies of the image within the film as a hieroglyphics—that is, as a kind of symbol system whose significance was directly readable as the expression of others.[112] For Bela Balázs, the facial close-up not only opened a window onto another subjectivity, it enabled that subjectivity to be communicated to audiences in a primordial and universal manner.[113] This intimate 'microphysiognomics' of the face offered the close-up as an escape from a purely narrative or metaphorical semantics, supplanting for the widely theorised language of film the face as a kind of utopian expressiveness in itself.[114] Such accounts mounted an admirable defence of the expressive capacities of film, emphasising the potential of this apparatus to bring an intimate experience of personhood to audiences.

However, guided by a desire to reinstate some form of authentic, innate empathy within modern everyday contexts and media forms that were widely believed to extinguish it, such writers also tended to overlook the everyday, normative conditions under which faces did not, and were not called upon, to emote. Yet, this fundamental ambivalence of the face, which gives individuals opportunities to use their faces for purposes other than individual-expressive communication, had also been extremely productive for the film industry from the beginning. Before 1910, films had not only worked through the communicative potential of the facial close-up, but had also exploited anxieties provoked by the idea that such forms of communication were no longer possible at all. As examples such as *The Cheese Mites*, with its 'Lilliputian' performers, begin to suggest, the moving pictures could couple an intimate experience of facial expression with grotesque, disproportionate representations of the human form. In such films, the capacity to foster empathy in distant audiences was arguably compromised by emphasising aspects of the body's spectacular display.

Trick genres regularly sought to penetrate into the body's economy in this way: shrinking, enlarging, transmogrifying, exploding, dismembering, and magically reassembling the body, sometimes reducing ideals of individual expressivity to a grotesque corporeality that seemed to defy the communicative potential of the medium.[115] More generally, from the exhibition of acrobatic talent to erotic display of the female body, every facet and capability of the human body was explored and exploited by early producers. Because the face promised to deliver the most intimate and expressive

162

aspects of early film performance, it was also especially prone to this type of corporeal display, and representations of faces from this period tend to switch fluidly between these possibilities. Still more significantly, far from guaranteeing the presence of distant performers, the photographic representation of faces could also provoke a profound anxiety concerning the nature of everyday life—what Georges Bataille, writing specifically about photographic reproduction of the human face in the late nineteenth century, would later describe as the 'absence of common measure among various human entities'.[116]

This negotiation of the ambivalent expressive potential of the face is most obviously identifiable in the early 'facial expressions' genre. In facials, performers were framed in close-up or extreme close-up in order to emphasise their performance of facial expressions. Sometimes performers attempted to communicate a range of emotional and expressive inner attitudes; at other times the mugging devolved into a series of absurd facial grotesques rendering little of the communicative intimacy promised. As I have demonstrated elsewhere, projected facials proved a popular feature of film programmes internationally between about 1897 and 1907, though these drew upon numerous earlier institutional precedents, not least in the work of Etienne Jules Marey and Ottomar Anschütz.[117] As early as 1894, Edison productions such as *Layman, the Man of 1,000 Faces* had also offered to the customers of kinetoscope parlours moving pictures of a series of emotional expressions in extreme close-up.[118] 1897 marks George Albert Smith's film, *Comic Faces*, which featured a mugshot of a man drinking a beer while talking with an off-screen barman and a second scene, which has not survived, featuring a woman taking snuff.[119] Judging by the numbers of these films appearing in catalogues, they appear to have been most popular with British audiences during 1901 and 1902, with George Albert Smith, in particular, specialising in their production.[120] Towards the end of the cycle, in 1907, Paul released a short series of 'studies of facial expression', including *How a Burglar Feels* (1907) and *Pity the Poor Blind* (1907). Catalogue descriptions suggest that these films were very similar to earlier productions, consisting of only a few brief scenes in which the varied expressions of a 'very good actor' remained at the heart of the attraction.[121]

In almost every example of this remarkably stable, though short-lived, genre, one or two protagonists were portrayed interacting with properties (or with each other) in a manner that made the significance of their facial contortions explicit, if not overdetermined. Catalogues continually referred to the success of acting activities within facials, and sometimes took the unusual step of publishing the names of the 'prominent Actors and Come-

163

dians' that accomplished them.[122] Describing Smith's *Two Old Sports* (1900), the first of a series of films featuring these 'old boy' stock characters, the Warwick catalogue noted that 'the faces were taken very large, the parts were played by two most experienced actors, and it is next to an impossibility to avoid catching the spirit of their fun'.[123] Warwick here emphasised the familiarity and empathy of audiences with the facial responses represented and exploited the common metaphor of contagious humour to impress upon exhibitors the comic effect on spectators of *Two Old Sports*. Furthermore, this effect is clearly signposted within the film itself: the two pore with excited pantomimic gestures over salacious images from a copy of 'Footlight Favourites'; one of them even glances conspiratorially at the camera in an open, though clearly gendered, gesture of inclusion. Similarly, in Smith's *The Dull Razor* (1900), the audience's gendered recognition of a familiar emotion or sensation, in this case the response to an especially painful shave, is the key to an expressive mode of address to audiences:

> The individual herein depicted is seen lathering and shaving himself to judge by his grimaces, evidently with a dull razor. His back being to the camera, the face and 'scraping' manoeuvres are plainly seen by reflection in the mirror. As most men have had a similar experience, this subject is bound to create much mirth among an audience.[124]

As in Smith's better known *A Quick Shave and Brush Up* (1900), the practice of shaving occasions a skilful display of grimacing from performer Tom Green, but in *The Dull Razor* the facial action is even more absurdly exaggerated and is reflected in a mirror, with the back of Green's head and shoulder visible in the right foreground.

Films such as *How a Burglar Feels*, *Two Old Sports* and *The Dull Razor* strongly emphasise the intimacy potentially elicited by facial expression, so that a supposedly private activity is reconstituted as a communicative activity. Similarly, in *A Study in Facial Expression* (Paul, 1898), an old gentleman is caught by his wife reading a risqué story, and in *Hair Soup; or The Disappointed Diner* (Paul, 1901) a 'marvellous example of facial expression' is generated when the diner swallows a hair.[125] Such films occasioned a specialised form of spectatorial voyeurism, in which everyday, but embarrassing or risqué scenarios served to justify the exaggerated facial performances. Other facials, such as *Sweet Suffragettes* (Cricks and Sharp, 1906), in which the suffragette 'receives several eggs in the face and a policeman's arms are seen hauling her off', simply called upon the audience's knowledge of existing stock characters, but exaggerated them into absurdity.[126]

However, most facials stretched their own minimal narrative logic in this way up to or beyond breaking point, ultimately presenting the magnified, mobile human face as a kind of spectacle in itself.[127] *The Dull Razor* lurches swiftly from one grimace to another during the course of the shave, and comes to a grand finale when Green wipes his face clean and puffs out his cheeks in an inscrutable instance of facial display. Similarly, in *Facial Expressions: The Fateful Letter* (BMBC, 1898), the outlandish facial expressions of the performer, Ben Nathan, pass from anxiety, to grief, to happiness with such absurd rapidity, that the context of this action—he has received a letter naming him as a beneficiary of a relative's will—seem relatively insignificant. There is little attempt made to communicate inner emotional experience, so that what remains is the corporeality of the face itself, an object which exhibitors might choose to contextualise in relation to the basic narrative action, or might prefer to offer as a grotesque attraction in its own right. In the latter scenario, the visible surface of the face, rather than its reflexive, inward-directed expressiveness, would have become the ultimate object of the spectator's attention, marking a potentially productive realignment of the relationship between performers and audiences.

Above all, this switch between modes of facial expression is accomplished during facials by a literal and symbolic adjustment of spectatorial focus from the eyes to the face's mobile features. The mouth, in particular, seems to take on a life of its own, directing the viewer's attention, according to some recent commentators, in a manner that parallels Mikhail Bakhtin's influential discussion of grotesque 'folk images' of the human body.[128] A few facials seem entirely divorced from any context besides that of carnival grotesquerie. In the unattributed film, *Masks and Faces* (c.1901), a series of fifteen different countenances, ranging from tribal masks to clown and tramp faces, are presented in rapid sequence. Most present exaggerated emotional attitudes, blowing out their cheeks or picking their noses, and the final face appears to follow a fly around the room, before catching and eating it.[129] Similarly, Hepworth and Co.'s 1901 film *Comic Grimacer* reportedly presented a single human face undergoing a series of unexplained distortions into 'frightful and hideous knots'.[130] The inscrutable comic effect of such spectacles proved extremely difficult to convey in catalogues: 'A human face shown the full size of the screen is always a comic and interesting sight', concluded the Hepworth catalogue of *Comic Grimacer* with typical ambiguity.

However, even in films such as these which seem to defy other explanations, application of the Bakhtinian model of the carnivalesque (originally applied to the works of Rabelais) tends to overgeneralise and overpoliticise the strongly institutionalised practices of film production, exhibition and reception at work at the end of the nineteenth century. Facials such as *Comic Grimacer* exploited long traditions of facial contortionists on the fairground, side-show, and freak show and of gurning competitions, wherein the competitor able to mug the ugliest face would win a prize. *Masks and Faces* seems to derive equally from the performative tradition of quick-change artistry, facilitating an especially rapid transition between different personae. John Barnes has also argued that facials borrowed from certain magic lantern entertainments in which the countenance of a face on-screen would slowly alter according to the drift of a spoken narrative.[131] More direct lines of inheritance can be drawn from music hall and pantomime, since known facial performers like Tom Green and Ben Nathan had been long associated with popular theatrical traditions.[132] Such traditions suggest the existence of a fascinating intermedial connection between nineteenth-century physiognomic images, prevalent traditions of facial pantomime in the music hall (of which Dan Leno was the acknowledged master at the turn of the century), and the facial play of Tom Green, and others, on-screen.

Institutionalised traditions such as these suggest that, even when the moving pictures appeared to present little more than a series of disturbing grotesques on the screen, the early film industry depended strongly upon existing and familiar conventions of performance and spectatorship. For example, Green's conventional clowning abilities suggest that *The Dull Razor* was more legible than a simple emphasis on the grotesque allows. Arguably, the film reproduced numerous styles of facial performance from legitimate theatre to freak show, but it also borrowed more specifically from the distinct performance routine of the shaving sketch. A rather unlikely Victorian fascination with beards, shaving and the sharpness of razors had appeared in a proliferation of 'How to Shave' books and parodies and in a series of shaving routines in the nineteenth century.[133] For example, Ralph Parr's *Shaving Done Here*, which was in its sixty-first edition by 1896, featured an unfortunate customer being painfully shaved by a succession of besmocked yokels and bumpkins.[134] A shaving subject entitled *Barber Shop* (1894), in which the unfortunate customer 'grimaces and winces when the razor takes off sections of his cuticle' had appeared amongst the first productions of the Kinetoscope, some years before the numerous other British and American films.[135] As I have already mentioned, Mitchell and Kenyon's local subject, *Whitsun Fair at Preston: 1906* shows a similar sketch performed on the parade of Sedgwick's Bioscope show. *The Dull Razor* therefore depended upon the tried and tested performance routine of the shaving sketch, had wholly predictable conclusions, and re-enacted popular controversies over etiquette and decency that were themselves largely traditional.

Most powerfully reminiscent of the dialogic subversiveness of folk humour, as Tom Gunning has suggested, were those facials offering the magnified image of the human mouth in action: eating, drinking, smoking, laughing, kissing, or indeed opening and closing without apparent cause.[136] Hepwix's *Macaroni Competition* (1899) was among numerous films dedicated to prodigious consumption presented 'more than life size upon the screen'. [137] In British Mutoscope and Biograph's (provisionally titled) *Herbert Campbell as 'Little Bobbie'* (1899), the music hall star messily consumes a plateful of food and a glass of beer in just a few seconds, all the while gazing glassily at the camera. Reversing subjects such as Warwick's *The Yokel's Dinner* (1900) and Smith's *The Hungry Countryman* (1899) delighted in the grotesque spectacle of performers retrieving food from their open mouths and laying it back on the plate. The thematisation of consumption and regurgitation offered by these films may be read, in part, as new manifestations of ancient traditions of folk imagery. But it is necessary to resist reading even these films simply as subversive embodiments of a popular feast. They are highly institutionalised products which depend strongly upon the stock characters and caricatures of the naïve rustic and the vulgar, boorish lout. At the same time, it should be noted, the reversal of footage reorients these stereotyped social interactions into a relationship with audiences wherein filmmaker, exhibitor and apparatus are also credited, much more directly, with an institutional responsibility for the bizarre action on-screen.

Facials reproduced highly institutionalised conventions, now long forgotten, which were likely to be familiar to most spectators. Among these, the promise of an intimate mode of address associated with the individual represented in close up was held in tension with representations of an incommunicative, but monstrously mobile, face. Facials oscillated between these possibilities, so that the face was presented both as a key to the individuality residing behind the eyes and as an anti-individual, startlingly dynamic kind of mask. They therefore capitalised fully on the ambivalence of the face, just as popular entertainments had done throughout the nineteenth century, exploiting not only the ability of spectators to read signs of expressive individuality from facial expression, but also their enjoyment of long-institutionalised conventions of facial grotesquerie. If such films also seem to resonate with a primordial sense of the unnatural and uncanny, perhaps bringing into aesthetic focus the general insinuation that everyday interpersonal relations were automatic, routine, and existentially empty, then this too can be seen as a productive reorientation of existing performative, artistic and literary traditions associated most obviously with the gothic or the supernatural. 'Ghosts, vampires, monsters,' writes Mladen Dolar, 'flourish in an era when you might expect them to be dead and buried, without a place. They are something brought about by modernity itself.'[138] They were brought to fruition in early film, I would add, because they possessed a distinct psychological and affective value of otherness, which modern media institutions have routinely exploited.

Otherness, Objectification—and Empathy

Spectacles of otherness represented a primary attraction for early film audiences, who often seem to have thrived on the capacity of the medium to distance, abstract and objectify that Bergson condemned within the apparatus. But as Bergson also acknowledged, such attitudes additionally served eminently practical purposes, enabling the objectifier to feel a sense of mastery over a world that continually threatened to slip out of his or her grasp.[139] This played directly into the institutional imperatives of the early film industry, enabling filmmakers and exhibitors, on the one hand, to reflect and manipulate the preferences and prejudices of their audiences, and viewers, on the other, to consolidate their own sense of normative experience and identity. Paradoxically, the construction of cultural, racial or bodily alterity within film could therefore succeed in fostering a sense of community among audiences, wherein bonds of kinship and empathy were strengthened (albeit in service of a potentially false, or morally suspect, order).

Arguably, this type of relationship was present within most early genres, coexisting with more direct relationships established between audiences and on-screen performers. Thus, for example, traditions of local filmmaking can be seen as serving apparently conflicting functions for audiences, both encouraging spectators to identify with the mundane experiences of the individuals depicted on-screen, but also defamiliarising and exoticising these everyday scenes, converting them into part of the cinematograph's definitively modern landscape. Similarly, in some examples of trick filmmaking, the depiction of particularly gruesome accidents also seems to elicit a sense of inclusion or community. In Smith's *Mary Jane's Mishap; or, Don't Fool with the Paraffin* (1903), the action proceeds when the servant Mary Jane is blown up a chimney and into the sky by a paraffin explosion, before her remains fall to earth. Returning to frighten off the mourners gathered around her grave, the ghost of Mary Jane seems to realise fully the phantom-like qualities of animated performance. But even as she seals her fate by pouring paraffin onto the fire, Mary Jane turns to camera, grinning and winking occasionally, in order to bring spectators in on the fatal joke being

168

played upon her. In other films, this sense of inclusion was achieved by playing upon well-known fears and insecurities. For example, widespread discourses concerning automobile accidents around the turn of the century received comic treatment in Hepworth and Co.'s (self-explanatory) 1900 films, *Explosion of a Motor Car* and *How it Feels to be Run Over*. The neurasthenic and hysterical pace of modern life, which the automobile and the cinematograph exemplified in 1900, as the railway had done for the previous fifty years, was thus transformed by filmmakers into a repeatable, and soon conventional, commodity of the film.[140] After an initial, widely advertised period of unease with the moving picture itself, the anxieties of the modern world were soon offered back to audiences in an unthreatening institution-alised form.

But in early film the representation of alterity is allied most obviously with genres of travel and ethnographic filmmaking. In such films the screen seems to offer a window upon the world, but, as William Uricchio has noted, 'the nature of the window itself' was of 'only sporadic interest'.[141] Spectators were attracted to a touristic or observational mode of seeing enacted by the apparatus and by its operator, and they were encouraged to identify with the visual and ideological perspective of the filmmaker relative to the foreign landscapes encountered. Thus, as in magic lantern travelogues, such films elicited two predominant relationships with audiences: the identification and reification of an outward-looking and often colonialist gaze on the one hand, and an objectification of foreign lands, people and practices on the other. For example, in the amateur British film, *Gang Making Railway— South Africa* (1898), a gang of black navvies are depicted at work, stripped to the waist, and posed in a frontal relationship to the camera. They are watched closely by a white supervisor whose proprietary, racially inflected, and mastering gaze offered a potential parallel to the gaze of the camera and of the British spectators for whom, most likely, the workers were arranged.

As this example implies, processes of objectification could place British spectators in potentially flattering and comfortable subject positions, on this occasion, shortly before the outbreak of the Boer War, reminding them of a shared imperialist past.[142] The apparatus proved singularly adept at representing the spectacle of otherness because, though it seemed to depend upon alienation for its effects, it actually developed a surrogate sense of intimacy founded upon cultural commonalities. The marketing of alterity was thus complicit with longstanding and highly institutionalised precedents and generated consistent and comfortable interpretational strategies in its audiences. At the same time, such films could also evoke very different, but equally commercially productive, sentiments in its viewers. As Gunning has shown in relation to certain traditions of ethnographic filmmaking, the film's protagonists did not always submit altogether passively to the camera's gaze.[143] For example, in more challenging moments of *Gang Making Railway—South Africa*, the navvies gaze back at the supervisor, camera operator, and spectator, sometimes threatening to overcome structures of objectification altogether.

Very occasionally, early films introduced a degree of discomfort into the viewing experience that audiences found much more difficult to process. For example, Doctor Eugène-Louis Doyen was an early and insistent proponent of the use of cinematograph in surgery, but his films, which were later distributed internationally by Gaumont, also tended to provoke heated debate when they were screened for audiences on the fairground.[144] Most controversial for the UK press, as on the continent, was Doyen's 1902 film depicting the medical separation of conjoined twins, Doodica and Radica, an operation which caused the death of Doodica days later, and which prolonged Radica's life by only a short while. The two girls, born in India in 1889, had been exhibited as freaks in European capitals from 1893 as 'The Orissa Sisters' and 'The Hindoo Twins' before Doodica fell ill with tuberculosis. Joined by a band of tissue between the two sternums, it was believed that this experimental surgical procedure was the only chance to rescue Radica. The British trade press, while sympathetic to Barnum and Bailey's Greatest Show on Earth', who had exhibited the twins, were quick to criticise accounts appearing within French newspapers that 'naturally gave gruesome and realistic details of the ceremony'.[145] Condemnation in *The Showman* fell most heavily upon a Mrs Coleman, the foster mother and manager of the twins, who had apparently 'stipulated that a number of persons should be present at the operation to cinematograph the proceedings' and had therefore prevented the operation from taking place in a hospital where 'doctors objected to allow the operation to be made a sort of spectacular display'.[146]

The film, which survives, shows Doyen, surrounded by journalists and other surgeons, making the first (remarkably brutal-seeming) incision. It remains difficult viewing, but was exhibited throughout continental Europe from May 1902 within Barnum and Bailey's show where, according to one review, it 'showed all the horrors of the dissecting room' and therefore had 'awakened considerable disgust' in its audiences.[147] In fact, such screenings were secured without the consent of Doyen himself.[148] However, in a period when few boundaries yet existed between popular and professional applications of moving pictures, and the Rontgen Ray still found a place in the fairground alongside the cinematograph, the negative public reaction to the film represents one defining moment in the consolidation of the moving pictures as an entertainment medium. Distancing itself from the spectacles of enfreakment on show within the operating theatre, early film culture also banished the freak show to the relative privacy of the medical sphere, where the cinematograph could record whatever was deemed necessary.

At the same time, freak discourses were revalidated and repackaged within the increasingly sophisticated narrative and generic patterns of early film, where human bodies were routinely compromised for the pleasure of paying audiences. Here, though the currency of grotesque representations of the human body persisted, audiences were reassured that the extraordinary and challenging bodies objectified on-screen were part of the harmless public spectacle provided by entertainment institutions. Among such films were a few which graphically realised the ambition to 'correct' enfreaked or transgressive human bodies, but which did not encroach upon the operating theatre in order to do so. Martin F. Norden has identified an entire comic sub-genre in the years before 1905, which was dedicated to the 'miraculous recovery' of disabled bodies. In films such as James Williamson's *The Fraudulent Beggars* (1898) and Cecil Hepworth's *The Beggar's Deceit* (1900), the mendicants recover use of their eyesight, hearing or legs in order to escape from policemen who have discovered their deceptions.[149] These films effectively erased the markers of bodily difference that set crippled beggars apart from criminals, converting bodily transgression into a form of moral monstrosity that might be unproblematically condemned. The barely concealed prejudice against the disabled (and the poor) expressed by these films was therefore part of the broader project of reassurance which would continue to inform representations of bodily otherness throughout the twentieth century.

Such films exemplify early film's fascination with alterity, but also demonstrate that this fascination was ultimately part of a broader project to confirm identity, to mask differences, and to generate intimacy based upon shared cultural allegiances. On ciné-variety programmes, the empathetic promise of expressive on-screen performance might be compromised by the grotesque bodily or facial gesture, by the sovereignty of an objectifying gaze from spectators, or even by the wholesale disintegration of on-screen bodies. However, regardless of the challenge some films seem to have posed for everyday practices going on in the world, the tendency of spectators to look for and find comfortable expressions of selfhood and personality within them lent a degree of stability to filmmaking institutions. At the same time, these institutions began to gather around themselves further markers of identity with which audiences could identify, interrogate and interact. From named personalities such as celebrity camera operators, to the more abstract agents associated with narration and authorship, film producers sought to co-ordinate early practices of spectatorship with activities that appeared to take place behind, as well as upon the screen.

5

Conjurors, Adventurers and Other Authors

Unlike on-screen film performers, whose relationships with audiences are determined in the first instance by their visibility, those personae understood to be literally or figuratively 'responsible for' a film's production have most often been associated with the forms of vision the apparatus seems to reproduce. In the context of later commercial cinemas, the dominant conventions for reading these personae have regularly circulated around ideas of authorship and narration, often embodied with reference to authorities such as studios, stars, producers, directors and screenwriters. However, within the early industry, where such interpretive conventions were not yet in place for audiences, and where the interests and capacities of the camera were diversifying, like its genres, rapidly and in multiple directions, the identities to be ascribed to this site of vision were often determined much more fluidly. Most often, they drew from a range of earlier institutional contexts and more generally from everyday viewing practices, as well as from personae associated with a film's production. This was one of the reasons that exhibitors expended so much time and effort on ensuring that films were legible, introducing a spoken lecture, title slides, or accompanying written material in order to instruct audiences concerning the significance of what they saw on the screen.

Early spectators were also remarkably adept at recognising and negotiating between the many possible cultural authorities that might be associated with early film shows, partly because they were extremely familiar with other entertainment institutions that required them to adopt a similarly knowing and knowledgeable position. Furthermore, their expertise was also prompted by formal characteristics within the films themselves, whose resemblance to everyday scopic practices or to existing visual conventions associated with other media did much to contextualise and guide possible interpretations of film. For example, in films such as *Tram Rides Through Nottingham* (M&K,

1902), and *Sheffield Street Accident* (M&K, 1902), both subjects commissioned by the showman Ralph Pringle, the attraction for local audiences did not only depend upon the recognition of familiar faces and places; the films also re-enacted the extremely varied everyday viewing practices that were at work within the contemporary street scene. Whether such films reproduced the mobility and detachment of the view from the tram, or the momentary, emotive fascination with a public accident, they brought easily recognisable viewing practices to exhibition venues that had not previously capitalised so directly upon this resource. A similar form of relatively straightforward identification with the camera was also prevalent in films based upon popular theatrical regimes such as *Little Tich and his Big Boots*, which replicated an advantageous viewing position in an auditorium.

However, many other films called upon a more complex series of possible relationships with audiences, associated especially with the agency of the camera operator or other agents behind the camera. For example, in Esmé Collings' *Boys Scrambling for Pennies under the West Pier, Brighton* (1896), the boys wait expectantly for an unseen benefactor on top of the pier to throw coins into the waves, which they busily attempt to retrieve. Some are thoroughly engaged in the rough-and-tumble, but others are clearly more interested in the operation of the camera, which is positioned next to the pier and faces out to sea, and stare back at it with the fascination common at this time. The film offers a number of characteristic attractions, among them the spectacle of a chaotic flurry of limbs, prevailing mischievous child stereotypes, and the possibility of an individualised response to an especially thoughtful or eager child. But, at the same time, the actions of the camera operator and of the coin-thrower are also apparent, and acknowledging this was another important part of the experience of watching the film.

The public interest in this type of subject was reflected by the production of Hepworth and Co.'s *Mud Larks* (c.1899), a film which represented identical actions, but whose title explicitly referred to the poor living to be obtained by screening the mud on the banks of the Thames for items of value. As the catalogue explained for the benefit of potential exhibitors and lecturers, an agreement had been reached between camera operator and children that not only could they keep the pennies, but a consolation prize would be awarded to 'him who, in his endeavours to find the pennies, gets the wettest'.[1] Such films instantly evoked Victorian class distinctions, perhaps imbricating these with the privileged form of vision the cinematograph appeared to deliver. A similar film of 1900, Warwick's *Coolie Boys Diving for Coins*, added the appeal of exotic travel (and a layer of racial stereotyping) to the formula. The description of this film published in *The Era* suggests that it was the passengers on board a steamer who threw the coins, but the avid attention of the boys to the camera suggests that their chief benefactor, once again, was the cameraman.[2]

All three of these films staged an interaction with the boys such that the off-screen adult agents responsible also become focal points of the action, suggesting in the Warwick film, for example, that the agency of the world traveller significantly influenced its interpretation. The possibility of identifying with figures associated with the camera was both reinforced and compromised by the material exchange of coins. This haptic contact serves as the premise for the sequence of gazes that are set in motion between children, camera operator and audience, but it also acknowledges the material conditions of this contact, emphasising that it has taken place in a distant region of time and space. Such films therefore seem less intent on reproducing an everyday experience of vision, such as that associated with presence on a city street, than on recounting an episode drawn from the adventures of the camera and its operator. The operator has an active and obvious (if not visible) role in creating the scene rather than passively recording it, and this role tends to co-ordinate the relationships potentially established with the children on-screen, fostering possibilities for audience identification with a suitably grown-up and touristic gaze.

The spectator's imaginative reconstruction of unseen agents such as these, who were credited with responsibility for the content of films, was an especially important aspect of their interpretive activities during the early period, when conventions for reading agents such as narrators from the image track had not yet become stabilised. Notwithstanding the potential presence of a lecturer to explain the action, early examples of film editing in story films were similarly explicit in the guidance they offered audiences, often adapting existing conventions drawn from lantern slide sequences. In George Albert Smith's *Let Me Dream Again* (1900) a middle-aged man is depicted drinking and flirting exaggeratedly with an attractive girl in bizarre fancy dress. Avoiding throughout the glance at the camera, this scene is revealed to be a dream when the camera racks out of focus and refocuses in a match cut (as we would call it today) upon the same man asleep in bed, eagerly embracing his ugly wife. Awakening to find herself the object of an unwelcome embrace, she rouses her husband and nags until they turn away from each other, faces churning with anger and unhappiness. The film thus reproduces a familiar gender-based joke played out between these characters, but once it is realised that the bizarre first shot is the product of the husband's erotic dream, the highly visible technique of racking focus tends to divert attention to the unseen agency of a 'joke teller', making it clear that both husband

and wife are victims of a gag shared by this figure with audiences. This type of agency, which is likely to be associated more strongly with the minimal narrative of the film than the conditions of its filming, is perhaps less obvious to audiences than seems to be the case in films such as *Boys Scrambling for Pennies under the West Pier, Brighton*, but it is just as effective in co-ordinating the relationships between audience and screen.

Consideration of figures such as these, who were not so much viewed as intuited by spectators, is an especially slippery job. The imaginative capacities and interests of spectators are largely unknowable, and their interpretations of these films would have depended strongly upon intangible factors such as their prior knowledge of other influential media forms, or their understanding of the models of vision reproduced by the camera. For example, it seems likely that, when screened to isolated rural audiences, the reaction to city scenes such as *Sheffield Street Accident* might have been more akin to a touristic view than a scenario of recognition. Moreover, because these relationships with the screen appear to have been so varied, drawing influences from a wide range of earlier media and entertainments as well as everyday viewing practices, it becomes extremely difficult to account for their exact orientation during any one exhibition, or even any one film. In the case of films such as *Mud Larks*, the range of signifying relationships potentially established with audiences seems especially nuanced and complex, and was perhaps unlikely to be repeated on any subsequent occasions. For this reason, it also becomes problematic to apply an inclusive terminology of agency, such as that proposed by modern narratology, without losing a meaningful sense of what these figures actually signified for their first audiences. For example, it is perfectly possible to describe the figure of the joke teller in *Let Me Dream Again* as a kind of narrator, but this term loses the institutional and social specificity implied by the idea of the gag, which seems likely to have been the chief motive and context guiding interpretation of the film. However, this is not to say that specific figures such as the joke teller were created randomly or on a purely individual basis: the creation of a number of relatively stable figures such as this was as important to the generic and stylistic development of the early industry as was the definition of performance styles on the screen.

This chapter will work through a selection of such figures, focussing especially on the pervasive figures of the conjuror and the adventurous camera operator, before describing the industry's identification and consolidation of discrete narrative personae within filmed fiction. The relationships between audiences and these figures differed markedly, not least because they occupied what Edward Branigan has called different 'levels of narration'; the camera operator is a real individual strongly associated with the film's production, whereas conjurors and narrators most often do not exist as such, independently of the spectator's interaction with the screen.[3] However, all such relationships depended upon the imaginative capacity of spectators to accredit a fundamental presence responsible, in some fashion, for the images on-screen. We can think about this kind of attribution of intentionality to the film as a process of 'embodiment'—literally giving a human form to personae that were not usually present during exhibition or represented on the screen. Audiences were not always conscious that this process was taking place, and they were most often cued into participating in it by the films themselves, if not by lecturers or other extratextual informants, but they were always actively involved in embodying distant agents credited with some form of responsibility for the action on-screen. As described by Giddens's principal of institutional duality of structure, spectators were therefore elicited by film institutions to read significant personae into the films they watched, but they did so creatively, and in a manner that might subsequently introduce changes to institutional structures. As the following sections will show, interactions of this kind were responsible for fundamental aspects of institutional change in the early industry, and the figures of the conjuror, the adventurous camera operator, and the narrator have been selected in order to expose some of the most significant of these: the formulation of specific modes of fictional film production; the creation of modes of factual film-making now most often associated with documentary genres; and the development of narrative authorities, which played an especially crucial role in allowing filmmakers to defend copyright on their productions.

Insofar as this line of enquiry seeks to trace the imaginative activities of film spectators, it might also seem to resurrect study of what Albert Laffay, in his 1964 work *Logique du Cinéma*, described as a 'grand imagier': a hypothetical figure somehow responsible for the film and answerable for its effects.[4] This idea has remained extremely significant for enunciation theorists of film ever since, and can be traced through Christian Metz's influential discussion in *Film Language: A Semiotics of Cinema* of the 'grand image-maker' in cinema as 'a sort of "potential linguistic focus" situated somewhere behind the film'.[5] The contradictions associated with the idea of a linguistic centre within a primarily visual medium have subsequently proven extremely productive within the work of theorists such as Francesco Casetti, Jan Simons, François Jost and André Gaudreault, and it will be useful to sketch one key aspect of this debate in order to clarify how the process I have described as embodiment was played out between audiences and the early screen.[6]

One of the central problems with theories of filmic enunciation has been that, unlike verbal language, the dominant signifying capacities of cinema are not attached to any identifiable enunciator and, excepting narrative interpositions such as intertitles or voice-overs, do not even possess the deictic grammatical markers that convey a sense of personhood in most literary forms.[7] For this and other reasons, David Bordwell, Noël Carroll, and others have strongly critiqued any implicit or explicit use of deictics to describe cinema, understanding such attempts as part of an untenable anthropomorphism also typified by traditions such as auteur criticism.[8] However, communication of a kind nonetheless takes place. Although filmmakers and spectators operate in time/space isolation, as Francesco Casetti has indicated, 'the bonds are far more numerous than it seems and the distances less irreducible'.[9] Above all, the film is characterised by an 'intrinsic availability', which is 'constantly confirmed by the most basic facts, such as when differences are cancelled, or absences compensated for, thanks to the co-operation of the viewer'.[10] Casetti's book-length exploration of this co-operation reintroduces the idea of enunciation, but carefully qualifies it by establishing that enunciators and enunciatees are best understood not as real 'bodies', but as ideal positions or 'roles' inscribed in the text.[11] These roles are then confronted and interpreted by spectators and filmmakers, guiding them in the processes of creating and interpreting film texts. Casetti therefore survives Bordwell and Carroll's objections because he suggests that it is the interaction between real individuals and the roles they identify for themselves within the film that enables these individuals, with some measure of control, to discover enunciators within the medium.[12] Regardless of the uncertain ontological status of these enunciators, they remain powerfully significant for spectators, whose supposed naïveté in this respect is therefore worthy of prolonged consideration in itself.

The desire to look for and discover these significant figures underpins the process I have called embodiment, a term which I prefer because it suggests more directly the immediacy and materiality of many of the individuals early film spectators identified. For example, the figure of the camera operator in films such as *Coolie Boys Diving for Coins* has a tangible and highly specific presence within this film, even though his body is never visible. I would also add to Casetti's account that, very often, it was possible to identify more than one such figure within a film, and that audiences might discover these outside as well as within the text. Such features drew attention to what Gaudreault has called the 'trickality' of the medium, bringing the illusionist premise upon which the medium depended to the surface of the show, and giving it a familiar human form.[13] Moreover, as Michael Chanan has suggested, the figure of the illusionist himself was routinely discerned by spectators in their interactions with the screen.[14] In this light, 'the magician with the instantaneous lens', as Charles Dawbarn described the filmmaker in 1911, became a prominent part of the imaginative projects of spectators, and might even be profitably regarded as a kind of master figure for cinematic illusionism during the early period.[15]

Conjurors and the Definition of Film Fiction

Observing that there was a only a 'fuzzy line' between 'the discovery of "special effects" in scientific films . . .; the use of similar techniques . . . in trick films which belong in the realms of humour, magic and fantasy; and the deception of the fake actuality', Chanan describes an ambiguity that proved extremely productive for the early industry.[16] All of these early genres depended upon the ability of the apparatus to reshape space and time, an ability which made the figurative associations between magic and the moving pictures seemingly irresistible for early filmmakers. These associations became most obvious when the cinematograph traded on hyper-realism, as in the phantom train journeys of Hale's Tours, which the *Kinematograph and Lantern Weekly* described in 1907 as 'one of the cleverest optical illusions of modern times'.[17] Borrowing from discourses associated with the spectacular realism of a variety of nineteenth-century entertainments, accounts such as these tended to play up the disorientating effect of these illusions, making the suspension of disbelief an important condition for the show's success: 'As we step out of the car with our auditory and visual faculties still vibrating,' the reviewer concluded, 'it seems a contradiction of nature to find ourselves still in Oxford Street, London.'[18] By 1907, this was a description that clearly differentiated the experience of Hale's Tours from the common run of film shows, whose varied illusionist qualities rarely merited such detailed attention. However, although familiar enough to have become largely invisible, the tricks played by the cinematograph in the majority of films tended to call much more extensively upon the expertise of audiences in discerning the motives behind illusionist effects. In particular, interpretation of films depended in large measure on whether they seemed intended to deceive or, as in the case of Hale's Tours, to make an open virtue of their deception. As I have shown in relation to the figure of the showman, this open play with trust and confidence was one of early film's primary attractions, but, in relation to film production, it was often codified in terms of trickery, faking and fiction—precisely the terrain of illusionist traditions such as magic theatre, and popular figures such as the stage conjuror. Hence,

179

popular constructions of the filmmaker-as-magician type tend to have a direct institutional focus in the early period, referring back to performance regimes with a complex history of their own.

The magic theatre was the institution that most obviously formalised the pervasive discourses concerning trickery that were circulating at the turn of the century, consistently encouraging audiences not only to enjoy the illusionist spectacle of the show, but also to conjecture concerning the mechanism of the trick.[19] In fact, for many of the most successful stage conjurors, entering into public debate concerning the nature of their tricks was a vital component of a show's success. Conjurors sought not only to engage the speculation of the audience during the show, but also that of the popular and trade press right the way through the life of the trick. Public discussion of the relationship between illusion and deception was very much the stock-in-trade, to take the most famous example, of the anti-spiritualists Maskelyne and Cooke, who struck a chord with a self-consciously enlightened popular press from the 1870s by debunking spiritualist séances, and who continued to do so throughout their careers at the Egyptian Hall, earning for this institution the title, 'England's Home of Mystery'.[20]

Maskelyne's book, *Modern Spiritualism*, sold at the Hall from 1875, was one of many publications that routinely sought to capitalise on this very public initiative to domesticate magic and spiritualism in the latter half of the nineteenth century. While the spiritualists might be admired for their craft, which played upon widely held superstitions and beliefs in their audiences, they were easily condemned, as Maskelyne put it, because 'the *false* pretence brought the money'.[21] By contrast, the form of pretence practised at the Hall was not false, but fictional, a lie which did not seek to deceive. It deliberately drew attention to the mystery of the trick, and posed audiences the challenge of solving it, sometimes, in pursuit of further publicity, offering cash rewards to any that could successfully decipher or repeat it. In this way, spectators were able, rather indirectly and vicariously, to enjoy entertainments that imbricated scientific discourses with taboo ideas of mysticism and the occult.

Late Victorian magic theatre internalised this project, putting the principle of rational enquiry at the centre of the show, so that its deceptions structured the relationship between conjuror and audience partly in the image of that between expert and initiate. This relationship proved enduringly productive for popular magicians and, by 1901, some performers were still specialising in the 'anti spiritualist séance', an entertainment which depended, as *The Showman* put it, on 'producing all the manifestations of so-called spiritualism in full glare of the gas light', and hence giving 'one or two hard knocks to the rappers'.[22] More extensive shows, such as that at the Egyptian Hall, offered a more complex series of attractions to audiences. At the turn of the century, the Hall offered a lengthy programme, which might include sleight of hand or memory experts, mesmerists, thought-readers or humorists, and many other tricks and short sketches. It also presented relatively long dramatic productions, which called upon traditions of spectacular theatre but which tended to focus the energies of audiences onto the spectacular illusions that punctuated the plot. These included ghost effects, as in the productions of *The Artist's Dream* and *The Miser*, and levitation effects, as in *The Entranced Fakir*. While, no doubt, the idea of animated, spectral presences or unworldly events enacted on the stage had a peculiar resonance for audiences in the same years that the cinematograph appeared, the principle attractions of these exhibits were likely to be far more mundane. As *The Showman* concisely explained of *The Artist's Dream*, in which the portrait of a dead woman appears to come to life, 'the audience who . . . saw this remarkable apparition, did not endeavour to look upon it as a vision, but knew it to be one of the most beautiful and perfect illusions ever devised'.[23]

Above all, it is this tone of knowing contemplation associated with the reception of illusionist shows, and especially the distinction made by Maskelyne between 'false pretence' and the kind of pretence that did not seek to deceive, which would have the most significant impact on the moving pictures, and which would make the conjuror such a significant figure for early filmmakers and spectators.[24] Play with this distinction, which had for so long co-ordinated the relationships between conjurors, audiences and exhibits in the magic theatre, can be seen as one of the key structuring tensions around which early genre discourses were formulated, but in the first years of film this was a fluid, contested, and often perplexing terrain. While the practice of deception typified by the séance was by now regularly and conventionally condemned within anti-spiritualist conjuring shows, the varieties of trick associated with early moving pictures were not so well known and the intentions of the filmmakers not so easily interpreted. Consequently, during the early 1900s, the ready trust that the moving pictures seemed to inspire in audiences quickly provoked questions resembling those that had long ago been answered by anti-spiritualist thinking. To what extent was it possible to trust the content of moving pictures? When were their illusionist practices to be deemed acceptable, and when illegitimate? These questions of dressage were ultimately addressed in a manner that also borrowed heavily from the tradition of magic theatre, and pervasive constructions of the filmmaker as conjuror were extremely significant within this process. Because illusion—the illusion of life and movement—

was the stock in trade of the cinematograph, the imaginative projection of such figures would have a profound impact on the ontological status of the moving image, closely informing the definition of legitimate relationships between audience, screen and world.

Questions concerning the trustworthiness of the medium were explicitly debated in the trade press, whose pages played a crucial role in mediating models of good practice between exhibitors and producers, and hence in disseminating effective patterns of dressage. From 1899, Henry V. Hopwood, the author of one of the earliest handbooks for film producers, was beginning to detail some 'errors and falsities' to which films were subject. Writing in *The Optician and Photographic Trades Review*, Hopwood noted that, although the public was by now familiar with the manipulation of photographs, the moving pictures presented a different kind of problem:

> Novelty and the mysterious have a peculiar charm, and loss of faith in single views does not necessarily imply a popular doubt of the veracity of 'Living Pictures'. Far be it from me to destroy the confidence of any simple creature who implicitly relies on receiving sixpennyworth of realistic truth, as well as a back seat, for a sixpence. I only desire to point out the various methods by which the view on the screen may be made to vary from the actual scene from which it was derived, in order that those engaged in the manufacture of films, may further develop my suggestions to their own profit. Trick Kinematography is probably more effective than any other photographic dodge, the realism of motion goes far towards dispelling natural disbelief in incredible things, seen but not believed.[25]

In much the same way that conjurors seemed willing to give away certain tricks of the trade, Hopwood goes on to explain the mechanism of a number of different trick cinematographic effects. His assertion, some four years after the introduction of projected moving pictures, that some 'simple' spectators might take such effects to be created without manipulation of the footage, seems rather specious—perhaps part of a rhetorical objective to set the expertise of professional filmmakers against the supposed naïveté of their customers. However this account does suggest, at the very least, that the distinction between (acceptable) trickery and (fraudulent) faking remained relatively tentative and imprecise at this point, and also that the slippage between these possibilities might be productive for the industry. Comparing trick cinematography with the showman's 'dodge', Hopwood described a marketplace in which belief became a quality as manipulable as the footage itself and in which the unreliability of the moving image therefore might become a primary attraction of the show.

The uncertainty concerning definitions of trick and fake films persisted during 1900 in the pages of *The Optical Magic Lantern Journal and Photographic Enlarger*. 'This winter,' wrote one commentator, 'fake cinematograph pictures will probably become very popular. Almost any impossible feats can be seen by the use of fake films, but in arranging, cutting up, and rejoining the negatives a tremendous amount of labour and skill is involved.'[26] The article went on to describe an unnamed film in which a magical musician duplicates himself eight times, with each copy standing up to play his own cornet before merging back into the original 'consolidated man', who finally walks, alone, out of frame.[27] Films such as these could be grasped relatively unproblematically within the context of magic theatre. Indeed, a large number of early trick films directly represented the figure of the conjuror in order to explain the action on-screen. For example, R.W. Paul's 1896 series of trick films, which included titles such as *Mr Maskelyne Spinning Plates and Basins*, *Devant's Exhibition of Paper Folding*, and *Devant's Hand Shadows*, directly advertised the appearance on-screen of the famous conjurors, Neville Maskelyne and David Devant, both of whom were still performing at the Egyptian Hall at this time. Bamforth's *The Would be Conjuror* (1900) embeds a simple trick, wherein a conjuror magically produces coins from a yokel's hat, within a familiar gag, in which the yokel unsuccessfully attempts to perform the same trick on his unfortunate wife. Other films reproduced more complex effects derived from traditions in magic theatre. In Paul's *Artistic Creation* (1902), a pierrot's sketches of a young girl come to life, piece by piece, until 'the lady as a whole steps forward', a cinematic trick effect which recalls the spectacular illusion at the heart of the sketch, *The Artist's Dream*, which was still in production at the Egyptian Hall at this time.[28] More frequently, magic subjects did not make such obvious references to existing conjuring tricks, but generated new ones that depended upon ingenious manipulations of the film apparatus. In *The Human Flies* (Paul, 1899), an anonymous conjuror figure is depicted on the screen, but his trick (he makes four observers stick to the ceiling) is created by profilmic manipulation of the scene and substitution effects produced during editing.

Even when no conjuror was presented on-screen, this figure may still have played an important role for audiences in justifying the appearance of trick effects, though here responsibility for the trick was more obviously displaced onto the filmmaker. In a reversing subject such as *The Bathers* (Hepworth and Co., 1900), the 'weird and extremely comic effect' of watching two men impossibly leaving the water feet first perhaps reminded audiences of the projectionists' occasional trick of reversing the apparatus, but there was also a suggestion of the manipulation of reality most pervasively associated with the popular illusionist.[29] Similarly, in James Williamson's *The Puzzled Bather and his Animated Clothes* (1901), the swimmer has even more difficulty staying in the water: his attempts to do so are thwarted when each item of clothing he removes magically reappears on his body. More extensive play with the nature of reality and with the film apparatus occurs in trick films such as *The Big Swallow* (Williamson, 1901). In this well-known film, which was popular enough to remain in catalogues for several years, a man, apparently angry at being cinematographed, approaches the camera and swallows it along with its operator, who is then seen tumbling down his throat. The film then provokes spectators to question the identity of the impossible body responsible afterwards for filming the man as he retreats, munching contentedly. Although such questions were (and are) likely to remain unresolved by spectators, the idea of the conjuror tends to mitigate them, making it clear that the most significant relationship in play was that between audiences and the figure credited with responsibility for arranging the trick. Meanwhile, the man on-screen, whose gaze at the camera persists throughout, perhaps offers a more familiar point of focus for this type of relationship, emphasising that the bizarre action of this film was still connected to a recognisable representative of everyday life.

In such films, the figure of the conjuror may be straightforwardly identified with the longstanding tradition of nineteenth-century illusionist entertainments, and especially with the qualities of spectacle, surprise, sleight of hand, and mastery over space and time associated with magic theatre. Such associations persisted whenever conjurors were associated with the screen, whether they were recognisable celebrities such as Devant, who profilmically arranged their own illusions, or the stock conjuror-figures often represented by Méliès, Paul and others, whose tricks depended substantially upon manipulation of footage, or figures embodied by audiences, whose significance was implied only by the presence of the trick effect. However, *The Optical Magic Lantern Journal and Photographic Enlarger's* definition of such films as 'fake' was already, by 1900, somewhat out of date within the early industry, whose genre classifications were becoming more precise than this. As the next issue reported, Charles Urban, then the managing director of the Warwick Trading Company, had requested that the journal clear up the confusion between cinematographic trickery and faking:

The style of picture we described should have been spoken of as a 'trick film'. This [Urban] explains, differs from a 'fake' inasmuch as the general understanding of a 'fake' film is that of producing a film of a counterfeit representation of an actual event, such as has been practised extensively with South African war subjects, many of which were made in the suburbs of London, beside France and New Jersey, USA.[30]

Urban's motivations for clarifying this point doubtless derived from his desire to establish a reputation for genuine war pictures; as the report pointedly continued, all of Warwick's Boer productions were 'actual photographs taken in the occurrence of the various events in Africa'.[31] But the distinction, which Urban would aggressively pursue on a number of subsequent occasions, was also part of an accretion of formal, stylistic and generic descriptions that cumulatively came to define the conditions under which a film might legitimately seek to mislead its audiences.[32] According to Urban's definition, the trick film called upon the complex conditions of scepticism that had been elaborated within magic theatre, which only required that filmmakers, exhibitors and audiences acknowledge the manifestly artificial premise of the trick. [33] However, in the case of films alleging to represent Boer War scenes, there was a clear agenda to establish what Thomas L. Carson, in his work concerning the social definition of lying, has called a 'warranty of truth', a guarantee that there was no intention to manipulate, falsify, or misrepresent events unfolding before the camera.[34] Urban's comments therefore participated in the process of co-ordinating the belief structures of audiences with qualities of representation on-screen, helping to establish the conditions under which the deception of audiences might be justifiably conducted.

More profound difficulties emerged when the intentional design behind the film was deemed by spectators to be not merely deceptive, but actively untrustworthy and corrupt. 'It is a fallacy to suppose that a photograph cannot lie,' declared the widely-circulated *Harmsworth Magazine* in 1898, and 'what may be done for recreation is also possible of application in more serious affairs'.[35] Sometimes the attitudes of spectators were characterised by optimism or by pragmatic acceptance that films could be trusted. However, the possibilities for manipulation of the truth that the apparatus offered also dictated that cynicism and distrust might be the most appropriate and pragmatic attitudes.

This sophisticated understanding of tricks and fakes was exemplified between 1899 and 1901 by the responses of men such as Urban to faked scenes of the Boer War and of the Boxer Rebellion. 'With the tide of patriotic fervour at the flood', as *The Showman* put it, the value of war footage in the winter of 1900–01 was such that the flow of topical events pictures supplied by world-wide operations like Lumière or the Warwick Trading Company could not match UK demand.[36] In this intensely competitive environment it is not surprising that several of the smaller producers opted to fake their own wartime scenes. Famously, James Williamson staged Boer War films on a golf course, and his *Attack on a China Mission* (1900) was filmed in Hove.[37] Certain other, apparently legitimate, films such as Warwick's *A Skirmish with the Boers near Kimberly* (1900), which was filmed amongst the British troops in South Africa, also contained aspects of staging, though this was clearly not a point that Urban was prepared to confess. This film comprises three shots depicting troop movements and fighting in which the solders scrupulously avoid glancing at the camera. However, the growing distrust of such films, coupled with strangely static fight scenes in which there is little evidence of any enemy to fight against, may also have encouraged exhibitors and spectators to acknowledge that there were elements of faking at work here, too. By late 1901 *The Sun* was reporting that 'certain Society folk' had begun to commission 'the recording and representation of stirring scenes on the field, in which members of the family were—or ought to have been—intimately associated'. [38]

But cinematographic faking was not only associated with wartime scenes. For example, the faking of the avalanche scenes during mountaineering subjects was well-known. By 1905, *The Daily Mail* was reporting in some detail on the manner in which 'Alpine "fatalities"' were reproduced 'for the benefit of the cinematograph':

> Now the operator who wishes to show an accident from this cause has many difficulties to contend with. It is obviously impossible for him to accompany a party of climbers to a dangerous chimney and wait until nature sends the rock. Nature never does send the rock when it is expected. But the cinematograph operator is accustomed to overcome difficulties. He searches the lower heights for a small chimney. Then he collects his climbing party, and looks for a natural 'royal box' from which the camera can observe the rehearsal in comfort . . . The climbers move in single file between the black walls; the cinematograph begins to whirr; the mock Jove tips over one of his rocky thunderbolts—whizz—crash— it flashes by the climbers, another scene has been added to the repertoire of the stage manager of Alpine accidents.[39]

As in the case of Boer war scenes, the staging of scenes such as Alpine accidents seems to have been of considerable interest to the public, and the rapidly growing popular press, exemplified by *The Sun* and *The Daily Mail*, capitalised upon this idea, playing the conjuror's game of demystifying the tricks played by the cinematographer.

This open public debate concerning film faking closely resembled that concerning the authenticity of the spiritualist show and the intentions of the spirit medium or conjuror. If a faked film were exhibited as authentic footage it risked the potentially disastrous criticism that filmmakers and exhibitors were simply lying; if elements of staging were acknowledged, lying could be seen as a fundamental property of the fiction. It was therefore possible for the most obvious of faked productions to find a favourable reception among British audiences. For example, as Frank Gray has argued concerning *Attack on a China Mission*, 'it was irrelevant to the late Victorian audience, that Williamson's film was staged in Hove, England, and displayed the Boxers in absurd ceremonial dress. The audience's applause, we can imagine, was for the victory of empire and Christendom, the defeat of the "yellow peril", and the wonder of animated photography.'[40] Similarly, Richard Brown has suggested that staged Boer War productions were usually distributed to exhibitors as 're-enactments' rather than genuine footage.[41] Provided exhibitors afforded the film a primarily fictional status, its palpably staged conditions of production were likely to appear fully justified, meaning that there was no need to guarantee the truth of its representations in the manner Urban, and others, had suggested. The consequences of this complex relationship with filmmaker and camera were potentially very varied, but certainly included the possibility that audiences would appreciate the knowing and well-humoured trick the filmmaker had played upon them.

Indeed, as Carson explains, 'the great majority of the cases in which the warranty of truth does not hold, involve storytelling or attempts to be humorous', and in the case of the early film these practices dovetailed neatly into the development of its own brand of fictionality, as the case of *Attack on a China Mission* suggests.[42] The point is eloquently made by *The Optical Lantern and Kinematograph Journal* in 1906, in an article that is remarkable for its clear insight into the growing value of fiction at this time:

> We are inclined to lay it down as a maxim that where there is no truth there must be other means taken to provide greater interest to balance the loss. We are led to make these remarks because we have recently seen a number of subjects, purporting to be records of real events, but palpably fakes, in which the aim of the makers has been to conceal their nature. Now we hold emphatically that the day when the public would believe

whatever it was told is long since past. If anything, excesses in the past have led to an excess of incredulity to-day, and many a genuine subject is regarded as a 'stage-managed' one. As a consequence, the subjects shown to us will not make the impression their makers hope; the public will recognise them as faked, and, what is more, it will recognise that an attempt has been made to pass them off as genuine, after which failure is a certainty. A far wiser plan, in our opinion, would have been to make no pretence about reality, show the films as faked and introduce incidents which would be impossible in a genuine picture. The public realises that no attempt is being made to deceive it and enjoys the picture none the less.[43]

In this case, as the 'editor' argues, spectators did not have to believe in the authenticity of film and the trustworthiness of filmmakers, but were able to arrange and evaluate the information on-screen in order to discover the relationship of the film to the world. As in the conjuror's practice of anti-spiritualist magic, the open de-mystification of the tricks that could be played by filmmakers contributed to a sense that the lies told within the show were not intended to deceive. In other words, they were openly fictional, and simply called upon the audience's prior understanding of the forms and functions of fiction.

Furthermore, the article continued, there were good pragmatic reasons for the industry to concentrate either on the production of what it called the 'genuine film' or on openly fictional films.[44] With respect to the latter style of production, it even drew attention to a recent patent that had described a new combination of the magic lantern and cinematograph, with the lantern providing a photographic backdrop for scenes that 'could neither be genuinely obtained or "faked" in the usual manner'.[45] Such films could be cheaply staged 'at the headquarters of the firm' but would not risk alienating audiences by masquerading as footage of unpremeditated events. By contrast, the advantage of marketing authentic actualité footage was that it required no such elaborate stage management:

> The public will be satisfied with a very meagre amount of action in the genuine film, but with an acted piece they demand exciting incidents to balance the lack of truth. That is why faked war films (which everybody knows to be faked) are invariably more bloodthirsty than the real thing, and this attitude of the public also explains the interest with which they watch both the remarkable series showing the growth of a plant and the clever trick films which are now so common.[46]

188

Fully crediting the intelligence of the viewing public in the 1900s, this article suggests that the connection made by Chanan between scientific films, trick films and fakes was already acknowledged and understood in some parts of the industry. It also implies the existence of a tacit agreement between film-makers and spectators, corresponding with that between conjuror and audience, that the illusions generated by the apparatus should not be intended to deceive anyone. The important point about the deceptions prac-tised by the cinematograph was therefore that they openly solicited the curiosity of their knowledgeable audiences, challenging spectators to come to an understanding of the relationship between the projected image and the world it claimed to represent.

I do not wish this line of thinking to suggest that, on those occasions it appeared within a film show, the sensational charge of illusionist spectacle was in any way weakened or mitigated by this knowing expertise of audi-ences. However, it is surely significant that, in 1906, when the influence of theatrical and literary fiction was irresistibly making itself felt and the trend for longer narrative filmmaking was gaining momentum, audiences were already practised at negotiating complex variations on the kinds of truth moving pictures were capable of representing. Derived from a long tradition of popular scepticism that had pervaded showman-led entertainments such as the magic show, the tricks played by the screen would continue to confound, intrigue, and challenge audiences, marking a fundamental conti-nuity in their interpretive activities between the nineteenth and twentieth centuries. Given the consistency of this type of relationship, it was not diffi-cult to anticipate some of the challenges that might lie ahead for these audiences. 'The cinematoscope,' wrote celebrated author and journalist Edward Verrall Lucas, also in 1906, 'has not, I believe, yet begun to lie seri-ously. The fibs it tells now are trifling . . . but there is a great field for really good falsification.'[47] Eagerly imagining the propagandistic uses to which the medium might yet be put, Lucas joined with audiences in embracing the medium's burgeoning capacity for falsehood, looking forward to the 'excel-lent fun' that was to be had as the knowing game of deception and revelation inexorably continued to play itself out.[48]

Keeping it Real: The Camera Operator as Adventurer

Perhaps because the early moving pictures so often made such productive and explicit play with their capacity to deceive audiences, when filmmakers wished to convince spectators that the representations on-screen were authentic, unfalsified slices of reality, they quickly developed formal, generically defined mechanisms for doing so.[49] On some occasions, as the 'editor' from *The Optical Lantern and Kinematograph Journal* has already implied, the 'meagre amount of action' associated with many actuality scenes was probably enough to guarantee their authenticity. Self-evidently, there was little opportunity or motive for a filmmaker to stage a street scene, such as *Electric Tram Rides from Forster Square, Bradford* (M&K, 1902), or a football subject, such as *Sunderland v Leicester Fosse* (M&K, 1907), in which the everydayness or unpredictability of the action was in any case a key part of the attraction. Equally, more obviously staged actualities, such as royal and celebrity subjects, possessed a different kind of authenticity, tending to reproduce the etiquette already popularly associated with publicity for these individuals.

When the realist nature of the films was more difficult to guarantee, early filmmakers would frequently support their productions with publicity that reinforced their claim to representational integrity. This, for example, was the guiding motive behind Urban's repeated efforts to recommend his own genuine war scenes to potential exhibitors. In more ambitious genre productions such as these, publicity materials and catalogue descriptions often emphasised the presence of the camera operator in order to corroborate the authenticity of the scenes represented. Furthermore, films such as *Coolie Boys Diving for Coins* actively made a point of including the operator within the action, thus enabling spectators to witness this individual's participation in exotic scenes. Sometimes camera operators might even be visible within the film, usually because there was more than one cinematograph present at the scene, but very occasionally the camera captured a mirror image of its own operation. In Smith's *The Dull Razor*, which I have previously discussed in relation to facial performance, the reflected image of the camera operator, most likely Smith himself, is also reflected in the bathroom mirror. The 1901 Warwick catalogue chose to ignore this element of the film, perhaps fearing that it might be perceived as an error exhibitors could not remedy nor spectators excuse.[50] But the American Selig catalogue for 1903 emphasised that 'the facial contortions of this man are so funny that the lens of the taking camera itself shared the jolity [*sic*] and turned out a great, happy, wonderful picture', suggesting that this open acknowledgement of the operator need not be a problem. Provided he too was incorporated into an institutional logic, here perhaps associated with the inclusive and diversionary environment of vaudeville, the operator could thus become a significant figure for audiences, even in comedy productions.[51]

Although apparently accidental moments such as that captured by *The Dull Razor* were unusual, Selig's attempt to encourage spectators to identify with figures such as camera operators was entirely characteristic. Across a range of genres, this enabled audiences to adopt identifiable perspectives upon potentially unfamiliar or surprising scenes. On such occasions, it is relatively easy to see how spectators were encouraged to occupy what Casetti describes as roles inscribed within the text, because these roles were immediately associated not only with the camera, but with the camera operator's point of view. Thus, the early erotic subject, *A Victorian Lady in her Boudoir* (Esmé Collings, 1896), presents not just the spectacle of the lady undressing but also the spectacle of undressing before the camera and its operator, as her regular glances both at and behind the lens seem to acknowledge. Similarly, in films such as *Gang Making Railway—South Africa*, which I have discussed in terms of the proprietorial, racially-inflected gaze of the camera, there are also opportunities for spectators to consider the actual body behind the camera, and perhaps even to question the motives of this individual for taking the film.

Such embodiments are no more than intriguing possibilities written into the texts, but they add one further complication to the idea of the 'view aesthetic', which, in Gunning's work, has described the idea that 'the camera literally acts as a tourist, spectator or investigator, and the pleasure in the film lies in this surrogate of looking'.[52] Once the role of the camera operator in capturing such scenes was acknowledged by audiences, their relationship with the film was less likely to depend upon identification with the surrogate camera, than in an imaginative projection of the process of filming. Under such conditions, the figure behind the camera could be more precisely identified, becoming a much more sharply defined, individualised presence than the analogy between visual and ideological points of view on foreign scenes suggests. In fact, it was common practice for early film shows and associated publicity to promote exactly this kind of more personal relationship with camera operators. For example, when *The Showman* described in 1902 a forthcoming film entertainment 'of a kind of trip round the world in an armchair', it emphasised that 'a photographer has been dispatched from London with the necessary instructions', and described the role of this traveller in the selection and composition of the exotic images on-screen.[53] As Luke McKernan has shown in his work concerning the Charles Urban Trading Company, sometimes even the names and faces of more celebrated operators were known to exhibitors and audiences, especially when these individuals were present during exhibitions to describe their adventures when taking the films.[54] On such occasions, the early film industry's remarkable accumulation of world views serves as evidence not only of modernity's passion for images, but also of its propensity to deploy these images according to familiar institutional precedents, including those associated with pervasive nineteenth-century traditions of adventure narrative.

Among the most significant of these precedents at the turn of the century was a range of popular and widely circulated illustrated periodicals, including titles such as *The Strand*, *The Harmsworth Magazine*, *Pearson's Magazine*, the *Windsor Magazine*, and *Black and White Budget* which regularly included non-fictional (though highly sensationalised) accounts of adventures on mountains, in foreign lands, and during well-known conflicts. In addition to these well-known titles a number of more specialised publications, such as *Wide World Magazine*, which first appeared in 1898, sought to advance niche publishing of such material. Frequently calling upon the patriotic sentiments of their readers, stories such as 'The Romance of Seal Hunting' and 'A Battle Royal with a Tiger' were, of course, structured by an array of colonialist and nationalist discourses. But they construed these sentiments primarily as a matter of personal obligation and risk, usually developing narratives of fortitude and heroism that could be authenticated, as the editorial for the first issue of *Wide World Magazine* clarified, with reference to the authority of its authors and photographers:

> There will be no fiction in the Magazine, but yet it will contain weird adventure, more thrilling than any conceived by the novelist in his wildest flights. There will be the plain, straightforward narratives of well-known travellers, explorers, and others. As a rule, the photo of each narrator will be reproduced, so that you may see for yourself what manner of man the story-teller is. And so wonderful will the pictures be found, so enthralling the letterpress, that the Magazine will be found to fascinate not merely serious men, but also women of all degrees and even the smallest children, who will learn many delightful lessons from its attractive pages.[55]

The tone evoked is one of a serious-minded, courageous storyteller, returning to the domestic hearth to impart the lessons of moral improvement that were to be had from voluntarily exposing oneself to hardship and risk. An essential part of this strategy was the inclusion of a photograph of the adventurer in question, which gave the storyteller a face and seemed intended to offer audiences a tangible point of identification within the narrative. Repeatedly, such journals encouraged their readers to entertain this sense of personal engagement with narrators and protagonists, introducing biographical details and carefully describing their ingenuity in overcoming the threats they had encountered. On some occasions, the risks that were undertaken in order to capture good photographs also entered the narratives, closing the distance between photographer and view in such a way that the very effort to construct a world picture became a palpable part of the attraction.

In a similar manner, the most successful travel lecturers in the 1890s also tended to adopt self-reflexive positions, taking their own roles as adventurers in foreign lands as their subjects, and frequently detailing the risks encountered when trying to gain a new experience or capture a spectacular image for audiences at home. For example, among Burton Holmes's most popular lectures was his 'Into Morocco', and here the camera took on a leading role within the entertainment. Emphasising throughout what he referred to as a 'Mahommedan prejudice' against image-making equipment, Holmes recounts in detail the lengths he and his companions had gone to in order to take pictures of local scenes and people. In the city of Selli, Holmes complained that 'So hostile is the populace that every attempt at picture-making brings a volley of stones from howling urchins and threatening murmurs from savage looking citizens. All that we remember of our visit to Selli is a rapid dash through narrow thoroughfares amid a sprinkling of missiles and maledictions.'[56] Later, he recounted his attempt to capture an image of a young Prince of Morocco, fully capitalising on the tension this created:

> As Abd-el-Aziz approaches, I am trembling with excitement and anxiety; if I succeed, I shall have accomplished what never before has been done; if I am detected in the act of copying the features of the scared youth, the consequences may be serious—men have been killed for lesser sacrilege. The Prince draws nearer; to my joy he halts directly before the men who shield me from his look. Just as he draws rein, the horses prance apart and leave an opening in the line. Through this gap the Prince looks wonderingly at me as I make a profound salute, and at the same time level my camera, and with trembling fingers press the button. The click of the shutter sends a cold chill through me.[57]

The lecture is punctuated with these sensationalised attempts to take pictures, making the relationship between photographer and subject into an elaborate game of cat and mouse. Several of the photographs reproduced in the published version of the lecture, such as 'Discovered!' and 'Capturing a Fort with Cameras', were also intended to illustrate this drama, once again making the adventurous accumulation of views into the principle focus of the entertainment (**Fig. 6**).

This starring role of the camera operator, written so strongly into the

CAPTURING A FORT WITH CAMERAS

a. Photography as the conquest of foreign scenes.

Fig. 6 An adventurous accumulation of views. Photographs derived from Burton Holmes' Travelogue entertainment, 'Into Morocco,' emphasising the risks encountered by the camera operator. (Burton Holmes, 'Into Morocco,' in *The Burton Holmes Lectures*, 10 vols (Battle Creek, Michigan: The Little Preston Company, 1901), I, pp. 174, 183). © The British Library Board. All rights reserved 21/08/08. Shelfmark: 10028.h.8. License no. 1023910.691.

b. The photographer is spotted by his unwilling subjects.

DISCOVERED!

adventure narratives of illustrated magazines and popular lectures, would reappear regularly in varied genes of early non-fiction production. Indeed, far from being an occasional point of focus within films depicting exotic travel, the adventurous operator was a pervasive presence in such films, and can productively be seen as a rather specialised and very early type of 'picture personality'. In the period before 1910, companies such as Warwick, Pathé, and the Charles Urban Trading Company, which dominated non-fiction sales in the UK, all exploited such figures. During the 1910s, as Gerry Turvey has explained, it would also be important for the British and Colonial Kinematograph Company, whose celebrity mountaineer-operator, Frederick Burlingham, would also specialise in adventure subjects such as *Descent into the Crater of Vesuvius* (British and Colonial Kinematograph Company, 1913), in which the climbing party seems to get remarkably close to the steaming vents at the centre of the volcano.[58] For these firms, war, current events, exotic travel, exploration, mountaineering, anthropology and big-game hunting were all popular subjects that thrived on publicising (and, often, wildly exaggerating) the dangers to which their operators were routinely exposed. Closer to home, films inspired by the *fin de siècle* generation of urban ethnographers brought the exploration trope to bear on the poorest areas of large cities. For example, catalogue descriptions of the lengthy four-film series, *Living London* (Urban, 1904), which took the camera from the East End slums to Trafalgar Square, emphasised the participation of George R. Simms, perhaps the most celebrated populariser of urban exploration at this time.[59] In all of these genres, the camera operator became an early figure around which patterns of empathy and identification appeared to gather naturally, largely because this idea was already popularly associated with existing traditions of pictorial adventure narrative. As in these traditions, because the actuality camera was obliged to visit the most spectacular, dangerous and unlikely locations, and because it had to get close to the action in order to record it, such films fostered the idea that spectators could vicariously witness the denouement of an adventure undertaken by the operator.

The telling of such stories contributed to the definition of a peculiarly modern form of adventure in which risk and uncertainty were deliberately courted in order to enable representative individuals to surmount them. This was a relationship concisely described in 1911 by Georg Simmel, who saw in the modern adventure a means for reinforcing the fragile and unstable models of selfhood and identity he had already described as characteristic of everyday life under conditions of modernity. In his essay, 'The Adventure', Simmel argued that the form of the adventure had the power to reassure individuals of their own sense of agency, shoring up the cherished principle that their actions had some potency and force in a modern world that contin-ually threatened to slip out of their grasp.[60] In other words, the form of the adventure gave slippery aspects of modern life, such as the business enter-prise or the love affair, a definable beginning and end, assuring participants in these activities that they had an important, if not heroic, role to play in bringing them to their conclusion. In this uncertain cultural environment, adventure narratives, which identified unambiguous ambitions and then presented their fulfilment as a natural consequence of an individual's labour, delivered an idealised model of personal achievement that was likely to have considerable value. The capacity of the cinematograph to provoke an expe-rience of empathy for its adventurous subjects and operators was therefore likely to be especially powerful for spectators.

Filmmakers eagerly exploited this potential attraction, frequently playing up the danger to which camera operators subjected themselves in order to gain the custom of potential exhibitors. Once again, a key part of this strategy was to make the camera and its operator as visible as possible, either by emphasising the difficult circumstances under which the films had been taken, or more simply by allowing one operator to record the undertakings of another, so that the cinematograph itself became a principle subject of the film. For example, in *Captain Deasy's Daring Drive: Ascent* (Deutsche Mutoskop und Biograph, 1903) and *Captain Deasy's Daring Drive: Descent* (Deutsche Mutoskop und Biograph, 1903), in which Deasy attempts to drive up and down the track of a funicular railway, the cinematograph itself is clearly a central object of attention. In the *Ascent*, one cinematograph records the ingenious method of attaching another cinematograph and its operator to the engine, thus explaining the following scenes of the car climbing the mountain. Although the camera on the engine occasionally pans to view the landscape, it is far more concerned to record the reactions of the five men in the car as they negotiate tricky corners and the presence of other camera operators beside the line, who secure additional views of the car and engine as they pass. The *Descent* is more interested in exhibiting the sheer drop down the mountainside and the careful judgment of the driver in keeping the wheels of the car either side of the track. At one moment, one man in the car visibly indicates the scale of the drop; at another, a similar glance off-screen is followed by a lengthy pan looking down into the valley. Both films attempted to spice up the scenic views often at this time taken from funic-ular railways by introducing the hazards associated with automobiles, but they also focused the attentions of spectators directly upon the dangers undergone by all participants, including the camera operators, whose roles seem more prominent even than that of the driver.

The visibility of operators was also accentuated within the publicity generated by early producers. In 1901, when James Kenyon of Mitchell and Kenyon decided to film a storm at sea from the lighthouse on Roker Pier in Sunderland, but lost his camera to a freak wave, he was quick to report the story to *The Showman*, which reported that 'in the endeavours to obtain startling and sensational cinematograph films, the cinematographer often has to run no little personal risks'.[61] He thus brought the anecdote to an audience of showmen-exhibitors—his usual customers—and a group who could make good use of such spicy material. Two weeks later, with characteristic commercial acumen, Charles Urban adopted a similar policy, recounting to the same journal his adventures when obtaining what he pointedly called 'the best cinematograph pictures of a stormy sea' on behalf of the Warwick Trading Company:

> 'To take a series of living pictures of the ocean during a storm is something akin to cinematographing a bull as it is madly charging at you and your camera; in both cases the operator is in a tight place,' says Mr. Urban. 'The day I selected to make my exposure, a mountainous sea was on, breaking all over the boat, being carried, indeed, over the navigation bridge, which is 65ft. above the water-line . . . I attempted to fix my Bioscope at the door of this deck and, assisted by a friendly hand, started to work. No sooner had I commenced, than a huge body of water came over the bow and rushed in a mighty flood through the door, carrying the outfit, myself, and assistant along in its path, leaving us bruised and damp, nearly 100ft aft.'[62]

Although Urban was a vocal advocate of the role of the cinematograph in education, this type of hyperbolic account of non-fiction production was equally characteristic of the publicity he produced for the Warwick Trading Company and then, after 1903, at the Charles Urban Trading Company.[63] Indeed, the dominance of these two firms in the UK market for non-fiction indicates something of the success of this strategy. Like *Wide World Magazine*, Urban delivered a series of sensationalised narratives, frequently centred on the figure of the adventurous operator, but also promised that his entertainments would be improving for audiences. Thus, while cultivating the vital showman market, Urban also promoted his films as a high-class entertainment, and in 1903 began using London's prestigious Alhambra Theatre to showcase many of them on this basis.

Urban's commitment to this style of instructive adventure filmmaking is easily discerned from the remarkable series of Warwick and Urban catalogues released between 1898 and 1907.[64] Repeatedly, these increasingly lavishly illustrated catalogues not only identified the operators responsible for taking sensational pictures, but also included photographs of these men at work on location and lengthy accounts of the adventures they encountered as they did so. Such descriptions were certainly intended to attract the interest of possible exhibitors and served as the basis for press releases to journals such as *The Showman*, but they are also an excellent example of the kind of precise instruction catalogues could give to film lecturers. In the case of *Living London*, the 1905 Urban catalogue even promised to anyone purchasing the entire series a free copy of the complete descriptive lecture given by Frank Stevens at the Alhambra.[65] Thus, although it was impossible for most exhibitors to reproduce the performances associated with celebrated lecturers, Urban did all he could to uphold connections with such men. He would subsequently become the UK distributor for films derived from Holmes's Travelogues, and surviving correspondence shows that Arthur Malden had (for a disputed fee) lectured Urban films at the London Polytechnic during 1906.[66]

More generally, the catalogue descriptions carefully echoed certain aspects of the performances of men such as Holmes, and especially those that emphasised the operation of the apparatus under perilous circumstances. Thus, camera operators such as Joseph Rosenthal (best known for his Boer and Russo-Japanese War films), Frank Ormiston-Smith (an Alpine specialist), H.R. Lomas (views of Borneo and Ceylon), George Rogers (who filmed the Russian army during the Russo-Japanese war), and Charles Rider Noble (who filmed the insurgents during the Macedonian uprising in 1905[67]), were all significant figures in Urban's catalogues, and the dangers they had undergone were routinely detailed. 'Mr Rosenthal', according to the *The Great Russo-Japanese War* supplement in 1905, 'was compelled to enter the firing line and expose himself and his instrument to many dangers.'[68] As Urban emphasised in subsequent editions of the catalogue, such incidents were common occurrences for his operators:

> Probably, most people will be surprised to learn that the life of a conscientious cinematographer is far more dangerous than that of the 'knight of the pencil', the war correspondent. But the fact of the matter is, that the latter has only himself, his pencil, the indispensable tooth-brush, and his note-book to carry about with him, while the bioscoper, wherever he goes, must take with him a comparatively bulky camera, boxes of films, and various other none too portable paraphernalia.
>
> *Still, there is, strangely enough, an indescribable fascination surrounding*

198

> *the quest of securing pictures under perilous conditions, and I know many men*
> *who, on being offered a choice between an easy and a dangerous expedition,*
> *will unhesitatingly choose the latter.*[69]

The exotic scenes produced by such men were not only intended to produce an immersive experience for spectators, enabling them to adopt the perspective of the camera, but also to provide evidence of the adventures that had been undertaken in order to secure spectacular views. At the same time, the established authority associated with such adventurer figures—men who actively dedicated themselves to perilous pursuits –helped to legitimise the footage they captured, making it possible for Urban to exaggerate the spectacular appeal of his films without incurring accusations that his productions had been faked.

The remarkable mountaineering films produced by Frank Ormiston-Smith for Urban both at Warwick and the Charles Urban Trading Company typify this kind of relationship with audiences. In film series such as *Switzerland: An Ascent of the Jungfrau* (WTC, 1901); *The Ascent of Mont Blanc, 15,781ft High* (WTC, 1902); *The Matterhorn (14,780 Feet)* (Urban, 1903); *An Ascent of the Wetterhorn* (Urban, 1905); *Conquering the Dolomites* (Urban, 1907); and *Ascent and Descent of the Dolomite Towers* (Urban, 1907), as well as a large number of individual mountain scenes, the catalogues emphasised with increasing exuberance the dangers experienced by the climbing party and reproduced by the camera.[70] By the time the Dolomite series appeared, the idea of the scenic view was barely registered within descriptions that affectively lingered over the experience of risk associated with these hazardous peaks:

> With rapidly changing films, the progress of the climbers through the *impressive wildness and sublime majesty* is watched with breathless interest: *perilous ascents* which cause the audience to gaze in eloquent silence and greet the accomplishment with hearty applause.
>
> They are shown a party of climbers start on their *dangerous journey;* they accompany them step by step along their *hazardous way,* gasp with apprehension as they negotiate some difficult rock path or treacherous 'traverse', hold their breath as for a moment one of the climbers seems apprehensive, and heave a sigh of thankfulness when they realise that the summit of the journey and their expectations is reached.[71]

As the surviving copy of *The Ascent of Mont Blanc, 15,781ft High* testifies, this sense of breathless expectation conveyed by catalogue and lecture had been presupposed by the films themselves, which followed the conventional narrative progress from the first scene, *Preparations for the Ascent and Descent of the Party*, to the last, *The Summit of Mont Blanc, 15781 Feet*, but always encouraged audiences to attend to the possibility of an accident. Although scenes such as *Reaching the Grands Mulets, 10,120 Feet* presented an evidently staged series of avalanches (again, in spite of Urban's protestations to the contrary), most scenes seem naturally drawn to the arduous, shuffling progress of the mountaineers back and forth across the frame. Encouraging spectators to attend closely to this sense of duration, the exaggerated contingency of the climb and the role of the adventurer with nothing but 'loose, rocking boulders . . . between him and a sheer drop into eternity' made every movement on-screen significant, and every movement of the camera between scenes an acknowledgment of an off-screen movement soliciting further risk.[72]

Other films capitalised further on the 'perilous adventures in search of animated photographs' undertaken by men such as Ormiston-Smith, by filming spots at which actual accidents had taken place.[73] Barely a month after the widely publicised death of two British climbers on the Wetterhorn Couloir, Ormiston-Smith obtained a panorama scene with two more climbers ghoulishly passing through the scene of the accident. 'This picture was only obtained at great risk,' the catalogue salaciously emphasised, 'as rocks and avalanches are liable to sweep down the couloir at any moment and without warning.'[74] Ormiston-Smith would also race to the scene of an accident on Mont Blanc the day after it occurred, and his *The Accident on the Great Schreckhorn* (WTC, 1902) fully dramatised the experience of risk that underpinned all of his Alpine subjects. In the series *An Alpine Catastrophe* (Urban, 1905), a search party were filmed as they attempted to recover the bodies of two climbers, who had died in the previous season, from a ravine. Later, the fictional productions released by Urban-Eclipse of films such as *A Mont Blanc Tragedy* (Urban-Eclipse, 1907) and *The Mountaineer's Flirtation* (Urban-Eclipse, 1907) would capitalise more openly, but less controversially, on the idea of the Alpine accident, using it to initiate rescue narratives without provoking the morbid sentiments associated with actuality scenes. In the latter production, for example, the catalogue presented a 'picture-story of love, jealousy, rivalry, and magnaminous forgiveness . . . interwoven with thrilling scenes of Alpine adventure, disaster and rescue'.[75]

Perhaps seeking to compete with the heightened affective responses now being proposed by openly fictional productions, by December 1906 Ormiston-Smith wrote to Urban with a more daring project, intended to raise the stakes still further in the fierce market for non-fiction film:

As soon as I have the details of my 'Alps from End to End' scheme ready I would like a chat with you.

It might be advisable to do the Matterhorn from its most difficult Italian side next summer, in view of the possibility of Pathé's man taking it into his head to try the Matterhorn after his trip this summer.

Then if he did so you would have a fine set off, as the Italian side is very sensational and difficult, and if he did not, you could hold over the pictures for inclusion in the final 'End to End' series.[76]

Probably looking to impress Urban with the necessity of funding another large scale excursion, Ormiston-Smith purposefully implies that the Charles Urban Trading Company was in danger of falling behind Pathé, at this point their most significant competition in non-fiction production. In order to stay ahead, Ormiston-Smith recommended a policy that mountaineers had been following for the past fifty years: he emphasised the uncertain and dangerous aspects of mountaineering, offering to attempt new peaks, or more difficult faces of the same peaks, or suggested climbing them during unfavourable seasons. Taking on the most 'sensational and difficult' of climbs, the point of this proposal was not (or at least, not primarily) to capture a sequence of views, nor to educate audiences concerning the Alpine scene, or even to delineate the narrative of an ascent, but to emphasise the dangers undertaken by the climbing party and the cinematographer. In a market saturated with Alpine views, Ormiston-Smith suggested, it was the operator's active soliciting of risk in the mountains that would give Urban a competitive edge.

Mountaineering was only one of several adventure genres during the 1900s and 1910s which emphasised the idea of risk. Whether watching the laborious progress of adventurers scaling a glacier, or trekking across treacherous Arctic wastes, or carefully negotiating a conflict zone, or painstakingly stalking big game animals, spectators were frequently obliged to experience some of the tension that weighed upon these scenes, undergoing a powerful experience of empathy for the camera's subjects and operators. Among these much-overlooked but highly significant genres, films depicting big game hunting, primarily in Africa and the Polar Regions, seem to have been especially popular in the early 1910s, and relatively large numbers survive, sometimes in the form of newsreels.[77] Similarly, the nature films of Cherry Kearton, who began his career with Urban, frequently detailed the adventures that had been undertaken in order to secure images of exotic species. In all such films, the intrepid camera operator was a uniquely visible, accountable, and frequently named lead player in the drama. He offered to audiences a privileged vantage point upon spectacular scenes, but in contrast to the touristic implications of scenic genres, his gaze opened up onto definitively unsafe spaces, where perils, conflicts and adventures might legitimately be had. In doing so, he potentially had a remarkably direct and emotive impact on the experience of audiences, comparable in some ways to the practised manipulation of emotions that would later come to characterise fictional filmmaking. Because the drama of adventure filmmaking deliberately exposed the risks undertaken by camera and operator, it encouraged audiences, as Simmel might also have noted, to reflect on possibilities for conquest in a modern world that increasingly seemed to flatten out the experience of everyday life. Like the authors and narrators of narrative fiction, the camera operator was a site of imaginative projection, a figure credited with responsibility for the heightened emotional responses that audiences hoped, on the routine basis which film institutions afforded them, to experience.

Telling Tales, Owning Films

The idea of adventure provided early audiences with institutionally sanctioned mechanisms for experiencing action that reached beyond the textures of their everyday lives. Thus, the tale of the lone protagonist, embarking on the sensationalised adventure of the conquest, the rescue, or the love affair, and taking unlikely risks in order to achieve his or her goals, would remain central to the narrative patterns of the moving pictures. Meanwhile, discourses associated with the faking or unreliability of early films ensured that, running parallel to the film's evolving narrativity, spectators had also come to a sophisticated understanding of the unstable nature of its fictionality, enabling them to anticipate, speculate upon, and regulate the relationship between themselves and the screen, and between the screen and the world. The development of such forms of expertise in spectators was intrinsic to the institutional development of the early industry from the beginning, but it was the consolidation of stable modes of film fiction during the 1890s and 1900s which would capitalise most effectively and enduringly on the skills they had acquired. Therefore, the processes of embodiment I have described in the early cinema are not to be opposed to the narrative economy associated with linear editing practices in subsequent cinemas: they were part of the same process that would continue to allow audiences to contextualise, personalise, and make sense of the flow of images that appeared on the screen.

Thus, as Thomas Elsaesser has argued in relation to narrative cinema, the early cinema thrived because it enabled spectators to recognise intentionality within the medium, 'to construe all movement as . . . potentially significant, by interpreting it as purposive and motivated'.[78] There were potentially innumerable figures to be credited with some measure of responsibility for a film, depending upon its formal properties and upon the institutional and social contexts in which it was screened. In order to demonstrate this point in the case of early cinema, we need only postulate a subtle alteration in the institutional context of exhibition for the films. If Warwick's *The Accident on the Great Schreckhorn*, one of the Ormiston-Smith series, were to appear in the course of a lecture concerning 'Scenic Switzerland' (as it may well have done), if aspects of faking were identified in the film, or if it were alternatively titled 'The Rescue', this single adventure film would instead evoke practices of embodiment associated more strongly with the tourist's view of foreign landscapes, with the trickery of untrustworthy filmmakers, or with storytelling practices. Thus, as Edward Branigan and other cognitive theorists have argued, again in relation to narrative cinema, the interpretation of early film very rarely rests on the application of only one interpretive frame, or one model of authorship:

> It would instead seem more useful to acknowledge a polyphony at work in film in which the 'camera' becomes a fiction—merely a fluid site for a series of speculations we make about the text. A text, then, is composed of the simultaneous advance of a multiple series of narrations, or lines, which overlap one another though each maintains a relatively independent compositional course.[79]

These speculations, I would add, continued to include all manner of agents from the most literal sources of authority, such as named camera operators, to abstract figures such as narrators. Rejecting metaphors of depth, it is the interaction of these figures rather than the attribution of an authentic state of mind to an individual agent which defines the interpretation of film.[80] Thus the adventurer, the tourist, the deceptive film producer and the storyteller were among the potential figures credited with responsibility for *The Accident on the Great Schreckhorn*, but their exact positioning was likely to differ to some extent from site to site, and from spectator to spectator. Among these figures, however, the role of the storyteller would gradually become increasingly important within explicitly fictional genres, and here the influence of earlier narrative traditions made itself strongly felt.

Of course, as historians of magic lantern have done most to demonstrate, the storytelling impetus of the moving image had already undergone several decades of institutional development before the appearance of film. The dissolving views of lantern entertainments and the screening of lantern sequences had already implied the idea of a basic temporal progression.[81] For Harry Furniss, the celebrated British lantern lecturer and American film scenarist, the practice of speaking to pictures had been 'the best of preparations for taking part in moving pictures'.[82] 'As for writing plots,' he continued, 'an impromptu speaker is of little use if he cannot, when the truth fails him, invent his own stories'. Similar claims can be made for other technologies and performance practices from puppetry and shadow theatre to the zoetrope. Marta Braun has even argued that the chronophotographer, Eadweard Muybridge, 'was not using his camera as an analytic tool at all but was using it for narrative representation, and the results are at least as absorbing as what he was ostensibly producing'.[83]

Thus the development of the narrative capacities of moving pictures, as described within many recent accounts of the early cinema, were predicated by the existence of narrative pictorial media with which early filmmakers and audiences were already familiar. In addition, the demand among the first film producers for fictional plot scenarios, which began long before the appearance of feature films and the construction of static picture theatres, also borrowed from earlier production traditions, such as those of life-model lantern producers. According to one contemporary account, lantern manufacturer James Bamforth's planning process began with the selection or commissioning of new stories and songs, and this was followed by the creation or acquisition of painted flats and props to serve as backgrounds for the action.[84] Similarly, Cecil Hepworth recalled of his early productions that, 'First we thought of a story; then we painted the scenery if it wasn't all open air, as it usually was. Then we acted and photographed it.'[85] More generally, Edward Azlant writes that in the period between 1898 and 1903, when narrative film was beginning to emerge, screenwriting 'could be fairly described as the pre-arrangement of scenes', and he suggests that even the first Lumière productions probably exploited ordered, if skeletal, pre-production designs.[86] Though relatively simple, such processes did not depend on whimsy and intuition and inevitably began with an initial stage of story development. In this way, filmmakers such as Hepworth, borrowing from existing production strategies, anticipated and facilitated the demands of spectators and exhibitors for the telling of simple stories.

There is also some evidence suggesting that the growth and consolidation of storytelling practices in early film responded not only to the demands of spectators, for whom simple pictorial stories had long been an attraction of entertainment institutions, but also to the requirements of industrial rationalisation. In particular, as Gaudreault has argued, the necessity for film-makers to obtain intellectual property rights on their pictures and prevent copying or duping by competitors had a powerful influence on the development of fictional filmmaking.[87] Thus, legitimisation within parliament or the courts dictated, in part, the kinds of signifying practices that dominated the screen. On such occasions, the idea of authorship, which arguably had always been a pertinent part of audiences' practices of embodiment, became much more explicitly a matter of institutional significance. Not only did such figures connect producers, exhibitors and audiences by constraining the range of interpretive responses that might be appropriately addressed to a film, they also became the premise for film production companies to claim copyright on fictional film subjects. Although, as this book has argued, early film shows were characterised by a proliferation of bodies and modes of address, any of which might establish effective lines of communication, identifying figures among these whose role was comparable to that of literary or dramatic authors linked the telling of stories to the ownership of the films. Furthermore, because the idea of film authorship emphasised the originality of film production as opposed to exhibition practices, it tended to reinforce the gradual transition of performative responsibility for the film from exhibitors to producers.

In fact, the system of ownership for the film came rapidly into operation within the first fifteen years of film in the UK. A considerable number of moving pictures after 1897 were registered in the UK at Stationers Hall as proof of ownership in intellectual property. Furthermore, as Richard Brown has confirmed, even though no specific legislation was introduced before the Copyright Act of 1911, there were surprisingly few British cases of infringement of copyright for a moving picture during this period.[88] Brown cites a selection of cases between 1896 and 1911, however, which demonstrate that 'copyright protection was always available in England to cover individual scenes in a film, if they had been registered as single photographs, but not for the combination, or sequence of photographs that constituted a film'.[89] Later, producers carefully copyrighted at least one frame of every scene of multi-shot films, effectively registering all pertinent elements of the mise-en-scène at Stationers Hall.

However, the practice of 'film filching' continued, and in 1905 *The Optical Magic Lantern and Cinematograph Journal* roundly condemned the 'dishonest laggards' who carried out this 'abominable trade'.[90] Furthermore, in spite of legal prevention of the mechanical copying of films, the law did not prevent films like *The Biter Bit* (Bamforth, 1901), which remade George Albert Smith's *A Joke on the Gardener* (1898), and the Lumières' very early

L'Arroseur Arrosé (1895) from reproducing the success of earlier films.[91] 'Far worse' than merely copying films according to the same commentator from the *Journal*, 'is it to steal the plot, scenes, and ideas of a successful film, to re-act (sometimes I admit with improvement) and produce the work without the slightest acknowledgement to the originators!'[92] In this hostile atmosphere it was difficult to protect film subjects legally, as Sam Ricketson explains, 'if they were not the result of any arrangement or ordering by the maker of the film'.[93] Therefore, it became essential for filmmakers that the specific forms of personal, stylistic investment employed within moving pictures be recognised as intellectual property in their own right. In this light, the increasing significance of storytelling agencies within films, whose presence was closely associated with longstanding and copyrightable artistic and narrative precedents, was a reflection not only of the tastes of audiences, but also of the commercial motive for each film production company to protect its products. In both the UK and the USA, earlier developments in dramatic copyright regulation proved especially important legal precedents for filmic representation.

Jennifer Forrest has detailed the growing sophistication in copyrighting practices before 1911 in the USA across a series of significant cases.[94] However, usefully in the context of my preceding intermedial study of the early industry, we can trace these developments across two landmark cases concerning the adaptation of *Ben-Hur* to the magic lantern and film screens. In the first of these cases Bradford slide manufacturers, Riley Bros, defended their adaptation of the story to the magic lantern.[95] Lew Wallace, the author of the novel, and Harper Bros, its New York publisher, alleged that the marketing of this item in the USA constituted an infringement of their dramatic copyright on the 'Story of Ben-Hur', which they had acquired several years before.[96] A letter from Riley Bros to the *Optical Magic Lantern Journal* in August 1896 (which cleverly publicised the court case, and the slides, in the UK) spelled out the case put by Harper Bros:

> Harpers, in their plaint, allege that a magic lantern exhibition is a dramatic representation, that the person demonstrating or lecturing and the operator at the machine are the *dramatis personae* as much as the living actors on the stage, and that, therefore, every exhibition of our pictures in conjunction with the lecture is an infringement of a drama on 'Ben Hur'.[97]

The Honourable Henry E. Lacombe would finally adjudge that the publishing and selling of the printed lecture would be prohibited in the USA, but that Riley Bros might legitimately sell the slides alone. Some light is shed on the decision by a remark reportedly made by the judge during the hearing:

> We understand that the judge, who, of course, said little, remarked to the plaintiff's counsel that if we have been setting it forth in the 'Vitascope', where there is such a real representation of life, he could have understood his argument, but it was difficult to imagine such being brought into a mere demonstration as in a lantern exhibition.[98]

In terms of copyright, Judge Lacombe's remark usefully defined the distinction between a 'demonstration', which here defined the form of the lantern lecture, and a 'representation', which defined the performance of the early American film projector, the Vitascope, which had made a much-publicised New York debut that April. A demonstration required that some object be shown, or some conclusion proven, and that an authoritative framing procedure be responsible for that showing or proving. In this case the shown lantern images (objects which, according to Lacombe, did not tell a story in themselves) were framed by the authoritative lecture (a discourse which did tell a story about the images). Consequently, the printed lecture was deemed an infringement of Harpers' copyright on the novel: the judge considered that it reproduced a narrative and stylistic centre of authority that had also epitomised the printed book. But the lantern images, which did not imply any narrative or stylistic centre of authority besides that superimposed by the lecture, could not in themselves infringe upon the copyright.[99]

By contrast the representation made by film would not have rendered the projected image in this same neutral, non-narrated manner. If the demonstration of slides depended entirely upon the presence and authority of a demonstrator, a dependence physically symbolised by the interposition of the pointer between narration and image, the representation of film substantially depended upon the 'presence' and authority attributed to the moving images on-screen. The point was reinforced in the second *Ben-Hur* case when Wallace sued the Kalem Company for their sixteen-scene version of his story (1907) and, for the first time in such a challenge on the movies, succeeded.[100] During the 1911 appeal hearing, Justice Holmes reinforced the court's opinion that, 'Action can tell a story, display all the most vivid relations between men, and depict every kind of human emotion', and that the film therefore infringed upon the dramatic copyright on *Ben-Hur*.[101] It was the very potential of the moving picture to tell a story effectively, and to do so with a definable style, which led to its effective prosecution in this case.

In the UK, a similar case was brought by music hall performer Fred Karno against Pathé Frères, on the grounds that their film *Au Music Hall* (1907) infringed Karno's copyright on his sketch 'The Mumming Birds or Twice Nightly' under the 1833 Dramatic Copyright Act.[102] In fact, the court found for the defendant on the grounds that the sketch did not constitute a dramatic performance in the first place. However, in his judgement, Judge Jelf, who had scrutinised both sketch and the film, added carefully that 'if the "Mumming Birds" were within the protection of the Act' the film would indeed constitute a culpable 'representation of the plaintiff's sketch':

> Mere pictures or even stationary *tableaux vivants* would not, I think, infringe the right of sole representation, but, as the cinematograph shows the figures moving, just as the living persons, I think this production would be held to be within the language as well as within the mischief of the Act.[103]

Unfortunately for Karno, Jelf acknowledged 'the general idea of "fun" and "ragging" with plenty of "business" and a considerable amount of "gag"' in the sketch, but added that 'there is no connected story or plot capable of being written down in literary form'.[104] In other words, as in the 1911 American case, the important point was that the 'representation' of the cinematograph—its ability to tell a story with a definable style—might well infringe upon a story told in another medium. By the same token, however, film producers were also protected from others duping their own successful stories. Thus, in both the UK and the USA, personal and stylistic investment in the moving pictures was now recognised in the courts, and could potentially be defended by manufacturers. This was further confirmed in Europe at the 1908 Berlin Conference on international copyright, which stated that 'Cinematographic productions shall be protected as literary or artistic works if, by the arrangement of the acting form or the combination of incidents represented, the author has given the work a personal and original character'.[105] Furthermore, for the delegates at the conference it became clear that the filming of a pre-existing work also 'required the application of a level of skill that qualified for the description of "authorship"'.[106] These changes were ratified in the UK by the 1911 Copyright Act, further consolidating the industry trend toward story films.[107]

Thus, though the telling of stories certainly represented an important attraction to audiences from the beginning, their significance for the industry was confirmed from the late 1900s by their copyrightable status in the courts. This relationship was not coincidental: early film producers had begun by capitalising on the persistently compelling and easily diversified attractions of narrative, and it is not surprising that they sought to consolidate this strategy within stable and easily regulated legal and institutional frameworks. This was just one of the ways in which these institutions married their own, principally commercial, imperatives with the everyday desires, values and practices of audiences. Indeed, numerous commentators have acknowledged that by 1910 a decisive shift towards story films and more consistent forms of spectatorship had taken place within the industry, though this was not a movement embraced evenly by all filmmakers, exhibitors and audiences. Lecturing itself ultimately retreated from its traditional role during exhibition to become part of the sales patter of distributors: 'While the original purpose of lectures is almost extinct,' wrote the American David S. Hulfish in 1915, 'their advertising value remains and they are used by manufacturers in large quantities.'[108] The lecture's move backwards from exhibition to production and distribution reflected the growing importance of institutions of production, though institutions of exhibition would retain a significant influence over spectatorial practices. Though permanent exhibition venues for film had appeared very early, 'Electric Theatres' were constructed in the UK from 1907, and many of these favoured longer programmes, longer films, and encouraged audiences to return each week and watch a new programme from beginning to end. The aggressive spread of electric theatre chains throughout the UK was an indication of this consolidation of patterns of spectatorship.[109]

An important 1909 article from *The World's Fair* describes the close connection between the emergence of the 'miniature theatres' in London and the longer 'miniature dramas' that were preoccupying film producers.[110] According to the London manager of Pathé-Frères, who was also cited in this article, 'the advance in the taste of the public, as in the means of pleasing it, has been enormous since the early days of the biograph, when audiences were content with a number of comic scenes imperfectly mounted'. Seeking now to 'increase and to satisfy the demand for miniature dramas', a policy which contrasted starkly with the ambitions of the numerous fairground and shop-front shows that continued to thrive within the UK during the 1910s, the business plans of such men clearly revolved around the development of narrative scenarios within their films. A series of guidebooks to screen-writing proliferated from this time, seeking to answer the growing demand for screenplays.[111] An early British example of advice to the aspiring screen-writer recommended films 'which by their simple story make a direct and successful appeal to audiences':

> The story of a picture, humorous or dramatic, must be very clear and easily followed. A simple line of progressive action, through a series of

scenes must be maintained until the climax is reached, each scene having a definite connection with the story.[112]

Such advice suggests the screenwriter's increasingly expert management of a film's narrative resources. Thus, the regulation of audience cognition and emotion, which had been largely the responsibility of a showman or lecturer in the first years of film, became the primary responsibility of filmmakers, and became closely tied to matters of style. Some performers, such as Harry Furniss, followed this transformative potential into screenwriting and production. Others, such as travelling showmen William Haggar or George Green, opted for invisibility and opened their own chains of static picture theatres during the 1910s.[113] More frequently, the showmen persisted in their itinerant trade, but now moved on to new forms of show as tastes at the fairground changed, leaving the moving pictures to other entrpreneurs.

If, however, the extraordinary heterogeneity of early exhibition practices was curtailed by narrative pressures, spectators persisted in their partly unpredictable practices of embodiment. Branigan has tentatively suggested that narrators in film might be seen as evidence of 'of an overriding faith in *ordinary causality* and in our presumed role as *actors* able to make order in the world'.[114] This proposal strongly supports the idea that narrative film nurtures an ideology of reassurance in which human agencies identified within the film neutralise anxieties concerning the chaotic and ungraspable nature of existence. The drift away from live performance practices to the varied modes of self presentation associated with the screen or with the film's production does not, therefore, imply that spectators were left stranded within the repressive discourses of a hegemonic institution. As in all processes of institutional change, this shift testifies to the impact of the creative activities of spectators as much as it does to the significance of institutional constraints. Furthermore, narration, like all institutional practices, has always easily fragmented along social and cultural lines, as any moviegoer, keen to discuss with other audience members what they have seen, can testify. Branigan adds that the process of 'personifying narration would seem to have a real function in our lives', and that this process requires explanation on that basis.[115] It seems to me that, when looking for explanations of this kind, the early cinema, which began by presenting a spectrum of reassuring personalities to audiences, must inform our considerations.

Conclusion

Early Institutional Cinemas

When it first appeared in the crowded Victorian entertainment marketplace, early film was adopted with varying degrees of success by numerous institutions. In doing so, the medium inevitably contributed to the reproduction of existing institutional structures. Indeed, the continuities in institutional practices explored in the preceding chapters are only representative of the full range of influences that took part in the definition and consolidation of early film shows. However, as Giddens's principle of duality of structure suggests, and the case studies presented in this book confirm, the new medium also generated the prospect of substantial institutional change. Film was not simply a new novelty to add to the roster of established Victorian attractions: like other successful novelties, it represented an opportunity for media producers, exhibitors and receivers to do new kinds of work within existing institutional frameworks—an opportunity that resulted in long-standing changes to these frameworks. From this point of view, the important point about the appearance of film was that it became enormously productive for existing institutions, generating discontinuities, ellipses and anxieties that could be worked through by those who produced, exhibited and consumed it.

Thus, the purveyors of early cinema applied performative practices derived principally from earlier entertainments, but also capitalised upon the multiple opportunities the medium offered to redevelop and repackage these practices. Doing so was good business practice since it enabled them to steer clear of the uncomfortable paradigm shifts that audiences neither desired nor were prepared to pay for, while continuing to diversify the range of commodities they had on offer. My contention has been that, for every institution seeking to make a profit from the medium, the preservation of a stable marketplace that constructed and answered the desires of audiences in a reliable and reassuring manner was at least as significant as any attempts to alter

211

existing relationships between audience and show. This type of stability, which depended upon the capacity to introduce incremental change whilst avoiding material and commercial crises, is exactly what we would expect of modern institutions more generally. Indeed, from an institutional perspective, the emergence of film was not really a special or isolated moment at all; it was just one part of the graduated, day-to-day process of managing continuities and change in a manner that allowed institutions to constitute themselves as commercially viable, ongoing concerns.

The key to the success of early film institutions was therefore to integrate existing commercial imperatives seamlessly into the lives of consumers, but also to respond to the gradually changing demands of these consumers by subtly reformulating their products, practices and policies. In doing so, competent early film entrepreneurs both exploited and, sometimes, sought to extend the already considerable interpretive capacities of their audiences. To an extent varied by their experience, audiences were curious, competent, and knowledgeable consumers of popular entertainments, and though they did not often practise their expertise in a conscious, self-referential manner, producers and exhibitors were careful to reproduce existing, comfortable habits of consumption more likely to flatter than challenge this expertise. Thus, for example, the popularity of diverse and shocking material in certain early film texts is not sufficiently explained by the idea that audiences were repeatedly willing to be shocked in the name of 'good fun'. As historians who have systematically investigated such phenomena have acknowledged, audiences already possessed expert knowledge concerning the longstanding market for novelty. They had learned this from decades of exposure to spectacular images, bizarre performances, and other commodifications of alterity on the fairground, in the lecture theatre, and elsewhere—environments in which these attractions were contextualised, at the very least, by the popular understanding of good showmanship.

But the expertise of audiences stretched much further than this, for even in the industrialising, technologising, commodity-driven environments of modern cities, individuals maintained the capacity for an even-paced and reflective mastery over the practices of everyday life, regardless of the undoubted increase in pace within certain aspects of it. For a period in the early part of the century, the moving pictures thrived partly because they afforded spectators a fertile opportunity to practise such mastery. Faced with the regular pronouncement in this period of the alleged alienation effects of modernity, a problem which the cinematograph appeared to exemplify, the film industry, like the showmen before it, found that it could capitalise upon such fears by answering them. Most importantly, the popular, widely disseminated characterisation of modernity as a propensity to unsettle, endanger or redefine apparent certainties of self-identity, community and communication, became enormously productive. In early cinemas, spectators were able to develop consistent readings of films and film shows by discerning various forms of intentionality within them, including those associated with live performances, those directly represented onscreen, and those implied by the image track. They were also able to discriminate between these, and playing out the sophisticated interchanges between them was one of the key pleasures to be had from the shows. Furthermore, the broader functions these personae served—to confirm identity, mask differences, and generate intimacy based upon shared cultural allegiances—have remained powerfully in place throughout the twentieth century, and can be tracked throughout the productions of the mainstream media industries.

The potential attractions associated with a film show were therefore remarkably varied, and this book has attempted to track only the most significant of these. In addition to the widely promoted capacity of such shows to offer spectacular, distractive material to audiences, they also functioned to reaffirm normative descriptions of social identity; to engage or align audiences with verbal performances and personalities appearing on the stage; to create structures of intimacy or empathy with distant individuals appearing on the screen or with other individuals credited with responsibility for these images; to foster contemplation of familiar scenes and faces; to enable critical observation of foreign scenes and current events; to generate curiosity concerning scientific and other educational topics; to repackage existing discourses and iconographies of celebrity; or, more generally, to reassure audiences that the emergent mass media (and, by extension, industrial modernity in general) need not be regarded as alienating features of modern life. Since this is so, the early cinema needs to be seen as a dynamic, responsive environment which developed multiple relationships—sometimes at the same time—with its varied audiences, and which therefore proliferated experiences of intimacy, empathy, curiosity, reassurance and mastery for individual spectators in place of those it was widely accused of undermining.

Finally, I have argued that the early film industry was especially significant in this respect, because it so openly exploited the increasing distance between conditions of production and consumption that had been opened up by modern institutional practices, but also sought to generate from this scenario a series of experiences better characterised in terms of proximity and comfort. In this light, early film shows are profitably regarded—in the broadest of senses—as one of the most important sites at which modern institutional structures stitched themselves into the fabric of everyday life, productively capitalising upon, but also introducing changes to, constructions of communication and self-identity that audiences cherished. Therefore, the term 'marketing modernity' refers to more than the process of allowing audiences to come to terms with the alienation effect popularly associated with everyday life at the turn of the century—though this was certainly one important function of popular entertainments such as early film shows. A substantial part of the enterprise of such shows involved a revalidation of existing conceptions of selfhood and community on behalf of audiences. Although the nascent film industry had a powerful interest in exaggerating its contribution to the newness of the new century, and though it was sometimes regarded as symptomatic of the breakdown of traditional notions of community, early film institutions also participated fully in modernity's fascination with, and repackaging of, very traditional social forms. In doing so, these institutions exploited fundamental continuities that underpinned structures of everyday life throughout this period, offering diversifying opportunities to fulfil much the same cultural functions that had long typified the nineteenth-century entertainment marketplace, and which would remain dominant in the enlarged media landscape of the twentieth century.

Notes

Introduction

1   Henry V. Hopwood, *Living Pictures: Their History, Photo-Production and Practical Working* (London: Optician and Photographic Trades Review, 1899), p. 226.

2   For this phrase, see Laurent Mannoni, *The Great Art of Light and Shadow: Archaeology of the Cinema* (Exeter: University of Exeter Press, 2001). Mannoni also provides an excellent description of this idea in his entry concerning the 'Archaeology of Cinema/Pre-cinema' in *Encyclopedia of Early Cinema*, ed. Richard Abel (London: Routledge, 2005), pp. 32–35. For a rare exploration of the idea of influence as it has been used in early film studies, see Paolo Cherchi Usai, 'On the Concept of "Influence" in Early Cinema', in *Cinéma sans Frontières 1896–1918*, ed. Roland Cosandey and François Albera (Quebec: Nuit Blanche, 1995), pp. 275–86.

3   For a full discussion of the controversial notion of 'primitivity', see Noël Burch, *Life to those Shadows*, trans. and ed. Ben Brewster (London: BFI, 1990), pp. 186–201. For introductory accounts of early film as teleological end-point of nineteenth-century development see Olive Cook, *Movement in Two Dimensions* (London: Hutchinson Press, 1963); and David Robinson, *From Peep Show to Palace: The Birth of American Film* (New York: Columbia University Press, 1996). For an extensive collection of source materials, which implicitly demonstrates the connections between nineteenth- and early twentieth-century media forms, see, Stephen Herbert, *A History of Pre-Cinema*, 3 vols (London: Routledge, 2000); and Stephen Herbert *A History of Early Film*, 3 vols (London: Routledge, 2000). For several representative accounts of early film and modernity see, *Cinema and the Invention of Modern Life*, ed. Leo Charney and Vanessa R. Schwartz (Berkeley: University of California Press, 1995).

4   But work on the US context has very recently begun to theorise the continuities that existed across this period. See, especially, Charles Musser, 'A Cinema of Contemplation, a Cinema of Discernment: Spectatorship, Intertextuality, and Attractions in the 1890s', in *The Cinema of Attractions Reloaded*, ed. Wanda Streuven (Amsterdam: Amsterdam University Press, 2006), pp. 159–80.

5   Stephen Bottomore, 'Out of this World: Theory, Fact and Film History', *Film History* 6 (1994), p. 10. For a further defence and discussion of the 'overarching and metacritical historical paradigm' that has informed early film studies, see Roberta E. Pearson, 'The Attractions of Cinema, or, How I learned to Start Worrying About Loving Early Film', in *Cinema: The Beginnings and the Future*, ed. Christopher Williams (London: University of Westminster Press, 1996), p. 158.

6   Alexander Black, 'The Camera and the Comedy', *Scribners* 20 (1896), p. 606.

7   For an excellent summary of such work on early film and modernity, and international

examples of anxieties associated with modern life, see Tom Gunning's entry on 'Modernity' in *Encyclopedia of Early Cinema*, ed. Richard Abel (London: Routledge, 2005), pp. 439–42.

8   David Bordwell, *Making Meaning: Inference and Rhetoric in the Interpretation of Cinema* (Cambridge, MA: Harvard University Press, 1989), p. 153.

9   David Bordwell, *Narration in the Fiction Film* (Madison: University of Wisconsin Press, 1985), p. 62.

10   Rudolf Arnheim offers a useful discussion of the pathetic fallacy in this context. See Rudolf Arnheim, *Art and Visual Perception: A Psychology of the Creative Eye* (London: Faber and Faber, 1956), p. 368.

11   Béla Balázs, *Theory of the Film: Character and Growth of a New Art* (New York: Arno Press, 1972), p. 92. For an account of the economic causes of this desire to discover human agency within the film, see especially pp. 44–46.

12   Anthony Giddens, *Modernity and Self-Identity: Self and Society in the Late Modern Age* (Stanford: Stanford University Press, 1991), pp. 84–85.

1   Performing Intimacy: An Institutional Account of Early Film

1   For an account of one attempt to consolidate the varied interests of the early film industry in the UK, see Jon Burrows, 'When Britain Tried to Join Europe: The Significance of the 1909 Paris Congress for the British Film Industry', *Early Popular Visual Culture* 4:1 (2006), pp. 1–19.

2   Between 1907 and 1908, the dedicated British film trade press, which initially comprised *The Kinematograph and Lantern Weekly* and *The Bioscope*, strongly supported development of picture theatres and of longer narrative scenarios within films, frequently arguing that such changes were a necessary part of the legitimisation of the industry. See Jon Burrows, 'Penny Pleasures: Film Exhibition in London during the Nickelodeon Era, 1906–1914', *Film History* 16 (2004), pp. 72–73.

3   Charles Urban, who worked initially within the Warwick Trading Company, and then set up a series of his own companies within the UK, was the film producer most strongly associated with the argument that film should be seen as an educative tool. For an account of Urban's position, see Luke McKernan, *'Something More than a Mere Picture Show': Charles Urban and the Early Non-Fiction Film in Great Britain and America, 1897–1925* (unpublished doctoral thesis, Birkbeck College, University of London, 2003), pp. 57–60.

4   Ben Singer, *Melodrama and Modernity: Early Sensational Cinema and its Contexts* (New York: Columbia University Press, 2001), p. 102.

5   For analysis of this movement, see Tom Gunning, 'Film History and Film Analysis: The Individual Film in the Course of Time', *Wide Angle* 12:3 (1990): 4–19. See also Susan Buck-Morss, 'The Flaneur, the Sandwichman and the Whore: The Politics of Loitering', *New German Critique* 39 (Fall 1986), pp. 99–140

6   Gunning, 'Modernity', *Encyclopedia of Early Cinema*, ed. Richard Abel (London: Routledge, 2005), pp. 440–41; Singer, *Melodrama and Modernity*, pp. 118–26.

7   Charles Baudelaire, 'The Painter of Modern Life', in *The Painter of Modern Life and other Essays*, trans. and ed. Jonathan Mayne (London: Phaidon Press, 1964), p. 13.

8   For conservative literary and artistic journals, for example, 'the modern' was often disdainfully characterised as the province of 'novelty-mongers', individuals with a talent

for producing 'the semblance of freshness' or 'the pretence of original thought' on behalf of a public unable to resist the charms of the new, whatever it might be. ('The Note of Modernity', in *The Dial: A Semi-Monthly Journal of Literary Criticism, Discussion, and Information* 41: 488 (16 October 1906), p. 226). More radical thinkers, such as René Doumic, embraced modernity and condemned those 'humdrum beings' with a false attachment to traditional value systems as 'an anachronism, and essentially ridiculous from their incongruity with their environment'. (Emphasis in original. René Doumic, 'The Craze for "Modernity"', in *Living Age* 7:219 (1898), p. 3.)

9   George R. Simms, *Living London: its Work and its Play, its Humour and its Pathos, its Sights and its Scenes*, 3 vols (London: Cassell, 1902–03); William Booth, *In Darkest England and the Way Out* (London: Salvation Army, 1890).

10   'Reflections on Modernity', in *Academy* 80 (1911), p. 273.

11   See especially, Walter Benjamin, *Charles Baudelaire: A Lyric Poet in the Age of High Capitalism*, trans. Harry Zohn (London: Verso, 1983); Walter Benjamin, 'The Work of Art in the Age of Mechanical Reproduction', in *Illuminations*, trans. Harry Zohn (New York: Schocken, 1969), pp. 219–53.

12   See especially, Anne Friedberg, *Window Shopping: Cinema and the Postmodern* (Berkeley: University of California Press, 1993), pp. 68–94.

13   Georg Simmel, 'The Metropolis and Mental Life', in *Sociology of Georg Simmel*, trans. and ed. Kurt H. Wolff (London: Collier-MacMillan, 1950), p. 410.

14   These can be considered as consolidations of ways of seeing and experiencing the world that had become implicit to metropolitan life. For Lynne Kirby, following Wolfgang Schivelbusch among others, the train and the cinema are even to be understood as 'two great machines of vision that give rise to similar modes of perception'; Lynne Kirby, 'Male Hysteria and Early Cinema', *Camera Obscura* 17 (1988), p. 113. Similar ideas have led another recent commentator to describe travel and film in the period as essentially the same phenomenon: 'The film "viewer" is a practitioner of viewing space—a tourist'; Giuliana Bruno, 'Site-Seeing: Architecture and the Moving Image', *Wide Angle* 19:4 (1997), p. 17.

15   For work concerning programming in the first picture theatres, see Nicholas Hiley, 'At the Picture Palace: The British Cinema Audience, 1895–1920', in *Celebrating 1895: The Centenary of Cinema*, ed. John Fullerton (London: John Libbey and Company, 1998), pp. 96–103; and Vanessa Toulmin, 'The Importance of the Programme in Early Film Presentation', in *KINtop* 11 (2002), pp. 19–34.

16   'Latest Cinematograph Freak', *The World's Fair* (1 December 1906), p. 1.

17   David Bordwell, *On the History of Film Style* (Cambridge, MA: Harvard University Press, 1997), pp. 141–46; Charlie Keil, '"Visualised Narratives", Transitional Cinema and the Modernity Thesis', in *Le Cinema au Tournant du Siècle / Cinema at the Turn of the Century*, eds Clair Dupré la Tour, André Gaudreault and Roberta Pearson (Lausanne/Quebec: Éditions Payot Lausanne / Éditions Nota Bene, 1999), pp. 133–47. For further work on this increasingly heated, but useful, debate, see Charlie Keil, 'From Here to Modernity: Style, Historiography, and Transitional Cinema', in *American Cinema's Transitional Era: Audiences, Institutions, Practises*, eds Charlie Keil and Shelly Stamp (Berkeley: University of California Press, 2004), pp. 51–65; Tom Gunning, 'Modernity and Cinema: A Culture of Shocks and Flows', in *Cinema and Modernity*, ed. Murray Pomerance (Piscatawny, NJ: Rutgers University Press, 2006), pp. 297–315; and Charlie Keil, 'Integrated Attractions: Style and Spectatorship in Transitional Cinema', in *The Cinema of Attractions Reloaded*, ed. Wanda Streuven (Amsterdam: Amsterdam

University Press, 2006), pp. 193–204.

18 Singer, *Melodrama and Modernity*, p. 128.

19 *Ibid.*, p. 117

20 *Ibid.*, p. 118.

21 Gunning, 'Modernity and Cinema', p. 305.

22 Ben Highmore, 'Street Life in London: Towards a Rhythmanalysis of London in the Late Nineteenth Century', *New Formations* 47 (2002), pp. 171–93. For a similar reading of street life in London (and film), see Lynda Nead, *The Haunted Gallery: Painting, Photography, Film c.1900* (New Haven: Yale University Press, 2007), pp. 129–30.

23 Doumic, 'The Craze for "Modernity"', p. 3.

24 T. Clifford Allbutt, 'Nervous Diseases and Modern Life', in *The Contemporary Review* 67 (January–June 1895), pp. 214, 216.

25 *Ibid.*, p. 226.

26 Henri Lefebvre, *Rhythmanalysis: Space, Time, and Everyday Life* (London: Continuum Press, 2004), pp. 38–45.

27 Sylvanus, 'Our First Kinematograph Show', in *The Kinematograph and Lantern Weekly* (4 July 1907), p. 128.

28 Tom Gunning, 'The Cinema of Attraction: Early Film, its Spectator, and the Avant-Garde', *Wide Angle* 8:3/4 (1986), p. 70; André Gaudreault and Tom Gunning, 'Le Cinéma des Premier Temps: Un défi a histoire du film?' in *Histoire du Cinéma: Nouvelles Approches*, ed. J. Aumont, André Gaudreault and M. Marie (Paris: Publications de la Sorbonne, 1989), pp. 49–63. For further observations on shock effect in early cinema, see Tom Gunning, '"Now You See It, Now You Don't": The Temporality of the Cinema of Attractions', in *The Velvet Light Trap* 32 (1993), pp. 3–12; and Leo Charney, 'In a Moment: Film and the Philosophy of Modernity', in *Cinema and the Invention of Modern Life*, eds Charney and Schwartz, pp. 279–93.

29 Charles Musser, 'A Cinema of Contemplation, a Cinema of Discernment: Spectatorship, Intertextuality, and Attractions in the 1890s', in *The Cinema of Attractions Reloaded*, ed. Streuven, p. 170.

30 Gunning, 'Modernity and Cinema', p. 306.

31 Tony Bennett, *The Birth of the Museum* (London: Routledge, 1995), pp. 59–89; Timothy Mitchell, 'Orientalism and the Exhibitionary Other', in *Colonialism and Culture*, ed. Nicholas B. Dirks (Ann Arbor: University of Michigan Press, 1992), pp. 289–318.

32 Bennett, *The Birth of the Museum*, p. 86.

33 On freak show, see Susan Stewart, *On Longing: Narratives of the Miniature, the Gigantic, the Souvenir, the Collection* (Durham, NC: Duke University Press, 1993), p. 109; Rosemarie Garland Thomson, 'Introduction: From Wonder to Error—A genealogy of freak discourse in modernity', in *Freakery: Cultural Spectacles of the Extraordinary Body*, ed. Rosemarie Garland Thomson (New York: New York University Press, 1996), pp. 1–22; and Rosemarie Garland Thomson, *Extraordinary Bodies: Figuring Physical Disability in American Culture and Literature* (New York: Columbia University Press, 1997). On ethnological and travelogue shows, see Alison Griffiths, *Wondrous Difference: Cinema, Anthroplogy, and Turn of the Century Visual Culture* (New York: Columbia University Press, 2001), pp. 3–45.

34 Georg Simmel, 'Bridge and Door', trans. Mark Ritter, *Theory, Culture, and Society* 11: 1 (1994), p. 10.

35 See Joe Kember, 'The Functions of Showmanship in Freak Show and Early Film', in *Early Popular Visual Culture* (April 2007), pp. 1–23.

36 See for example, Kelly Hurley, *The Gothic Body: Sexuality, Materialism, and Degenera-tion at the Fin de Siècle* (Cambridge: Cambridge University Press, 1996), pp. 3–7.

37 Anthony Giddens, *Modernity and Self-Identity: Self and Society in the Late Modern Age* (Stanford: Stanford University Press, 1991), p. 26.

38 'The Modernity Hospital', in *Atlantic Monthly* 75 (1895), pp. 714–15.

39 Maxim Gorky, review of the Lumière programme at the Nizhni-Novgorod fair (4 July 1896), repr. in *In the Kingdom of the Shadows: A Companion to Early Cinema*, eds Colin Harding and Simon Popple, (London: Cygnus Arts, 1996), pp. 5–6; O. Winter, 'The Cinematograph', *New Review* 14 (May 1896), pp. 507–13.

40 O. Winter, 'The Cinematograph', p. 511.

41 Gorky, Review, pp. 5–6.

42 Joseph Pennell, 'Is Photography Among the fine Arts?' in *The Contemporary Review* 72 (December 1897), p. 833.

43 D.Z., 'The Imagination and the Cinematograph', in *Month* 126:613 (1915), p. 80.

44 Henri Bergson, *Creative Evolution*, trans. Arthur Mitchell (London: Macmillan, 1911), p. 322. For earlier work concerning the nature of modern subjectivity, see especially Bergson's 1889 essay *Time and Free Will: An Essay on the Immediate Data of Consciousness* (London: Swan Sonnenschein and Co., 1910); and his 1896 essay *Matter and Memory*, trans. Nancy Margaret Paul and W. Scott Palmer (London: Swan Sonnenschein and Co., 1911). For work on Bergson's attitude to cinema (and consciousness), see Paul Douglass, 'Bergson and Cinema: Friends or Foes?' in *The New Bergson*, ed. John Mullarkey (Manchester: Manchester University Press, 1999), pp. 209–27.

45 Bergson, *Creative Evolution*, p. 8.

46 In Italy, by 1911, the perceptual confusions the cinematograph seemed to generate were being researched by Mario Ponzo, who investigated the synaesthetic effects moving images appeared to have on susceptible spectators, demonstrating that even when sound effects were not 'produced behind the stage by the ingenious showman', spectators were 'apt to imagine that we see or hear what we think we should see or hear under the circum-stances'; 'Illusions of the Cinematograph', *The Literary Digest* 44:19 (11 May 1912), p. 985.

47 'At The Palace', in *Punch* 115 (6 August 1898), p. 57.

48 For examples of the British debate at this time see, 'Bad Effects of Moving Pictures', *The Bioscope* (6 November 1908), p. 10; and 'Bioscope and Eye', *The Bioscope* (27 November 1908), p. 15. For analysis of similar issues on the continent, see, Thierry Lefebvre, 'Une "Maladie" au Tournant du Siècle: La Cinématophtalmie', in *Cinéma des Premiers Temps: Nouvelles Contributions Françaises*, ed. Thierry Lefebvre and Laurent Mannoni (Toulouse: Presses de la Sorbonne, 1996), pp. 131–36.

49 Lynne Kirby, 'Male Hysteria and Early Cinema', *Camera Obscura* 17 (1988), pp. 113–31; Lynne Kirby, *Parallel Tracks: The Railroad and Silent Cinema* (Exeter: University of Exeter Press, 1997), pp. 57–73

50 'Reflections on Modernity', p. 273

51 Miriam Hansen, *Babel and Babylon: Spectatorship in American Silent Film* (Cambridge, MA: Harvard University Press, 1991), p. 77; see also Miriam Hansen, 'Universal Language and Democratic Culture: Myths of Origin in Early American Cinema', in *Myth and Enlightenment in American Literature: In Honour of Hans-Joachim Lang*, ed. Dieter Meindl and Friedrich W. Horlacher (Erlangen: University of Erlangen-Nürn-berg Press, 1985), pp. 321–51.

52 'The Lantern as Illustrator', *The Showman* (October 1900), p. 35.

53 The Charles Urban Trading Company Catalogue (November 1903), front cover;

Montagu A. Pyke, *Focussing the Universe* (London: Waterloo Brothers, [1912]), p. 5; see also [Montagu A. Pyke], 'The Making of a Picture, no. 1', *The Rinking World and Picture Theatre News* (4 December 1909), pp. 20–23.

54 David Bordwell, Janet Staiger and Kristin Thompson, *The Classical Hollywood Cinema: Film Style and Mode of Production to 1960* (London: Routledge and Kegan Paul, 1985), p. 4.

55 See Rick Altman, 'General Introduction: Cinema as Event', *Sound Theory Sound Practice*, ed. Rick Altman (London: Routledge, 1992), pp. 1–14. See also, Rick Altman, 'Film Sound: All of It', *Iris* 27 (1999), pp. 31–47; 'An Interview with Rick Altman', *Velvet Light Trap* 51 (2003), pp. 67–72; and Rick Altman, *Silent Film Sound* (New York: Columbia University Press, 2004).

56 See Tom Gunning, 'An Unseen Energy Swallows Space: The Space in Early Film and its Relation to American Avant-Garde Film', in *Film Before Griffith*, ed. John L. Fell (Berkeley: University of California Press, 1983), pp. 355–66; and Noël Burch, 'Primitivism and the Avant-Gardes: A Dialectical Approach', in *Narrative, Apparatus, Ideology: A Film Theory Reader* (New York: Columbia University Press, 1986), pp. 483–506.

57 See especially, Germain Lacasse, 'Du Boniment Quebecois comme Pratique Résistant', *Iris* 22 (Autumn 1996), p. 63. Steven J. Ross, in his work on labour activism in American film, even suggests that the political conservatism typical of Hollywood narrative film only developed painfully out of conflict and via repression of subversive worker-friendly films in the early years of the century; see Steven J. Ross, 'Struggles for the Screen: Workers, Radicals, and the Political Uses of Silent Film', in *American Historical Review* 96 (1991), pp. 333–67; and Steven J. Ross, *Working-class Hollywood: Silent Film and the Shaping of Class in America* (Princeton: Princeton University Press, 1998). For similar work on British film, see Alan Burton, 'The Emergence of an Alternative Film Culture: Film and the British Consumer Co-operative Movement before 1920', in *Celebrating 1895*, ed. Fullerton, pp. 71–81; and Alan Burton, *The British Film Co-Operative Movement Film Catalogue* (Trowbridge: Flicks Books, 1997).

58 Germain Lacasse's chief emphasis has been on cinema in the Quebec area. His PhD dissertation attempts an international survey of the significance of early film lecturing, and does not show that resistant practices formed a significant part of the exhibition contexts of colonial powers such as the UK; Germain Lacasse, *Le Bonimenteur et Le Cinema Oral: Le Cinema Muet entre Tradition et Modernité* (unpublished doctoral thesis, University of Montreal, 1997).

59 Richard Brown and Barry Anthony, *A Victorian Film Enterprise: The History of the British Mutoscope and Biograph Company, 1897–1915* (Trowbridge: Flicks Books, 1999).

60 The notion of an 'evolutionary' model of film has been strongly criticised in recent years. However, provided that the term 'evolution' is not mistakenly regarded as synonymous with 'teleology', or with an equally mistaken description of Darwinian theory as simply the survival of the fittest, I believe that it remains useful. In my account it describes, as in its biological sense, the idea of a complex and multi-directional interaction between individuals and their environment, and suggests that this interaction generates an incremental pattern of institutional development, not toward perfection, but simply from one paradigm to the next.

61 McKernan, *'Something More than a Mere Picture Show'*.

62 Burrows, 'Penny Pleasures': Film Exhibition in London during the Nickelodeon Era, 1906–1914', *Film History* 16 (2004), pp. 77–86. For an account of the survival of several fairground shows, see Vanessa Toulmin, 'Bioscope Biographies', in *In the Kingdom of the Shadows*, eds Harding and Popple, pp. 249–61.

63 Charlie Keil and Shelley Stamp, 'Introduction', *American Cinema's Transitional Era*, eds Keil and Stamp, p. 1.

64 Ben Brewster, 'Periodization of Early Cinema', in *American Cinema's Transitional Era*, eds Keil and Stamp, p. 74.

65 Anthony Giddens, *The Constitution of Society: Outline of the Theory of Structuration* (Cambridge: Polity Press, 1984).

66 Structuration theory has proven enormously productive in the social sciences during the last twenty years, and the debate which has surrounded it has some profound ramifications for the institution of film generally, as well as for the study of early film. See especially Derek Gregory, 'Presences and Absences: Time-Space Relations and Structuration Theory', in *Social Theory of Modern Societies: Anthony Giddens and his Critics*, eds David Held and John B. Thompson (Cambridge: Cambridge University Press, 1989), pp. 185–215, and Giddens's reply, pp. 275–81; and the various debates concerning communication and modernity in *Anthony Giddens: Consensus and Controversy*, eds Jon Clark, Celia Modgil and Sohan Modgil (London: Fulmar Press, 1990).

67 Giddens, *The Constitution of Society*, p. 25.

68 Anthony Giddens, *Modernity and Self-Identity: Self and Society in the Late Modern Age* (Stanford: Stanford University Press, 1991), p. 27

69 The application of these ideas to a relatively narrow empirical project is endorsed by Giddens's approach to field research; Giddens, *The Constitution of Society*, pp. 281–93.

70 Stephen Bottomore, 'The Panicking Audience? Early Cinema and the Train Effect', *Historical Journal of Film, Radio and Television* (June 1999), pp. 177–216.

71 John B. Thompson, 'The Theory of Structuration', in *Social Theory of Modern Societies*, eds Held and Thompson, pp. 56–76 (especially pp. 73–74).

72 Richard Maltby has offered a comparable account of institutional stability and change within the institution of Hollywood cinema; Richard Maltby, *Hollywood Cinema: An Introduction* (Oxford: Blackwell, 1995), pp. 40–46.

73 Giddens, *The Constitution of Society*, p. 174.

74 Thompson, *The Media and Modernity*, p. 84

75 Thompson, *Ideology and Modern Culture: Critical Social Theory in the Era of Mass Communication* (Cambridge: Polity Press, 1990), p. 149. Emphasis in original.

76 Richard Crangle, '"Next Slide Please": The Lantern Lecture in Britain', *The Sounds of Early Cinema*, eds Richard Abel and Rick Altman (Bloomington: Indiana University Press, 2001), pp. 39–48.

77 See especially, Jay David Bolter and Richard Grusin, *Remediation: Understanding New Media* (Boston: MIT Press, 2000), pp. 64–84.

78 David Berry, *Wales and Cinema: The First Hundred Years* (Cardiff: University of Wales Press, 1994), p. 46.

79 Tom Gunning, *D.W. Griffith and the Origins of American Narrative Film: The Early Years at Biograph* (Chicago: University of Illinois Press, 1994), p. 262. For Gunning's detailed definition of the narrator system, see pp. 25–28.

80 Miriam Hansen, 'Early Cinema, Late Cinema: Transformations of the Public Sphere', *Screen* 34:3 (Autumn 1993), p. 210. Her emphasis in original. A similar gesture has enabled critics like Rick Altman to position the monolithic ideal of film classicism within a field of competing institutional paradigms sharing much in common with the earliest practices of production, exhibition and spectatorship. Rick Altman, 'Dickens, Griffith, and Film Theory Today', in *Silent Film*, ed. Richard Abel (Piscatawny, NJ: Rutgers University Press, 1996), pp. 145–62 (first publ. in *South Atlantic Quarterly* 88:2 [1989], pp. 321–59).

81　In this respect, this model is opposed to that of André Gaudreault, who has produced the most sophisticated account of institutional change to date, and with which my own account otherwise shares some resemblances. Most recently, Gaudreault and Phillipe Marion have introduced the metaphor of the prism in order to explain institutional change. The 'hodge podge' of early film practice, like diffuse beams of light, are converted by this mechanism into a 'single "organic" and directed light', and thus the institutionalisation of cinema occurs. This metaphor seems to imply, however, that earlier practices were relatively chaotic, and later practices possessed some kind of 'natural' coherence. I do not believe this to be the case. I would add that this metaphor seems to add an unnecessary degree of abstraction to a process that, as Giddens shows, was occasioned by a diversity of materially located practices; André Gaudreault and Philippe Marion, 'The Neo-Institutionalisation of Cinema as a New Medium', in *Visual Delights Two: Exhibition and Reception*, eds Simon Popple and Vanessa Toulmin (Eastleigh: John Libbey, 2005), p. 94.

82　Anthony Giddens, *The Consequences of Modernity* (Cambridge: Polity Press, 1990), pp. 21–29.

83　See especially, Charles M. Berg, 'The Human Voice and the Silent Cinema', *Journal of Popular Film* 4:2 (1975), pp. 165–77; Martin Sopocy, 'A Narrated Cinema: The Pioneer Story Films of James A. Williamson', *Cinema Journal* 18:1 (Fall 1978), pp. 1–28; Charles Musser, 'The Nickelodeon Era Begins: Establishing the Framework for Hollywood's Mode of Representation', *Framework* 22/23 (Autumn 1983), pp. 4–11; Norman King, 'The Sound of Silents', *Screen* 25:3 (1984), pp. 2–25; Charles Musser, *Before the Nickelodeon. Edwin Porter and the Edison Manufacturing Company* (Berkeley: University of California Press, 1991); Charles Musser and Carol Nelson, *Lyman H. Howe and the Forgotten Era of Travelling Exhibition 1880–1920* (Princeton: Princeton University Press, 1991); Martin Sopocy, *James Williamson: Studies and Documents of a Pioneer of the Film Narrative* (Rutherford, NJ: Fairleigh Dickinson University Press, 1998); Richard Abel and Rick Altman (eds), *The Sounds of Early Cinema* (Bloomington: Indiana University Press, 2001); Rick Altman, *Silent Film Sound* (New York: Columbia University Press, 2004).

84　Stephen Bottomore, 'An International Survey of Sound Effects in Early Cinema', *Film History* 11:4 (1999), pp. 485–98; Stephen Bottomore, 'The Story of Percy Peashaker: Debates about Sound Effects in the Early Cinema', *The Sounds of Early Cinema*, eds Abel and Altman, pp. 129–42.

85　Musser, 'The Early Cinema of Edwin S. Porter', *Cinema Journal* 19:1 (1979), p. 3.

86　See Rick Altman, 'The Silence of the Silents', *Musical Quarterly* 80:4 (1996), 648–718.

87　See especially, Roberta Pearson, *Eloquent Gestures: The Transformation of Performance Styles in the Griffith Biograph Films* (Berkeley: University of California Press, 1992); Ben Brewster and Lea Jacobs, 'Pictorial Styles of Film Acting in Europe in the 1910s', in *Celebrating 1895*, ed. Fullerton, 253–62; Ben Brewster and Lea Jacobs, *Theatre to Cinema: Stage Pictorialism and the Early Feature Film* (Oxford: Oxford University Press, 1997); Jon Burrows, *Legitimate Cinema: Theatre Stars in Silent British Films, 1908–1918* (Exeter: University of Exeter Press, 2003).

88　See André Gaudreault, 'Showing and Telling: Image and Word in Early Cinema', in *Early Cinema: Space Frame Narrative*, ed. Thomas Elsaesser (London: British Film Institute, 1990), pp. 274–81.

89　As Michel Foucault has explained in his work on the 'author function' in literature, such figures therefore function as a 'principle of thrift in the proliferation of meaning', enabling spectators to pinpoint institutionally appropriate strategies of interpretation for each film; Michel Foucault, 'What is an Author?' in *Textual Strategies: Perspectives in Post-Structuralist Criticism*, ed. Josué V. Harari (London: Methuen and Co., 1979), p. 159.

90   See especially Giddens, *The Consequences of Modernity*, pp. 74–80.

2   Expertise and Trust

1   We might profitably regard this visibility of early operators as an aspect of the influence of magic lantern entertainments, wherein the skill of lanternists was a key attraction. When exhibiting lantern sequences, for example, the ability of the operator to dissolve seamlessly from one image to the next by dextrous operation of biunial or triunial apparatus was arguably just as critical as a good lecture in ensuring the success of the show, as trade publications sometimes emphasised. See, for example, Thos. McMeian, 'Lantern Operators', *The Magic Lantern Journal and Photographic Enlarger Almanac and Annual 1897–8* (London: Magic Lantern Journal Co., 1898), pp. 81–83.

2   In fact, practices of showmanship derived from a series of centuries-old traditions, and recent research has shown that the illustrated lecture began as early as the mid-seventeenth century. See Hauke Lange-Fuchs, 'Samuael Reyher of the University of Kiel: The First Audio Visual Lecturer?' in *Realms of Light: Uses and Perceptions of the Magic Lantern from the 17th to the 21st Century*, eds Richard Crangle, Mervyn Heard, and Ine van Dooren (London: Magic Lantern Society, 2005), pp. 135–37.

3   Tom Gunning, 'The Scene of Speaking: Two Decades of Discovering the Film Lecturer', *Iris* 27 (1999), pp. 67–79.

4   Helmut Gernsheim and Alison Gernsheim, *L.J.M. Daguerre: The History of the Diorama and the Daguerreotype* (London: Sacker and Warburg, 1956), pp. 13–45; Stephan Oettermann, *The Panorama: History of a Mass Medium*, trans. Deborah Lucas Schneider (New York: Zone Books, 1997).

5   For accounts of panoramas and dioramas, see John Timbs, *Curiosities of London* (London: Virtue and Co., 1855); 'Panoramas', *Chambers's Journal of Popular Literature* 13 (21 January 1860), pp. 33–35; Gernsheim and Gernsheim, *L.J.M. Daguerre*; Richard D. Altick, *The Shows of London* (Cambridge, MA: Belknap Press, 1978), pp. 117–98; Ralph Hyde, *Panoramania* (London: Trefoil Publications, 1988); Laurent Mannoni, Donata Pesenti Campagnoni, and David Robinson, *Light and Movement: Incunabula of the Motion Picture 1420–1896* (Gemona: Le Giornate del Cinema Muto, 1995), pp. 155–87; and Angela Miller, 'The Panorama, the Cinema, and the Emergence of the Spectacular', *Wide Angle* 18: 2 (1996), pp. 34–69.

6   For the original schematics of Barker's original London Panorama building and the Paris Diorama, which closely resembled the London building, see Mannoni, Campagnoni, and Robinson, *Light and Movement*, pp. 157–58, 185–87; and Arthur T. Gill, 'The London Diorama', *History of Photography* 1:1 (January 1977), pp. 31–36.

7   *The Times* (4 October 1823), p. 7.

8   For this position, see especially Jonathan Crary *Techniques of the Observer: On Vision and Modernity in the Nineteenth Century* (Cambridge, MA: MIT Press, 1990). For a critique of Crary's position, focusing upon the visual regime of the microscope, see Isobel Armstrong, 'The Microscope: Mediations of the Sub-Visible World', *Transactions and Encounters: Science and Culture in the Nineteenth-Century*, eds Roger Luckhurst and Josephine McDonagh (Manchester: Manchester University Press, 2002), pp. 30–54. In

a subsequent book, Crary has argued more forthrightly that visual regimes were only part of a broader perceptual apparatus; Jonathan Crary, *Suspensions of Perception: Attention, Spectacle, and Modern Culture* (Cambridge, MA: MIT Press, 2001), pp. 2–3.

9 Nicholas Green, *The Spectacle of Nature: Landscape and Bourgeois Culture in Nineteenth-Century France* (Manchester: Manchester University Press, 1990), p. 133. See also Denis E. Cosgrove, *Social Formation and Symbolic Landscape*, 2nd edn. (Madison: University of Wisconsin, 1998), pp. 234–37.

10 Andrew E. Hershberger, 'Performing Excess/Signaling Anxiety: Towards a psychoanalytic theory of Daguerre's Diorama', *Early Popular Visual Culture* 4:2 (2006), p. 88. His emphasis in original. The popularity of exhibitions of British cityscapes, such as the famous panorama of London to be seen at the Colosseum during the 1830s, lends further credence to this idea. See 'Re-opening of the Colosseum, Regent's Park', in *The Illustrated London News* (3 May 1845).

11 Examples are preserved at the John Johnson Collection, Oxford. See *Explanation of the View of Lisbon from Almada Hill* (1812), and *Description of the View of Moscow* (1813). Bodleian Library, University of Oxford: John Johnson Collection; Dioramas 1.

12 For an excellent example, see 'On Dioramic Painting', in *The Saturday Magazine* (23 December 1843).

13 Barker's efforts to capture 'the most picturesque point of view' on the behalf of audiences were routinely mentioned in pamphlets for Barker's Panorama during the 1910s. See, for example, *Description of the View of Moscow* (1813), Bodleian Library, University of Oxford: John Johnson Collection; Dioramas 1. For Burford's experience of a snowstorm spent stuck in a chalet on the Bernese Alps, see 'Panoramas', p. 34.

14 August Lewald, *Gesammelte Schriften* (Leipzig: 1845), (repr. and trans. in Gernsheim and Gernsheim, *L.J.M. Daguerre*, pp. 29–31).

15 *Ibid.*, p. 31.

16 The absence of lengthy studies of nineteenth-century public lecturing, which was extremely popular and pervasive from this period, is, perhaps, worthy of examination in its own right. However, for a useful account of public lecturing in the USA during the 1840s and 1850s, see Donald M. Scott, 'The Popular Lecture and the Creation of a Public in Mid-Nineteenth-Century America', in *The Journal of American History* 66:4 (1980), pp. 791–809. On public lecturing in Manchester in the same period, see Martin Hewitt, 'Ralph Waldo Emerson, George Dawson and the control of the lecture platform in mid-nineteenth-century Manchester', in *Nineteenth-Century Prose* 25:2 (1998), pp. 1–24.

17 Gernsheim and Gernsheim print a list, too long to include here, of all the sites in London where these so-called 'dioramic' entertainments were exhibited. See Gernsheim and Gernsheim, *L.J.M. Daguerre*, p. 44. For a full list of the other '-oramas' available to the London public, see Raymund Fitzsimons, *The Baron of Piccadilly: The Travels and Entertainments of George Albert Smith, 1816–1860* (London: Geoffery Bles., 1967), p. 100. On the development of moving panoramas, see Robert MacDonald, 'The Route of the Overland Mail to India', in *The New Magic Lantern Journal* 9:6 (2004), pp. 83–84.

18 Miller, 'The Panorama . . .', p. 41.

19 For example, Damer Waddington has chronicled the remarkable variety of touring panoramas that came to Jersey (from both Britain and France) from the 1810s to the 1910s. Damer Waddington, *Panoramas, Magic Lanterns, and Cinemas: A Century of 'Light' Entertainment in Jersey 1814–1914* (Jersey: Tocan Books, 2003), pp. 1–26.

20 A remarkable collection of diorama and panorama handbills survives at the John Johnson collection, Oxford, at the Guildhall Library, London, and the Bill Douglas Centre,

Exeter. Together, these sources give a good impression of the scale and diversity of these shows.

21 *The Diorama of the Ganges*, handbill. Bodleian Library, University of Oxford: John Johnson Collection; Dioramas 1.

22 Review from *The Sunday Times*, repr. in *The Diorama of the Ganges*, handbill.

23 *Descriptive Book of the Tour of Europe, the Largest Moving Panorama in the World* (Frankfurt: C. Horstmann, 1853). Bodleian Library, University of Oxford: John Johnson Collection; Dioramas 3.

24 *Grand Moving Panorama Illustrative of the Great African and American Slave Trade!*, pamphlet. Bodleian Library, University of Oxford: John Johnson Collection; Exhibitions 24.

25 See Jens Ruchatz, 'The Magic Lantern in Connection with Photography: Rationalisation and Technology', in *Visual Delights: Essays on the Popular and Projected Image in the 19th Century*, eds Simon Popple and Vanessa Toulmin (Trowbridge: Flicks Books, 2000), p. 44.

26 For a good account of Robert Ball, perhaps the most celebrated astronomical lecturer, see Mark Butterworth, 'A Lantern Tour of Star-Land: The Astronomer Robert Ball and his Magic Lantern Lectures', in *Realms of Light*, eds Crangle, Heard and van Dooren, pp. 162–73. Several examples of publicity for earlier itinerant shows survive at the John Johnson Collection, Oxford. See, for example, the poster for Theodore Habersohn's *Popular Lecture on Astronomy* (1859). Bodleian Library, University of Oxford: John Johnson Collection; London Play Places 1.

27 See Lester Smith, 'Entertainment and Amusement, Educations and Instruction: Lectures at the Royal Polytechnic Institution', in *Realms of Light*, eds Crangle, Heard and van Dooren, pp. 138–45. For a good contemporary account of lectures at the Royal Polytechnic during the 1850s, see J.O. Choules, *Young Americans Abroad; or Vacations in Europe: Travels in England, France, Holland, Belgium, Prussia and Switzerland* (Boston: Gould and Lincoln, 1852), p. 127.

28 See [Report on the design of the Polytechnic], *The Builder* 9 (December 1851), p. 802.

29 *Royal Panopticon of Science and Art, Leicester Square*, publicity leaflet accompanying the launch of this institution. Bodleian Library, University of Oxford: John Johnson Collection; London Play Places 4.

30 'Holiday Amusements' *The Morning Chronicle* (18 April 1854), p. 7.

31 On the culture of self-help, see Peter W. Sinnema, 'Introduction', in Samuel Smiles, *Self-help: with Illustrations of Conduct and Perseverance* (Oxford: Oxford University Press, 2002), pp. vii–xxviii.

32 *Royal Panopticon of Science and Art, Leicester Square*, publicity leaflet.

33 For example, Grieve and Telbin's *New Moving Diorama of the Events of the War with Russia* employed a Mr Stocqueler 'whose acquaintance with Mulitary matters peculiarly qualifies him to Lecture upon this subject'. *Events of the War*, pamphlet. Bodleian Library, University of Oxford: John Johnson Collection; Dioramas 3. Mr W. Frith's 1866 lectures on *The Wonders of Chemistry* assured audiences that he was the author of the books, *How to Detect Adulterations* and *Chemistry and Chemical Illusions*. *Mr W. Frith, Entertainment of Exhibition of Arts*, poster. Bodleian Library, University of Oxford: John Johnson Collection; London Play Places, 1.

34 Anthony Giddens, *Modernity and Self-Identity: Self and Society in the Late Modern Age* (Stanford: Stanford University Press, 1991), p. 30.

35 *New Oriental Diorama, Life and Scenes in India Illustared in an Imaginary Tour*, pamphlet.

Bodleian Library, University of Oxford: John Johnson Collection; Dioramas 2), p. 2.

36 Erving Goffman, 'The Lecture', in *Forms of Talk* (Philadelphia: University of Philadelphia Press, 1981), p. 194.

37 Goffman's 'frame analyses' of face-to-face interactions have recently begun to inform analysis of Victorian entertainments and remain highly suggestive in relation to archival material concerning performance. See Peter Lamont, 'Magician as Conjuror: A Frame Analysis of Victorian Mediums', *Early Popular Visual Culture* 4:1 (2006), pp. 21–33; and Erving Goffman, *Frame Analysis: An Essay on the Organization of Experience* (London: Harper and Row, 1974).

38 Charles Dickens, 'The American Panorama', in *The Works of Charles Dickens*, 36 vols (London: Chapman and Hall, 1911), XXXVI, p. 139.

39 Dickens, 'The American Panorama', p. 139.

40 Among innumerable late-nineteenth-century testimonials to Smith, see Walter Goodman, *The Keeleys: On Stage and at Home* (London: Bentley, 1895), pp. 224–34; Edmund Yates, *Edmund Yates: His Recollections and Experiences*, 2 vols (London: Richard Bentley and Son, 1884), I, pp. 224–32; George Augustus Sala, *The Life and Adventures of George Augustus Sala*, 3rd edn. (London: Cassell and Co., 1896), pp. 161–73; Charles Edward Matthews, *The Annals of Mont Blanc: A Monograph* (London: T. Fisher Unwin, 1898), pp. 176–96; Henry James, *A Small Boy and Others* (London: Macmillan, 1913), pp. 329–30.

41 Smith had developed a mastery for self-advertisement during his years in the London press. Smith published in *Punch*, among numerous other journals, and during the 1840s consistently contributed both articles and serialised novels to *Bentley's Miscellany* and his own journal, *The Man in the Moon*. Here, he developed the confessional style that would later reappear in the 'personal narrative' of the ascent. He had also sought to identify himself with P.T. Barnum, whom he had twice met. In 1857, Smith turned the relationship to direct advantage when he introduced a new character, the thinly-disguised Yankee showman, 'Phineas Cutecraft' to the entertainment. See Albert Smith, 'A Go-A-Head Day with Barnum', *Bentley's Miscellany* 27 (1847), p. 522. See also, Albert Smith, 'A Little Talk about Bartholomew Fair—Past and Present', *Bentley's Miscellany* 12 (1842), pp. 390–94; Albert Smith, 'A Visit to Greenwich Fair', *Bentley's Miscellany* 11 (1842), pp. 511–20; and Albert Smith, 'Recollections of a Cheap Tour', *Bentley's Miscellany* 24 (1848), pp. 408–16, 484–91.

42 Goodman, *The Keeleys*, p. 225.

43 It was only in the final seasons that the tale of the Ascent, which Smith had performed many hundreds of times, often for repeat audiences, was reduced to a pictorial *entr'acte* between other sections of the show.

44 By 1850, the railway to Chamonix had been completed (the hotel trade had been flourishing for years); by 1855, Thomas Cook was taking tourist groups to central Europe; and by 1863, he was taking them to Mont Blanc where, for one franc, they could fire a cannon to make the entire Chamonix Valley echo to their arrival.

45 Altick, *The Shows of London*, p. 478.

46 An undated pamphlet for the post-Smith *Mont Blanc* entertainment survives, apparently using similar routines to Smith. It does not name the new lecturer. Bodleian Library, University of Oxford: John Johnson Collection; Dioramas 2.

47 *Mr T. Lawrence, Popular Entertainment, Illustrative and Descriptive* (1858). Bodleian Library, University of Oxford: John Johnson Collection; Dioramas 3.

48 Surviving handbills suggest that by the 1870s such entertainments included a substantial

element of variety, depending, presumably, upon the kinds of second hand materials that were available. For example, a handbill for the *Beautiful Pictorial Dioramic Panorama*, exhibited at the Old Temperance Hall on Vauxhall Walk in 1874 included images of a gunpowder explosion in Regents Park, scenic views from England, and scenes from *A Christmas Carol*, amongst many other attractions. Bodleian Library, University of Oxford: John Johnson Collection; Dioramas 2.

49 *Snazelle*, poster. Bodleian Library, University of Oxford: John Johnson Collection; London Play Places 1.

50 *Artemus Ward's Lecture (As Delivered at the Egyptian Hall, London)*, ed. T.W. Robertson and E. Hingston (London: John Camden Hotten, 1869), p. 54. For a good general description of Ward's style, see Curtis Dahl, 'Artemus Ward: Comic Panoramist', *New England Quarterly* 32:4 (1959), pp. 476–85.

51 E. Hingston, 'Prefatory Note', in Ward, *Artemus Ward's Lecture*, p. 27.

52 For an early reference, see Charles Dickens, 'The Uncommercial Traveller', *All the Year Round* 9 (1863), p. 349; for a later reference, see George E. Brown, 'The Lanternist as Lecturer', in *The Optical Magic Lantern Journal and Photographic Enlarger* 11:134 (1900), p. 90.

53 See Giddens, *Modernity and Self-Identity*, pp. 109–44.

54 Roberstson and Hingston, *Artemus Ward's Lecture*, p. 16.

55 'Artemus Ward among the Mormons'. Pamphlet held in the Guildhall Collection, London.

56 'Artemus Ward', *Chambers's Journal* 76 (10 June 1865), p. 358.

57 *Mr Alexander Lamb's Royal Diorama, Scotland its Cities Lakes and Mountains!*, posters. Bodleian Library, University of Oxford: John Johnson Collection; Dioramas 3.

58 See Hudson John Powell, *Poole's Myriorama!: A Story of Travelling Panorama Showmen* (Bradford-on-Avon: ELSP, 2002).

59 'Panoramas and all the Other 'Ramas: An Interview with Mr. Poole', in *Pall Mall Budget* (5 September 1889), p. 1140.

60 *Panorama of the Defence of Paris against the German Armies* (1875), booklet. Bodleian Library, University of Oxford: John Johnson Collection; Dioramas 2, p. 16.

61 *Ibid.*; See also, *Panorama of the Siege of Paris* (1881), pamphlet. Bodleian Library, University of Oxford: John Johnson Collection; London Play Places 3.

62 Laurent Mannoni, 'Elbow to Elbow: The Lantern/Cinema Struggle', *The New Magic Lantern Journal* 7:1 (Jan 1993), p. 3.

63 Newspaper cutting from the 'Poole Family Scrapbook', repr. in Powell, *Poole's Myriorama*, p. 101.

64 By 1908, Victor Hamilton was the manager of the America Animated Picture Co., a touring film show. See 'Hamilton's Excursions Recalled', in *The Bioscope* (13 November 1908), p. 6. The Pooles finally finished touring in 1909, but had opened permanent cinemas since 1905. See Powell, *Poole's Myriorama*, pp. 138–40.

65 Deac Rossell, 'Double Think: The Cinema and Magic Lantern Culture', in *Celebrating 1895: The Centenary of Cinema*, ed. John Fullerton (London: John Libbey and Co., 1998), p. 29.

66 Richard Crangle, '"Next Slide Please": the Lantern Lecture in Britain, 1890–1910', in *The Sounds of Early Cinema*, eds Richard Abel and Rick Altman (Bloomington: Indiana University Press, 2001), pp. 46–47.

67 David Jay Bolter and Richard Grusin, *Remediation: Understanding New Media* (Cambridge, MA: MIT Press, 2000), pp. 20–84.

68 These publications often have an encyclopaedic quality, designed to bring to light the vast amount of information concerning the lantern show during the nineteenth century and earlier. See especially Hermann and Ann Hecht, *Pre-Cinema History: an Encyclopedia and Annotated Bibliography of the Moving Image before 1896* (London: Bowker Saur/British Film Institute, 1993); David Robinson, Stephen Herbert and Richard Crangle, *Encyclopedia of the Magic Lantern* (London: The Magic Lantern Society, 2001); and *Realms of Light*, eds Crangle, Heard and van Dooren.

69 For a fascinating transcription of a magic lantern show of the early 1840s, see 'A Magic Lantern Entertainment by Timothy Toddle', in *Magic Images: The Art of Hand-Painted and Photographic Lantern* Slides, eds Dennis Crompton, David Henry, and Stephen Herbert (London: Magic Lantern Society, 1990), pp. 47–59. On lantern slides, see *The Lantern Image: Iconography of the Magic Lantern 1420–1880*, ed. David Robinson (London: Magic Lantern Society, 1993). On the magic lantern and conjuring, see Mervyn Heard, 'Now You See it, Now You Don't: The Magician and the Magic Lantern', in *Realms of Light*, eds Crangle, Heard and van Dooren, pp. 13–24.

70 For an excellent description of a children's lantern show, see 'Little Ones at Limehouse', in *Belgravia: A London Magazine* 10 (1869), pp. 61–68. For working-class lantern shows on London's infamous Mile End Road, a location better known for its freak and waxwork shows, see 'East-end experiences', *Chambers's Journal of Popular Literature* 809 (1879), pp. 407–09.

71 Richard Crangle, *Hybrid Texts: Modes of Representation in the Early Moving Picture and some Related Media in Britain* (unpublished doctoral thesis, University of Exeter, 1996), p. 130. Jens Ruchatz, 'The Magic Lantern in Connection with Photography: Rationalisation and Technology', in *Visual Delights*, eds Popple and Toulmin, pp. 38–49.

72 W.J. Chadwick, *The Magic Lantern Manual* (London: Frederick Warne and Co., 1878), p. 83.

73 'Pictures by the Million: A Chat with a Lantern Slide Maker', repr. in *The New Magic Lantern Journal* 5:3 (1988), p. 13.

74 Terry and Debbie Borton, 'How many lantern shows in a year?' in *Realms of Light*, eds Crangle, Heard and van Dooren, pp. 105–15; Stephen Herbert, 'A Slice of Lantern Life: Lantern presentations in and around Hastings in early 1881', in *Realms of Light*, eds Crangle, Heard and van Dooren, pp. 185–92; Waddington, *Panoramas, Magic Lanterns, and Cinemas*, pp. 55–138.

75 Crangle, *Hybrid Texts*, p. 118.

76 Catalogues consulted at The Bill Douglas Centre, University of Exeter. For example, *Newton and Co.'s Catalogue of Lantern Slides (Pt II)* (London: Newton and Co's, [n.d.]) was divided into the following sections: Educational, Scientific, Medical, Travel, Church, Art and Literature, Sunday School, and Children's Entertainments. In his work on York and Son, David Henry finds a similar division of themes, but adds that by the late 1890s, the illustrated song genre was also becoming popular. David Henry, 'York and Son, Part 1', in *New Magic Lantern Journal* 3:1 (1984), pp. 12–13.

77 Crangle, *Hybrid Texts*, pp. 130–32.

78 Revd J.M. Lewis, *Lantern Readings: A Thousand Miles up the Congo River* (London: J. Tamblin, [n.d.]).

79 Robert Craven, 'The Little Match Girl', in *Short Lantern Readings, Series no. 8* (Bradford: Riley Bros., [n.d.], pp. 3–6.

80 Mervyn Heard and Richard Crangle, 'The Temperance Phantasmagoria', in *Realms of Light*, eds Crangle, Heard and van Dooren, pp. 53–54.

81   J.W. Kirton, *Buy your own Cherries* (London: Jerrold and Sons, [n.d.]). This was an often reproduced title, which, famously, was subsequently be adapted to the cinematograph.

82   'Lantern Lectures: 1899–1900', pamphlet. Bodleian Library, University of Oxford: John Johnson Collection; London Play Places 2).

83   Examples are preserved at the Bill Douglas Centre, University of Exeter. See the composite variety lecture entitled *Magic Lantern Reading to Accompany Slides*, apparently fabricated by lecturer, J. Hollins; and the composite temperance lecture entitled *Which Side Wins*.

84   For example, see 'Little Ones at Limehouse', pp. 61–68; G.R.Bryce, 'Lantern Lectures', in *Optical Magic Lantern Journal and Photographic Enlarger* 8:94 (1897), p. 29; and The Showman, 'Lecturer's Profits', in *Optical Magic Lantern Journal and Photographic Enlarger* 11:130 (1900), p. 39.

85   See, for example, T.C. Hepworth, *The Book of the Lantern* (London: Wyman and Sons, 1888), pp. 264–73; *The Art of Projection and Complete Magic Lantern Manual, by An Expert* (London: E.A. Beckett, 1893), pp. 105–09; and Revd J.M. Lewis, *Lantern Readings: A Thousand Miles up the Congo River* (London: J. Tamblin, [n.d.]), p. 4.

86   The books and articles surveyed are as follows:

       From books: T.C. Hepworth, *The Book of the Lantern*, pp. 264–73; A.A. Wood, *Magic Lanterns: How Made and How Used with Practical Advice to Unpractised Lecturers*, 4th edn (London: E.G. Wood and Horne, 1891); *The Art of Projection*, pp. 105–09; *The Lantern Buyer's Guide: Being Hints on the Purchase of Lantern Outfits* (Bradford: Riley Bros., 1894).

       From the *Optical Magic Lantern Journal*: G.R. Bryce, 'Lantern Lectures' (March 1897), pp. 29–30; Revd H. Bedford, 'Hints on Lantern Lectures' (October 1899), pp. 131–33; George E. Brown, 'The Lanternist as Lecturer, Pt I' (July 1900), pp. 90–91; and 'The Lanternist as Lecturer, Pt II' (July 1900), pp. 95–96; T. Perkins, 'Our Lantern Lectures' (January 1902), pp. 105–06; A.B., 'Lecturers Should Learn their Lectures' (February 1902), p. 125.

       From the *Optical Lantern and Cinematograph Journal*: J.W. Wright, 'How to Deliver Lantern Lectures' (March 1905), pp. 65–68; Revd T. Perkins, 'Three Requisites for a Successful Lantern Lecture' (August 1905), pp. 156–58.

       From *The Showman*: 'Lantern and Cinematograph Exhibiting, Pt. II' (14 June 1901), pp. 389–90; 'The Sorrows of the Lantern Lecturer' (21 June 1901), pp. 399–400; Professor Oakden, 'Elocution Made Easy, Pt. I' (5 July 1901), pp. 432–34; 'Elocution Made Easy, Pt. II' (12 July 1901), pp. 452–53; and 'Elocution Made Easy, Pt. III' (19 July 1901), pp. 459–60.

       From *The Photographic News*: Allan Blair, 'How to Prepare a Lantern Lecture' (27 October 1899), p. 703.

       From *Hobbies* 1896/7(repr. in Stephen Herbert, *A History of Pre-Cinema* 3 vols (London: Routledge, 2000): 'The Lantern for Pleasure and Profit', II, pp. 459–60; 'Lecturing', II, pp. 471–72; and 'Lecturing, continued', II, pp. 473–74.

87   A.B., 'Lecturers Should Learn their Lectures', *The Optical Magic Lantern Journal* (February 1902), p. 125.

88   Harry Furniss, *Confessions of a Caricaturist* (London: Unwin, 1901) (repr. in David Robinson, 'Harry Furniss—Lantern Showman', *The New Magic Lantern Journal* 6:3 [1992], p. 2.

89   George E. Brown, 'The Lanternist as Lecturer', *The Optical Magic Lantern Journal and Photographic Enlarger* 11:134 (July 1900), p. 90.

90   Revd H. Bedford, 'Hints on Lantern Lectures.—II', *The Optical Magic Lantern Journal*

10:126 (December 1899), p. 143.

91 Tom Gunning, 'The Scene of Speaking: Two Decades of Discovering the Film Lecturer', *Iris* 27 (1999), p. 77.

92 Germain Lacasse, 'The Lecturer and the Attraction', in *The Cinema of Attractions Reloaded*, ed. Wanda Streuven (Amsterdam: Amsterdam University Press, 2006), p. 187.

93 Notices for female lecturers did appear, although infrequently, and were chiefly noted as exceptions to normal practice. See, for example, the brief notice of Miss Jessie Noble's lecture on South Africa. 'Another Lady Lecturer', *The Optical Lantern and Cinematograph Journal* (July 1905), p. 143.

94 Nicholas Hiley, '"At the Picture Palace": The British Cinema Audience, 1895–1920', in *Celebrating 1895*, ed. Fullerton, p. 97.

95 André Gaudreault with Jean-Pierre Sirois-Trahan, 'Le retour du [bonimenteur] refoulé . . . (ou serait-ce le bonisseur-conférencier, le commentateur, le conférencier, le présentateur ou le "speaker"?)', *Iris* 22 (1996), p. 20.

96 See, for example, Martin Sopocy, 'James A. Williamson: American View', in *Cinema 1900/1906: An Analytical Study*, compiled by Roger Holman (Brussels: FIAF, 1982), p. 299.

97 Germain Lacasse, *Le Bonimenteur et Le Cinema Oral*, pp. 23–42.

98 Gaudreault and Sirois-Trahan, 'Le Retour du [bonimenteur] refoulé . . .', p. 23.

99 James Parkes, 'Dearth in Lanterndom', *The Optical Magic Lantern Journal and Photographic Enlarger* (October 1901), pp. 67–68.

100 [Editorial], *The Showman* (20 September 1901), p. 24.

101 T. Perkins, 'Our Lantern Lectures', *The Optical Magic Lantern Journal and Photographic Enlarger* (January 1902), p. 105

102 L. Gaumont and Company advised customers that they could write for a 'special pamphlet' concerning their film, *Boer Atrocities*. [Gaumont advertisement], *The Showman* (27 September 1901), advertisement p. 2.

103 'The Printed Lecture', in *The Bioscope* (17 December 1908), p. 21.

104 *Newton and Co.'s Catalogue of Lantern Slides (Pt II)*, p. vii.

105 The Showman, 'Lecturer's Profits', in *The Optical Magic Lantern Journal* (March 1900), pp. 37–40.

106 This sum compared unfavourably even with the lowest billed performers on the music hall stage, who five years earlier might have expected £400 per annum. See G.H. Duckworth, 'Art and Amusement', in *Life and Labour of the People in London*, ed. Charles Booth, 8 vols (London: Macmillan and Co., 1896), VIII, p. 138.

107 See, for example, E. Dockree, 'Lecturer's Expenses', in *The Photographic News* (1 January 1897), pp. 8–9.

108 *Newton and Co's Catalogue of Lantern Slides (Pt II)*, p. 900a.

109 For two useful illustrative images confirming this (but which were reproduced on comic postcards, and are not wholly reliable), see Crangle, 'Next Slide Please', pp. 40–41.

110 Famously, the first ever film screenings in the UK, by Birt Acres on 10 and 15 January 1896, were made for two different photographic societies, and Robert Paul presented his Theatrograph at the Royal Institution on 28 February 1896. More generally in the first few years of film, lectures of all kinds often included brief descriptions of the apparatus used in the screening and the method by which the illusion of living pictures had been achieved.

111 See especially, Charles Musser and Carol Nelson, *High-Class Moving Pictures: Lyman H. Howe and the Forgotten Era of Travelling Exhibition, 1880–1920* (Princeton: Princeton

University Press, 1991); X. Theodore Barber, 'The Roots of Travel Cinema: John L. Stoddard, E. Burton Holmes and the Nineteenth-Century Illustrated Travel Lecture', *Film History*, 5:3 (1993), pp. 68–84; Alison Griffiths, *Wondrous Difference: Cinema, Anthroplogy and Turn-of the-Century Visual* Culture (New York: Columbia University Press, 2001), pp. 203–28; and Rick Altman, 'From Lecturer's Prop to Industrial Product: The Early History of Travel Films', in *Virtual Voyages: Cinema and Travel*, ed. Jeffrey Ruoff (Durham, NC: Duke University Press, 2006), pp. 61–78.

112 See [Review of Hibbert lecture], *The Showman* (22 March 1901), p. 168; and [Review of Hibbert lecture], *The Showman* (12 April 1901), p. 232. Hibbert synopsised elements of his lecture for *The World's Fair* some years later; Harold R. Hibbert, 'How to Spend Three Days in Paris', in *The World's Fair* (4 February 1908), p. 4. For an informal account of Hibbert's enormously successful career in the North of England, see G.J. Mellor, *Movie Makers and Picture Palaces: A Century of Cinema in Yorkshire 1896–1996* (Bradford: Bradford Libraries, 1996), pp. 72–83.

113 'A Successful Living Picture Lecture', in *The Optical Lantern and Cinematograph Journal* (May 1906), p. 93. See also, 'Pictorial Lecture at Margate', *The Bioscope* (13 November 1908), p. 6.

114 'Mr Arthur B. Malden', in *The Optical Lantern and Cinematograph Journal* (May 1906), p. 92.

115 For Holmes' British shows, see Charles Urban, *A Yank in Britain: The Lost Memoirs of Charles Urban, Film Pioneer*, ed. Luke McKernan (Hastings: The Projection Box, 1999), pp. 60–62, 65–66.

116 [Review of Holmes' Travelogues], *The Optical Lantern and Cinematograph Journal* (September 1905), p. 170.

117 Musser and Nelson, *High-Class Moving Pictures*, p. 54. Alison Griffiths has described these shows as 'a consumable package of voyeuristic pleasure and rationalist rhetoric of uplift, comfort, and affordability'. Griffiths, *Wondrous Difference*, p. 205.

118 Alan Burton, *The British Consumer Co-operative Movement and Film, 1890s–1960s* (Manchester: Manchester University Press, 2005).

119 [Letters], *The Optical Lantern and Cinematograph Journal* (June 1905), p. 104. See also 'Pictures and Politics in the West', *The Optical Lantern and Cinematograph Journal* (May 1905), p. 98.

120 [Report on Primrose League screening], *The Optical Lantern and Cinematograph Journal* (February 1906), p. 41.

121 [Editorial on film and the election], *The Optical Lantern and Cinematograph Journal* (March 1906), p. 50. See also 'The Election', *The Optical Lantern and Cinematograph Journal* (May 1906), p. 91.

122 This has been one of the initial findings of the 'Projected and Moving Image Entertainments in the SW, 1820–1914' project, directed by John Plunkett and myself at the University of Exeter, which has discovered that lantern culture remained powerfully active in urban and provincial centres during the first decades of the twentieth century.

123 Peter Cherches, *Star Course: Popular Lectures and the Marketing of Celebrity* (unpublished doctoral dissertation, New York University, 1997), p. 12.

124 See John Barnes, *The Beginnings of the Cinema in England, 1894–1901*, 5 vols (Exeter: University of Exeter Press, 1996), IV, pp. 97–102; and *Who's Who of Victorian Cinema: A Worldwide Survey*, ed. Stephen Herbert and Luke McKernan (London: British Film Institute, 1996), pp. 149–50. For his own account of his first attempts at a show, see Alfred West, 'The Birth of the Kinema: Some Interesting Details of a Show that had an Unin-

terrupted Run for Fifteen Years', *The Kinematograph and Lantern Weekly* (1 March 1917), pp. 9–11; and Alfred West, *Sea Salts and Celluloid* (unpublished autobiography, available at 'Our Navy' website: http://www.ournavy.org.uk/)

125 [Review of 'Our Navy'], *The Optical Magic Lantern Journal and Photographic Enlarger* (December 1899), p. 143.

126 Richard Brown, 'The British Film Copyright Archive', *The Kingdom of Shadows*, eds Harding and Popple, p. 242.

127 *British Journal of Photography* (13 October 1899), p. 642 (repr. in Barnes, *The Beginnings of the Cinema in England*, IV, p. 98).

128 [Review of West's show], *The Showman* (25 January 1901), p. 65.

129 Thomas Byford, 'Concerning Two Remunerative Callings', *The Optical Magic Lantern Journal and Photographic Enlarger* 12146 (December 1901), pp. 88–89.

130 *The Showman* (September 1900), p. 17.

131 'The Side Shows of London', *The Showman* (22 February 1901), p. 127.

132 Mannoni, 'Elbow to Elbow', p. 3.

133 Henry V.Hopwood, *Living Pictures: Their History, Photo-Production and Practical Working* (London: Optician and Photographic Trades Review, 1899), p. 212.

134 Cecil M. Hepworth, *Animated Photography: The ABC of the Cinematograph* (London: Hazell, Watson and Viney, 1900), p. 74.

135 'At England's Home of Mystery', *The Showman* (26 April 1901), p. 265. For further details on film at the Egyptian Hall, see David Devant, *My Magic Life* (Bideford, Devon: The Supreme Magic Co., [n.d.]), pp. 70–79; and George A. Jenness, *Maskelyne and Cooke: Egyptian Hall, London, 1873–1904* (London: H. Clarke and Co., 1967), pp. 71–72.

136 See 'C.W. Locke', in *The Showman* (11 October 1901), p. 71.

137 'How to Give a Good Cinematograph Show', *The Showman* (6 September 1901), p. 571. On title slides, which were regularly promoted by the press, see [Commentary on titles slides], *The Showman* (27 September 1901), p. 47.

138 'Animated Pictures and Elocution', *The Showman* (20 September 1901), p. 24.

139 Sometimes these novelties seem bizarre and remain difficult for us to reconstruct. For example, in 1906 Ann Holland used film within her travelling show to assist in a lottery. See [Cinematograph Lottery], *The World's Fair* (12 May 1906), p. 1.

140 Charles Urban, *A Yank in Britain : The Lost Memoirs of Charles Urban, Film Pioneer*, ed. Luke McKernan (Hastings: The Projection Box, 1999); and Luke McKernan, '*Something More than a Mere Picture Show': Charles Urban and the Early Non-Fiction Film in Great Britain and America, 1897–1925* (Unpublished doctoral thesis, Birkbeck University of London, 2004).

141 A fascinating collection of letters, accepting or declining an invitation to the show, survive among the Charles Urban Papers, National Media Museum, Bradford.

142 For example, see the work of cinema chain owner Montagu A. Pyke, *Focussing the Universe* (London: Waterloo Brothers, [1912]).

143 For an account of Styles' career up until 1910, when he retired, see 'Mr James Styles— Describer', *The World's Fair* (24 September 1910), p. 14.

144 'Il est comme un surface où se rencontrent des forces opposées, surface où ces forces vont d'amalgamer au cours d'un processus dynamique d'attirance et de répulsion'. Lacasse, *Le Bonimenteur et le Cinema Oral*, p. 28. My translation.

145 'The Lecturer's Worth', *The Bioscope* (20 November 1908), p. 12.

146 Tom Gunning, *D.W. Griffith and the Origins of American Narrative Film: The Early Years at Biograph* (Chicago: University of Illinois Press, 1991), p. 91. See also Miriam Hansen,

Babel and Babylon: Spectatorship in American Silent Film (Cambridge, MA: Harvard University Press, 1991), pp. 96–97. For a brief account of this phenomenon in relation to British film shows, see Hiley, 'At the Picture Palace', p. 97.

147   Peter McLachlan, 'A Suggestion to Manufacturers', *The Bioscope* (31 January 1909), p. 23.

148   'An Analytical Programme', *The Bioscope* (21 January 1909), p. 13. For work on lecturing as an early manifestation of narrative voice-over techniques in film, see Sarah Kozloff, *Invisible Storytellers: Voice-Over Narration in American Fiction Film* (Berkeley: University of California Press, 1988), pp. 8–26; for work on lecturing in relation to intertitling, see Martin Sopocy, 'The Role of the Intertitle in Film Exhibition, 1904–1910', in *Cinema: The Beginnings and the Future*, ed. Williams, pp. 123–34.

149   B.B., 'Social Welfare and the Kinematograph', in *Charity Organization Review* 196 (1913), p. 182.

150   *Ibid.*

151   *Motion Picture Handbook: A Guide for Managers and Operators of Motion Picture Theatres* (New York: Moving Picture World, 1910), p. 169. His emphasis in original.

152   A.S., 'Explain the Pictures!', *The Bioscope* (10 December 1908), p. 11.

153   'The Printed Lecture', *The Bioscope* (17 December 1908), p. 21.

154   'The Lecturing Idea', *The Bioscope* (7 January 1909), p. 5.

155   A.S., 'Explain the Pictures!', p. 11.

156   *Ibid.*

157   For example, for detailed work on the cult of the character actor in British film during the 1910s, see Jon Burrows, *Legitimate Cinema: Theatre Stars in Silent British Films 1908–1918* (Exeter: University of Exeter Press, 2003), pp. 141–79.

158   This was a situation repeated in Holland, as is uniquely demonstrated by the biography of film lecturer Max Nabarro. Max Nabarro, 'This is My Life', trans. Ivo Blom and Tom Gunning, *Iris* 22 (1996), pp. 183–200.

3   Knowing Better

1   There is a growing literature on fairground bioscope show performance. See especially Father Greville, 'Brief Particulars of Bioscope Shows', in *Merry-Go-Round* 7:1–11(1951–53); Arthur Fay, *Bioscope Shows and their Engines* (Lingfield: The Oakwood Press, 1966); Mark E. Schwartz, 'An Overview of Cinema on the Fairgrounds', in *Film Reader* 6 (1985), pp. 65–77; Vanessa Toulmin, 'Telling the Tale: The Story of the Fairground Bioscope Shows and the Showmen who Operated them', in *Film History* 6 (1994), pp. 219–37; Toulmin, 'Travelling Shows and the First Static Cinemas', in *Picture House* 21 (1996), pp. 5–12; Toulmin, *Randall Williams, King of Showmen: From Ghost Show to Bioscope* (London: The Projection Box, 1998); Joe Kember, '"It was not the show, it was the tale that you told": Film Lecturing and Showmanship on the British Fairground', in *Visual Delights: Essays on the Popular and Projected Image in the 19th Century*, eds Simon Popple and Vanessa Toulmin (Trowbridge: Flicks Books, 2000), pp. 56–64; Mervyn Heard, '"Come in Please, come out pleased": the Development of British Fairground Bioscope Presentation and Performance', in *Moving Performance: British Stage and Screen, 1890s–1920s*, eds Linda Fitzsimons and Sarah Street (Trowbridge: Flicks Books, 2000), pp. 101–11; Vanessa Toulmin, '"We take them and make them": Mitchell and Kenyon and the Travelling Exhibition Showmen', in *The Lost World of Mitchell and*

Kenyon: Edwardian Britain on Film, eds VanessaToulmin, Patrick Russell and Simon Popple (London: British Film Institute, 2004), pp. 59–68.

2 Deac Rossell, 'A Slippery Job: Travelling Exhibitors in Early Cinema' in *Visual Delights*, ed. Popple and Toulmin, pp. 50–60

3 Jon Burrows, 'Penny Pleasures: Film Exhibition in London during the Nickelodeon Era, 1906–1914', *Film History* 16 (2004), pp. 60–91.

4 Vanessa Toulmin, 'Cuckoo in the Nest: Edwardian Exhibition and the Transition to Cinema', forthcoming. Many thanks to Vanessa Toulmin for furnishing me with a draft version of this article.

5 On music hall exhibition, see especially, Richard Brown and Barry Anthony, *A Victorian Film Enterprise: The History of the British Mutoscope and Biograph Company, 1897–1915* (Trowbridge: Flicks Books, 1999). For a brief survey of sound in early US film, see Rick Altman, 'The Living Nickelodeon', in *The Sounds of Early Cinema*, eds Richard Abel and Rick Altman (Bloomington: Indiana University Press, 2001), pp. 232–40. See also Stephen Bottomore, 'An International Survey of Sound Effects in Early Cinema', *Film History* 11 (1999), pp. 485–99.

6 Peter Bailey, *Popular Culture and Performance in the Victorian City* (Cambridge: Cambridge University Press, 1998), pp. 128–50.

7 *Ibid.*, p. 128. See also Peter Bailey, 'Custom, Capital and Culture in the Victorian Music Hall', in *Popular Custom and Culture in Nineteenth-Century England*, ed. R. Storch (London: Croom Helm, 1982), pp. 180–208; and Bailey, 'A Community of Friends: Business and Good Fellowship in London Music Hall Management c. 1860–1885', in *Music Hall: The Business of Pleasure*, ed. Peter Bailey (Milton Keynes: Open University Press, 1986), pp. 33–52

8 Bailey, *Popular Culture*, pp. 140–41.

9 *Ibid.*, p. 140.

10 For a contemporary account of the gentrification of the halls, see Andrew Wilson, 'Music Halls', *Contemporary Review* 58 (July 1900), pp. 134–41. Evidence is especially scarce concerning the performance of film lecturers in music halls, but certain accounts of 'ingeniously-connected films' (especially concerning wars or current events concerning royalty) do imply that the lecturer had some role to play in these institutions too. 'Showmen at the Alhambra', *The Showman* (29 March 1901), p. 206.

11 Walter Benjamin, *Charles Baudelaire: A Lyric Poet in the Era of High Capitalism*, trans. Harry Zohn (London: Verso, 1983); Simmel, 'The Stranger', in *Sociology of Georg Simmel*, trans. and ed. Kurt H. Wolff (London: Collier-Macmillan, 1950), pp. 402–08; Guy Debord, *The Society of the Spectacle*, trans. Donald Nicholson (New York: ZONE, 1994); Michel de Certeau, *The Practice of Everyday Life*, trans. Steven Rendall (Berkeley: University of California Press, 1984). For a summary of influential 'textual' urban studies see *Social and Cultural Forms of Modernity*, eds Robert Bocock and Kenneth Thompson (Cambridge: Polity Press in association with the Open University, 1992), pp. 417–61.

12 De Certeau, *The Practice of Everyday Life*, p. xix.

13 'The Successful Exhibitor', *The Bioscope* (6 November 1908), p. 10.

14 But earlier generations of film historians have made some interesting and informed use of anecdote. See especially Leslie Wood's narrative account of the beginning of the movies; Leslie Wood, *The Romance of the Movies* (London: Heinemann, 1937).

15 *Photographic News* (14 January 1898), (repr. in *In the Kingdom of the Shadows: A Companion to Early Cinema*, ed. Colin Harding and Simon Popple [London: Cygnus Arts, 1996], p. 79).

16   Lily May Richards, *Biography of William Haggar: Actor, Showman and Pioneer of the Film Industry* (University of Sheffield Library, National Fairground Archive MS), p. 33.

17   Vanessa Toulmin, unpublished interview with Miss Celine Williams (University of Sheffield Library, National Fairground Archive MS).

18   Cecil Hepworth, *Came the Dawn: Memoires of a Film Pioneer* (London: Phoenix House, 1951), pp. 33–34; Cecil Hepworth, 'Those Were the Days', in *Film Makers on Film Making: Statements on their Art by Thirty Directors*, ed. Harry M. Geduld (Bloomington: Indiana University Press, 1967), pp. 29–30 (first publ. in *Penguin Film Review* 6 [April 1948], pp. 33–39).

19   This assumption has been made most recently in Lacasse, *Le Bonimenteur et Le Cinema Oral*, p. 71; see also Michael Chanan, *The Dream That Kicks: The Prehistory and Early Years of Cinema in Britain*, 2nd edn (London: Routledge, 1996), pp. 6–7. Hepworth's claim to the anecdote is strengthened, albeit tenuously, by evidence that on at least one other occasion his late autobiographical writing had borrowed from his own pseudonymous articles in contemporary journals. An anecdotal article written for *The Showman* in 1901 by a C. Milton Haydon, whose name is encouragingly similar to Cecil Milton Hepworth, all but proves that they were in fact the same person. See C. Milton Haydon, 'Tight Corners, and Such Like', *The Showman* (28 June 1901), pp. 421–22; Hepworth, 'Those Were the Days', p. 30.

20   'Side Shows at Bazaars', *The Showman* (November 1900), p. 50.

21   Richards, *Biography of William Haggar*, p. 21. For further details on Haggar's career, see David Berry, 'William Haggar: Film Pioneer, Actor and Showman', in *Moving Performance: British Stage and Screen, 1890s–1920s* (Trowbridge: Flicks Books, 2000), pp. 112–22.

22   Richard Altick, *The Shows of London: A Panoramic History of Exhibitions, 1600–1862* (Cambridge, MA: Belknap Press, 1978), p. 425.

23   In Dickens, see especially the Crummle family in *Nicholas Nickleby*; Mr Sleary in *Hard Times*; and the numerous fairground and penny gaff showmen described in *Sketches by Boz*, and *The Old Curiosity Shop*. For an excellent overview of Dickens' approach to entertainment, see Paul Schlicke, *Dickens and Popular Entertainment* (London: Unwin Hyman, 1985). For fictional representations appearing toward the end of the Victorian period, see Reid Kerr, 'The Showman: A Story', in *Temple Bar* 116 (April 1899), pp. 535–47; and Revd Thomas Horne, *Humorous and Tragic Stories of Showman Life* (London: The Era, [1909]).

24   E. Raree, *Walk Up! Walk Up! and See the Fool's Paradise with the Many Wonderful Adventures There as Seen in the Strange Surprising PEEP SHOW of Professor Wolley Cobble Showman these Five and Twenty Years NB Money Returned if Performance not Approved of* (London: John Camden Hotten, 1871), prefatory note. For work on this and similar publications, see John Plunkett 'Moving Books/Moving Images: Optical Recreations and Children's Publishing 1800–1900', in *19: Interdisciplinary Studies in the Long Nineteenth Century* 5 (2007). Article accessed at http://www.19.bbk.ac.uk/issue5/index5.htm.

25   'A Wonderful Baby', *The Showman* (21 February 1902), p. 6.

26   See, for example, 'William Clark', *The Showman* (1 February 1901), p. 73; and *The Showman* (15 November 1901), p. 146.

27   I am indebted to Professor Vanessa Toulmin for this information. For a full account of the operation of the Guild, see Toulmin, *Fun without Vulgarity: Community, Women and Language in Showland Society, from 1890 to the Present Day* (unpublished doctoral thesis, University of Sheffield, 1997).

28   'The Showman's Guild', in *The Showman* (1 February 1901), p. 82.

29   Many thanks to Vanessa Toulmin for providing me with this estimate.

30   G.H. Duckworth, 'Art and Amusement', in *Life and Labour of the People in London*, 8 vols. ed. Charles Booth (London: MacMillan and Co., 1896), VIII, p. 107.

31   'The Showman's Guild', p. 82.

32   *Ibid.*

33   For an exhaustive account of the development of the Guild, see Toulmin, *Fun without Vulgarity*.

34   See, for example, the account of the first annual meeting of the Yorkshire Union of Showmen, 'Showmen's Notes', *The Music Hall and Theatre Review* (7 November 1902), p. 309; and an account of a public meeting held at a showground at Eccles Wakes, 'Showmen's Notes', *The Music Hall and Theatre Review* (5 September, 1902), p. 65.

35   See *The Showman* (17 January 1902), p. 293.

36   'Special to all Entertainers: "The Showman" Entertainment Bureau', in *The Showman* (31 May 1901), p. 345.

37   'Side Shows at Bazaars', in *The Showman* (November 1900), p. 50.

38   'James Chipperfield: An All-Round Showman', in *Music Hall and Theatre Review* (10 June 1904), p. 381.

39   Some of these individuals were able to negotiate for higher salaries or a cut of the profits, and sometimes moved to other shows when a better offer was made, bringing with them the exaggerated self-portraits that adorned the facades of the shows. See 'Show-Life Secrets', *The Showman* (20 September 1901), p. 27. But the point is highly contested. See David A. Gerber, 'Volition and Valorization in the Analysis of the 'Careers' of People Exhibited in Freak Shows', *Disability, Handicap & Society* 7:1 (1992), pp. 53–69; and Robert Bogdan, 'In Defense of Freak Show', *Disability, Handicap & Society* 8:1 (1993), pp. 91–94.

40   Lord George Sanger, *Seventy Years a Showman* (London: C.Arthur Preston, 1908).

41   For good accounts of Barnum's role in the development of popular entertainment, see Eric Fretz, P.T. Barnum's Theatrical Selfhood and the Nineteenth-Century Culture of Exhibition', in *Freakery: Cultural Spectacles of the Extraordinary Body*, ed. Rosemary Garland Thomson (New York: New York University Press, 1996), pp. 97–107; and John Springhall, 'On with the Show': American Popular Entertainment as Cultural and Social History', in *History Compass* 2:1 (2004).

42   'Showmen's Notes', in *The Music Hall and Theatre Review* (18 July 1902), p. 47.

43   On Kemp and Howard, see 'George Kemp', in *The Showman* (December 1900), p. 68; and 'Prof. Howard', in *The Showman* (10 May 1901), pp. 299–300.

44   Jon Burrows, 'Penny Pleasures II: Indecency, Anarchy, and Junk Film in London's Nickelodeons', 1906–1914', in *Film History* 16 (2004), p. 174.

45   Montagu Williams QC bemoaned the fact that the law was often unable to track down men such as Norman, charging the showmen within the premises instead. Montagu Williams QC, *Round London: Down East and Up West* (London: MacMillan and Co, 1892), p. 16

46   Altick, *The Shows of London*, pp. 428–29.

47   *The Era Almanack Advertiser* (December 1893), advertising page.

48   Vanessa Toulmin, '"Curios things in curios places": Temporary exhibition venues in the Victorian and Edwardian entertainment environment', in *Early Popular Visual Culture*, 4:2 (2006), pp. 113–37.

49   See 'Side Shows at Bazaars', *The Showman* (November 1900), p. 50; and 'Exhibitions and How they are Run', *The Showman* (28 June 1901), pp. 411–12.

50 Toulmin, 'Curios things in curios places', pp. 16–18.

51 This was the case on the Mile End Road, opposite the London Hospital, which became a flare up point between the showmen and the authorities during the 1880s.

52 'Exhibitions and How they are Run', p. 411.

53 'The Side Shows of London', in *The Showman* (22 February 1901), p. 127.

54 Tom Norman, *Memoirs of Tom Norman: The Silver King* (Sheffield University Library, National Fairground Archive MS), p. 12.

55 *Ibid.*

56 Val Royle, 'Smartness in Shows', in *The Showman* (October 1900), p. 27.

57 Williams, *Round London*, pp. 12–13.

58 Royle, 'Smartness in Shows', p. 27

59 Toulmin notes that the prices of shop shows were typically much lower than those of museums or of grand exhibition spaces such as the annual World's Fair at the Agricultural Hall, Islington. Toulmin, 'Curios things in curios places', p. 134.

60 Williams, *Round London*, p. 13.

61 'The Side Shows of London, Pt. 3' in *The Showman* (15 March 1901), p. 174.

62 'The Side Shows of London, Pt. 2' in *The Showman* (1 March 1901), p. 144.

63 'The Side Shows of London', p. 127.

64 Arthur St John Adcock, 'Sideshow London', in *Living London*, ed. George R. Sims, 3 vols (London: Cassell and Company, 1903), II, p. 286.

65 For a fascinating, but highly prejudiced, 1889 account of the bank holiday crowds at the fairground, which focused upon the drunkenness of working-class visitors, see George Gissing, *The Nether World* (Oxford: Oxford University Press, 1999), pp. 104–13.

66 W.M.A., 'A Glimpse of Showman's Life', in *The Showman* (29 November 1901), p. 190.

67 This appears to have been the case at the ancient Coventry Whitsuntide Fair in 1902, at which showmen were informed that, in addition to submitting to an abnormally high ground rent, they could no longer trade between the very profitable hours of 11pm and 12am, nor could they use any organ, whistle or horn in any public place in order to attract the crowds. See 'Showmen's Notes', in *The Music Hall and Theatre Review* (16 May 1902), p. 317. Some local councils used the 1865 Locomotive Act to prosecute showmen for transporting loads over twelve tons, at speeds in excess of 10 mph, or in more than two articulated carriages. Transportation by rail was not always possible, and the cost of doing so also grew, with certain companies distinguishing between trades in a way that seemed to some showmen discriminatory. See 'Correspondence', in *The Showman* (28 February 1902), p. 56.

68 'Hull Fair', in *The Showman* (November 1900), p. 53.

69 'Birmingham Fair', *The Showman* (7 June 1901), p. 367.

70 Toulmin, *Randall Williams*, pp. 13, 14.

71 Pat Collins was reportedly responsible for the establishment of a twice-annual Smethwick Fair during 1901. 'Smethwick Fair', in *The Showman* (14 June 1901), p. 389.

72 See 'Showman's Notes', in *The Music Hall and Theatre Review* (9 May 1902), p. 301.

73 A remarkable collection of waxwork catalogues survives at the John Johnson Collection. Bodleian Library, University of Oxford: John Johnson Collection, Waxworks 1 and 2.

74 Val Royle, 'To Attract the Public', *The Showman* (September 1900), p. 16.

75 One showman even exhibited a waxwork depicting Jeremia Carrington, who had been charged, but was not yet convicted, with the murder of Hannah Shea. The police and solicitor for the defence made representations to the Director of Public Prosecutions, but it was not clear what action could be taken against the showman. 'Showmen's Notes',

in *The Music Hall and Theatre Review* (7 November 1902), p. 309.

76 'The Side Shows of London, Pt.2', p. 143.

77 See, for example, 'Entertainers' Patter', in *The Showman* (7 February 1902), p. 343; and 'Entertainers' Patter', in *The Showman* (14 March 1902), p. 98.

78 See, for example, 'Telling the Tale', *The World's Fair* (15 December 1906), p. 4.

79 The book had first appeared in 1895, but was translated into English in 1896. Gustave Le Bon, *The Crowd: A Study of the Popular Mind*, 19th edn. (London: Ernest Benn, 1947), pp. 118–19. For a populist account of the fascination with crowds, see Jeremy Broome, 'Crowds', *The Strand Magazine* (July 1898–December 1898), pp. 558–66.

80 Le Bon, *The Crowd*, p. 118.

81 Henry Mayhew, *London Labour and the London Poor*, 4 vols (New York: Dover Publications, 1968), IV, p. 209.

82 Eric Partridge, 'Parlyaree: Cinderella Among Languages', in *Here, There and Everywhere: Essays upon Language* (London: Hamish Hamilton, 1950), p. 116.

83 Toulmin, *Fun Without Vulgarity*, p. 217. For a full explanation of the distinctions between traveller languages, see pp. 217–22.

84 David Birch, 'Travellers' Cant, Shelta, Mumpers' Talk and Minklers' Thari', in *Lore and Language* 3 (July 1983), p. 16.

85 W.M.A.','A Glimpse of Showman's Life', p. 190.

86 The difficulty with this account appears because of a programme for the 1873–74 Christmas Bazaar at the Royal Agricultural Hall, which is preserved in Islington Public Library, Local Studies (dated 26 December 1873 to 16 February 1874), which lists 'Tom Norman' as one of the lower billed attractions. I am indebted to Vanessa Toulmin for this information.

87 Norman, *Memoirs*, p. 8.

88 Norman explains the trick in some detail; Norman, *Memoirs*, p. 68.

89 On the creation of biographical details for the freaks, see Robert Bogdan, *Freak Show: Presening Human Oddities for Amusement and Profit* (Chicago: University of Chicago Press, 1988), pp. 102–06.

90 Norman, *Memoirs*, 8.

91 For this suggestion, see 'Show-Life Secrets', p. 27.

92 'The Side Shows of London', in *The Showman* (22 February 1901), p.128.

93 See especially, Susan Stewart, *On Longing: Narratives of the Miniature, the Gigantic, the Souvenir, the Collection* (Durham, NC: Duke University Press, 1993), p. 109.

94 E.H. Montagu, 'In the Days when Films were Rented on the Deposit System', *The Kinematograph and Lantern Weekly* (Special Supplement: Twenty-First Anniversary of Kinematography) (1 March 1917), p. 9.

95 'Notes on Current Topics', in *The Kinematograph and Lantern Weekly* 7 (20 June 1907), p. 89.

96 For an example of the nostalgic representation of travelling showmen, see Sylvanus, 'Our First Kinematograph Show', in *The Kinematograph and Lantern Weekly* 8 (4 July 1907), p. 128. On the relationship between the film trade press and the penny showmen within London, see Burrows, 'Penny Pleasures', pp. 72–77.

97 For example, Tony Fletcher has chronicled in exhaustive detail the London County Council records of the Theatre and Music Hall Committee relating to the safety of cinematograph exhibitions. Tony Fletcher, 'The London County Council and the Cinematograph, 1896–1900', *Living Pictures: The Journal of the Popular and Projected Image Before 1914*, 1:2 (2001), pp. 69–83; and Tony Fletcher, 'A Tapestry of Celluloid,

1900–1906', in *Early Popular Visual Culture* 4:2 (2006), pp. 175–221.

98 For example, the execution of Leon Czogolz, who assassinated President McKinley, attracted reproductions of all kinds in the USA, not to mention—reputedly—several attempts to recover his body for exhibition within Museums of Curiosity. Beside several films dedicated to the execution, Messrs Stewart, Sons & De Witt offered multiple wax figures for sale. See 'Notes of the Week' in *The Showman* (8 November 1901), p. 1.

99 For example, see the series of *Madame Tussaud's* catalogues from the turn of the century in the John Johnson Collection, which repeatedly have Peace at the heart of the Chamber of Horrors. Bodleian Library, University of Oxford: John Johnson Collection, Waxworks 2.

100 In 1909 Mr Walter Winans patented a device which enabled film to be used for target practice. See 'Big Game Hunting by Cinematograph', *The World's Fair* (3 July 1909) (repr. in *In the Kingdom of the Shadows*, ed. Harding and Popple, p. 40).

101 For example, Henry Mayhew's account of a former freak-show exhibitor who had found that 'photography was attracting more attention than giants and dwarfs', strongly suggests the potential of his own discourse to undermine the referentiality of his portraits. Mayhew, *London Labour and the London Poor*, III, p. 204.

102 Lily May Richards, *Biography of William Haggar*, p. 28.

103 'Animated Pictures and Elocution', p. 24.

104 For an account of the difficulties of an inexperienced operator, see 'The Upstart', 'Experiences in Animated Photography', in *The Showman* (3 January 1902), p. 272.

105 'Animated Pictures and Elocution', p. 24.

106 See Barnes, *The Beginnings of the Cinema in England*, III, pp. 87–93.

107 'Cinematograph Lanterns , &c., and the L.C.C.', in *The Photographic News* 43 (13 January 1899), p. 29.

108 This position is put most strongly (but also caricatured) by an account of a seaside showman appearing in a contemporary journal intended for professional photographers. 'The Kinematograph Man', in *The Photographic News* (25 May 1900), pp. 328–29.

109 'Side Shows at Bazaars', p. 50.

110 Burrows, 'Penny Pleasures', p. 62. Burrows cites John Barnes in evidence of this assertion: Barnes, *The Beginnings of the Cinema in England*, III, p. 71.

111 Fletcher, 'A Tapestry of Celluloid', p. 191.

112 One 1901 report claimed that 'shop shows seem somewhat off just now in Ipswich' and that even 'a first class cinematograph and concert phonograph' had done poor business. This implies, however, that such shows had been a relatively common feature of the town. 'Notes from the Provinces', in *The Showman* (15 November 1901), p. 152.

113 'Prof. Howard', p. 299.

114 Frederic A. Talbot, *Moving Pictures: How they are Made and Worked*, 2nd edn (London: William Heinemann, 1923), p. 161.

115 Rachel Low, *The History of the British Film 1896–1906* (London: George Allen and Unwin, 1948), pp. 38–39 (first publ. in George Pearson, 'Lambeth Walk to Leicester Square', *Sight and Sound* 7:28 [Winter 1938], p. 150).

116 For this date see Deac Rossell, *Living Pictures: The Origin of the Movies* (Albany, NY: State University of New York Press, 1998), p. 89. For an example of a waxwork show, which included automatics as an auxiliary attraction, see the 1897 account of Madame Bosworth's establishment in Manchester: 'The Showmen World', in *The Era* (11 September 1897), p. 20.

117 'Busking Extraordinary', in *The Optical Magic Lantern and Photographic Enlarger*

(February 1901), p. 19.

118 'Indecent Cinematographic Exhibition', in *The Optician and Photographic Trades Review* (29 September 1899), p. 34.

119 'Prof. Stone', *The Showman* (21 June 1901), pp. 395–96

120 See 'An Open-Air Living Picture Show', *The Kinematograph and Lantern Weekly* (29 August 1907), p. 255.

121 See Barnes, *The Beginnings of the Cinema in England*, III, pp. 72–74; Rossell, *Living Pictures*, pp. 152–55.

122 Advertisement for 'Hughes Animated Living Picture Outdoor Peep Show', in *The Era* (23 April 1898), p. 31. See also the advertisement for the large 'Duplex' model of the apparatus: 'New Apparatus: Duplex Photo-Rotoscope', *The Optical Magic Lantern Journal and Photographic Enlarger* (June 1899), p. 79.

123 'An Expert', *The Art of Projection and Complete Magic Lantern Manual*, 2nd edn (London: E.A. Beckett, 1901), p. 9.

124 [Report on street cinematographs], *British Journal of Photography* 45, Monthly supplement (7 October 1898), pp. 73–74.

125 Advertisements regularly appeared in the classified pages of *The Era* and *The Showman* alongside a variety of other sideshow exhibits. See, for example, *The Era* (4 September 1897), p. 18; and *The Showman* (December 1900), p. v. Entertainment agents such as M.Wicks of London offered a number of services to the showmen, including the provision of a permanent address or engagements at music halls and other venues, but capitalised upon the cinematograph by buying and selling second-hand films. See [Advertisement for Wicks], in *The Showman* (September 1900), p. vi.

126 'Editor's Page', in *The Showman* (15 February 1901), p. 106.

127 'The House for Films', in *The Showman* (4 October 1901), p. 63.

128 On the development of film rental during this period, see Richard Brown, 'War on the Home Front: The Anglo-Boer War and the Growth of Rental in Britain. An Economic Perspective', *Film History* 16:1 (2004), pp. 28–36.

129 'The House for Films', in *The Showman* (4 October 1901), p. 63.

130 For example, the Universal Agency at Finsbury Pavement, London, made similar claims at the end of 1900. [Advertisement], *The Showman* (December 1900), p. 2.

131 See Jon Burrows, 'Walter Jeff's Scrapbooks', in *Picture House: Journal of the Cinema Theatre Association* 29 (2004), pp. 44–55; Richard Brown, 'New Century Pictures: Regional Enterprise in Early British Film Exhibition', in *The Lost World of Mitchell and Kenyon*, eds Toulmin, Popple and Russell, pp. 69–82; and Toulmin, 'Cuckoo in the Nest'.

132 'Showmen's Notes', in *The Music Hall and Theatre Review* (9 May 1902), p. 301. The development of the bioscope shows has been exhaustively detailed elsewhere. For a concise account, see Toulmin, 'Telling the Tale', pp. 219–37.

133 'Hull Fair', p. 53.

134 Freda Allen and Ned Williams, *Pat Collins: King of Showmen* (Wolverhampton: Uralia Press, 1991), p. 119.

135 'Editor's Page', in *The Showman* (2 August 1901), p. 497.

136 *The Kinematograph and Lantern Weekly* (4 July 1907), p. 114; 'William Clark', *The Showman* (1 February 1901), p. 78; Richards, *Biography of William Haggar*, p. 16.

137 Richards, *Biography of William Haggar*, p. 17.

138 'The Cinney that Sinned and the Audience that Wanted their Money Back', in *The World's Fair* (28 April 1906), p. 6.

139 W.M.A., 'A Glimpse of Showman's Life', p. 190.

140 [Report on a fairground film show], *The Kinematograph and Lantern Weekly* (4 July 1907), p. 114.

141 Early bioscope operator Jimmy Lynton recalled that turns were usually provided by a 'comedian or a girl dancer' in one of his shows. See 'Old Time Picture Shows', *The World's Fair* (27 November 1954), p. 25.

142 Horne, *Humorous and Tragic Stories of Showman Life*, pp. 65–68.

143 For the showmen's role in commissioning and shooting local films, see Vanessa Toulmin, 'Local Films for Local People: Travelling Showmen and the Commissioning of Regional Films, 1900–1902', *Film History*, 13:2 (2001), pp. 118–38.

144 'Notes on Current Topics', p. 89.

145 By 1918, however, the Showman's Guild was fighting to reopen the 200 fairs that had been allowed to lapse since the beginning of the war. 'Fairs in War Time', *The Times* (23 January 1918), p. 3

146 'Introducing Variety Turns', in *The Bioscope* (4 December 1908), p. 18.

147 'The Bioscope Parliament', in *The Bioscope* (10 December 1908), p. 13.

148 'The Variety Discussion', in *The Bioscope* (17 December 1908), p. 15.

149 John B. Rathbun, *Motion Picture Making and Exhibiting* (London: Werner Laurie, 1914), p. 111. The same point is made by David S. Hulfish, *Motion Picture Work: A General Treatise on Picture Taking, Picture Making, Photo-Plays, and Theater Management and Operation* (Chicago: American Technical Society, 1915), pp. 196–97.

150 'Gain Public Confidence', *The Bioscope* (4 December 1908), p. 3.

151 *How To Run a Picture Theatre* (London: The Kinematograph Weekly, [1911]), p. 56.

152 'Gain Public Confidence', p. 3

4 'Oh, there's our Mary!'

1 'Cinematography Burlesqued', *The Photographic News* (28 January 1898), p. 50; Charles Francis Jenkins, *Animated Pictures* (Washington: H.L. McQueen, 1898), pp. 83–84.

2 Jenkins, *Animated Pictures*, p. 83.

3 'Cinematography Burlesqued', p. 50.

4 Burch argues that these visionary qualities of early British filmmakers were generated by their middle-class origins and their familiarity with aspects of lantern culture. I would add to this account that these qualities were also implicit to their understanding of the commercial basis of the lantern industry, which had depended for decades upon the ability to diversify genres and styles of performance. See Noël Burch, *Life to those Shadows* (London: British Film Institute, 1990), p. 95.

5 Warwick Trading Company catalogue supplement (1897–98), p. 19.

6 Charles Urban Trading Company catalogue (November 1903).

7 Hepwix catalogue supplement (June 1905), pp. 22–23.

8 Maxim Gorky, newspaper review of the Lumiere programme at the Nizhni-Novgorod fair (4 July 1896), reprinted in *In the Kingdom of the Shadows: A Companion to Early Cinema*, eds Colin Harding and Simon Popple (London: Cygnus Arts, 1996), p. 6.

9 A selection of early examples is available in *Victorian Film Catalogues: A Facsimile Collection* (Hastings: The Projection Box, 1996).

10 Warwick Trading Company catalogue (1897–98), pp. 24, 27.

11 See for example, Warwick's separate listings of films depicting the USA, Jamaica, and

Switzerland. Warwick Trading Company catalogue (1902), pp. 87–93.

12 Hepwix catalogue (1903), pp. 3–5.

13 Frank Scheide, 'The Influence of the English Music-Hall on Early Screen Acting', in *Moving Performance: British Stage and Screen, 1890s–1920s*, eds Linda Fitzsimmons and Sarah Street (Trowbridge: Flicks Books, 2000), pp. 69–79.

14 See especially, Janet Staiger, '"The eyes are really the focus": Photoplay Acting and Film Form and Style', *Wide Angle* 6 (1985), pp. 14–23; Roberta Pearson, *Eloquent Gestures: The Transformation of Performance Styles in the Griffith Biograph Films* (Berkeley: University of California Press, 1992); and Richard deCordova, *Picture Personalities: The Emergence of the Star System in America* (Chicago: University of Illinois Press, 1990), pp. 23–49.

15 In spite of deviations, the guiding distinction made within several studies of film acting in the early 1910s is still closely related to that between Lev Kuleshov's 'film actor-mannequin' and V.I. Pudovkin's method for 'incarnating oneself into' the image. Lev Kuleshov, *Kuleshov on Film: Writings by Lev Kuleshov*, trans. and ed. Ronald Levaco (Berkeley: University of California Press, 1974), p. 135; V.I. Pudovkin, *Film Acting: A Course of Lectures Delivered at the State Institute of Cinematography, Moscow*, trans. Ivor Montagu (London: George Newnes, [1935]), p. 110. See, for example, Roberta Pearson on the distinction between what she calls 'histrionic' and 'verisimilar' codes of acting. Pearson, *Eloquent Gestures*, p. 50. Tom Gunning also adopts aspects of this distinction in his work on Griffith's films of this period. Gunning, *D.W. Griffith and the Origins of American Narrative Film*, pp. 225–26.

16 Ben Brewster and Lea Jacobs, 'Pictorial Styles of Film Acting in Europe in the 1910s', in *Celebrating 1895: The Centenary of Cinema*, ed. John Fullerton (London: John Libbey and Company, 1998), p. 253. For an excellent summary of nineteenth-century lexicons of gesture in relation to acting performance, see Ben Brewster and Lea Jacobs, *Theatre to Cinema: Stage Pictorialism and the Early Feature Film* (Oxford: Oxford University Press, 1997), pp. 85–98.

17 Jonathan Crary, *Suspensions of Perception: Attention, Spectacle, and Modern Culture* (Cambridge, MA: MIT Press, 2001), p. 344.

18 Prestwich catalogue (1898), p. 6.

19 Warwick catalogue (1897), pp. 59–60.

20 For biographical details on Terry, which her autobiography ignored (she had married three times, borne two illegitimate children, and conducted various affairs), see Nina Auerbach, *Ellen Terry: A Player in her Time* (London: Phoenix Press, 1987); and Tracy C. Davis, *Actresses as Working Women: Their Social Identity in Victorian Culture* (London: Routledge, 1991), p. 106.

21 See Stephen Bottomore, '"She's just like my granny! Where's her crown?" Monarchs and Movies, 1896–1916', in *Celebrating 1895*, ed. Fullerton, pp. 172–81. For a discussion of Victoria as 'media monarch', see John Plunkett, *Queen Victoria: First Media Monarch* (Oxford: Oxford University Press, 2003).

22 Richard Brown and Barry Anthony, *A Victorian Film Enterprise: The History of the British Mutoscope and Biograph Company, 1897–1915* (Trowbridge: Flicks Books, 1999), p. 57.

23 These are preserved among the Charles Urban Papers, National Media Museum, Bradford.

24 For example, shortly before Edward VII's coronation, Hepworth and Co. advertised that they had 'already secured two or three positions, but intend booking other stands as well', thus hoping to gain a substantial advantage over competitors. See 'A Visit to "Hepworth's"', *The Showman* (6 March 1902), p. 45.

25 See, for example the range of adverts in *The Showman* for 15 February 1901. These included: Mitchell and Kenyon, p. vi; Hepworth and Co., p. 3; Walter Gibbons, p. 4; and The Prestwich Manufacturing Co., p. 9. In fact, of the funeral films had been available at least as early as 8 February, only eighteen days after Victoria's death. See *The Showman* (8 February 1901), p. 95.

26 See, for example, the Warwick Trading Company catalogue for 1897–98, which includes films such as *Gladstone Funeral: The Lying in State, Gladstone Funeral: The Procession*, and seven films, collectively titled *Coronation of the Queen of Holland*. Already, the Warwick Trading Company signalled an awareness in their catalogue of the significance of public personalities, regularly emphasising the views that had been obtained of prominent royals. Warwick Trading Company catalogue (1897–98), pp. 3, 12.

27 'New "Hepwix" Films: Funeral of Queen Victoria', *The Showman* (15 February 1901), p. 3

28 'First in 1893: L. Gaumont and Co.', *The Showman* (22 February 1901), p. 2.

29 'Funeral of the Queen: Impressive and Solemn Spectacle', *The Showman* (15 February 1901), p. 4.

30 For example, Richard Brown and Barry Anthony's list of films produced by the British Biograph and Mutoscope Company between 1897 and 1907 lists 76 films featuring British royalty, far outnumbering other celebrity subjects. See Brown and Anthony, *A Victorian Film Enterprise*, p. 313.

31 'Cinematograph Films', *The Showman* (15 November 1901), p. 152.

32 See David Russell, 'The Football Films', in *The Lost World of Mitchell and Kenyon: Edwardian Britain on Film*, eds Vanessa Toulmin, Simon Popple and Patrick Russell (London: BFI, 2004), pp. 169–80.

33 Warwick Trading Company catalogue (1902), p. 217.

34 'Cinematograph Films', *The Showman* (1 November 1901), p. 127. There was also some well-publicised evidence that the King and Queen enjoyed watching the moving pictures. They had seen a full programme at Balmoral on 14 October 1901. For details, see, 'An Ideal Cinematograph Show', *The Showman* (15 November 1901), pp. 157–58.

35 'Cinematograph Notes', *The Showman* (21 March 1902), p. 77.

36 Hepwix Catalogue (1903), p. 46.

37 See the various discussions from the 1994 Amsterdam Workshop on non-fiction, in *Non-fiction from the Teens*, eds Daan Hertogs and Nico de Klerk (London: British Film Institute, 1994).

38 Sylvanus, 'Our First Kinematograph Show', in *The Kinematograph and Lantern Weekly* (4 July 1907), p. 128.

39 Warwick Trading Company catalogue (1897–98), p. 19.

40 'To the Cinematograph Showmen of To-day', *The Showman* (9 August 1901), advertising page 3. On the attractions of accidental features of early non-fiction films, see Mark-Paul Meyer, 'Moments of Poignancy: The Aesthetics of the Accidental and the Casual in Early Non-fiction Film', in *Uncharted Territory: Essays on Early Non-fiction Film*, eds Daan Hertogs and Nico de Klerk (Amsterdam: Nederlands Filmmuseum, 1997), pp. 51–60.

41 Tom Gunning, 'Pictures of Crowd Splendor: The Mitchell and Kenyon Factory Gate Films', in *The Lost World of Mitchell and Kenyon*, eds Toulmin, Popple and Russell, p. 54

42 For example, the strategy of the Prestwich Manufacturing Company was to sell cameras to travelling exhibitors. See 'Types of Cinematograph Films', *The Showman* (9 August 1901), p. 509. See also, Stephen Bottomore, 'From the Factory Gate to the "Home

Talent" Drama: A International Overview of Local Films in the Silent Era', in *The Lost World of Mitchell and Kenyon*, eds Toulmin, Popple and Russell, pp. 36–37.

43 See 'Prices for taking, developing, and Printing Cinematograph films of Special Subjects', Warwick Trading Company catalogue supplement (1897–98), back cover.

44 'Notes from the Provinces', *The Showman* (5 July 1901), p. 434.

45 'Representative Kinematograph Shows 1. An Example from Poplar', *The Kinematograph and Lantern Weekly* (11 July 1907), p. 142.

46 Bottomore, 'From the Factory Gate to the "Home Talent" Drama', p. 34.

47 'More Show-Life Secrets' (advertisement feature), *The Showman* (2 August 1901), frontispiece.

48 *The Showman* (December 1900), p. 57.

49 'Showmen's Notes', *The Music Hall and Theatre Review* (9 May 1902), p. 301.

50 'Free Cinematograph Films of Local Subjects', *Warwick Trading Company Catalogue 1902*, p. 283.

51 'Cinematograph Films', *The Showman* (11 October 1901), p. 77.

52 Walter Benjamin, 'The Work of Art in the Age of Mechanical Reproduction', in *Illuminations*, trans. Harry Zohn (New York: Schocken, 1969), pp. 233–34.

53 See Barry Anthony, *The Kinora: Motion Pictures for the Home 1896–1914* (Hastings: The Projection Box, 1996), pp. 6–11.

54 Warwick Trading Company catalogue supplement (1902), p. 3.

55 Anthony, *The Kinora*, pp. 8–9.

56 See, for example, the review in *The Photographic News* of R.W. Paul's Theatrograph projector, whose subjects, screened at several halls, were also 'mostly selected from popular plays and from the favourite "turns" at the music-halls'. 'The "Theatrograph"', *The Photographic News* (27 March 1896), p. 194.

57 For example, Brown and Anthony note that this was the case at London's Palace Theatre from 1897; Brown and Anthony, *A Victorian Film Enterprise*, pp. 215–16.

58 Warwick Trading Company catalogue (1902), pp. 32–33.

59 Scheide, 'The Influence of English Music Hall', p. 74. Emphasis in original.

60 Harry Randall, *An Old Time Comedian by Himself* (London: Sampson Low, 1930), p. 68.

61 Peter Bailey, 'A Community of Friends: Business and Good Fellowship in London Music Hall management c. 1860–1885' in *Music Hall: The Business of Pleasure*, ed. Peter Bailey (Milton Keynes: Open University Press, 1986), p. 43.

62 For an account of this process in relation to music hall audiences, see Dagmar Höher, 'The Composition of Music Hall Audiences 1850–1900', in *Music Hall*, ed. Bailey, pp. 73–92.

63 Randall, *An Old Time Comedian*, p. 145.

64 Warwick Trading Company catalogue (1901), p. 156.

65 The 1902 American Mutoscope and Biograph Company catalogue description is reproduced by Brown and Anthony, *A Victorian Film Enterprise*, p. 299.

66 Elizabeth Coffman, 'Women in Motion: Loie Fuller and the "Interpenetration" of Art and Science', in *Camera Obscura* 17: 1 (2002), pp. 73–105.

67 Berry, *Cinema and Wales*, p. 31. Famously, attempts to standardise and mechanise the aural components of exhibition had begun as early as 1887 according to Thomas Edison who claimed that 'all motion and sound could be recorded and reproduced simultaneously'. Thomas Edison's preface to W.K.L. Dickson and Antonia Dickson, *History of the Kinetograph, Kinetoscope , and Kineto-phonograph* (New York: Arno Press, 1970).

68 For example, Ernst Ruhmer, the inventor of the experimental 1901 sound-on-film

machine, the 'Photographophone', had looked forward in *The Showman* to the 'film that shall combine both sound reproduction and picture representation' in such a manner that 'the illusion would become almost perfect'; 'The "Photographophone"', *The Showman* (6 September 1901), p. 577. In 1907, Professor Korn's 'photo-cinematophone' also promised an illusionist perfection derived in part from the technology of the phototelegraphy service he had recently developed. 'The Coming Method of Living Pictures with Sound', *The Kinematograph and Lantern Weekly* (30 May 1907), p. 47. For 1908 examples of phototelegraphic images of faces see *Industrialisation and Culture 1830–1914*, eds Christopher Harvie, Graham Martin and Aaron Scharf (London: Macmillan and the Open University Press, 1970) p. 351.

69   See John Barnes, *The Beginnings of the Cinema in England*, 5 vols (Exeter: University of Exeter Press, 1997), V, p. 115.

70   'Cinematograph Notes', *The Showman* (December 1900), p. 62.

71   See, for example, the flattering extracts of reviews reprinted within the 1906 Gaumont and Co. catalogue. 'The voices of R.G. Knowles, Joe Mack, Hamilton Hill and other well-known artistes', reported the *South Wales and Daily Post*, 'make one feel he is in a variety hall'. Gaumont and Co. catalogue (1906), p. 14.

72   [The Chronophone], *The Kinematograph and Lantern Weekly* (20 June 1907), p. 89. On William Taylor, see Father Greville, 'Fair Ground Cinemas', in *Merry-Go-Round* 7:2 (1951), p. 2.

73   See Freda Allen and Ned Williams, *Pat Collins: King of Showmen* (Wolverhampton: Uralia Press, 1991), p. 119; Berry, *Wales and Cinema*, p. 31.

74   See 'Representative Kinematograph Shows: Singing Pictures at the Hippodrome', *The Kinematograph and Lantern Weekly* (5 September 1907), p. 259. For recommendations on the provision of sound effects, see 'Helps and Hints', *The Kinematograph and Lantern Weekly* (4 July 1907), p. 121; and 'Notes on Current Topics', *The Kinematograph and Lantern Weekly* (5 September 1907), p. 258. For a much earlier account of the use of music and effects during film shows, see T.C. Hepworth, 'Music and "Effects" in Cinematography', *The* Showman (6 September 1901), p. 574.

75   'Helps and Hints', p. 121

76   Indeed, parallel work concerning forms of celebrity performance in early television suggests that the construction of remarkably intimate, highly personalised relationships with spectators has been a vital part of the emergence and popularisation of new media industries throughout the twentieth century. See Donald Horton and R. Richard Wohl, 'Mass Communication and Para-Social Interaction: Observations on Intimacy at a Distance', *Psychiatry* 19 (1956), p. 216.

77   Bailey, 'A Community of Friends', p. 49.

78   Warwick Trading Company catalogue (1901), p. 156.

79   However, in the UK, the use of such scenes was restricted by an Act of Parliament, which defended the legitimate theatres' monopoly on dramatic productions.

80   Jon Burrows, *Legitimate Cinema: Theatre Stars in Silent British Films 1908–1918* (Exeter: University of Exeter Press, 2003), p. 21.

81   *Ibid.*

82   deCordova, *Picture Personalities*, pp. 25–26.

83   Richard Crangle, *Hybrid Texts: Modes of Representation in the Early Moving Picture and some Related Media in Britain* (unpublished doctoral thesis, University of Exeter, 1996), p. 140. Although Crangle clarifies that this is only a 'working technical definition', it accurately describes the majority of life model output. Crangle's work on life model

sequences remains the most substantial account of their production and aesthetics, and has been influential on my own understanding of this industry.

84 'Mr James Bamforth's Lantern Slides', *The Optician and Photographic Trades Review* (29 September 1899), p. 140.

85 'Life Model Studies. 1.—A Peep Behind the Scenes', *The Photogram* (February 1899); and 'Life Model Studies. 2.—The Models Themselves', *The Photogram* (March 1899). Both articles reprinted in the *New Magic Lantern Journal* 5:3 (April 1988), pp. 2–3.

86 'Life Model Studies. 2', p. 3

87 For an account of acting performance that does not elide the earliest films in this way, see Amy Sargent, 'Darwin, Duchenne, Delsarte', in *Moving Performance: British Stage and Screen, 1890s–1920s*, eds Linda Fitzsimmons and Sarah Street (Trowbridge: Flicks Books, 2000), pp. 26–43.

88 Warwick Trading Company catalogue (1897–98), p. 59.

89 Warwick Trading Company catalogue supplement (1897–98), pp. 17–19.

90 Warwick Trading Company catalogue supplement (1897–98), p. 17.

91 The explicitly political plot and the moral of the slide sequence are indicated by the lantern reading intended to accompany them:

> And now behold the champions of every woman's right
> Now screaming for *protection* and for help with all their might . . .
> And off they both ran different ways a once with all their might,
> And from that day they were ashamed to talk of women's rights.

Though it seems unlikely that this thematic complexity was conveyed by any oral accompaniment to the film, the basic premise that shrewish gossips deserved retribution is certainly carried by the moving image alone. 'Women's Rights', *Short Lantern Readings* 3 (Holmfirth: Bamforth and Co., *c*.1891), p. 18.

92 Frank Kessler and Sabine Lenk, 'L'Expression des Sentiments Dans la Comédie des Premiers Temps', *La Licorne* 37 (1996), pp. 7–15.

93 Miriam Hansen, *Babel and Babylon: Spectatorship in American Silent Film* (Cambridge, MA: Harvard University Press, 1991), p. 39.

94 For further work on the implications of the idioms of music hall performance in early film, see Michael Chanan, *The Dream that Kicks: The Prehistory and Early Years of Cinema in Britain*, 2nd edn (London: Routledge, 1996), pp. 221–25.

95 The films both represent the entry of a train into a tunnel, followed by an interior shot of a cabin where a young man and woman kiss, then a shot of the train leaving the tunnel. There is a more obvious distinction between the films: Smith's film has the camera mounted on the front of the train, whereas Riley Brothers' offers long shots of the train entering and leaving the tunnel. John Barnes, *The Beginnings of the Cinema in England*, IV, pp. 42–45.

96 'Film-Picture Actors', *The Bioscope* (2 October 1908), p. 18.

97 As Charles Dawbarn wrote in his 1911 account of a film rehearsal, 'the "natural" is exalted, while the stiff and artificial stand condemned'. Charles Dawbarn, 'The Popular Theatre of Today. Behind the Scenes at a Cinematograph Rehearsal', *Pall Mall Magazine* 48: July–December (1911), p. 271. See also, William J. Elliott, *How to Become a Film Actor* (London: The Picture Palace News Co., 1917); and Aurèle Labat de Lambert, *General Advice on Film Acting*, Cinema Course Series, IV (London: Standard Art Book Company, 1920).

98 'Behind the Scenes: A Cinematograph Rehearsal', *The World's Fair* (18 November 1911), p. 11.

99 See Patrizia Magli, 'The Face and the Soul', in *Zone Four: Fragments for a History of the Human Body*, eds Michel Feher with Nadia Taza and Ramona Nadaff, 3 vols (New York: Zone, 1989), II, p. 87.

100 Samuel R. Wells, *New Physiognomy, or Signs of Character* (New York: Fowler and Wells, 1896), ps. 582, 227.

101 'The Artistic Value of the Kinematograph', *The Kinematograph and Lantern Weekly* (28 June 1907), p. 111.

102 Warwick Trading Company catalogue (1901), p. 157.

103 *Ibid.*

104 *Ibid.*

105 Warwick Trading Company catalogue (1897–98), p. 23.

106 R.W. Paul catalogue (1902), no page no.

107 *Ibid.*

108 See, for example, François Delsarte, 'Delsarte's Own Words' (taken from notes), in *Delsarte System of Oratory: Including the Complete Work of M. L'Abbe Delamosne and Mme. Angelique Arnaud (Pupils of Delsarte) with the Lieterary Remains of François Delsarte* (New York: Edgar S. Werner, 1887); and Gustave Garcia, *The Actor's Art: A Practical Treatise on Stage Declamation, Public Speaking and Deportment* (London: T. Pettitt, 1882), pp. 82–112.

109 Theodor Lipps, 'Empathy and Aesthetic Pleasure', in *Aesthetic Theories: Studies in the Philosophy of Art* (1906), eds Karl Aschenbrenner and Arnold Isenberg (Englewood Cliffs: Prentice-Hall, 1965), pp.401–14; Georg Simmel, 'The Aesthetic Significance of the Face' (1901), in *Georg Simmel 1858–1918: A Collection of Essays with Translations and a Bibliography*, ed. Kurt H. Wolff (Columbus: Ohio State University, 1959), pp. 276–81. Simmel intriguingly concludes that 'if perfectly solved [the problem of the face] would lead to the solution of those other problems which involve soul and appearance'. (p. 281)

110 Lipps, 'Empathy and Aesthetic Pleasure', p. 409.

111 See Frank Kessler and Sabine Lenk, '". . . levant les bras au ciel, se tapant sur les cuisses". Réflexions sur L'Universalité du Geste dans le Cinéma des Premiers Temps', in *Cinéma sans Frontiéres 1896–1918: Images Across Borders*, eds Roland Cosandey and François Albera (Quebec: Nuit Blanche, 1995), pp. 133–45.

112 Vachel Lindsay, *The Art of the Moving Picture* (New York: Macmillan, 1916), p. 20.

113 Béla Balázs, *Theory of the Film: Character and Growth of a New Art* (New York: Arno Press, 1972), p. 44.

114 *Ibid.*, p. 65.

115 For work on dismemberment in early magic trick films, see Jacques Malthête, 'Quand Méliès n'en faisait qu'a sa tête', in *Pour une Histoire des Trucages*, ed. Thierry Lefebvre (Charente: Pleinchant à Bassac, 1999), pp. 21–32.

116 Georges Bataille, 'Human Face', in *October*, 36 (1986), p. 18.

117 Joe Kember, 'Face to Face: The Facial Expressions Genre in Early British Films', in *The Showman, The Spectacle, and the Two-Minute Silence: Performing British Cinema before 1930*, eds Alan Burton and Laraine Porter (Trowbridge: Flicks Books, 2001), pp. 28–39. I have also briefly summarised some key aspects of the facials genre, including its reappearance in the 1910s, in Simon Popple and Joe Kember, *Early Cinema: From Factory Gate to Dream Factory* (London: Wallflower Press, 2004), pp. 91–93. On the chronophotographers, see Deac Rossell, 'Altered States: Modernism, Chronophotography and the Historical Record', (paper delivered at the Literature Film, and Modernity Conference, University of London, 13 January 2000).

118 See Ray Phillips, *Edison's Kinetoscope: A History to 1896* (Trowbridge: Flicks Books, 1997), p. 165.

119 For a detailed examination of this film, see Garrett Monaghan, 'Performing the Passions: Comic Themes in the Films of George Albert Smith', in *Pimples, Pranks, and Pratfalls: British Film Comedy Before 1930*, eds Alan Burton and Laraine Porter (Trowbridge: Flicks Books, 2000), p. 26.

120 See for example the Warwick catalogue (1902), pp. 9–10.

121 R.W. Paul catalogue supplement (May 1907).

122 Description of Smith's *Two Old Sports' Political Discussion* (1901), which featured Tom Green and Mr Hunter. Warwick catalogue (1901), p. 167.

123 Warwick catalogue (1901), p. 141.

124 *Ibid.*, p. 167.

125 R.W. Paul catalogue (1902).

126 Cricks and Martin catalogue (1908), p. 32.

127 See Tom Gunning, 'In Your Face: Physiognomy, Photography, and the Gnostic Mission of Early Film', *MODERNISM/modernity* 4 (1997), pp. 25–27.

128 For a primarily Bakhtinian perspective on Smith's facials, see Monaghan, 'Performing the Passions'. See also Gunning, 'In your face'. For relevant passages in Bakhtin, see M.M. Bakhtin, *Rabelais and His World*, trans. Hélène Iswolsky (Cambridge, MA: MIT Press, 1968), p. 316.

129 The BFI catalogue of *British Silent Comedy Films* lists this film as *Masques and Grimaces* (*c.*1901). However, the 1903 Pathé catalogue lists *Masks and Faces* with an illustration that identifies this as the same film.

130 Hepworth and Co. catalogue (1903), p. 43.

131 See Barnes, *The Beginning of the Cinema in England*, V, pp. 32–35.

132 Green had performed in Brighton, where Smith probably first encountered him at the Aquarium. Nathan, an agent for British Biograph, had a long history of performance in London music halls. See Barnes, *The Beginning of the Cinema in England*, V, pp. 45–47; and Brown and Anthony, *A Victorian Film Enterprise*, p. 225.

133 Among the numerous guide books on how to shave, and the equally numerous treaties on why not to, see John Teetgen, *My Razor and Shaving Tackle . . . How to Shave etc.* (London: [n. pub], 1844).

134 Ralph Parr, *Shaving Done Here on the Shortest Notice versus Yeds wi' Summut in Um: A Comic Dialogue* (London: John Heywood, 1896). See also *Easy Shaving: A Farce in One Act* (New York: Robert de Witt, [n.d.]).

135 *Northern Queensland Herald* (4 September 1895) (repr. in Phillips, *Edison's Kinetoscope*, p. 120).

136 Gunning, 'In your Face'.

137 Hepwix catalogue (1903), p. 43.

138 Mladen Dolar, '"I Shall be with you on your Wedding Night": Lacan and the Uncanny', *October* 58 (1991), p. 7.

139 As Bergson explained, 'I am so because I have everything to gain by being so'. Henri Bergson, *Time and Free Will: An Essay on the Immediate Data of Consciousness*, (London: Swan Sonnenschein and Co., 1910), p. 168.

140 On the representation of the dangers of rail travel, see Nicholas Daly, 'Blood on the Tracks: Sensation Drama, the Railway, and the Dark Face of Modernity', *Victorian Studies* 42:1 (Autumn 1998/1999) pp. 47–76.

141 William Uricchio, 'Ways of Seeing: The New Vision of Early Non-fiction Film', in

Uncharted Territory, eds Hertogs and de Klerk, p. 121.

142 During the war itself, film shows were usually highly charged with a sense of national community, as in the reported case of a 1901 show at the Royal Aquarium that featured 'the serio-comic films, Kruger's Dream of Empire, and Kruger *v.* John Bull' in a boxing match. 'How the latter scene would have been received had not Paul been knocked out is not hard to guess', reported the reviewer; 'The Royal Aquarium', in *The Showman* (18 Jan 1901), p. 48.

143 See Gunning on the American film, *Native Woman Washing a Negro Baby in Nassau, B.I.* (Edison, 1903). Gunning, '"The Whole World Within Reach": Travel Images Without Borders', in *Cinéma sans Frontières,* ed. Cosandey and Albera, pp. 32–34.

144 Virgilio Tosi, *Cinema before Cinema: The Origins of Scientific Cinematography* (London: BUFVC, 2005), p. 168.

145 'Death of Doodica', and 'Radica's Future', *The Showman* (21 February 1902), p. 6. For an account of the reactions of the European popular press to this procedure and to the film, see Thierry Lefebvre, 'Die trennung der Siamesischen Zwillinge Doodica und Radica durch Dr Doyen', *KINtop* 6 (1997), pp. 97–101. For a full account of the controversy concerning the film and of Doyen's work, see Thierry Lefebvre, *La Chair et le Celluloid: Le Cinéma Chirurgical du Docteur Doyen* (Brionne: Jean Doyen, 2004).

146 'Notes of the Week', *The Showman* (14 February 1902), p. 1.

147 'Showmen's Notes', *Music Hall and Theatre Review* (16 May 1902), p. 317.

148 Tosi, *Cinema before Cinema*, p. 168.

149 Martin F. Norden, *The Cinema of Isolation: A History of Physical Disability in the Movies* (New Brunswick, NJ: Rutgers University Press, 1994), p. 16.

5 Conjurors, Adventurers and other Authors

1 Hepworth and Co. catalogue (1903), p. 18.

2 *The Era* (10 November 1900), p. 30 (repr. in John Barnes, *Beginnings of the Cinema in England, 1894–1901,* 5 vols (Exeter: University of Exeter Press, 1996) V, p. 241).

3 Edward Branigan, *Narrative Comprehension and Film* (London: Routledge, 1992), p. 87.

4 Albert Laffay, *Logique du Cinéma* (Paris: Masson, 1964), p. 81.

5 Christian Metz, *Film Language: A Semiotics of Cinema* (Oxford: Oxford University Press, 1974), p. 21.

6 For an account of the significance of this work within early film studies, see Joe Kember, 'The Cinema of Affections: The Transformation of Authorship in British Cinema before 1907', in *The Velvet Light Trap* 57 (2006), pp. 3–17. Gaudreault's work concerning early cinema has strongly influenced my own understanding of the narrative theory appropriate to early film studies. André Gaudreault, *Du Littéraire au Filmique: Système du Récit* (Paris: Méridiens Klincksieck, 1988), p. 10. See also André Gaudreault, 'Film, Narrative, Narration: The Cinema of the Lumière Brothers', in *Early Cinema: Space Frame Narrative*, ed. Thomas Elsaesser (London: British Film Institute, 1990), pp. 68–75; André Gaudreault, 'Showing and Telling: Image and Word in Early Cinema', in *Early Cinema*, ed. Elsaesser, pp. 274–81; and André Gaudreault and François Jost, *Le Récit Cinématographique* (Condé sur Noireau: Editions Nathan, 1994), pp. 39–77.

7 Therefore, in the film, as Jan Simons asserts, 'enunciation is seen as the place where the subject of language emerges as the mediating locus between *langue* and *parole*, the actual "mise-en-discours" of this formal apparatus'; Jan Simons, 'Enunciation: From Code to

Interpretation', in *The Film Spectator: From Sign to Mind*, ed. Warren Buckland (Amsterdam: University of Amsterdam, 1995), p. 193.

8   David Bordwell, *Narration in the Fiction Film* (Madison: University of Wisconsin Press, 1985), p. 62. See also, Noël Carroll, *Mystifying Movies: Fads and Fallacies in Contemporary Film Theory* (New York: Columbia University Press, 1988), pp. 150–60.

9   Francesco Casetti, 'Looking for the Spectator', *Iris* 1:2 (1983), p. 23.

10 *Ibid.*

11 Francesco, Casetti, *Inside the Gaze: The Fiction Film and its Spectator*, trans. Neil Andrew with Charles O'Brien (Bloomington: Indiana University Press, 1998), p. 40.

12 *Ibid.*, p. 42.

13 André Gaudreault, 'Theatricality, Narrativity and "Trickality": Re-evaluating the Cinema of George Méliès', in *Journal of Popular Film and Television* 15 (1987), pp. 110–19.

14 See Michael Chanan, 'The Treats of Trickery', in *Cinema: The Beginnings and the Future*, ed. Christopher Williams (London: University of Westminster Press, 1996), pp. 117–22.

15 Charles Dawbarn, 'The Popular Theatre of the Day. Behind the Scenes at a Cinematograph Rehearsal', *Pall Mall Magazine* 48 (1911), p. 271.

16 Chanan, 'The Treats of Trickery', p. 121

17 'A Clever Optical Illusion', *Kinematograph and Lantern Weekly* (31 May 1907), p. 44. For an account of the hyper-reality of Hale's tours, see Lauren Rabinowitz, 'From Hale's Tours to Star Tours: Virtual Voyages, Travel Ride Films, and the Delirium of the Hyper-Real', in *Virtual Voyages: Cinema and Travel*, ed. Jeffrey Ruoff (Durham, NC: Duke University Press, 2006), pp. 42–60.

18 'A Clever Optical Illusion', p. 44.

19 On early twentieth-century magic theatre, see Edwin A. Dawes, 'The Magic Scene in Britain in 1905', in *Early Popular Visual Culture* 5:2 (2007), pp. 109–26. For work concerning the psychological complexity associated with reception of the conjuring trick, see Peter Lamont and Matthew Wiseman, *Magic in Theory: An Introduction to the Theoretical and Psychological Elements of Conjuring* (Hatfield: Hertfordshire University Press, 1999); and Peter Lamont, 'Magician as Conjuror', in *Early Popular Visual Culture* 4:1 (2006), pp. 21–33.

20 The story is among the most frequently told concerning Victorian magic theatre. See, for example, George A Jenness, *Maskelyne and Cooke: Egyptian Hall, London, 1873–1904* (London: Enfield Press, 1967).

21 Quoted in Jenness, *Maskelyne and Cooke*, p. 57.

22 'Personal Pars', *The Showman* (1 November 1901), p. 127.

23 'Maskelyne and Cooke's Mysteries', *The Showman* (25 October 1901), p. 109. For an account of this trick, see Lynda Nead, *The Haunted Gallery: Painting, Photography, Film c.1900* (New Haven, CT: Yale University Press, 2007), pp. 86–88.

24 For pertinent work on the relationship between magic theatre and early film shows, see especially Eric Barnouw, *The Magician and the Cinema* (Oxford: Oxford University Press, 1981); Dan North, 'Illusory Bodies', in *Early Popular Visual Culture* 5:2 (2007), pp. 175–88; and Matthew Solomon, 'Up-to-Date Magic: Theatrical Conjuring and the Trick Film', in *Theatre Journal* 58 (2006), pp. 595–615.

25 Henry V. Hopwood, 'Kinetographic Pictures: Their Errors and Falsities', *The Optician and Photographic Trades Review* (29 September 1899), p. 69.

26 'Fake Cinematograph Pictures', *The Optical Magic Lantern Journal and Photographic Enlarger* (November 1900), p. 138.

27 *Ibid.*

28 'Artistic Creation', R.W.Paul catalogue (1902).

29 Hepwix catalogue (1903), 27.

30 'Fake or Trick Cinematograph Pictures', *The Optical Magic Lantern Journal and Photographic Enlarger* (December 1900), pp. 153–54.

31 *Ibid.*, p. 153.

32 See Luke McKernan, '*Something More than a Mere Picture Show': Charles Urban and the Early Non-Fiction Film in Great Britain and America, 1897–1925* (unpublished doctoral thesis, Birkbeck College, University of London, 2003), pp. 82–83.

33 However, in spite of Urban's best efforts, the term 'fake' would continue to be applied to examples of trick filmmaking for years to come. See, for example, the description of increasingly unfashionable 'silly fakes' in 'From the Editor's Pen', *The Optical Lantern and Kinematograph Journal* (March 1907), p. 115.

34 Thomas L. Carson, 'The Definition of Lying', *Nous* 40:2 (2006), p. 293.

35 'Photographic Lies: Proving the Uselessness of the Camera as a Witness', *The Harmsworth Magazine* 1:3 (September 1898), p. 264.

36 M.W., 'Cinematograph Notes', *The Showman* (December 1900), p. 62.

37 See Michael Chanan, *The Dream that Kicks: The Prehistory and Early Years of Cinema in Britain*, 2nd edn (London: Routledge, 1996), pp. 240–41; Martin Sopocy, 'James A.Williamson: American View', in *Cinema 1900/1906: An Analytical Study*, compiled by Roger Holman (Brussels: FIAF, 1982), pp. 297–319.

38 'Novel Films', *The Showman* (20 December 1901), p. 239.

39 [Review of *Daily Mail* article], *The Optical Lantern and Cinematograph Journal* (October 1905), p. 192.

40 Frank Gray, 'James Williamson's 'Composed Picture': *Attack on a China Mission—Bluejackets to the Rescue* (1900)', in *Celebrating 1895: The Centenary of Cinema*, ed. John Fullerton (London: John Libbey and Company, 1998), pp. 210–11.

41 Richard Brown, 'War on the Home Front: The Anglo-Boer War and the Growth of Rental in Britain. An Economic Perspective', *Film History* 16:1 (2004), pp. 28–36.

42 Carson, 'The Definition of Lying', p. 295.

43 'From the Editor's Pen', *The Optical Lantern and Kinematograph Journal* (August 1906), p. 199.

44 *Ibid.*

45 *Ibid.*

46 *Ibid.*

47 E.V. Lucas, 'The Cinematoscope—A Power', repr. in *The Optical Lantern and Cinematograph Journal* (June 1906), p. 94.

48 *Ibid.*

49 For a useful description of such mechanisms at work in travelogue films of the 1910s, see Jennifer Peterson, 'Truth is Stranger than Fiction: Travelogues from the 1910s at the Nederlands Filmmuseum', in *Uncharted Territory: Essays on Early Non-fiction Film*, eds Daan Hertogs and Nico de Klerk (Amsterdam: Nederlands Filmmuseum, 1997), pp. 75–90.

50 Warwick catalogue (1901), p. 167.

51 The *American Film Institute Catalogue 1893–1910*, compiled by Elias Savada (London: Scarecrow Press, 1995), p. 292.

52 Tom Gunning, 'Before Documentary: Early Non-fiction Films and the "View" Aesthetic', in *Uncharted Territory*, eds Hertogs and de Klerk, p. 14. See also Tom

Gunning, '"The Whole World within Reach": Travel Images without Borders', Roland Cosandey and François Albera, *Cinéma sans Frontières 1896–1918: Images Across Borders* (Quebec: Nuit Blanche, 1995), pp. 21–36; William Uricchio, 'Ways of Seeing: The New Vision of Early Non-fiction Film', in *Uncharted Territory*, eds Hertogs and de Klerk, pp. 119–31.

53 [Report on forthcoming production], *The Showman* (17 January 1902), p. 293.

54 McKernan, *'Something More than a Mere Picture Show'*, pp. 76–77

55 'Introduction', *The Wide World Magazine* 1:1 (April 1898), p. 3

56 Burton Holmes, *The Burton Holmes Lectures* 10 vols (Battle Creek, Michigan: The Little Preston Company, 1901), I, p. 299.

57 *Ibid.*, pp. 323–24

58 Gerry Turvey, 'Frederick Burlingham: Exploration, Mountaineering and the Origins of Swiss Documentary Cinema', *Historical Journal of Film, Radio, and Television* 27:2 (2007), pp. 167–91. Burlingham's contribution to Alpine cinematography is described in detail in his book *How to Become an Alpinist* (London: T.Werner Laurie, 1914), which is punctuated with accounts of the dangers of cinematographing on the mountains.

59 Charles Urban Trading Company catalogue (1906), p. 99. Ten minutes of this forty-minute production survive at the National Film and Sound Archive in Australia.

60 Georg Simmel, 'The Adventure', in *Georg Simmel, 1858–1918: A Collection of Essays with Translations and a Bibliography*, ed. Kurt H. Wolff (Columbus: Ohio State University Press, 1959), pp. 257–58.

61 [Report on James Kenyon in Sunderland], *The Showman* (29 November 1901), p. 178.

62 [Reported correspondence from Charles Urban], *The Showman* (13 December 1901), p. 210.

63 For an account of Urban's dedication to educational filmmaking, see McKernan, *'More than a Living Picture Show'*, pp. 113–19.

64 *Ibid.*, pp. 40–113.

65 Charles Urban Trading Company catalogue (1905), p. 193.

66 Letter from Arthur Malden to Charles Urban, 11 October 1906. Charles Urban papers, National Media Museum, Bradford.

67 Charles Rider Noble had also been named by Walter Gibbons as his chief cinematographer in South Africa during 1900. 'Special Films from Pretoria', *The Showman* (December 1900), p. 4.

68 *The Great Russo-Japan War*, Charles Urban Trading Company catalogue supplement (1905), p. 1.

69 Charles Urban Trading Company catalogue (1907), p. 8. Emphasis in original.

70 In the case of *Switzerland: An Ascent of the Jungfrau*, Ormiston-Smith was accompanied by Urban and by George Albert Smith, who was then working at Warwick, making the conquest of the mountain into a visibly institutional concern.

71 Charles Urban Trading Company catalogue (1905), pp. 2–3. Emphasis in original.

72 Warwick Trading Company catalogue supplement (October 1902), p. 15.

73 'Bioscoping in the High Alps', in Warwick Trading Company catalogue supplement no. 3 (October 1902), p. 13. The emphasis on the Alpine accident also drew heavily from earlier narrative traditions. For a particularly salacious account, see 'Dangers of Alpine Mountaineering', *Temple Bar* 52 (February 1878), pp. 213–24.

74 Warwick Trading Company catalogue supplement (October 1902), p. 10.

75 Urban-Eclipse catalogue (1907–08), p. 30.

76   Letter from Frank Ormiston-Smith to Charles Urban. Charles Urban Papers, National Media Museum, Bradford.

77   The National Film and Television Archive, London, has numerous examples available for viewing. Many of these seem grotesque to modern viewers, which perhaps explains why the genre has been so consistently overlooked. For example, in the uncredited and undated *Hunting Hippopotami, Upper Nile*, native Africans corral the hippos into the river, where they are shot, then skinned, before the final tableau of a severed head is displayed.

78   Thomas Elsaesser, 'Narrative Cinema and Audience-Oriented Aesthetics', in *Popular Television and Film*, eds Tony Bennett, Susan Boyd-Bowman, Colin Mercer and Janet Woollacott (London: British Film Institute, 1981), p. 280.

79   Edward Branigan, 'Diegesis and Authorship in Film', *Iris* 3:7 (1986), p. 53.

80   See François Jost, 'The Polyphonic Film and the Spectator', in *The Film Spectator: From Sign to Mind*, ed. Warren Buckland (Amsterdam: Amsterdam University Press, 1995), p. 190.

81   See especially Gaudreault, *Du Littéraire au Filmique*, p. 38.

82   Harry Furniss, *Our Lady Cinema: How and Why I went into the Photo-Play World and What I Found There* (Bristol: J.W. Arrowsmith, 1914; repr. London: Garland Publishing, 1978), p. xi.

83   Marta Braun, *Picturing Time: The Work of Etienne-Jules Marie (1830–1904)* (London: University of Chicago, 1992), p. 248.

84   'Life Model Studies. 1.—A Peep Behind the Scenes', *The Photogram* (February 1899). Reprinted in the *New Magic Lantern Journal* 5:3 (April 1988), p. 2.

85   Cecil Hepworth, 'Those Were the Days', in *Film Makers on Film Making: Statements on their Art by Thirty Directors*, ed. Harry M. Geduld (Bloomington: Indiana University Press, 1967), p. 29.

86   Edward Azlant, 'Screenwriting for the Early Silent Film: Forgotten Pioneers, 1897–1911', *Film History* 9 (1997), p. 230.

87   Gaudreault, *Du Littéraire au Filmique*, p. 135. See also André Gaudreault, 'The Infringement of Copyright Laws and its Effects', in *Early Cinema*, ed. Elsaesser, pp. 114–22.

88   Richard Brown, 'The British Film Copyright Archive', in *In the Kingdom of the Shadows: A Companion to Early Cinema*, eds Colin Harding and Simon Popple (London: Cygnus Arts, 1996), p. 241.

89   *Ibid.*, p. 242. For further details on two important cases, see 'The British Mutoscope and Bioscope Company and Others v. Burns and Oates (limited)', *The Times* (25 March 1899), p. 4; and 'The Mutoscope and Biograph Syndicate (limited) and the British Mutoscope and Biograph Company (limited) v. The British Stereopticon Company (limited)', *The Times* (12 January 1900), p. 13.

90   [On 'film filching'], *The Optical Magic Lantern and Cinematograph Journal* (December 1905), p. 275.

91   See Jennifer Forrest and Leonard R. Koos, *Dead Ringers: The Remake in Theory and Practice* (New York: SUNY Press, 2001), pp. 89–126; and Jane M. Gaines, 'Early Cinema's Heyday of Copying: The Too Many Copies of L'Arroseur Arosé', *Cultural Studies* 20: 2–3 (2006), pp. 227–44.

92   [On 'film filching'], p. 276.

93   Sam Ricketson, *The Berne Convention for the Protection of Literary and Artistic Works: 1886–1986* (London: Centre for Commercial Law Studies, 1986), p. 550.

94   Jennifer Forrest, 'The "Personal" Touch: The Original, the Remake, and the Dupe in

Early Cinema', in *Dead Ringers: The Remake in Theory and Practice*, eds Jennifer Forrest and Leonard R. Koos (New York: SUNY Press, 2001), pp. 89–126.

95 For a full account of this case, see '*Ben Hur*: Francis Frederic Theophilus Weeks and Patent No 8615 of 1894', *New Magic Lantern Journal* 5:1 (1987), pp. 2–5.

96 On Wallace's cautious attitude to the theatrical production, see Lew Wallace, *Lew Wallace: An Autobiography*, 2 vols (New York: Harper Bros, 1906), II, pp. 1000–01.

97 'Harper Bros & Gen Lew Wallace v. Riley Brothers', *The Optical Magic Lantern Journal and Photographic Enlarger* (August 1896), p. 135.

98 *Ibid.*, p. 136.

99 For a full description of the case, which was followed closely each month by the *Journal*, and its conclusion, see 'Wallace and others v. Riley Brothers, New York', *The Optical Magic Lantern Journal and Photographic Enlarger* (October 1896), pp. 166–67.

100 For an account of this film, see David Mayer, *Playing Out the Empire: Ben-Hur and Other Toga Plays and Films 1883–1908. A Critical Anthology* (Oxford: Oxford University Press, 1994), pp. 298–99.

101 The case 'Kalem Co. v. Harper Bros, 1911', may be found in (1911) 222 US 55, 56 L Ed 92.

102 'The Dramatic Copyright Act, 1833', *Chitty's Statutes* (1894), pp. 11–13. The judgement on 'Karno v. Pathé Frères, London (Sept 26, 1908)' may be found in (1908) 99 L.T., 115–19. For reviews of this case, see Gavin McFarlane, *Copyright Through the Cases* (London: Waterlow Law Books, 1986), pp. 44–46; and Brown, 'The British Film Copyright Archive', pp. 242–43.

103 'Karno v. Pathé Frères, London (Sept 26, 1908)', p. 119. See also 'Karno v. Pathé Frères. Appeal from the King's Bench Division (April 17, 1909)', in (1909) 100 L.T. pp. 260–62.

104 'Karno v. Pathé Frères, London (Sept 26, 1908)', p. 117.

105 Cited in Ricketson, *The Berne Convention*, p. 550. See also J.A.L. Sterling, *Intellectual Property Rights in Sound and Recordings, Film and Video* (London: Sweet and Maxwell, 1992), pp. 212–19.

106 Ricketson, *The Berne Convention*, p. 551.

107 'Copyright Act, 1911', 1 & 2 GEO.5., pp. 182–205.

108 David S. Hulfish, *Motion-Picture Work: A General Treatise on Picture Taking, Picture Making, Photo-Plays, and Theater Management and Operation* (Chicago, IL: American Technical Society, 1915), p. 112.

109 See, for example, 'Picture Theatre Finance', *The Rinking World and Picture Theatre News* (11 December 1909), p. 18; 'Picture Pars', *The Rinking World and Picture Theatre News* (8 January 1910), p. 11; 'The Picture Theatre Boom', *The Rinking World and Picture Theatre News* (19 February 1910), pp. 14–15.

110 'Advance of the Cinematograph: Its Place in the Entertainment World', *The World's Fair* (9 January 1909), p. 7.

111 See, for example, Eustace Hale Ball, *The Art of the Photoplay* (New York: Veritas Press, 1913); and Hulfish, *Motion-Picture Work*, pp. 76–94. For a thorough review of such guide-books, see Kristin Thompson, 'Narrative Structure in Early Classical Cinema', in *Celebrating 1895*, ed. Fullerton, pp. 225–37.

112 'Plots for Picture Plays: Concocting Thrilling Dramas and Farcical Fakes for the Cinematograph', *The World's Fair* (24 June 1911), p. 11.

113 On Haggar, see Lily May Richards, *Biography of William Haggar: Actor, Showman and Pioneer of the Film Industry* (University of Sheffield Library, National Fairground Archive MS) , p. 34. On Green, see Adrienne Scullion, 'Geggies, Empires, Cinemas: The Scottish Experience of Early Film', *Picture House* 21 (1996), pp. 13–19. On the general

movement of showmen into static cinemas, see Vanessa Toulmin, 'Travelling Shows and the First Static Cinemas', *Picture House* 21 (1996), pp. 5–12.

114 Emphases in original. Branigan, *Narrative Comprehension and Film*, p. 110.

115 *Ibid.*

Bibliography

Films Cited

Abbreviations for film production companies:

Bamforth	Bamforth and Company
BMBC	British Mutoscope and Biograph Company
Edison	Edison Manufacturing Company
GAS	George Albert Smith Company
Hepworth	Hepworth and Company, or Hepwix (until 1904)
	Hepworth Manufacturing Company (1904 onwards)
M&K	Mitchell and Kenyon
Paul	Paul's Animatograph Works
Urban	Charles Urban Trading Company
WTC	Warwick Trading Company
Williamson	Williamson Kinematograph Company

20,000 Employees Entering Lord Armstrong's Elswick Works (M&K, 1902)
The Accident on the Great Schreckhorn (WTC, 1902)
An Alpine Catastrophe (Urban, 1905)
Amann, the Great Impersonator (BMBC, 1898)
Annabelle Serpentine Dance (Edison, 1895)
L'Arroseur Arrosé (Lumière, 1895)
Artistic Creation (Paul, 1902)
As Seen Through a Telescope (GAS, 1900)
Ascent and Descent of the Aigulles des Grandes Charmoz, 11,293 feet (WTC, 1902)
Ascent and Descent of the Dolomite Towers (Urban, 1907)
The Ascent of Mont Blanc, 15,781 Feet High [Series] (WTC, 1902)
1. *Preparations for the Ascent and Departure Party*
2. *Crossing a Mountain Torrent*
3. *Party Leaving the Pierre Pointue Inn, 6,800 feet*
4. *Crossing the Glacier des Bossons*
5. *The 'Junction' of Glaciers de Taconnaz and de Bossons*
6. *Traversing the Glacier de Taconnaz*
7. *Climbing Ice Pinnacles on the same Glacier*
8. *Reaching the Grands Mulets, 10,120 feet*

9. *Arrival of the Party at the Grands Mulets*
10. *Life at the Grands Mulets, Partaking of Refreshments*
11. *Sunset Panorama from the Grands Mulets, 7 p.m.*
12. *Leaving by Moonlight for the Summit, 1.30 a.m.*
13. *Ascending the Snow Slopes towards the Petit Plateau, 3 a.m.*
14. *A Cloud Sea from the Petit Plateau, 4 a.m.*
15. *Crossing a Snow Bridge near the Grand Plateau, 15,000 feet*
16. *Finding a way over a Great Crevasse near La Tournette, 15,300 feet*
17. *Ascending the Slope below the Summit over a Snow Bridge during a Snowstorm, 15,300 feet*
18. *The Summit of Mont Blanc, 15,781 feet*

An Ascent of the Wetterhorn (Urban, 1905)
Attack on a China Mission (Williamson, 1900)
Au Music Hall (Pathé Frères, 1907)
Barber Shop (Edison, 1895)
The Bathers (Hepworth, 1900)
The Beggar's Deceit (Hepworth, 1900)
Ben Hur (Kalem, 1907)
The Big Swallow (Williamson, 1901)
The Biter Bit (Bamforth, 1900)
Boys Cricket Match and Fight (Bamforth,1900)
Boys Scrambling for Pennies under the West Pier, Brighton (Esmé Collings, 1896)
The Bride's First Night (Haydon and Urry, 1898)
Buller's Last Appearance at Aldershot (Gaumont, 1901)
Buy Your Own Cherries (Paul, 1904)
Captain Deasy's Daring Drive: Ascent (Deutsche Mutoskop und Biograph, 1903)
Captain Deasy's Daring Drive: Descent (Deutsche Mutoskop und Biograph, 1903)
The Cheese Mites; or, Lilliputians in a London Restaurant (Paul, 1901)
Children in the Nursery (Paul, 1896)
Children's Sports No. 3 (M&K, 1902)
Circulation of Blood in the Frog's Foot (Urban, 1903)
Come Along Do! (Paul, 1898)
Comic Faces (GAS, 1897)
Comic Grimacer (Hepworth, 1901)
Coolie Boys Diving for Coins (WTC, 1900)
Conquering the Dolomites (Urban, 1907)
The Countryman and the Cinematograph (Paul, 1901)
Dr W.G. Grace, Batting (WTC, 1901)
Dr W.G. Grace, Bowling (WTC, 1901)
Devant's Exhibition of Paper Folding (Paul, 1896)
Devant's Hand Shadows (Paul, 1896)
Descent into the Crater of Vesuvius (British and Colonial Kinematograph Company, 1913)
Difficulties of an Animated Photographer (Paul, 1898)

The Dull Razor (GAS, 1900)

The Egg-Laying Man (Paul, 1896)

Electric Tram Rides from Forster Square, Bradford (M&K, 1902)

Explosion of a Motor Car (Hepworth, 1900)

Facial Expressions: The Fateful Letter (BMBC, 1898)

Feeding the Pigeons in St. Mark's Square (BMBC, 1898)

The Fraudulent Beggars (Williamson, 1898)

Funeral of Queen Victoria (Hepworth, 1901)

Gang Making Railway—South Africa (amateur, 1898)

The German Emperor Reviewing his Troops at Fall Manœuvres (WTC, 1902)

Hair Soup; or The Disappointed Diner (Paul, 1901)

Hanging out the Clothes (GAS, 1897)

[Herbert Campbell as 'Little Bobbie'] (BMBC, 1899)

The House that Jack Built (GAS, 1900)

How a Burglar Feels (Paul, 1907)

How it Feels to be Run Over (Hepworth, 1900)

The Human Flies (Paul, 1899)

The Hungry Countryman (GAS, 1899)

A Joke on the Gardener (GAS, 1898)

King John (BMBC, 1899)

The Kiss in the Tunnel (GAS, 1899)

The Kiss in the Tunnel (Riley Bros, 1899)

Layman, the Man of 1000 Faces (Edison, 1894)

Let Me Dream Again (GAS, 1900)

The Life of Charles Peace (William Haggar, 1905)

The Little Breadwinner (Paul, 1898)

Little Tich and his Big Boots (Gaumont, 1902)

A Lively Dispute (Paul, 1898)

Living London (Charles Urban Trading Company, 1904)

London: Victoria Station (Gaumont, 1901)

Lord Roberts Leaving for South Africa (WTC, 1899)

[Lover Kisses Husband] (Bamforth, [1900])

Macaroni Competition (Hepworth, 1899)

Mary Jane's Mishap; or, Don't Fool with the Paraffin (GAS, 1903)

Masks and Faces (c.1901)

The Matterhorn (14,780 Feet) (Urban, 1903)

Milling the Militants; A Comical Absurdity (Clarendon Film Company, 1913)

Miss Ellen Terry [Series] (GAS, 1897)

    At her country cottage window

    Gathering flowers in her garden

    Afternoon tea with a friend in the garden

A Mont Blanc Tragedy (Urban-Eclipse, 1907)

The Mountaineer's Flirtation (Urban-Eclipse, 1907)

Mr Dan Leno, Assisted by Mr Herbert Campbell, Editing the 'Sun' (BMBC, 1902)

Mr Maskelyne Spinning Plates and Basins (Paul, 1896)

Mud Larks (Hepworth, c.1899)

The New Baby (Walturdaw, 1910)

Oh! That Cat (Gaumont, 1907)

The Old Maid's Valentine (GAS, 1900)

One Mile Champion Belt Race (WTC, c.1900)

One Sort of Sunday Crowd at Hyde Park (WTC, c.1901)

Our New Errand Boy (Williamson, 1905)

Pity the Poor Blind (Paul, 1907)

Poison or Whiskey? (Hepworth, 1904)

The Puzzled Bather and his Animated Clothes (Williamson, 1901)

A Quick Shave and Brush Up (GAS, 1900)

Rescued by Rover (Hepworth, 1905)

Russian Officers Attached to the President (WTC, c.1897)

Santa Claus (GAS, 1898)

Scenes at Balmoral (unknown, 1896)

Séparation des Souers Xiphopages Doodica et Radica (Eugène-Louis Doyen, 1902)

Sheffield Street Accident (M&K, 1902)

A Skirmish with the Boers near Kimberly (WTC, 1900)

Sliding Down an Alpine Glacier (WTC, 1902)

Snapshotting an Audience (GAS, 1900)

The Strikers at Grimsby (Hepworth, 1901)

A Study in Facial Expression (Paul, 1898)

Sunday in a Provincial Town (WTC, c.1901)

Sunderland v Leicester Fosse (M&K, 1907)

Sweet Suffragettes (Cricks and Sharp, 1906)

Switzerland: An Ascent of the Jungfrau [Series] (WTC, 1901)

Their Majesties, Edward VII and Queen Alexandra Starting for a Motor Ride (Biograph Company—France, 1901)

Trams in Sheffield (M&K, 1900)

Tram Rides Through Nottingham (M&K, 1902)

The Twins' Tea Party (Paul, 1896)

Two Old Sports (GAS, 1900)

Two Old Sports' Political Discussion (GAS 1901),

The Unclean World (Hepworth, 1903)

A Victorian Lady in her Boudoir (Esmé Collings, 1896)

Visit of the King and Queen to Dartmouth to lay the Foundation Stone of the New Naval College (Hepworth, 1902)

Weary Willie (Bamforth, 1898)

Wedding Ceremony in a Church (GAS, 1900)

When Daddy Comes Home (Hepworth, 1902)

When Mamma's Out (Precision Film Company, 1909)

Whitsun Fair at Preston: 1906 (M&K, 1906)

Will Evans, the Musical Eccentric (WTC, 1899)

Winky and the 'Dwarf' (Bamforth, 1914)
Women's Rights (Bamforth, 1899)
Workforce of Ormerod's Mill, Great Moor Street, Bolton (M&K, 1900)
The Would-Be Conjurer (Bamforth, 1898)
The Yokel's Dinner (WTC, 1900)

Primary Sources

Warwick Trading Company and Charles Urban Trading Company catalogues consulted from the Charles Urban papers collection, National Media Museum, Bradford and from the private collections.

All other references to early film catalogues are taken from *Early Rare British Film-makers Catalogues, 1896–1913*, 8 reels microfilm (World Microfilms, 1993).

'10 Minutes Chat with Celebrities: No. 1.—Mr. Montagu Alexander Pyke', *The Rinking World and Picture Theatre News* (4 December 1909), 19–20

A.B., 'Lecturers Should Learn their Lectures', *Optical Magic Lantern Journal* (February 1902), 125

A.S., 'Explain the Pictures!', *The Bioscope* (10 December 1908), 11

Adcock, Arthur St John, 'Sideshow London', George R. Sims, ed., *Living London*, 3 vols (London: Cassell and Company, 1903), II, 281–85

'Advance of the Cinematograph: Its Place in the Entertainment World', *The World's Fair* (9 January 1909), 7

[Advertisement for Wicks], *The Showman* (September 1900), vi

Allbutt, T. Clifford, 'Nervous Diseases and Modern Life', *The Contemporary Review* 67 (January–June 1895), 210–31

'An Analytical Programme', *The Bioscope* (21 January 1909), 13

'Animated Pictures and Elocution', *The Showman* (20 September 1901), 24

'Another Lady Lecturer', *The Optical Lantern and Cinematograph Journal* (July 1905), 143

The Art of Projection and Complete Magic Lantern Manual, by An Expert (London: E. A. Beckett, 1893)

'Artemus Ward', *Chambers's Journal* 76 (10 June 1865), 358

'The Artistic Value of the Kinematograph', *The Kinematograph and Lantern Weekly* (28 June 1907), 111

'The Ascent of Mont Blanc', *Illustrated London News* (25 December 1852), 565

'At England's Home of Mystery', *The Showman* (26 April 1901), 265

'At The Palace', *Punch* 115 (6 August 1898), 57

'Bad Effects of Moving Pictures', *The Bioscope* (6 November 1908), 10

Ball, Eustace Hale, *The Art of the Photoplay* (New York: Veritas, 1913)

Baudelaire, Charles, 'The Painter of Modern Life' in *The Painter of Modern Life and Other Essays*, trans. and ed. Jonathan Mayne (London: Phaidon, 1964), 1–40

Bayley, Child, *Modern Magic Lanterns and their Management* (London: L. Upcott and Gill, 1896)

B.B., 'Social Welfare and the Kinematograph', *Charity Organization Review* 196 (1913), 182

Bedford, Rev. H., 'Hints on Lantern Lectures', *Optical Magic Lantern Journal* (October 1899), 131–33

Behind the Scenes: A Cinematograph Rehearsal', *The World's Fair* (18 November 1911), 10–11

Bergson, Henri, *Creative Evolution*, trans. Arthur Mitchell (London: Macmillan, 1911)

—, *Matter and Memory*, trans. Nancy Margaret Paul and W. Scott Palmer (London: Swan Sonnenschein and Co., 1911)

—, *Time and Free Will: An Essay on the Immediate Data of Consciousness* (London: Swan Sonnenschein and Co., 1910)

'Bioscope and Eye', *The Bioscope* (27 November 1908), 15

'The Bioscope Parliament', *The Bioscope* (10 December 1908), 13

'Birmingham Fair', *The Showman* (7 June 1901), 367

Black, Alexander, 'The Camera and the Comedy', *Scribners* 20 (1896), 605–10

—, 'Photography in Fiction: "Miss Jerry," the First Picture Play', *Scribners* 18 (1895), 348–60

Blair, Allan, 'How to Prepare a Lantern Lecture' *The Photographic News* (27 October 1899), 703

'The British Mutoscope and Bioscope Company and Others v. Burns and Oates (limited)', *The Times* (25 March 1899), 4

Booth, William, *In Darkest England and the Way Out* (London: Salvation Army, 1890)

Broome, Jeremy, 'Crowds', *The Strand Magazine* (December 1898), 558–66

Brown, George E., F.I.C., 'The Lanternist as Lecturer', *The Optical Magic Lantern Journal and Photographic Enlarger* 11: 134 (July 1900), 90–91

—, 'The Lanternist as Lecturer, Pt II' (July 1900), 95–96

Bryce, G.R., 'Lantern Lectures', *Optical Magic Lantern Journal* (March 1897), 29–30

Burlingham, Frederick, *How to Become an Alpinist* (London: T. Werner Laurie, [1914])

'Busking Extraordinary', *The Optical Magic Lantern Journal and Photographic Enlarger* (February 1901), 19

Byford, Thomas, 'Concerning Two Remunerative Callings', in *The Optical Magic Lantern Journal and Photographic Enlarger* (November 1901), 88–89

'C.W.Locke', *The Showman* (11 October 1901), 71

Calvert, Charles, 'Foreword', in William J. Elliot, *How to Become a Film Actor* (London: The Picture Palace News Co., 1917)

Chadwick, W.J., *The Magic Lantern Manual* (London: Frederick Warne and Co., 1878)

Choules, J.O., *Young Americans Abroad; or Vacations in Europe: Travels in England, France, Holland, Belgium, Prussia and Switzerland* (Boston: Gould and Lincoln, 1852)

[The Chronophone], *The Kinematograph and Lantern Weekly* (20 June 1907), 89

'The Cinematograph Bill: Text of the Amended Measure', *The World's Fair* (9 October 1909), 12

'Cinematography Burlesqued', *The Photographic News* (28 January 1898), 50

'Cinematograph Films', *The Showman* (11 October 1901), 77

'Cinematograph Films', *The Showman* (1 November 1901), 127

'Cinematograph Films', *The Showman* (15 November 1901), 152

'Cinematograph Films', *The Showman* (22 November 1901), 175

'Cinematograph Lanterns , &c., and the L.C.C.', *The Photographic News* 43 (13 January 1899), 29

[Cinematograph Lottery], *The World's Fair* (12 May 1906), 1

'Cinematograph Notes', *The Showman* (December 1900), 62

'Cinematograph Notes', *The Showman* (21 March 1902), 77

'The Cinney that Sinned and the Audience that Wanted their Money Back', *The World's Fair* (28 April 1906), 6

'A Clever Optical Illusion', *Kinematograph and Lantern Weekly* (31 May 1907), 44

'The Coming Method of Living Pictures with Sound', *The Kinematograph and Lantern Weekly* (30 May 1907), 47

[Commentary on titles slides], *The Showman* (27 September 1901), 47

'Copyright Act, 1911', 1 & 2 GEO.5., 182–205

'Correspondence', *The Showman* (28 February 1902), 56

Craven, Robert, 'The Little Match Girl', *Short Lantern Readings, Series no.8* (Bradford: Riley Bros, [n.d.]), 3–6

D.Z., 'The Imagination and the Cinematograph', in *Month* 126:613 (1915), 80

'Dangers of Alpine Mountaineering', *Temple Bar* 52 (February 1878), 213–24

Dawbarn, Charles, 'The Popular Theatre of Today. Behind the Scenes at a Cinematograph Rehearsal', *Pall Mall Magazine* 48 (1911), 271

'Death of Doodica', *The Showman* (21 February 1902), 6

Delamosne, M. L'Abbe, 'Delamosne on Delsarte', in *Delsarte System of Oratory: Including the Complete Work of M. L'Abbe Delamosne and Mme. Angelique Arnaud (Pupils of Delsarte) with the Literary Remains of François Delsarte* (New York: Edgar S. Werner, 1887)

Delsarte, François, 'Delsarte's Own Words' (taken from notes), in *Delsarte System of Oratory: Including the Complete Work of M. L'Abbe Delamosne and Mme. Angelique Arnaud (Pupils of Delsarte) with the Lieterary Remains of François Delsarte* (New York: Edgar S. Werner, 1887)

Devant, David, *My Magic Life* (Bideford: The Supreme Magic Co., [n.d.])

Dickens, Charles, 'The American Panorama', in *The Works of Charles Dickens*, 36 vols (London: Chapman and Hall, 1911), XXXVI, 139–41

—, 'The Uncommercial Traveller', *All the Year Round* 9 (1863), 348–52

Dockree, E., 'Lecturer's Expenses', *The Photographic News* (1 January 1897), 8–9

Doumic, René, 'The Craze for "Modernity"', *Living Age* 7:219 (1898), 3

'The Dramatic Copyright Act, 1833', *Chitty's Statutes* (1894), 11–13

Duckworth, G.H., 'Art and Amusement', in *Life and Labour of the People in London*, 8 vols, ed. Charles Booth (London: MacMillan and Co., 1896), VIII, 106–48

'East-end Experiences', *Chambers's Journal of Popular Literature* 809 (1879), 407–09

Easy Shaving: A Farce in One Act (New York: Robert de Witt, [nd])

Edison, Thomas, 'Preface', in W.K.L. Dickson and Antonia Dickson, *History of the Kinetograph, Kinetoscope, and Kineto-phonograph* (New York: A.Bunn, 1895; repr. New York: Arno Press, 1970)

[Editorial], *The Showman* (20 September 1901), 24

[Editorial on film and the election], *The Optical Lantern and Cinematograph Journal* (March 1906), 50

'Editor's Page', *The Showman* (15 February 1901), 106

'Editor's Page', *The Showman* (2 August 1901), 497

'The Election', *The Optical Lantern and Cinematograph Journal* (May 1906), 91

Elliott, William J., *How to Become a Film Actor* (London: Picture Palace News Co., [1917])

'Entertainers' Patter', *The Showman* (7 February 1902), 343

'Entertainers' Patter', *The Showman* (14 March 1902), 98

Esenswein, J. Berg, and Arthur Leeds, *Writing the Photoplay* (Springfield, MA: Home Correspondence School, 1913)

'Exhibitions, and How they are Run', *The Showman* (28 June 1901), 411–12

'An Expert', *The Art of Projection and Complete Magic Lantern Manual*, 2nd edn (London: E. A. Beckett, 1901)

'Fairs in War Time', *The Times* (23 January 1918), 3

'Fake Cinematograph Pictures', *The Optical Magic Lantern Journal and Photographic Enlarger* (November 1900), 138

'Fake or Trick Cinematograph Pictures', *The Optical Magic Lantern Journal and Photographic Enlarger* (December 1900), 153–54

'A Famous Describer', *The World's Fair* (19 November 1910), 1

'Film-Picture Actors', in *The Bioscope* (2 October 1908), 18

'First in 1893: L. Gaumont and Co.', *The Showman* (22 February 1901), 2

'From the Editor's Chair', *The Photographic News* (14 January 1898), 19

'From the Editor's Pen', *The Optical Lantern and Kinematograph Journal* (August 1906), 199

'From the Editor's Pen', *The Optical Lantern and Kinematograph Journal* (March 1907), 115

'[Front cover image]' (Warwick advertisement), *The Showman* (25 January 1901), cover page

'Funeral of the Queen: Impressive and Solemn Spectacle', *The Showman* (15 February 1901), 4

Furniss, Harry, *Our Lady Cinema: How and Why I went into the Photo-Play World and What I Found There* (Bristol: J. W. Arrowsmith, 1914; repr. London: Garland Publishing, 1978)

'Gain Public Confidence', *The Bioscope* (4 December 1908), 3

Garcia, Gustave, *The Actor's Art: A Practical Treatise on Stage Declamation, Public Speaking and Deportment* (London: T. Pettitt, 1882)

[Gaumont advertisement], *The Showman* (27 September 1901), advertisement page 2

'George Kemp', *The Showman* (December 1900), 68

Gissing, George, *The Nether World* (Oxford: Oxford University Press, 1999)

Goodman, Walter, *The Keeleys: On Stage and at Home* (London: Bentley, 1895)

Gorky, Maxim, Newspaper review of the Lumiere programme at the Nizhni-Novgorod fair (4 July 1896), repr. in *In the Kingdom of the Shadows: A Companion to Early Cinema*, eds Colin Harding and Simon Popple (London: Cygnus Arts, 1996), 5–6

'Hamilton's Excursions Recalled', in *The Bioscope* (13 November 1908), 6

'Harper Bros & Gen Lew Wallace v. Riley Brothers', *The Optical Magic Lantern Journal and Photographic Enlarger* (August 1896), 135–36

Hasluck, Paul H., *Optical Lanterns and Accessories: How to Make and Manage Them* (London: Cassell and Company, 1901)

Haydon, C. Milton, 'Tight Corners, and Such Like', *The Showman* (28 June 1901), 421–22

'Helps and Hints', *The Kinematograph and Lantern Weekly* (4 July 1907), 121

Hepworth, Cecil M., *Animated Photography: The ABC of the Cinematograph* (London: Hazell, Watson and Viney ltd, 1900)

—, *Came the Dawn: Memoires of a Film Pioneer* (London: Phoenix House, 1951)

—, 'Preface' in John Scotland, *The Talkies* (London: Lockwood and Son, 1930)

—, 'Those Were the Days', in *Film Makers on Film Making: Statements on their Art by Thirty Directors*, ed. Harry M. Geduld (Bloomington: Indiana University Press, 1967), 26–32 (first publ. in *Penguin Film Review* 6 (April 1948), 33–39)

Hepworth, T. C., *The Book of the Lantern* (London: Wyman and Sons, 1888)

—, 'Music and "Effects" in Cinematography', *The Showman* (6 September, 1901), 575

Hibbert, Harold R., 'How to Spend Three Days in Paris', in *The World's Fair* (4 February 1908), 4

Hingston, E.P., 'Prefatory Note', in Artemus Ward, *Artemus Ward's Lecture (As Delivered at the Egyptian Hall, London)*, ed. T.W. Robertson and E. Hingston (London: John Camden Hotten: 1869)

'Holiday Amusements', *The Morning Chronicle* (18 April 1854), 6–7

Hollins, J., *Magic Lantern Reading to Accompany Slides* (University of Exeter, Bill Douglas Centre MS)

Holmes, Burton, *The Burton Holmes Lectures* 10 vols (Battle Creek, Michigan: The Little Preston Company, 1901)

'Home Office Regulations. Dated February 18, 1910, made by the Secretary of State under the Cinematograph Act, 1909', in *The Modern Bioscope Operator* (London: Gaines, 1910), 2

Hopkins, Albert A., *Magic: Stage Illusions, Special Effects and Trick Photography* (London: Sampson Low, Marston, 1897; repr. New York: Dover Publications, 1976)

Hopwood, Henry V., 'Kinetographic Pictures: Their Errors and Falsities', *The Optician and Photographic Trades Review* (29 September 1899), 69–70

—, *Living Pictures: Their History, Photo-Production and Practical Working* (London: Optician and Photographic Trades Review, 1899)

Horne, Rev. Thomas, *Humorous and Tragic Stories of Showman Life* (London: The Era, [1909])

'The House for Films', *The Showman* (4 October 1901), 63

'How to Give a Good Cinematograph Show', *The Showman* (6 September 1901), 571

How To Run a Picture Theatre (London: The Kinematograph Weekly, c1911)

'Hughes Animated Living Picture Outdoor Peep Show', *The Era* (23 April 1898), 31

Hulfish, David S., *Motion Picture Work: A General Treatise on Picture Taking, Picture Making, Photo-Plays, and Theater Management and Operation* (Chicago, IL: American Technical Society, 1915)

'Hull Fair', *The Showman* (November 1900), 53

'An Ideal Cinematograph Show', *The Showman* (15 November 1901), 157–58

'Illusions of the Cinematograph', *The Literary Digest* 44:19 (11 May 1912), 985

'Indecent Cinematographic Exhibition', *The Optician and Photographic Trades Review* (29 September 1899), 34

'Introducing Variety Turns', *The Bioscope* (4 December 1908), 18

'James Chipperfield: An All-Round Showman', *Music Hall and Theatre Review* (10 June 1904), 381

James, Henry, *A Small Boy and Others* (London: Macmillan, 1913)

Jenkins, Charles Francis, *Animated Pictures* (Washington: H.L. McQueen, 1898)

'Kalem Co. v. Harper Bros, 1911' (1911) 222 US, 92–96

'Karno v. Pathé Frères, London (Sept 26, 1908)' (1908) 99 L.T., 115–19

'Karno v. Pathé Frères. Appeal from the King's Bench Division (April 17, 1909)' (1909) 100 L.T. , 260–62

Kerr, Reid, 'The Showman: A Story', in *Temple Bar* 116 (April 1899), 535–47

'The Kinematograph Man', *The Photographic News* (25 May 1900), 328–29

Kirton, J.W., *Buy your own Cherries* (London: Jerrold and Sons, [n.d.])

Lambert, Aurèle Labat de, *General Advice on Film Acting*, Cinema Course Series, IV (London: Standard Art Book Company, [1920])

'The Lantern for Pleasure and Profit' (1896), repr. in Stephen Herbert, ed., *A History of Pre-Cinema*, 3 vols (London: Routledge, 2000) II, 459–60

'Lantern and Cinematograph Exhibiting, Pt. II', *The Showman* (14 June 1901), 389–90

'The Lantern as Illustrator', *The Showman* (October 1900), 35–36

The Lantern Buyer's Guide: Being Hints on the Purchase of Lantern Outfits (Bradford: Riley Bros, 1894)

'Latest Cinematograph Freak', *The World's Fair* (1 December 1906), 1

'Latest Productions', *The Kinematograph and Lantern Weekly* (29 August 1907), 253–54

Le Bon, Gustave, *The Crowd: A Study of the Popular Mind*, 19th edn (London: Ernest Benn, 1947)

'Lecturing' (1897), repr. in Stephen Herbert, ed., *A History of Pre-Cinema*, 3 vols (London: Routledge, 2000) II, 471–72

'Lecturing, continued' (1897) repr. in Stephen Herbert, ed., *A History of Pre-Cinema*, 3 vols (London: Routledge, 2000) II, 473–74

'The Lecturing Idea', *The Bioscope* (7 January 1909), 5

'The Lecturer's Worth', *The Bioscope* (20 November 1908), 12

[Letters], *The Optical Lantern and Cinematograph Journal* (June 1905), p. 104

Lewis, Rev. J. M., *Lantern Readings: A Thousand Miles up the Congo River* (London: J. Tamblin, [n.d.])

'Life Model Studies. 1.—A Peep Behind the Scenes', *The Photogram* (February 1899), repr. in the *New Magic Lantern Journal* 5:3 (April 1988), 2

'Life Model Studies. 2.—The Models Themselves', *The Photogram* (March 1899), repr. in the *New Magic Lantern Journal* 5:3 (April 1988), 3

Lipps, Theodor, 'Empathy and Aesthetic Pleasure', in *Aesthetic Theories: Studies in the Philosophy of Art*, ed. Karl Aschenbrenner and Arnold Isenberg (Englewood Cliffs, NJ: Prentice-Hall, 1965), 401–14; first publ. as 'Einfuhlung und Asthetischer Genuss', *Die Zukunft* 54 (1906), 106–19

'Little Ones at Limehouse', in *Belgravia: A London Magazine* 10 (1869), 61–68

Lucas, E. V., 'The Cinematoscope—A Power', *The Optical Lantern and Cinematograph Journal* (May 1906), 94

Lynton, Jimmy, 'Old Time Picture Shows', *The World's Fair* (27 November 1954), 25

M.W., 'Cinematograph Notes', *The Showman* (December 1900), 62

Mansbergh, Mrs Henry, 'An Idyll of the Cinematograph', *Windsor Magazine* 7 (December 1897–May 1898), 363–68

Matthews, Charles Edward, *The Annals of Mont Blanc: A Monograph* (London: T. Fisher Unwin, 1898)

'Maskelyne and Cooke's Mysteries', *The Showman* (25 October 1901), 108–10

Mayhew, Henry, *London Labour and the London Poor*, 4 vols (London: Griffen, Bohn and Company, 1851; repr. New York: Dover Publications, 1968)

McLachlan, Peter, 'A Suggestion to Manufacturers', *The Bioscope* (31 January 1909), 23

McMeian, Thos., 'Lantern Operators', *The Magic Lantern Journal and Photographic Enlarger Almanac and Annual 1897–8* (London: Magic Lantern Journal Co., 1898), 81–83

The Modern Bioscope Operator (London: Gaines, 1910)

'The Modernity Hospital', *Atlantic Monthly* 75 (1895), 714–15

Montagu, E.H., 'In the Days when Films were Rented on the Deposit System', *The Kinematograph and Lantern Weekly* (Special Supplement: Twenty-First Anniversary of Kinematography) (1 March 1917), 9

'More Show-Life Secrets' (advertisement feature), *The Showman* (2 August 1901), frontispiece

Motion Picture Handbook: A Guide for Managers and Operators of Motion Picture Theatres (New York: Moving Picture World, 1910)

'Mr Arthur B. Malden', *The Optical Lantern and Cinematograph Journal* (May 1906), 92

'Mr James Bamforth's Lantern Slides', *The Optician and Photographic Trades Review* (29 September 1899), 140

'Mr. James Styles', *The World's Fair* (24 September 1910), 14

'Mr Wyld's Globe', *The Times* (18 April 1854)

'The Mutoscope and Biograph Syndicate (limited) and the British Mutoscope and Biograph Company (limited) v. The British Stereopticon Company (limited,)' *The Times* (12 January 1900), 13

Nabarro, Max, 'This is My Life', trans. Ivo Blom and Tom Gunning, *Iris* 22 (1996), 183–200

'New Apparatus: Duplex Photo-Rotoscope', *The Optical Magic Lantern Journal and Photographic Enlarger* (June 1899), 79

'New "Hepwix" Films: Funeral of Queen Victoria', *The Showman* (15 February 1901), 3

Newton and Co. Slide Catalogue, 1900 (London: Newton and Co., 1900)

Norman, Tom, *Memoirs of Tom Norman: The Silver King* (Sheffield University Library, National Fairground Archive MS)

'Notes of the Week', *The Showman* (14 February 1902), 1

'Notes from the Provinces', *The Showman* (5 July 1901), 434

'Notes from the Provinces', *The Showman* (15 November 1901), 152

'The Note of Modernity', *The Dial: A Semi-Monthly Journal of Literary Criticism, Discussion, and Information* 41: 488 (16 October 1906), 226

'Notes of the Week' *The Showman* (8 November 1901), 1

'Notes on Current Topics', *The Kinematograph and Lantern Weekly* (20 June 1907), 89

'Notes on Current Topics', *The Kinematograph and Lantern Weekly* (5 September 1907), 258

'Novel Films', *The Showman* (20 December 1901), 239

Oakden, Professor, 'Elocution Made Easy, Pt. I', *The Showman* (5 July 1901), 432–34

—, 'Elocution Made Easy, Pt. II', *The Showman* (12 July 1901), 452–53

—, 'Elocution Made Easy, Pt. III', *The Showman* (19 July 1901), 459–60

'On Dioramic Painting', *The Saturday Magazine* (23 December 1843)

[On 'film filching'], The Optical Magic Lantern and Cinematograph Journal (December 1905), 275

'An Open-Air Living Picture Show', *The Kinematograph and Lantern Weekly* (29 August 1907), 255

'Panoramas', *Chambers's Journal of Popular Literature* 13 (21 January 1860), 33–35

'Panoramas and all the Other 'Ramas: An Interview with Mr. Poole', in *Pall Mall Budget* (5 September 1889), 1140

Parkes, James, 'Dearth in Lanterndom', *The Optical Magic Lantern Journal and Photographic Enlarger* (October 1901), 67–68

Parr, Ralph, *Shaving Done Here on the Shortest Notice versus Yeds wi' Summut in Um: A Comic Dialogue* (London: John Heywood, 1896)

Pennell, Joseph, 'Is Photography Among the Fine Arts?' *The Contemporary Review* 72 (1897), 824–36

Perkins, T., 'Our Lantern Lectures', *Optical Magic Lantern Journal* (January 1902), 105–06

—, 'Three Requisites for a Successful Lantern Lecture', *Optical Lantern and Cinematograph Journal* (August 1905), 156–58

'Personal Pars', *The Showman* (1 November 1901), 127

'Photographic Lies: Proving the Uselessness of the Camera as a Witness', *The Harmsworth Magazine* 1 (September 1898), 259–64

'The "Photographophone"', *The Showman* (6 September 1901), 577

'Pictorial Lecture at Margate', *The Bioscope* (13 November 1908), 6

'Picture Pars', *The Rinking World and Picture Theatre News* (8 January 1910), 11

'Pictures and Politics in the West', *The Optical Lantern and Cinematograph Journal* (May 1905), 98

'The Picture Theatre Boom', *The Rinking World and Picture Theatre News* (19 February 1910), 14–15

'Picture Theatre Finance', *The Rinking World and Picture Theatre News* (11 December 1909), 18

'Plots for Picture Plays: Concocting Thrilling Dramas and Farcical Fakes for the Cinematograph', *The World's Fair* (24 June 1911), 11

'Introduction', *The Wide World Magazine* 1:1 (April 1898), 3

'The Printed Lecture', in *The Bioscope* (17 December 1908), 21

'Prof Howard', *The Showman* (10 May 1901), 299–300

'Prof. Stone', *The Showman* (21 June 1901), 395–96

Pyke, Montagu A., *Focussing the Universe* (London: Waterloo Brothers, [1912])

[Pyke, Montagu A.], 'The Making of a Picture, no. 1.', *The Rinking World and Picture Theatre News* (4 December 1909)., 20–23

'Radica's Future', *The Showman* (21 February 1902), 6

Harry Randall, *Harry Randall: Old Time Comedian by Himself* (London: Sampson Low, 1930)

Raree, E., *Walk Up! Walk Up! and See the Fool's Paradise with the Many Wonderful Adventures There as Seen in the Strange Surprising PEEP SHOW of Professor Wolley Cobble Showman these Five and Twenty Years NB Money Returned if Performance not Approved of* (London: John Camden Hotten, 1871), prefatory note

Rathbun, John B., *Motion Picture Making and Exhibiting* (London: Werner Laurie, 1914)

'Reflections on Modernity', *Academy* 80 (1911), p. 273

'Re-opening of the Colosseum, Regent's Park', in *The Illustrated London News* (3 May 1845)

[Report on a fairground film show], *The Kinematograph and Lantern Weekly* (4 July 1907), 114

[Report on coming production], *The Showman* (17 January 1902), 293

[Report on James Kenyon in Sunderland], *The Showman* (29 November 1901), 178

[Report on the design of the Polytechnic], *The Builder* 9 (December 1851), 802

[Report on Primrose League screening], *The Optical Lantern and Cinematograph Journal* (February 1906), 41

[Report on street cinematographs], *British Journal of Photography* 45, Monthly supplement (7 October 1898), 73–74

[Reported correspondence from Charles Urban], *The Showman* (13 December 1901), 210

'Representative Kinematograph Shows. An Example from Poplar', *The Kinematograph and Lantern Weekly* (11 July 1907), 142

'Representative Kinematograph Shows: Singing Pictures at the Hippodrome', *The Kinematograph and Lantern Weekly* (5 September 1907), 259

'[Review of *Daily Mail* Article]', *Optical Lantern and Cinematograph Journal* (October 1905), 192

[Review of Hibbert lecture], *The Showman* (22 March 1901), 168

[Review of Hibbert lecture], *The Showman* (12 April 1901), 232

[Review of Holmes' Travelogues], *The Optical Lantern and Cinematograph Journal* (September 1905), 170

[Review of 'Our Navy'], *The Optical Magic Lantern Journal and Photographic Enlarger* (December 1899), 143

[Review of West's show], *The Showman* (25 January 1901), 65

Robertson, T.W., and E. Hingston, eds, *Artemus Ward's Lecture (As Delivered at the Egyptian Hall, London* (London: John Camden Hotten, 1869)

'The Royal Aquarium', *The Showman* (18 January 1901), 49

Royle, Val, 'Smartness in Shows', *The Showman* (October 1900), 27

—, 'To Attract the Public' *The Showman* (September 1900), 16

Sala, George Augustus, *The Life and Adventures of George Augustus Sala*, 3rd edn (London: Cassell and Co., 1896)

Sanger, Lord George, *Seventy Years a Showman* (London: C.Arthur Preston, 1908)

Scott, Leo, 'Reminiscences of Major Mite', *The World's Fair* (31 August 1935), 18

'Sham War Cinematograph Films', *The Optical Magic Lantern Journal and Photographic Enlarger* (March 1900), 30

'Show-Life Secrets', *The Showman* (20 September 1901), 27

The Showman, 'Lecturer's Profits', in *The Optical Magic Lantern Journal* (March 1900), 37–40

'The Showman's Guild', *The Showman* (1 February 1901), 82

'Showmen at the Alhambra', *The Showman* (29 March 1901), 206

'Showmen and the Cinematograph Bill', *The World's Fair* (25 September 1909), 7

'Showmen's Notes', *The Music Hall and Theatre Review* (9 May 1902), 301

'Showmen's Notes', *The Music Hall and Theatre Review* (16 May 1902), 317

'Showmen's Notes', *The Music Hall and Theatre Review* (18 July 1902), 47

'Showmen's Notes', *The Music Hall and Theatre Review* (5 September, 1902), 65

'Showmen's Notes', *The Music Hall and Theatre Review* (7 November 1902), 309

'The Showmen World', *The Era* (11 September 1897), 20

'Side Shows at Bazaars', *The Showman* (November 1900), 50

'The Side Shows of London, Pt 1', *The Showman* (22 February 1901), 127–28

—, 'Pt 2' (1 March 1901), 143–44

—, 'Pt 3' (15 March 1901), 173–74

Simmel, Georg, 'The Adventure', in *Georg Simmel 1858–1918: A Collection of Essays with Translations and a Bibliography*, ed. Kurt H. Wolff (Columbus: Ohio State University Press, 1959), 243–58; first publ. as 'Das Abenteuer', *Phiosophische Kultur. Gesammelte Essays* ([1911] 2nd ed.; Leipzig: Alfred Kroner, 1919), 7–24

—, 'The Aesthetic Significance of the Face', in *Georg Simmel 1858–1918: A Collection of Essays with Translations and a Bibliography*, ed. Kurt H. Wolff (Columbus: Ohio State University, 1959), 276–81; first publ. as 'Die ästhetische Bedeutung des Gesichts', in *Der Lotse. Hamburgische Wochenschrift für Deutsche Kultur* (1 June 1901), 280–84

—, 'Bridge and Door', trans. Mark Ritter, *Theory, Culture, and Society* 11:1 (1994), 5–10; first publ. as 'Brücke und Tür', in *Moderne Illustrierte Zeitung* (15 September 1909), 1–3

—, 'The Metropolis and Mental Life', in *Sociology of Georg Simmel*, trans. and ed. Kurt H. Wolff (London: Collier-Macmillan, 1950), 409–24; first publ. as 'Die Grosstädte und das Geistesleben', in *Die Grossstadt. Vorträge und Aufsätze zur Städteausstellung* 9 (1903), 185–206

—, 'The Stranger', in *Sociology of Georg Simmel*, trans. and ed. Kurt H. Wolff (London: Collier-Macmillan, 1950), 402–08; first publ. in Georg Simmel, *Soziologie: Untersuchungen über die Formen der Vergesellschaftung* (Leipzig: Duncker and Humblot, 1908), 685–91

Simms, George R., *Living London: its Work and its Play, its Humour and its Pathos, its Sights and its Scenes*, 3 vols (London: Cassell, 1902–03)

'Singing Pictures at the Hippodrome', *The Kinematograph and Lantern Weekly* (5 September 1907), 265

'Smethwick Fair', *The Showman* (14 June 1901), 389

Smith, Albert, 'A Go-A-Head Day with Barnum', *Bentley's Miscellany* 27 (1847) vol. 27, 522–27, 623–28

—, *A Handbook of Mr. Albert Smith's Ascent of Mont Blanc* (London, [n.pub.], 1852)

—, 'A Little Talk about Bartholomew Fair—Past and Present', *Bentley's Miscellany* 12 (1842), 390–94

—, *The Story of Mont Blanc*, 2nd edn (London: David Bogue, 1854)

—, 'A Visit to Greenwich Fair', *Bentley's Miscellany* 11 (1842), 511–20

'The Sorrows of the Lantern Lecturer', *The Showman* (21 June 1901), 399–400

'Special Films from Pretoria', *The Showman* (December 1900), 4

'Special to all Entertainers: "The Showman" Entertainment Bureau', *The Showman* (31 May 1901), 345

Steelcroft, Framley, 'Some Peculiar Entertainments, Pt 1', *Strand Magazine* 11 (April 1896), 328–35

—, 'Some Peculiar Entertainments, Pt 2', *The Strand Magazine* 11 (June 1896), 466–75

'The Successful Exhibitor', *The Bioscope* (6 November 1908), 10

'A Successful Living Picture Lecture', *The Optical Lantern and Cinematograph Journal* (May 1906), 93

Sylvanus, 'Our First Kinematograph Show', *The Kinematograph and Lantern Weekly* (4 July 1907), 128

'*Tableaux Vivants*', *Strand Magazine* 2 (1891), 3

Talbot, Frederick A., *Moving Pictures: How They are Made and Worked*, 2nd edn (London: William Heinemann, 1923)

'The Talking Photograph', *The Bioscope* (31 December 1908), 5

Teetgen, John, *My Razor and Shaving Tackle . . . How to Shave etc.* (London: [n. pub], 1844)

'Telling the Tale', *The World's Fair* (15 December 1906), 4

'The "Theatrograph"', *The Photographic News* (27 March 1896), 194

Thorington, James Monroe, *Mont Blanc Side-show: The Life and Times of Mr. Albert Smith* (Philadelphia, PA: John C. Winston Co., 1934)

Timbs, John, *Curiosities of London* (London: Virtue and Co., 1855)

'To the Cinematograph Showmen of To-day', *The Showman* (9 August 1901), advertising page 3

'Types of Cinematograph Films', *The Showman* (9 August 1901), 509

The Upstart, 'Experiences in Animated Photography', *The Showman* (3 January 1902), 272

Urban, Charles, *A Yank in Britain: The Lost Memoirs of Charles Urban, Film Pioneer*, ed., Luke McKernan (Hastings: The Projection Box, 1999)

'The Variety Discussion', *The Bioscope* (17 December 1908), 15

'A Visit to "Hepworth's"', *The Showman* (6 March 1902), 45

W.M., 'Cinematograph Notes', *The Showman* (December 1900), 62

W.M.A., 'A Glimpse of Showman's Life', *The Showman* (29 November 1901), 190

'Wallace and others v. Riley Brothers, New York', *The Optical Magic Lantern Journal and Photographic Enlarger* (October 1896), 166–67

Wallace, Lew, *Lew Wallace: An Autobiography*, 2 vols (New York: Harper Bros, 1906)

Ward, Artemus, 'Artemus Ward: His Book', in *Artemus Ward Complete* (London: Chatto and Windus, 1890)

Wells, Samuel R., *New Physiognomy, or Signs of Character* (New York: Fowler and Wells, 1896)

West, Alfred, 'The Birth of the Kinema: Some Interesting Details of a Show that had an Uninterrupted Run for Fifteen Years', *The Kinematograph and Lantern Weekly* (1 March 1917), 9–11

—, *Sea Salts and Celluloid*, unpublished autobiography, 'Our Navy' website (2004) (http://www.ournavy.org.uk/) [accessed 28 August 2008]

Which Side Wins (University of Exeter, Bill Douglas Centre MS)

'William Clark', *The Showman* (1 February 1901), 73

Williams, Montagu, QC, *Round London: Down East and Up West* (London MacMillan and Co., 1892)

Wilson, Andrew, 'Music Halls', *Contemporary Review* 58 (July 1900), 134–41

Winter, O., 'The Cinematograph', *New Review* 14 (May 1896), 507–13

'A Wonderful Baby', *The Showman* (21 February 1902), 6

Wood, A.A., *Magic Lanterns: How Made and How Used with Practical Advice to Unpractised Lecturers*, 4th edn (London: E.G. Wood and Horne, 1891)

Wood, Leslie, *The Romance of the Movies* (London: Heinemann, 1937)

'Women's Rights', *Short Lantern Readings* 3 (Holmfirth: Bamforth and Co., c.1891), 18

Wright, J.W., 'How to Deliver Lantern Lectures', *Optical Lantern and Cinemato-*

graph Journal (March 1905), 65–68
Yates, Edmund, *Edmund Yates: His Recollections and Experiences*, 2 vols (London: Richard Bentley and Son, 1884)

Secondary Sources

Abel, Richard, ed., *Encyclopedia of Early Cinema* (London: Routledge, 2005)
Allen, Freda and Ned Williams, *Pat Collins: King of Showmen* (Wolverhampton: Uralia Press, 1991)
Altick, Richard D., *The Shows of London: A Panoramic History of Exhibitions, 1600–1862* (Cambridge, MA: Belknap Press, 1978)
Altman, Rick, 'Dickens, Griffith, and Film Theory Today', in *Silent Film*, ed. Richard Abel (New Brunswick, NJ: Rutgers University Press, 1996), 145–62
—, 'Film Sound: All of It', *Iris* 27 (1999), 31–47
—, 'From Lecturer's Prop to Industrial Product: The Early History of Travel Films', in *Virtual Voyages: Cinema and Travel*, ed. Jeffrey Ruoff (Durham, NC: Duke University Press, 2006), 61–78
—, 'General Introduction: Cinema as Event', in *Sound Theory Sound Practice*, ed. Rick Altman (London: Routledge, 1992), 1–14
—, 'An Interview with Rick Altman', *Velvet Light Trap* 51 (2003), 67–72
—, 'The Living Nickelodeon', in *The Sounds of Early Cinema*, eds Richard Abel and Rick Altman (Bloomington: Indiana University Press, 2001), 232–40
—, 'The Silence of the Silents', *Musical Quarterly* 80:4 (1996), 648–718
—, *Silent Film Sound* (New York: Columbia University Press, 2004)
—, *Sound Theory Sound Practice*, ed. (London: Routledge, 1992)
Anthony, Barry, *The Kinora: Motion Pictures for the Home 1896–1914* (Hastings: The Projection Box, 1996)
Armstrong, Isobel, 'The Microscope: Mediations of the Sub-Visible World', in *Transactions and Encounters: Science and Culture in the Nineteenth Century*, eds Roger Luckhurst and Josephine McDonagh (Manchester: Manchester University Press, 2002), 30–54
Arnheim, Rudolf, *Art and Visual Perception: A Psychology of the Creative Eye* (London: Faber and Faber, 1956)
Auerbach, Nina, *Ellen Terry: A Player in Her Time* (London: Phoenix House, 1987)
Azlant, Edward, 'Screenwriting for the Early Silent Film: Forgotten Pioneers, 1897–1911', *Film History* 9 (1997), 228–56
Backer, Noèmia, 'Reconfiguring Annabelle's *Serpentine* and *Butterfly* Dance Films in Early Cinema History', in *Visual Delights: Essays on the Popular and Projected Image in the 19th Century*, eds Simon Popple and Vanessa Toulmin (Trowbridge: Flicks Books, 2000), 93–104
Bailey, Peter, 'A Community of Friends: Business and Good Fellowship in London Music Hall Management c. 1860–1885', in *Music Hall: The Business of Pleasure*, ed. Peter Bailey (Milton Keynes: Open University Press, 1986), 33–52

—, 'Custom, Capital and Culture in the Victorian Music Hall', in *Popular Custom and Culture in Nineteenth-Century England*, ed. R. Storch (London: Croom Helm, 1982), 180–208

—, *Popular Culture and Performance in the Victorian City* (Cambridge: Cambridge University Press, 1998)

Bakhtin, M.M., *Rabelais and His World*, trans. Hélène Iswolsky (Cambridge, MA: MIT Press, 1968)

Balázs, Béla, *Theory of the Film: Character and Growth of a New Art* (New York: Arno Press, 1972)

Balides, Constance, 'Scenarios of Exposure in the Practice of Everyday Life: Women in the Cinema of Attractions', *Screen* 34:3 (Spring 1993), 19–37

Barber, X. Theodore, 'The Roots of Travel Cinema: John L. Stoddard, E. Burton Holmes and the Nineteenth-Century Illustrated Travel Lecture', *Film History*, 5:3 (1993), 68–84

Barnes, John *The Beginnings of the Cinema in England, 1894–1901*, 5 vols (Exeter: University of Exeter Press, 1996)

Barnouw, Erik, *The Magician and the Cinema* (Oxford: Oxford University Press, 1981)

Bataille, Georges, 'Human Face', *October* 36 (1986), 17–21

'*Ben Hur*: Francis Frederic Theophilus Weeks and Patent No 8615 of 1894', *New Magic Lantern Journal* 5:1 (1987), 2–5

Bennett, Tony, *The Birth of the Museum* (London: Routledge, 1995)

Benjamin, Walter, *Charles Baudelaire: A Lyric Poet in the Age of High Capitalism*, trans. Harry Zohn (London: Verso, 1983)

—, 'The Work of Art in the Age of Mechanical Reproduction', in *Illuminations*, trans. Harry Zohn (New York: Schocken, 1969), 219–53

Berg, Charles M., 'The Human Voice and the Silent Cinema', *Journal of Popular Film* 4:2 (1975), 165–77

Berry, David, *Wales and Cinema: The First Hundred Years* (Cardiff: University of Wales Press, 1994)

—, 'William Haggar: Film Pioneer, Actor and Showman', in *Moving Performance: British Stage and Screen, 1890s–1920s* (Trowbridge: Flicks Books, 2000), 112–22

Birch, David, 'Travellers' Cant, Shelta, Mumpers' Talk and Minklers' Thari', *Lore and Language* 3 (July 1983), 8–29

Blom, Ivo, and Ine van Dooren, '"Ladies and Gentlemen, hats off, please." Dutch Film Lecturing and the Case of Cor Schuring', *Iris* 22 (1996), 81–101

Bocock, Robert, and Kenneth Thompson, eds, *Social and Cultural Forms of Modernity* (Cambridge: Polity Press in association with the Open University, 1992)

Bogdan, Robert, *Freak Show: Presenting Human Oddities for Amusement and Profit* (Chicago, IL: University of Chicago Press, 1988)

—, 'In Defense of Freak Show', *Disability, Handicap & Society* 8:1 (1993), 91–94

Bolter, Jay David, and Richard Grusin, *Remediation: Understanding New Media* (Cambridge, MA: MIT Press, 2000)

Bordwell, David, *Making Meaning: Inference and Rhetoric in the Interpretation of Cinema* (Cambridge, MA: Harvard University Press, 1989)

—, *Narration in the Fiction Film* (Madison, WI: University of Wisconsin Press, 1985)

—, *On the History of Film Style* (Cambridge, MA: Harvard University Press, 1997)

Bordwell, David, Janet Staiger and Kristin Thompson, *The Classical Hollywood Cinema: Film Style and Mode of Production to 1960* (London: Routledge and Kegan Paul, 1985)

Bottomore, Stephen, 'An International Survey of Sound Effects in Early Cinema', *Film History* 11 (1999), 485–98

—, 'From the Factory Gate to the "Home Talent" Drama: A International Overview of Local Films in the Silent Era', in *The Lost World of Mitchell and Kenyon: Edwardian Britain on Film*, eds Vanessa Toulmin, Simon Popple and Patrick Russell (London: British Film Institute, 2004), 33–48

—, 'Out of this World: Theory, Fact and Film History', *Film History* 6 (1994), 7–25

—, 'The Panicking Audience? Early Cinema and the Train Effect', *Historical Journal of Film, Radio and Television* (June 1999), 177–216

—, '"She's just like my Granny! Where's her crown?" Monarchs and Movies, 1896–1916', in *Celebrating 1895: The Centenary of Cinema*, ed. John Fullerton (London: John Libbey and Company, 1998), 172–81

—, 'The Story of Percy Peashaker: Debates about Sound Effects in the Early Cinema', in *The Sounds of Early Cinema*, eds Richard Abel and Rick Altman (Bloomington: Indiana University Press, 2001), 129–42

Branigan, Edward, 'Diegesis and Authorship in Film', *Iris* 3:7 (1986), 37–54

—, *Narrative Comprehension and Film* (London: Routledge, 1992)

Braun, Marta, *Picturing Time: The Work of Etienne-Jules Marie (1830–1904)* (Chicago, IL: University of Chicago, 1992)

Brewster, Ben, 'Periodization of Early Cinema', in *American Cinema's Transitional Era: Audiences, Institutions, Practices*, eds Charlie Keil and Shelley Stamp (Berkeley: University of California Press, 2004), 66–75

Brewster, Ben, and Lea Jacobs, 'Pictorial Styles of Film Acting in Europe in the 1910s', in *Celebrating 1895: The Centenary of Cinema*, ed. John Fullerton (London: John Libbey and Company, 1998), 253–62

—, *Theatre to Cinema: Stage Pictorialism and the Early Feature Film* (Oxford: Oxford University Press, 1997)

Brown, Richard, 'The British Film Copyright Archive', in *In the Kingdom of the Shadows: A Companion to Early Cinema*, eds Colin Harding and Simon Popple (London: Cygnus Arts, 1996), 240–45

—, 'New Century Pictures: Regional Enterprise in Early British Film Exhibition', in *The Lost World of Mitchell and Kenyon*, eds Toulmin, Popple and Russell, 69–82;

—, 'War on the Home Front: The Anglo-Boer War and the Growth of Rental in Britain. An Economic Perspective', *Film History* 16:1 (2004), 28–36.

Brown, Richard, and Barry Anthony, *A Victorian Film Enterprise: The History of the British Mutoscope and Biograph Company, 1897–1915* (Trowbridge: Flicks Books, 1999)

Bruno, Giuliana, 'Site-Seeing: Architecture and the Moving Image', *Wide Angle* 19:4

(1997), 8–24

—, *Street Walking on a Ruined Map: City Films of Elvira Notari* (Princeton, NJ: Princeton University Press, 1993)

Buckland, Warren, ed., *The Film Spectator: From Sign to Mind* (Amsterdam: Amsterdam University Press, 1995)

Buck-Morss, Susan, 'The Flaneur, the Sandwichman and the Whore: The Politics of Loitering', *New German Critique* 39 (Fall 1986), 99–140

Burch, Noël, *Life to Those Shadows*, trans. and ed. Ben Brewster (London: British Film Institute, 1990)

—, 'Primitivism and the Avant-Gardes: A Dialectical Approach', in *Narrative, Apparatus, Ideology: A Film Theory Reader*, ed. Philip Rosen (New York: Columbia University Press, 1986), 483–506

Burrows, Jon, *Legitimate Cinema: Theatre Stars in Silent British Films 1908–1918* (Exeter: University of Exeter Press, 2003)

—, 'Penny Pleasures: Film Exhibition in London during the Nickelodeon Era, 1906–1914', *Film History* 16:1 (2004), 60–91

—, 'Penny Pleasures II: Indecency, Anarchy, and Junk Film in London's Nickelodeons, 1906–1914', *Film History* 16:2 (2004), 172–97

—, 'Waller Jeffs' Scrapbooks', in *Picture House* 29 (2004), 44–55

—, 'When Britain Tried to Join Europe: The Significance of the 1909 Paris Congress for the British Film Industry', *Early Popular Visual Culture* 4:1 (2006), 1–19

Burton, Alan, *The British Consumer Co-operative Movement and Film, 1890s–1960s* (Manchester: University of Manchester Press, 2005)

—, *The British Film Co-Operative Movement Film Catalogue* (Trowbridge: Flicks Books, 1997)

—, 'The Emergence of an Alternative Film Culture: Film and the British Consumer Co-operative Movement before 1920', in *Celebrating 1895: The Centenary of Cinema*, ed. John Fullerton (London: John Libbey and Company, 1998), 71–81

Burton, Alan, and Laraine Porter, eds, *Pimples, Pranks, and Pratfalls: British Film Comedy Before 1930* (Trowbridge: Flicks Books, 2000)

Butterworth, Mark, 'A Lantern Tour of Star-Land: The Astronomer Robert Ball and his Magic Lantern Lectures', in *Realms of Light: Uses and Perceptions of the Magic Lantern from the 17th to the 21st Century*, eds Richard Crangle, Mervyn Heard and Ine van Dooren (London: Magic Lantern Society, 2005), 162–73

Carroll, Noël, *Mystifying Movies: Fads and Fallacies in Contemporary Film Theory* (New York: Columbia University Press, 1988)

Carson, Thomas L., 'The Definition of Lying', *Nous* 40:2 (2006), 293

Casetti, Francesco, *Inside the Gaze: The Fiction Film and its Spectator*, trans. Neil Andrew with Charles O'Brien (Bloomington: Indiana University Press, 1998)

—, 'Looking for the Spectator', *Iris* 1:2 (1983), 15–29

Chanan, Michael, *The Dream that Kicks: The Prehistory and Early Years of Cinema in Britain*, 2nd edn (London: Routledge, 1996)

—, 'The Treats of Trickery', in *Cinema: The Beginnings and the Future*, ed. Christopher Williams (London: Univerity of Westminster Press, 1996), 117–22

Charney, Leo, 'In a Moment: Film and the Philosophy of Modernity', in *Cinema and the Invention of Modern Life*, eds Leo Charney and Vanessa R. Schwartz (Berkeley: University of California Press, 1995), 279–93

Charney, Leo, and Vanessa R. Schwartz, eds, *Cinema and the Invention of Modern Life* (Berkeley: University of California Press, 1995)

Cherches, Peter, *Star Course: Popular Lectures and the Marketing of Celebrity* (unpublished doctoral dissertation, New York University, 1997)

Clark, Jon, Celia Modgil, Sohan Modgil, eds, *Anthony Giddens: Consensus and Controversy* (London: Fulmar Press, 1990)

Coffman, Elizabeth, 'Women in Motion: Loie Fuller and the "Interpenetration" of Art and Science', *Camera Obscura* 17: 1 (2002), 72–105

Cook, Olive, *Movement in Two Dimensions* (London: Hutchinson, 1963)

Cosandey, Roland, and François Albera, *Cinéma sans Frontières/Images Across Borders 1896–1918* (Quebec: Nuit Blanche, 1995)

Cosgrove, Denis E., *Social Formation and Symbolic Landscape*, 2nd edn (Madison: University of Wisconsin Press, 1998)

Crangle, Richard, *Hybrid Texts: Modes of Representation in the Early Moving Picture and Some Related Media in Britain* (unpublished doctoral thesis, Exeter University, 1996)

—, '"Next Slide Please": the Lantern Lecture in Britain, 1890–1910', in *The Sounds of Early Cinema*, eds Richard Abel and Rick Altman (Bloomington: Indiana University Press, 2001), 39–48

—, 'Saturday Night at the X-Rays—The Moving Picture and 'The New Photography' in Britain, 1896', in *Celebrating 1895: The Centenary of Cinema*, ed. John Fullerton (London: John Libbey and Company, 1998), 138–44

Crangle, Richard, Mervyn Heard and Ine van Dooren, eds, *Realms of Light: Uses and Perceptions of the Magic Lantern from the 17th to the 21st Century* (London: Magic Lantern Society, 2005)

Crary, Jonathan, *Suspensions of Perception: Attention, Spectacle, and Modern Culture* (Cambridge, MA: MIT Press, 2001)

—, *Techniques of the Observer: On Vision and Modernity in the Nineteenth Century* (Cambridge, MA: MIT press, 1990)

—, 'Unbinding Vision: Manet and the Attentive Observer in the Late Nineteenth Century', in *Cinema and the Invention of Modern Life*, eds Leo Charney and Vanessa R. Schwartz (Berkeley: University of California Press, 1995), 46–71

Crompton, Dennis, David Henry and Stephen Herbert, eds, *Magic Images: The Art of Hand-Painted and Photographic Lantern Slides* (London: Magic Lantern Society, 1990)

Dahl, Curtis, 'Artemus Ward: Comic Panoramist', *New England Quarterly* 32:4 (1959), 476–85

Daly, Nicholas, 'Blood on the Tracks: Sensation Drama, the Railway, and the Dark Face of Modernity', *Victorian Studies* 42:1 (Autumn 1998/1999) 47–76

Davis, Tracy C., *Actresses as Working Women: Their Social Identity in Victorian Culture* (London: Routledge, 1991)

Dawes, Edwin A., 'The Magic Scene in Britain in 1905', *Early Popular Visual Culture* 5:2 (2007), 109–26

Debord, Guy, *The Society of the Spectacle*, trans. Donald Nicholson (New York: Zone Books, 1994)

de Certeau, Michel, *The Practice of Everyday Life*, trans. Steven Rendall (Berkeley: University of California Press, 1984)

deCordova, Richard, *Picture Personalities: The Emergence of the Star System in America* (Chicago, IL: University of Illinois Press, 1990)

Deleuze, Gilles, *Cinema 1: The Movement Image*, trans. Hugh Tomlinson and Barbara Habberjam (London: Athlone Press, 1992)

de Vries, Tjitte, 'Arthur Melbourne-Cooper, Film Pioneer: Wronged by Film History', *KINtop* 3 (1994), 143–60

—, 'Letter to the Editor: The Case for Melbourne-Cooper', *Film History* 12 (2000), 300–05

Dirks, Nicholas B., ed., *Colonialism and Culture* (Ann Arbor, MI: University of Michigan Press, 1992)

Dolar, Mladen, '"I Shall be with you on your Wedding Night": Lacan and the Uncanny', *October* 58 (1991), 5–23

Douglass, Paul, 'Bergson and Cinema: Friends or Foes?' in *The New Bergson*, ed. John Mullarkey (Manchester: Manchester University Press, 1999), 209–27

Elsaesser, Thomas, ed., *Early Cinema: Space Frame Narrative* (London: British Film Institute, 1990)

—, 'Narrative Cinema and Audience-Oriented Aesthetics', in *Popular Television and Film*, ed. Tony Bennett, Susan Boyd-Bowman, Colin Mercer and Janet Woollacott (London: British Film Institute, 1981), 270–82

Fay, Arthur, *Bioscope Shows and their Engines* (Lingfield: The Oakwood Press, 1966)

Fitzsimons, Linda, and Sarah Street, eds, *Moving Performance: British Stage and Screen, 1890s–1920s* (Trowbridge: Flicks Books, 2000)

Fitzsimons, Raymund, *The Baron of Piccadilly: The Travels and Entertainments of George Albert Smith, 1816–1860* (London: Geoffery Bles., 1967)

Fletcher, Tony, 'The London County Council and the Cinematograph, 1896–1900', *Living Pictures: The Journal of the Popular and Projected Image Before 1914*, 1:2 (2001), 69–83

—, 'A Tapestry of Celluloid, 1900–1906', *Early Popular Visual Culture* 4:2 (July 2006), 175–221

Forrest, Jennifer and Leonard R. Koos, *Dead Ringers: The Remake in Theory and Practice* (New York: SUNY Press, 2001)

Foucault, Michel, 'What is an Author?' in *Textual Strategies: Perspectives in Post-Structuralist Criticism*, ed. Josué V. Harari (London: Methuen and Co., 1979), 141–60

Fretz, Eric 'P.T. Barnum's Theatrical Selfhood and the Nineteenth-Century Culture of Exhibition', in *Freakery: Cultural Spectacles of the Extraordinary Body*, ed. Rosemary Garland Thomson (New York: New York University Press, 1996), 97–107

Friedberg, Anne, *Window Shopping: Cinema and the Postmodern* (Berkeley: University of California Press, 1993)

John Fullerton, ed., *Celebrating 1895: The Centenary of Cinema* (London: John Libbey and Company, 1998)

Gaines, Jane M., 'Early Cinema's Heyday of Copying: The Too Many Copies of *L'Arroseur Arosé*', *Cultural Studies* 20: 2–3 (2006), 227–44

Gaudreault, André, 'The Diversity of Cinematographic Connections in the Inter-medial Context of the Turn of the 20th Century', in *Visual Delights: Essays on the Popular and Projected Image in the 19th Century*, eds Simon Popple and Vanessa Toulmin (Trowbridge: Flicks Books, 2000), 8–15

—, *Du Littéraire au Filmique: Système du Récit* (Paris: Méridiens Klincksieck, 1988)

—, 'Film, Narrative, Narration: The Cinema of the Lumière Brothers', in *Early Cinema: Space Frame Narrative*, ed. Thomas Elsaesser (London: British Film Institute, 1990), 68–75

—, 'The Infringement of Copyright Laws and its Effects', in *Early Cinema: Space Frame Narrative*, ed. Thomas Elsaesser (London: British Film Institute, 1990), 114–22

—, 'Showing and Telling: Image and Word in Early Cinema', in *Early Cinema: Space Frame Narrative*, ed. Thomas Elsaesser (London: British Film Institute, 1990), 274–81

—, 'Theatricality, Narrativity and "Trickality": Re-evaluating the Cinema of George Méliès', *Journal of Popular Film and Television* 15 (1987), 110–19

Gaudreault, André, and François Jost, *Le Récit Cinématographique* (Condé sur Noireau: Éditions Nathan, 1994), 39–77

Gaudreault, André, and Philippe Marion, 'The Neo-Institutionalisation of Cinema as a New Medium', in *Visual Delights Two: Exhibition and Reception*, eds Simon Popple and Vanessa Toulmin (Eastleigh: John Libbey and Company, 2005), 87–95

Gaudreault, André, with Jean-Pierre Sirois-Trahan, 'Le retour du [bonimenteur] refoulé . . . (ou serait-ce le bonisseur-conférencier, le commentateur, le conférencier, le présentateur ou le "speaker"?)', *Iris* 22 (1996), 17–28

Gaudreault, André, and Tom Gunning, 'Le Cinéma des Premier Temps: Un défi a histoire du film?' in *Histoire du Cinéma: Nouvelles Approches*, eds J. Aumont André Gaudreault and M. Marie (Paris: Publications de la Sorbonne, 1989), 49–63

Gerber, David A., 'Volition and Valorization in the Analysis of the 'Careers' of People Exhibited in Freak Shows', *Disability, Handicap & Society* 7:1 (1992), 53–69

Gernsheim, Helmut, and Alison Gernsheim, *L.J.M. Daguerre: The History of the Diorama and the Daguerreotype* (London: Sacker and Warburg, 1956)

Giddens, Anthony, *The Consequences of Modernity* (Cambridge: Polity Press, 1990)

—, *The Constitution of Society: Outline of the Theory of Structuration* (Cambridge: Polity Press, 1984)

—, *Modernity and Self-Identity: Self and Society in the Late Modern Age* (Stanford, CA: Stanford University Press, 1991)

Gill, Arthur T., 'The London Diorama', *History of Photography* 1:1 (January 1977), 31–36

Goffman, Erving, *Frame Analysis: An Essay on the Organization of Experience* (London: Harper and Row, 1974)

—, 'The Lecture', in *Forms of Talk* (Philadelphia, PA: University of Philadelphia Press, 1981), 162–95

Gray, Frank, 'James Williamson's 'Composed Picture': *Attack on a China Mission—Bluejackets to the Rescue* (1900)', in *Celebrating 1895: The Centenary of Cinema*, ed. John Fullerton (London: John Libbey and Company, 1998), 203–11

—, 'Smith versus Melbourne-Cooper: History and Counter-History', *Film History* 11 (1999), 246–61

Green, Nicholas, *The Spectacle of Nature: Landscape and Bourgeois Culture in Nineteenth-Century France* (Manchester: Manchester University Press, 1990)

Gregory, Derek, 'Presences and Absences: Time-Space relations and Structuration Theory', in *Social Theory of Modern Societies: Anthony Giddens and his Critics*, eds David Held and John B. Thompson (Cambridge: Cambridge University Press, 1989), 185–215

Greville, Father P., 'Brief Particulars of Bioscope Shows', in *Merry-Go-Round* 7:1–11 (1951–53)

Griffiths, Alison, *Wondrous Difference: Cinema, Anthroplogy, and Turn of the Century Visual Culture* (New York: Columbia University Press, 2001)

Gunning, Tom 'An Aesthetic of Astonishment: Early Film and the (In)credulous Spectator', *Art and Text* 34 (1989), 31–45

—, 'Before Documentary: Early Non-fiction Films and the "View" Aesthetic', in *Uncharted Territory: Essays on Early Non-fiction Film*, eds Daan Hertogs and Nico de Klerk (Amsterdam: Nederlands Filmmuseum, 1997), 9–24

—, 'The Cinema of Attraction: Early Film, its Spectator, and the Avant-Garde', *Wide Angle* 8:3/4 (1986), 63–70

—, *D.W. Griffith and the Origins of American Narrative Film: The Early Years at Biograph* (Chicago: University of Illinois, 1991)

—, 'Film History and Film Analysis: The Individual Film in the Course of Time', *Wide Angle* 12:3 (1990), 4–19

—, 'In Your Face: Physiognomy, Photography, and the Gnostic Mission of Early Film', *MODERNISM/modernity* 4 (1997), 1–29

—, 'Modernity', in *Encyclopedia of Early Cinema*, ed. Richard Abel (London: Routledge, 2005), 439–42

—, 'Modernity and Cinema: A Culture of Shocks and Flows', in *Cinema and Modernity*, ed. Murray Pomerance (Piscatawny, NJ: Rutgers, 2006), 297–315

—, '"Now You See It, Now You Don't": The Temporality of the Cinema of Attractions', *The Velvet Light Trap* 32 (1993), 3–12

—, 'Pictures of Crowd Splendor: The Mitchell and Kenyon Factory Gate Films', in *The Lost World of Mitchell and Kenyon: Edwardian Britain on Film*, eds Vanessa Toulmin, Simon Popple and Patrick Russell (London: British Film Institute, 2004), 49–58

—, 'The Scene of Speaking: Two Decades of Discovering the Film Lecturer', *Iris* 27 (1999), 67–79

—, 'An Unseen Energy Swallows Space: The Space in Early Film and its Relation to American Avant-Garde Film', in *Film Before Griffith*, ed. John L. Fell (Berkeley: University of California Press, 1983), 355–66

—, '"The Whole World Within Reach": Travel Images Without Borders', in *Cinéma sans Frontières/Images Across Borders 1896–1918*, eds Roland Cosandey and François Albera (Quebec: Nuit Blanche, 1995), 21–36

Hansen, Miriam Bratu, 'America, Paris, the Alps: Kracauer (and Benjamin) on Cinema and Modernity', in *Cinema and the Invention of Modern Life*, eds Leo Charney and Vanessa R. Schwartz (Berkeley: University of California Press, 1995), 362–402

—, *Babel and Babylon: Spectatorship in American Silent Film* (Cambridge, MA: Harvard University Press, 1991)

—, 'Early Cinema, Late Cinema: Transformations of the Public Sphere', *Screen* 34:3 197–210

—, 'Universal Language and Democratic Culture: Myths of Origin in Early American Cinema', in *Myth and Enlightenment in American Literature: In Honour of Hans-Joachim Lang*, eds Dieter Meindl and Friedrich W. Horlacher (Erlangen: University of Erlangen-Nürnberg, 1985), 321–51

Harding, Colin, and Simon Popple, eds, *In the Kingdom of the Shadows: A Companion to Early Cinema* (London: Cygnus Arts, 1996)

Harvie, Christopher, Graham Martin and Aaron Scharf, eds, *Industrialisation and Culture 1830–1914* (London: Macmillan and the Open University Press, 1970)

Heard, Mervyn, '"Come in Please, come out pleased": The Development of British Fairground Bioscope Presentation and Performance', in *Moving Performance: British Stage and Screen, 1890s–1920s*, eds Linda Fitzsimons and Sarah Street (Trowbridge: Flicks Books, 2000), 101–11

—, 'Now You See it, Now You Don't: The Magician and the Magic Lantern', in *Realms of Light: Uses and Perceptions of the Magic Lantern from the 17th to the 21st Century*, eds Richard Crangle, Mervyn Heard and Ine van Dooren (London: Magic Lantern Society, 2005), 13–24

Heard, Mervyn, and Richard Crangle, 'The Temperance Phantasmagoria', in *Realms of Light: Uses and Perceptions of the Magic Lantern from the 17th to the 21st Century*, eds Richard Crangle, Mervyn Heard and Ine van Dooren (London: Magic Lantern Society, 2005)

Hecht, Hermann, and Ann Hecht, *Pre-Cinema History: an Encyclopedia and Annotated Bibliography of the Moving Image before 1896* (London: Bowker Saur/ British Film Institute, 1993)

Held, David, and John B. Thompson, eds, *Social Theory of Modern Societies: Anthony Giddens and his Critics* (Cambridge: Cambridge University Press, 1989)

Henry, David, 'York and Son, Part 1', *New Magic Lantern Journal* 3:1 (1984), 12–13

Herbert, Stephen, *A History of Early Film*, 3 vols (London: Routledge, 2000)

—, *A History of Pre-Cinema*, 3 vols (London: Routledge, 2000)

Herbert, Stephen, and Luke McKernan, *Who's Who of Victorian Cinema: A Worldwide Survey* (London: British Film Institute, 1996)

Hershberger, Andrew E., 'Performing Excess/Signaling Anxiety: Towards a Psycho-analytic Theory of Daguerre's Diorama', *Early Popular Visual Culture* 4:2 (2006), 85–101

Hertogs, Daan, and Nico de Klerk, eds, *Non-fiction from the Teens* (London: British Film Institute, 1994)

—, eds, *Uncharted Territory: Essays on Early Non-fiction Film* (Amsterdam: Neder-lands Filmmuseum, 1997)

Hewitt, Martin, 'Ralph Waldo Emerson, George Dawson and the Control of the Lecture Platform in Mid-Nineteenth-Century Manchester', *Nineteenth-Century Prose* 25:2 (1998), 1–24

Highmore, Ben, 'Street Life in London: Towards a Rhythmanalysis of London in the Late Nineteenth Century', *New Formations* 47 (2002), 171–93

Hiley, Nicholas, 'At the Picture Palace: The British Cinema Audience, 1895–1920', in *Celebrating 1895: The Centenary of Cinema*, ed. John Fullerton (London: John Libbey and Company, 1998), 96–103

Höher, Dagmar, 'The Composition of Music Hall Audiences 1850–1900', in *Music Hall*, ed. Bailey, 73–92

Hollyman, Burnes St. Patrick, 'Alexander Black's Picture Plays, 1893–1894', in *Film Before Griffith*, ed. John L. Fell (Berkeley: University of California Press, 1983), 236–43

Holman, Roger, compiler, *Cinema 1900/1906: An Analytical Study, Cinema 1900/1906: An Analytical Study* (Brussels: FIAF, 1982)

Horton, Donald and R. Richard Wohl, 'Mass Communication and Para-Social Interaction: Observations on Intimacy at a Distance', *Psychiatry* 19 (1956), 215–29

Hurley, Kelly, *The Gothic Body: Sexuality, Materialism, and Degeneration at the Fin de Siecle* (Cambridge: Cambridge University Press, 1996)

Hyde, Ralph, *Panoramania* (London: Trefoil Publications, 1988)

Jenness, George A., *Maskelyne and Cooke: Egyptian Hall, London, 1873–1904* (London: H. Clarke and Co., 1967)

Jost, François. 'The Authorized Narrative', in *The Film Spectator: From Sign to Mind*, ed. Warren Buckland (Amsterdam: Amsterdam University Press, 1995), 164–80

—, 'The Polyphonic Film and the Spectator', in *The Film Spectator: From Sign to Mind*, ed. Warren Buckland (Amsterdam: Amsterdam University Press, 1995), 181–91

Keil, Charlie, 'From Here to Modernity: Style, Historiography, and Transitional Cinema', in *American Cinema's Transitional Era: Audiences, Institutions, Practices*, eds Charlie Keil and Shelley Stamp (Berkeley: University of California Press, 2004), 51–65

—, 'Integrated Attractions: Style and Spectatorship in Transitional Cinema', in *The Cinema of Attractions Reloaded*, ed. Wanda Streuven (Amsterdam: Amsterdam University Press, 2006), 193–204

—, 'Visualised Narratives, Transitional Cinema and the Modernity Thesis', in *Le Cinema au Tournant du Siècle / Cinema at the Turn of the Century*, eds Clair Dupré la Tour, André Gaudreault and Roberta Pearson (Lausanne/Quebec: Éditions

Payot Lausanne / Éditions Nota Bene, 1999), 133–47

Keil, Charlie and Shelley Stamp, eds, *American Cinema's Transitional Era: Audiences, Institutions, Practices* (Berkeley: University of California Press, 2004)

Kember, Joe, 'The Cinema of Affections: The Transformation of Authorship in British Cinema before 1907', *The Velvet Light Trap* 57 (2006), 3–17

—, 'Face to Face: The Facial Expressions Genre in Early British Films', in *The Showman, The Spectacle, and the Two-Minute Silence: Performing British Cinema before 1930*, eds Alan Burton and Laraine Porter (Trowbridge: Flicks Books, 2001), 28–39

—, 'The Functions of Showmanship in Freak Show and Early Film', *Early Popular Visual Culture* (April 2007), 1–23

—, '"It was not the show, it was the tale that you told": Film Lecturing and Showmanship on the British Fairground', in *Visual Delights: Essays on the Popular and Projected Image in the 19th Century*, eds Simon Popple and Vanessa Toulmin (Trowbridge: Flicks Books, 2000), 56–64

Kern, Stephen, *The Culture of Time and Space* (Cambridge, MA: Harvard University Press, 1983)

Kessler, Frank, and Sabine Lenk, '". . . levant les bras au ciel, se tapant sur les cuisses." Réflexions sur L'Universalité du Geste dans le Cinéma des Premiers Temps', in *Cinéma sans Frontières/Images Across Borders 1896–1918*, eds Roland Cosandey and François Albera (Quebec: Nuit Blanche, 1995), 133–45

—, 'L'Expression des Sentiments Dans la Comédie des premiers temps', *La Licorne* 37 (1996), 7–15

King, Norman, 'The Sound of Silents', *Screen* 25:3 (1984), 2–25

Kirby, Lynne, 'Male Hysteria and Early Cinema', *Camera Obscura* 17 (1988), 113–31

—, *Parallel Tracks: The Railroad and Silent Cinema* (Exeter: University of Exeter Press, 1997)

Kozloff, Sarah, *Invisible Storytellers: Voice-Over Narration in American Fiction Film* (Berkeley: University of California Press, 1988)

Kuleshov, Lev, *Kuleshov on Film: Writings by Lev Kuleshov*, trans. and ed. Ronald Levaco (Berkeley: University of California Press, 1974)

Lacasse, Germain, 'Du Boniment Quebecois comme Pratique Résistant', *Iris* 22 (Autumn 1996), 53–66

—, *Le Bonimenteur et Le Cinema Oral: Le Cinema Muet entre Tradition et Modernité* (unpublished doctoral thesis, University of Montreal, 1997)

—, 'The Lecturer and the Attraction', in *The Cinema of Attractions Reloaded*, ed. Wanda Strauven (Amsterdam: Amsterdam University Press, 2006), 181–91

Laffay, Albert, *Logique du Cinéma* (Paris: Masson, 1964)

Lamont, Peter, 'Magician as Conjuror', *Early Popular Visual Culture* 4:1 (2006), 21–33

Lamont, Peter, and Matthew Wiseman, *Magic in Theory: An Introduction to the Theoretical and Psychological Elements of Conjuring* (Hatfield: Hertfordshire University Press, 1999)

Lange-Fuchs, Hauke, 'Samuael Reyher of the University of Kiel: The First Audio

Visual Lecturer?' in *Realms* in *Realms of Light: Uses and Perceptions of the Magic Lantern from the 17th to the 21st Century*, eds Richard Crangle, Mervyn Heard and Ine van Dooren (London: Magic Lantern Society, 2005), 135–37

Lefebvre, Henri, *Rhythmanalysis: Space, Time, and Everyday Life* (London: Continuum, 2004)

Lefebvre, Thierry, *La Chair et le Celluloid: Le Cinéma Chirurgical du Docteur Doyen* (Brionne: Jean Doyen, 2004)

—, 'Internationalité, Influences, Réception: Le Cas de la Diffusion des Films Américains en France (1894–1916)', in *Cinéma des Premiers Temps: Nouvelles Contributions Françaises*, eds Thierry Lefebvre and Laurent Mannoni (Toulouse: Presses de la Sorbonne Nouvelle, 1996), 55–66

—, 'Une "Maladie" au Tournant du Siècle: La Cinématophtalmie', in *Cinéma des Premiers Temps: Nouvelles Contributions Françaises*, eds Thierry Lefebvre and Laurent Mannoni (Tolose: Presses de la Sorbonne, 1996), 131–36

—, 'Die trennung der Siamesischen Zwillinge Doodica und Radica durch Dr Doyen', *KINtop* 6 (1997), 97–101

Levy, David, 'Sentimental Journeys of the Big-Eyed Sightseer: Tourism and the Early Cinema', in *Cinéma sans Frontières/Images Across Borders 1896–1918*, eds Roland Cosandey and François Albera (Quebec: Nuit Blanche, 1995), 37–49

Lindsay, Vachel, *The Art of the Moving Picture* (New York: Macmillan, 1916)

Low, Rachel, *The History of the British Film 1896–1906* (London: George Allen and Unwin, 1948)

Luckhurst, Roger, and Josephine McDonagh, eds, *Transactions and Encounters: Science and Culture in the Nineteenth-Century* (Manchester: Manchester University Press, 2002)

MacDonald, Robert, 'The Route of the Overland Mail to India', *The New Magic Lantern Journal* 9:6 (2004), 83–87

'A Magic Lantern Entertainment by Timothy Toddle', in *Magic Images: The Art of Hand-Painted and Photographic Lantern Slides* (London: Magic Lantern Society, 1990), 47–59

Magli, Patrizia, 'The Face and the Soul', in *Zone Four: Fragments for a History of the Human Body*, 3 vols, ed. Michel Feher with Nadia Taza and Ramona Nadaff (New York: Zone Books, 1989), II, 87–127

Maltby, Richard, *Hollywood Cinema: An Introduction* (Oxford: Blackwell, 1995)

Malthête, Jacques, 'Quand Méliès n'en faisait qu'a sa tête', in *Pour une Histoire des Trucages*, ed. Thierry Lefebvre (Charente: Pleinchant à Bassac, 1999), 21–32

Mannoni, Laurent, 'Elbow to Elbow: The Lantern/Cinema Struggle', *New Magic Lantern Journal* 7:1 (Jan 1993), 3

—, 'Archaeology of Cinema/Pre-cinema', in *Encyclopedia of Early Cinema*, ed. Richard Abel (London: Routledge, 2005), 32–35

—, The Great Art of Light and Shadow: Archaeology of the Cinema (Exeter: University of Exeter Press, 2001)

Mannoni, Laurent, Donata Pesenti Campagnoni and David Robinson, *Light and Movement: Incunabula of the Motion Picture 1420–1896* (Gemona: Le Giornate del

Cinema Muto, 1995)

Mayer, David, 'Learning to See in the Dark', *Nineteenth-Century Theatre* 25:2 (1997), 92–114

—, *Playing Out the Empire: Ben Hur and Other Toga Plays and Films 1883–1908. A Critical Anthology* (Oxford: Oxford University Press, 1994)

Mcfarlane, Gavin, *Copyright Through the Cases* (London: Waterlow Law Books, 1986)

McKernan, Luke, *'Something More than a Mere Picture Show': Charles Urban and the Early Non-Fiction Film in Great Britain and America, 1897–1925* (unpublished doctoral thesis, Birkbeck College, University of London, 2003)

—, ed., *A Yank in Britain: the Lost Memoirs of Charles Urban, Film Pioneer* (Hastings: The Projection Box, 1999)

McMahan, Alison, 'The Quest for Motion: Moving Pictures and Flight', in *Visual Delights: Essays on the Popular and Projected Image in the 19th Century*, eds Simon Popple and Vanessa Toulmin (Trowbridge: Flicks Books, 2000), 181–93

Mellor, G. J., *Movie Makers and Picture Palaces: A Century of Cinema in Yorkshire 1896–1996* (Bradford: Bradford Libraries, 1996)

Metz, Christian, *Film Language: A Semiotics of Cinema* (Oxford: Oxford University Press, 1974)

—, 'The Impersonal Enunciation, or the Site of Film (In the margin of recent works on enunciation in cinema)', *New Literary History* 22 (1991), 747–72

Meyer, Mark-Paul, 'Moments of Poignancy: The Aesthetics of the Accidental and the Casual in Early Non-fiction Film', in *Uncharted Territory: Essays on Early Non-fiction Film*, eds Daan Hertogs and Nico de Klerk (Amsterdam: Nederlands Filmmuseum, 1997), 51–60

Miller, Angela, 'The Panorama, the Cinema, and the Emergence of the Spectacular', *Wide Angle* 18:2 (1996), 34–69

Mitchell, Timothy, 'Orientalism and the Exhibitionary Other', in *Colonialism and Culture*, ed. Nicholas B. Dirks (Ann Arbor: University of Michigan Press, 1992), 289–318

—, 'The World as Exhibition', *Comparative Studies in Society and History: An International Quarterly* 31 (1989), 217–236

Monaghan, Garrett, 'Performing the Passions: Comic Themes in the Films of George Albert Smith', in *Pimples, Pranks, and Pratfalls: British Film Comedy Before 1930*, eds Alan Burton and Laraine Porter (Trowbridge: Flicks Books, 2000), 24–32

Musser, Charles, *Before the Nickelodeon. Edwin Porter and the Edison Manufacturing Company* (Berkeley: University of California Press, 1991)

—, 'A Cinema of Contemplation, a Cinema of Discernment: Spectatorship, Intertextuality, and Attractions in the 1890s', in *The Cinema of Attractions Reloaded*, ed. Wanda Streuven (Amsterdam: Amsterdam University Press, 2006), 159–80

—, 'The Early Cinema of Edwin S. Porter', *Cinema Journal* 19:1 (Fall 1979), 1–38

—, 'The Nickelodeon Era Begins: Establishing the Framework for Hollywood's Mode of Representation', *Framework* 22/23 (Autumn 1983), 4–11

Musser, Charles, and Carol Nelson, *Lyman H. Howe and the Forgotten Era of Travelling Exhibition 1880–1920* (Princeton, NJ: Princeton University Press, 1991)

Nead, Lynda, *The Haunted Gallery: Painting, Photography, Film c.1900* (New Haven, CT: Yale University Press, 2007)

Norden, Martin F., *The Cinema of Isolation: A History of Physical Disability in the Movies* (New Brunswick, NJ: Rutgers University Press, 1994)

North, Dan, 'Illusory Bodies', *Early Popular Visual Culture* 5:2 (2007), 175–88

Stephan Oettermann, *The Panorama: History of a Mass Medium*, trans. Deborah Lucas Schneider (New York: Zone Books, 1997)

Partridge, Eric, 'Parlyaree: Cinderella Among Languages', in *Here, There and Everywhere: Essays upon Language*, ed. Eric Partridge (London: Hamish Hamilton, 1950), 116–25

Pearson, George, 'Lambeth Walk to Leicester Square', *Sight and Sound* 7:28 (Winter 1938), 150–51

Pearson, Roberta E., 'The Attractions of Cinema, or, How I Learned to Start Worrying About Loving Early Film', in *Cinema: The Beginnings and the Future*, ed. Christopher Williams (London: University of Westminster, 1996), 150–58

—, *Eloquent Gestures: The Transformation of Performance Styles in the Griffith Biograph Films* (Berkeley: University of California Press, 1992)

Peterson, Jennifer, 'Truth is Stranger than Fiction: Travelogues from the 1910s at the Nederlands Filmmuseum', in *Uncharted Territory: Essays on Early Non-fiction Film*, eds Daan Hertogs and Nico de Klerk (Amsterdam: Nederlands Filmmuseum, 1997), 75–90

Phillips, Ray, *Edison's Kinetoscope: A History to 1896* (Trowbridge: Flicks Books, 1997)

Plunkett, John, *Queen Victoria: First Media Monarch* (Oxford: Oxford University Press, 2003)

— 'Moving Books/Moving Images: Optical Recreations and Children's Publishing 1800–1900', in *19: Interdisciplinary Studies in the Long Nineteenth Century* 5 (2007), (http://www.19.bbk.ac.uk/issue5/index5.htm.), [article accessed 28 August 2008]

Pope, Dennis, and Frank Sharp, 'Interview with Lily May Richards' (University of Sheffield, National Fairground Archive, MS)

Popple, Simon and Joe Kember, *Early Cinema: From Factory Gate to Dream Factory* (London: Wallflower Press, 2004)

Popple, Simon, and Vanessa Toulmin, eds, *Visual Delights: Essays on the Popular and Projected Image in the 19th Century* (Trowbridge: Flicks Books, 2000)

—, eds, *Visual Delights Two: Exhibition and Reception* (Eastleigh: John Libbey and Company, 2005)

Powell, Hudson John, *Poole's Myriorama!: A Story of Travelling Panorama Showmen* (Bradford-on-Avon: ELSP, 2002)

Pudovkin, V.I., *Film Acting: A Course of Lectures Delivered at the State Institute of Cinematography, Moscow*, trans. Ivor Montagu (London: George Newnes, [1935])

Rabinowitz, Lauren, 'From Hale's Tours to Star Tours: Virtual Voyages, Travel Ride Films, and the Delirium of the Hyper-Real', in *Virtual Voyages: Cinema and Travel*, ed. Jeffrey Ruoff (Durham, NC: Duke University Press, 2006), 42–60

Richards, Lily May, *Biography of William Haggar: Actor, Showman and Pioneer of the Film Industry* (University of Sheffield Library, National Fairground Archive MS)

Ricketson, Sam, *The Berne Convention for the Protection of Literary and Artistic Works: 1886–1986* (London: Centre for Commercial Law Studies, 1986)

Robbins, David, 'Sport, Hegemony and the Middle Class: the Victorian Mountaineers', *Theory, Culture & Society* 4 (1987), 579–601

Robertson, David, 'Mid-Victorians Amongst the Alps', in *Nature and the Victorian Imagination*, ed. U.C. Knoepflmacher and G.B. Tennyson (Berkeley: University of California Press, 1977), 113–36

Robinson, David, *From Peep Show to Palace: The Birth of American Film* (New York: Columbia University Press, 1996)

—, 'Harry Furniss—Lantern Showman', *New Magic Lantern Journal* 6:3 (1992), 1–4

—, ed., *The Lantern Image: Iconography of the Magic Lantern 1420–1880* (London: Magic Lantern Society, 1993)

Robinson, David, Stephen Herbert and Richard Crangle, *Encyclopedia of the Magic Lantern* (London: The Magic Lantern Society, 2001)

Rosen, Philip, 'Disjunction and Ideology in a Preclassical Film: *A Policeman's Tour of the World*', *Wide Angle* 12:3 (1990), 20–36

Ross, Steven J., 'Struggles for the Screen: Workers, Radicals, and the Political Uses of Silent Film', *American Historical Review* 96 (1991), 333–67

—, *Working-Class Hollywood: Silent Film and the Shaping of Class in America* (Princeton, NJ: Princeton University Press, 1998)

Rossell, Deac, 'Double Think: The Cinema and Magic Lantern Culture', in *Celebrating 1895: The Centenary of Cinema*, ed. John Fullerton (London: John Libbey and Company, 1998), 27–36

—, *Living Pictures: The Origin of the Movies* (Albany: State University of New York, 1998)

—, 'A Slippery Job: Travelling Exhibitors in Early Cinema', in *Visual Delights: Essays on the Popular and Projected Image in the 19th Century*, eds Simon Popple and Vanessa Toulmin (Trowbridge: Flicks Books, 2000), 50–60

Ruchatz, Jens, 'The Magic Lantern in Connection with Photography: Rationalisation and Technology', in *Visual Delights: Essays on the Popular and Projected Image in the 19th Century*, eds Popple and Toulmin (Trowbridge: Flicks Books, 2000), 38–49

Ruoff, Jeffrey, ed., *Virtual Voyages: Cinema and Travel* (Durham, NC: Duke University Press, 2006)

Russell, David, 'The Football Films', in *The Lost World of Mitchell and Kenyon: Edwardian Britain on Film*, eds Vanessa Toulmin, Simon Popple and Patrick Russell (London: British Film Institute, 2004), 169–80

Sargent, Amy, 'Darwin, Duchenne, Delsarte', in *Moving Performance: British Stage and Screen, 1890s–1920s*, eds Linda Fitzsimmons and Sarah Street (Trowbridge: Flicks Books, 2000), 26–43

Savada, Elias, ed., *American Film Institute Catalogue 1893–1910* (London: Scarecrow Press, 1995)

Scheide, Frank, 'The Influence of the English Music-Hall on Early Screen Acting', in *Moving Performance: British Stage and Screen, 1890s–1920s*, eds Linda Fitzsimmons and Sarah Street (Trowbridge: Flicks Books, 2000), 69–79

Schwartz, Mark E., 'An Overview of Cinema on the Fairgrounds', *Film Reader* 6 (1985), 65–77

Scott, Donald M., 'The Popular Lecture and the Creation of a Public in Mid-Nineteenth-Century America', *The Journal of American History* 66:4 (1980), 791–809

Scullion, Adrienne, 'Geggies, Empires, Cinemas: The Scottish Experience of Early Film', *Picture House* 21 (1996), 13–19

Simkin, Mike, 'Albert Smith: Entrepreneur and Showman', *Living Pictures: The Journal of the Popular and Projected Image before 1914* 1 (2001), 18–28

—, 'Albert Smith: A Nineteenth-Century Showman', *New Magic Lantern Journal* 4 (1986), 68–71

Simons, Jan, 'Enunciation: From Code to Interpretation', in *The Film Spectator: From Sign to Mind*, ed. Warren Buckland (Amsterdam: University of Amsterdam Press, 1995), 192–206

Sinnema, Peter W., 'Introduction', in Samuel Smiles, *Self-Help: With Illustrations of Conduct and Perseverance* (Oxford: Oxford University Press, 2002), vii–xxviii

Singer, Ben, *Melodrama and Modernity: Early Sensational Cinema and its Contexts* (New York: Columbia University Press, 2001)

—, 'Modernity, Hyperstimulus, and the Rise of Popular Sensationalism', in *Cinema and the Invention of Modern Life*, eds Leo Charney and Vanessa R. Schwartz (Berkeley: University of California Press, 1995), 72–99

Smith, Lester, 'Entertainment and Amusement, Education and Instruction: Lectures at the Royal Polytechnic Institution', in *Realms of Light: Uses and Perceptions of the Magic Lantern from the 17th to the 21st Century*, eds Richard Crangle, Mervyn Heard and Ine van Dooren (London: Magic Lantern Society, 2005), 138–45

Solomon, Matthew, 'Up-to-Date Magic: Theatrical Conjuring and the Trick Film', *Theatre Journal* 58 (2006), 595–615

Sopocy, Martin, 'A Narrated Cinema: The Pioneer Story Films of James A. Williamson', *Cinema Journal* 18:1 (Fall 1978), 1–28

—, 'James A. Williamson: American View', in *Cinema 1900/1906: An Analytical Study*, compiled by Roger Holman (Brussels: FIAF, 1982), 297–319

—, *James Williamson: Studies and Documents of a Pioneer of the Film Narrative* (Rutherford, NJ: Fairleigh Dickinson University Press, 1998)

—, 'The Role of the Intertitle in Film Exhibition, 1904–1910', in *Cinema: The Beginnings and the Future*, ed. Christopher Williams (London: University of Westminster Press, 1996), 123–34

Springhall, John, 'On with the Show': American Popular Entertainment as Cultural and Social History', *History Compass* 2:1 (2004)

Staiger, Janet, '"The eyes are really the focus": Photoplay Acting and Film Form and Style' *Wide Angle* 6 (1985), 14–23

Sterling, J.A.L., *Intellectual Property Rights in Sound and Recordings, Film and Video*

(London: Sweet and Maxwell, 1992)

Stewart, Susan, *On Longing: Narratives of the Miniature, the Gigantic, the Souvenir, the Collection* (Durham, NC: Duke University Press, 1993)

Strain, Ellen, 'Exotic Bodies, Distant Landscapes: Touristic Viewing and Popularized Anthropology in the Nineteenth Century', *Wide Angle* 18:2 (1996), 71–100

Streuven, Wanda, ed., *The Cinema of Attractions Reloaded* (Amsterdam: Amsterdam University Press, 2006)

Thomson, Rosemarie Garland, *Extraordinary Bodies: Figuring Physical Disability in American Culture and Literature* (New York: Columbia University Press, 1997)

—, ed., *Freakery: Cultural Spectacles of the Extraordinary Body* (New York: New York University Press, 1996)

—, 'Introduction: From Wonder to Error—A Genealogy of Freak Discourse in Modernity', in *Freakery: Cultural Spectacles of the Extraordinary Body*, ed. Rosemarie Garland Thomson (New York: New York University Press, 1996), 1–22

Thompson, John B., *Ideology and Modern Culture: Critical Social Theory in the Era of Mass Communication* (Cambridge: Polity Press, 1990)

—, *The Media and Modernity: A Social Theory of the Media* (Oxford: Blackwell, 1995)

—, 'The Theory of Structuration', in *Social Theory of Modern Societies: Anthony Giddens and his Critics*, eds David Held and John B. Thompson (Cambridge: Cambridge University Press, 1989), 56–76

Thompson, Kristin, 'Narrative Structure in Early Classical Cinema', in *Celebrating 1895: The Centenary of Cinema*, ed. John Fullerton (London: John Libbey and Company, 1998), 225–37

Tosi, Virgilio, *Cinema before Cinema: The Origins of Scientific Cinematography* (London, BUFVC, 2005)

Toulmin, Vanessa, 'Bioscope Biographies', in *In the Kingdom of the Shadows: A Companion to Early Cinema*, eds Colin Harding and Simon Popple (London: Cygnus Arts, 1996), 249–61

—, 'Cuckoo in the Nest: Edwardian Exhibition and the Transition to Cinema', forthcoming (2009).

—, 'Curios Things in Curios Places': Temporary Exhibition Venues in the Victorian and Edwardian Entertainment Environment', *Early Popular Visual Culture*, 4:2 (2006), 113–37

—, *Fun Without Vulgarity: Community, Women, and Language in Showland Society* (unpublished doctoral thesis, University of Sheffield, 1997)

—, 'Local Films for Local People': Travelling Showmen and the Commissioning of Local Films 1900–1902', *Film History* 13:2 (2001), 118–38

—, *Randall Williams, King of Showmen: From Ghost Show to Bioscope* (London: The Projection Box, 1998)

—, 'Telling the Tale: The Story of the Fairground Bioscope Shows and the Showmen who Operated them', *Film History* 6 (1994), 219–37

—, 'Travelling Shows and the First Static Cinemas', in *Picture House* 21 (1996), 5–12

—, unpublished interview with Miss Celine Williams (University of Sheffield Library, National Fairground Archive MS)

288

—, '"We take them and make them": Mitchell and Kenyon and the Travelling Exhibition Showmen', in *The Lost World of Mitchell and Kenyon: Edwardian Britain on Film*, eds Vanessa Toulmin, Patrick Russell and Simon Popple (London: British Film Institute, 2004), 59–68

Turvey, Gerry, 'Frederick Burlingham: Exploration, Mountaineering and the Origins of Swiss Documentary Cinema', *Historical Journal of Film, Radio, and Television* 27:2 (2007), 167–91

Uricchio, William, 'Ways of Seeing: The New Vision of Early Non-fiction Film', in *Uncharted Territory: Essays on Early Non-fiction Film*, eds Daan Hertogs and Nico de Klerk (Amsterdam: Nederlands Filmmuseum, 1997), 119–31

Usai, Paolo Cherchi, 'On the Concept of "Influence" in Early Cinema', in *Cinéma sans Frontières/Images Across Borders 1896–1918*, eds Roland Cosandey and François Albera (Quebec: Nuit Blanche, 1995), 275–86

Vaughan, Christopher A., 'Ogling Igorots: The Politics and Commerce of Exhibiting Cultural Otherness, 1898–1913', in *Freakery: Cultural Spectacles of the Extraordinary Body*, ed. Rosemarie Garland Thomson (New York: New York University Press, 1996), 219–33

Victorian Film Catalogues: A Facsimile Collection (Hastings: The Projection Box, 1996)

Waddington, Damer, *Panoramas, Magic Lanterns, and Cinemas: A Century of 'Light' Entertainment in Jersey 1814–1914* (Jersey: Tocan Books, 2003)

Williams, Christopher, ed., *Cinema: The Beginnings and the Future* (London: University of Westminster Press, 1996)

Index